Solaris™ Application Programming

Solaris™ Application Programming

Darryl Gove

Sun Microsystems Press

PRENTICE
HALL

Upper Saddle River, NJ • Boston • Indianapolis • San Francisco
New York • Toronto • Montreal • London • Munich • Paris • Madrid
Capetown • Sydney • Tokyo • Singapore • Mexico City

The publisher offers excellent discounts on this book when ordered in quantity for bulk purchases or special sales, which may include electronic versions and/or custom covers and content particular to your business, training goals, marketing focus, and branding interests. For more information, please contact: U.S. Corporate and Government Sales, (800) 382-3419, corpsales@pearsontechgroup.com.

For sales outside the United States, please contact International Sales, international@pearsoned.com.

Visit us on the Web: www.prenhallprofessional.com.

This Book Is Safari Enabled

The Safari® Enabled icon on the cover of your favorite technology book means the book is available through Safari Bookshelf. When you buy this book, you get free access to the online edition for 45 days.

Safari Bookshelf is an electronic reference library that lets you easily search thousands of technical books, find code samples, download chapters, and access technical information whenever and wherever you need it.

To gain 45-day Safari Enabled access to this book:

• Go to http://www.prenhallprofessional.com/safarienabled

• Complete the brief registration form

• Enter the coupon code SXKI-4M3J-DDKI-UWJP-661P

If you have difficulty registering on Safari Bookshelf or accessing the online edition, please e-mail customer-service@safaribooksonline.com.

Library of Congress Cataloging-in-Publication Data

Gove, Darryl.
  Solaris application programming / Darryl Gove.
     p. cm.
  Includes index.
  ISBN 978-0-13-813455-6 (hardcover : alk. paper)
  1. Solaris (Computer file) 2. Operating systems (Computers) 3. Application software—Development. 4. System design. I. Title.
  QA76.76.O63G688 2007
  005.4'32—dc22

                                       2007043230

ISBN-13: 978-0-13-813455-6
ISBN-10:   0-13-813455-3
Text printed in the United States on recycled paper at Courier in Westford, Massachusetts.
First printing, December 2007

Contents

PART II
Developer Tools   47

PART III
Optimization   **277**

PART V
Concluding Remarks   435

Preface

About This Book

This book is a guide to getting the best performance out of computers running the Solaris operating system. The target audience is developers and software architects who are interested in using the tools that are available, as well as those who are interested in squeezing the last drop of performance out of the system.

The book caters to those who are new to performance analysis and optimization, as well as those who are experienced in the area. To do this, the book starts with an overview of processor fundamentals, before introducing the tools and getting into the details.

One of the things that distinguishes this book from others is that it is a practical guide. There are often two problems to overcome when doing development work. The first problem is knowing the tools that are available. This book is written to cover the breadth of tools available today and to introduce the common uses for them. The second problem is interpreting the output from the tools. This book includes many examples of tool use and explains their output.

One trap this book aims to avoid is that of explaining how to manually do the optimizations that the compiler performs automatically. The book's focus is on identifying the problems using appropriate tools and solving the problems using the easiest approach. Sometimes, the solution is to use different compiler flags so that a particular hot spot in the application is optimized away. Other times, the solution is to change the code because the compiler is unable to perform the optimization; I explain this with insight into why the compiler is unable to transform the code.

Goals and Assumptions

The goals of this book are as follows.

- Provide a comprehensive introduction to the components that influence processor performance.
- Introduce the tools that you can use for performance analysis and improvement, both those that ship with the operating system and those that ship with the compiler.
- Introduce the compiler and explain the optimizations that it supports to enable improved performance.
- Discuss the features of the SPARC and x64 families of processors and demonstrate how you can use these features to improve application performance.
- Talk about the possibilities of using multiple processors or threads to enable better performance, or more efficient use of computer resources.

The book assumes that the reader is comfortable with the C programming language. This language is used for most of the examples in the book. The book also assumes a willingness to learn some of the lower-level details about the processors and the instruction sets that the processors use. The book does not attempt to go into the details of processor internals, but it does introduce some of the features of modern processors that will have an effect on application performance.

The book assumes that the reader has access to the Sun Studio compiler and tools. These tools are available as free downloads. Most of the examples come from using Sun Studio 12, but any recent compiler version should yield similar results. The compiler is typically installed in `/opt/SUNWspro/bin/` and it is assumed that the compiler does appear on the reader's path.

The book focuses on Solaris 10. Many of the tools discussed are also available in prior versions. I note in the text when a tool has been introduced in a relatively recent version of Solaris.

Chapter Overview

Part I—Overview of the Processor
- Chapter 1—The Generic Processor
- Chapter 2—The SPARC Family
- Chapter 3—The x64 Family of Processors

Acknowledgments

A number of people contributed to the writing of this book. Ross Towle provided an early outline for the chapter on multithreaded programming and provided comments on the final version of that text. Joel Williamson read the early drafts a number of times and each time provided detailed comments and improvements. My colleagues Boris Ivanovski, Karsten Gutheridge, John Henning, Miriam Blatt, Linda Hsi, Peter Farkas, Greg Price, and Geetha Vallabhenini also read the drafts at various stages and suggested refinements to the text. A particular debt of thanks is due to John Henning, who provided many detailed improvements to the text.

I'm particularly grateful to domain experts who took the time to read various chapters and provide helpful feedback, including Rod Evans for his input on the linker, Chris Quenelle for his assistance with the debugger, Brian Whitney for contributing comments and the names of some useful tools for the section on tools, Brendan Gregg for his comments, Jian-Zhong Wang for reviewing the materials on compilers and source code optimizations, Alex Liu for providing detailed comments on the chapter on floating-point optimization, Marty Izkowitz for comments on the performance profiling and multithreading chapters, Yuan Lin, Ruud van der Pas,

Alfred Huang, and Nawal Copty for also providing comments on the chapter on multithreading, Josh Simmons for commenting on MPI, David Weaver for insights into the history of the SPARC processor, Richard Smith for reviewing the chapter on x64 processors, and Richard Friedman for comments throughout the text.

A number of people made a huge difference to the process of getting this book published, including Yvonne Prefontaine, Ahmed Zandi, and Ken Tracton. I'm particularly grateful for the help of Richard McDougall in guiding the project through the final stages.

Special thanks are due to the Prentice Hall staff, including editor Greg Doench and full-service production manager Julie Nahil. Thanks also to production project manager Dmitri Korzh from Techne Group.

Most importantly, I would like to thank my family for their support and encouragement. Jenny, whose calm influence and practical suggestions have helped me with the trickier aspects of the text; Aaron, whose great capacity for imaginatively solving even the most mundane of problems has inspired me along the way; Timothy, whose enthusiastic sharing of the enjoyment of life is always uplifting; and Emma, whose arrival as I completed this text has been a most wonderful gift.

PART I

Overview of the Processor

1

The Generic Processor

1.1 Chapter Objectives

In the simplest terms, a processor fetches instructions from memory and acts on them, fetching data from or sending results to memory as needed. However, this description misses many of the important details that determine application performance. This chapter describes a "generic" processor; that is, it covers, in general terms, how processors work and what components they have. By the end of the chapter, the reader will be familiar with the terminology surrounding processors, and will understand some of the approaches that are used in processor design.

1.2 The Components of a Processor

At the heart of every computer are one or more Central Processing Units (CPUs). A picture of the UltraSPARC T1 CPU is shown in Figure 1.1. The CPU is the part of the computer that does the computation. The rest of the space that a computer occupies is taken up with memory chips, hard disks, power supplies, fans (to keep it cool), and more chips that allow communication with the outside world (e.g., graphics chipsets and network chipsets). The underside of the CPU has hundreds of "pins";[1] in the figure these form a cross-like pattern. Each pin is a connection between the CPU and the system.

---

1. Pins used to be real pins sticking out of the base of the processor. A problem with this packaging was that the pins could bend or break. More recent chip packaging technology uses balls or pads.

Figure 1.1 The UltraSPARC T1 Processor

Inside the packaging, the CPU is a small piece of silicon, referred to as the "die." A CPU contains one or more cores (to do the computation), some (local or on-chip) memory, called "cache" (to hold instructions and data), and the system interface (which allows it to communicate with the rest of the system).

Some processors have a single core. The processor shown in Figure 1.1, the UltraSPARC T1, has eight cores, each capable of running up to four threads simultaneously. To the user of the system this appears to be 32 virtual processors. Each virtual processor appears to the operating system as a full processor, and is capable of executing a single stream of instructions. The die of the UltraSPARC T1 is shown in Figure 1.2. The diagram is labeled with the function that each area of the CPU performs.

1.3 Clock Speed

All processors execute at a particular clock rate. This clock rate ranges from MHz to GHz.[2] A higher clock rate will usually result in more power consumption. One or more instructions can be executed at each tick of the clock. So, the number of instructions that can be executed per second can range between millions and billions. Each tick of the clock is referred to as a "cycle."

The clock speed is often a processor's most identifiable feature, but it is not sufficient to use clock speed as a proxy for how much work a processor can perform.

---

2. Megahertz (MHz) = 1 million cycles per second. Gigahertz (GHz) = 1 billion cycles per second.

Figure 1.2 Die of the UltraSPARC T1

This is often referred to as the "Megahertz Myth." The amount of work that a processor can perform per second depends on a number of factors, only one of which is the clock speed. Other factors include how many instructions can be issued per cycle, and how many cycles are lost because no instructions can be issued, which is a surprisingly common occurrence. A processor's performance is a function of both the processor's design and the workload being run on it.

The number of instructions that can be executed in a single cycle is determined by the number of execution pipes available (as discussed in Section 1.6) and the number of cores that the CPU has.

The number of cycles in which the processor has no work depends on the processor's design, plus characteristics such as the amount of cache that has been provided, the speed of memory, the amount of I/O (e.g., data written to disk), and the particular application.

A key processor design choice often concerns whether to add cache, which will reduce the number of cycles spent waiting for data from memory, or whether to devote the same die space to features such as more processor cores, or more complex (higher-performance) circuitry in each processor core.

1.4 Out-of-Order Processors

There are two basic types of processor design: in-order and out-of-order execution processors. Out-of-order processors will typically provide more performance at a given clock speed, but are also more complex to design and consume more power.

On an in-order processor, each instruction is executed in the order that it appears, and if the results of a previous instruction are not available, the processor will wait (or "stall') until they are available. This approach relies on the compiler to do a good job of scheduling instructions in a way that avoids these stalls. This is not always possible, so an in-order processor will have cycles during which it is stalled, unable to execute a new instruction.

One way to reduce the number of stalled cycles is to allow the processor to execute instructions out of order. The processor tries to find instructions in the instruction stream that are independent of the current (stalled) instruction and can be executed in parallel with it. The x64 family of processors are out-of-order processors. A downside to out-of-order execution is that the processor becomes rapidly more complex as the degree of "out-of-orderness" is increased.

Out-of-order execution is very good at keeping the processor utilized when there are small gaps in the instruction stream. However, if the instruction stream has a large gap—which would occur when it is waiting for the data to return from memory, for instance—an out-of-order processor will show diminished benefits over an in-order processor.

1.5 Chip Multithreading

Chip multithreading (CMT) is an alternative to the complexity of out-of-order processors. An in-order processor is simpler to design and consumes less power than an out-of-order processor, but it will spend more time stalled, waiting for the results of previous instructions to become available. The CMT approach, which is used in the UltraSPARC T1, has multiple threads of instructions executing on the same core. So, when one thread stalls, one or more other threads will be ready for execution. As a result, each core of the processor will be executing an instruction almost every cycle—the processor is better utilized.

Previously, the emphasis has been on getting the best possible performance for a single thread, but CMT places the emphasis on how much work can be done per unit time (throughput) rather than how long each individual piece of work takes (response time).

A Web server is an example of an application that is very well suited to running on a CMT system. The performance of a Web server is typically measured in the number of pages it can serve per second, which is a throughput metric. Having multiple hardware threads available to process requests for pages improves system performance. On the other hand, the "responsiveness" of the server is (usually) dominated by the time it takes to send the page over the network, rather than the time it takes the Web server to prepare the page, so the impact of the processor's response time in serving the page is small compared to the time it takes to transmit the page over the network.

1.6 Execution Pipes

To be able to execute a number of instructions on each cycle a processor will have multiple "pipes," each capable of handling a particular type of instruction. This type of processor is called a *superscalar processor*. Typically there are memory pipes (which handle operations on memory, such as loads and stores), floating-point pipes (which handle floating-point arithmetic), integer pipes (which handle integer arithmetic, such as addition and subtraction), and branch pipes (which handle branch and call instructions). An example of multiple execution pipes is shown in Figure 1.3.

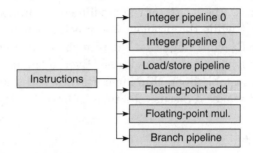

Figure 1.3 Example of Multiple Instruction Pipes

Another approach that improves processor clock speed is for the execution of instructions to be *pipelined*, which means that each instruction actually takes multiple cycles to complete, and during each cycle the processor performs a small step of the complete instruction.

An example of a pipeline might be breaking the process of performing an instruction into the steps of fetching (getting the next instruction from memory), decoding (determining what the instruction tells the processor to do), executing (doing the work), and retiring (committing the results of the instruction), which would be a four-stage pipeline; this pipeline is shown in Figure 1.4. The advantage of doing this is that while one instruction is going through the fetch logic, another instruction can be going through the decode logic, another through the execute logic, and another through the retire logic. The speed at which the pipeline can progress is limited by the time it takes an instruction to complete the slowest stage.

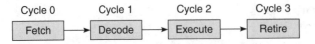

Figure 1.4 Four-Stage Pipeline

It is tempting to imagine that a high-performance processor could be achieved by having many very quick stages. Unfortunately, this is tricky to achieve because many stages are not easily split into simpler steps, and it is possible to get to a point where the overhead of doing the splitting dominates the time it takes to complete the stage. The other problem with having too many stages is that if something goes wrong (e.g., a branch is mispredicted and instructions have been fetched from the wrong address), the length of the pipeline determines how many cycles of processor time are lost while the problem is corrected. For example, if the processor determines at the Execute stage that the branch is mispredicted, it will have to start fetching instructions from a new address. Even if the instructions at the new address are already available in on-chip memory, they will take time to go through the Fetch and Decode stages. I discuss the topic of branch misprediction further in Section 1.6.4.

1.6.1 Instruction Latency

An instruction's execution latency is the number of cycles between when the processor starts to execute the instruction and when the results of that instruction are available to other instructions. For simple instructions (such as integer addition), the latency is often one cycle, so the results of an operation will be available for use on the next cycle; for more complex instructions, it may take many cycles for the results to be available. For some instructions, for example, load instructions, it may not be possible to determine the latency of the instruction until runtime, when it is executed. A load instruction might use data that is in the on-chip cache, in which case the latency will be short, or it might require data located in remote memory, in which case the latency will be significantly longer.

One of the jobs of the compiler is to schedule instructions such that one instruction completes and produces results just as another instruction starts and requests those results. In many cases, it is possible for the compiler to do this kind of careful scheduling. In other cases, it is not possible, and the instruction stream will have stalls of a number of cycles until the required data is ready. Different processors, even those within the same processor family, will have different instruction latencies, so it can be difficult for the compiler to schedule these instructions, but it can nevertheless have a large impact on the performance of an application.

1.6.2 Load/Store Pipe

A processor will have a pipe that performs loads and stores. A load will typically check to see whether the data is already present on the chip, in the nearest cache, or in the memory associated with another processor, before loading it from main memory. The time it takes for a load to complete will depend on how far away the required data is; this is called the *memory latency* or the *cache latency*, depending on whether the data is fetched from memory or from cache. It is not uncommon for memory latency to be well over 100 cycles.

Stores are more complex than loads. A store often updates just a few bytes of memory, and this requires that the new data be merged with the existing data. The easiest way to implement this is to read the existing data, update the necessary bytes, and then write the updated data back to memory.

1.6.3 Integer Operation Pipe

Integer arithmetic (additions and subtractions) is the basic set of operations that processors perform. Operations such as "compare" are really just a variant of subtraction. Adds and subtracts are very simple operations, and they are typically completed very quickly. Other logical operations (ANDs and ORs) are also completed quickly. Rotations and shifts (where a bit pattern is moved within a register) may take longer. Multiplication and division operations on integer values can be quite time-consuming and often slower than the equivalent floating-point operation.

Sometimes simply changing the way a value is calculated, or changing the details of a heuristic, can improve performance, because although the calculation looks the same on paper, the underlying operations to do it are faster. This is called *strength reduction*, or substituting an equivalent set of lower-cost operations. An example of this is replacing integer division by two with an arithmetic right-shift of the register, which achieves the same result but takes significantly less time.

1.6.4 Branch Pipe

Branch instructions cause a program to start fetching instructions from another location in memory. There are two ways to do this: branching and calling. A branch tells the processor to start fetching instructions from a new address. The difference with calling is that the address of the branch is recorded so that the program can return to that point later. One example of where branches are necessary is a conditional statement, as shown in Figure 1.5. In this example, the IF test has two blocks of conditional code, one executed if the condition is true and one if it is false. There has to be a branch statement to allow the code to continue at the FALSE code block, if the condition is false. Similarly, there has to be a branch at the end of the TRUE block of code to allow the program to continue code execution after the IF statement.

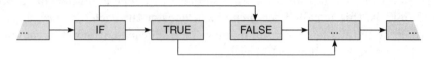

Figure 1.5 Conditional Statement

There are costs associated with branching. The primary and most obvious cost is that the instructions for a taken branch are fetched from another location in memory, so there may be a delay while instructions from that location are brought onto the processor. One way to reduce this cost is for the processor to predict whether the branch is going to be taken. Branch predictors have a range of complexity. An example of a simple branch predictor might be one that records whether a branch was taken last time and, if it was, predicts that it will be taken again; if it wasn't, it predicts that it will not be taken. Then, the processor anticipates the change in instruction stream location and starts fetching the instructions from the new location before knowing whether the branch was actually taken. Correctly predicted branches can minimize or even hide the cost of fetching instructions from a new location in memory.

Obviously, it is impossible to predict branches correctly all the time. When branches are mispredicted there are associated costs. If a mispredicted branch causes instructions to be fetched from memory, these instructions will probably be installed in the caches before the processor determines that the branch is mispredicted, and these instructions will not be needed. The act of installing the unnecessary instructions in the caches will probably cause useful instructions (or data) to be displaced from the caches.

The other issue is that the new instructions have to work their way through the processor pipeline and the delay that this imposes depends on the length of the pipeline. So, a processor that obtained a high clock speed by having many quick pipeline stages will suffer a long mispredicted branch penalty while the correct instruction stream makes its way through the pipeline.

1.6.5 Floating-Point Pipe

Floating-point operations are more complex than integer operations, and they often take more cycles to complete. A processor will typically devote one or more pipes to floating-point operations. Five classes of floating-point operations are typically performed in hardware: add, subtract, multiply, divide, and square root. Floating-point arithmetic is covered in Chapter 6. Note that although computers are excellent devices for handling integer numbers, the process of rendering a floating-point number into a fixed number of bytes and then performing math operations on it leads to a potential loss of accuracy.

Consequently, a standard has been defined for floating-point mathematics. The IEEE-754 standard defines the sizes in bytes and formats of floating-point values. It also has ways of representing non-numeric "values" such as Not-a-Number (NaN) or infinity.

A number of calculations can produce results of infinity; one example is division by zero. According to the standard, division by zero will also result in a trap; the software can choose what to do in the event of this trap.

Some calculations, such as infinity divided by infinity, will generate results that are reported as being NaN. NaNs are also used in some programs to represent data that is not present. NaNs are defined so that the result of any operation on a NaN is also a NaN. In this way, the results of computation using NaNs can cascade through the calculation, and the effects of unavailable data become readily apparent.

1.7 Caches

Caches are places where the most recently used memory is held. These are placed close to the cores, either on-chip or on fast memory colocated with the CPU. The time it takes to get data from a cache will be less than the time it takes to get data from memory, so the effect of having caches is that the latency of load and store instructions is, on average, substantially reduced. Adding a cache will typically cause the latency to memory to increase slightly, because the cache needs to be examined for the data before the data is fetched from memory. However, this extra cost is small in comparison to the gains you get when the data can be fetched from the cache rather than from memory. Not all applications benefit from caches. Applications that use, or reuse, only a small amount of data will see the greatest benefit from adding cache to a processor. Applications that stream through a large data set will get negligible benefit from caches.

Caches have a number of characteristics. The following paragraphs explain these characteristics in detail.

The *line size* of a cache is the number of consecutive bytes that are held on a single *cache line* in the cache. It is best to explain this using an example. When data is fetched from memory, the request is to transfer a chunk of data which includes the data that was requested. A program might want to load a single byte, but the memory will provide a block of 64 bytes that contains the one byte. The block of 64 bytes is constrained to be the 64-byte aligned block of bytes. As an example, consider a request for byte 73. This will result in the transfer of bytes 64–127. Similarly, a request for byte 173 will result in the transfer of bytes 128–191. See Figure 1.6. The benefit of handling the memory in chunks of a fixed number of bytes is that it reduces the complexity of the memory interface, because the interface can be optimized to handle chunks of a set size and a set alignment.

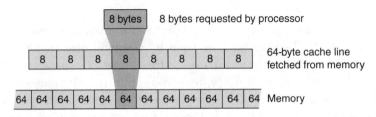

Figure 1.6 Fetching a Cache Line from Memory

The number of lines in the cache is the number of unique chunks of data that can be held in the cache. The size of the cache is the number of lines multiplied by the line size. An 8MB cache that has a line size of 64 bytes will contain 262,144 unique cache lines.

In a *direct mapped* cache, each address in memory will map onto exactly one cache line in the cache, so many addresses in memory will map onto the same cache line. This can have unfortunate side effects as two lines from memory repeatedly knock each other out of the cache (this is known as *thrashing*). If a cache is 8MB in size, data that is exactly 8MB apart will map onto the same cache line. Unfortunately, it is not uncommon to have data structures that are powers of two in size. A consequence of this is that some applications will thrash direct mapped caches.

A way to avoid thrashing is to increase the *associativity* of the cache. An N-way associative cache has a number of sets of N cache lines. Every line in memory maps onto exactly one set, but a line that is brought in from memory can replace any of the N lines in that set. The example illustrated in Figure 1.7 shows a 64KB cache with two-way associativity and 64-byte cache lines. It contains 1,024 cache lines divided into 512 sets, with two cache lines in each set. So, each line in memory can map onto one of two places in the cache. The risk of thrashing decreases as the associativity of the cache increases. High associativity is particularly important when multiple cores share a cache, because multiple active threads can also cause thrashing in the caches.

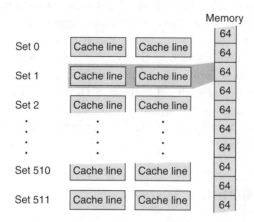

Figure 1.7 64KB Two-Way Associative Cache with 64-byte Line Size

The *replacement algorithm* is the method by which old lines are selected for removal from the cache when a new line comes in. The simplest policy is to randomly remove a line from the cache. The best policy is to track the least-recently-used line (i.e., the oldest line) and evict it. However, this can be quite costly to implement on the chip. Often, some kind of "pseudo" least-recently-used algorithm is used for a cache. Such algorithms are picked to give the best performance for the least implementation complexity.

The line sizes of the various caches in a system and the line size of memory do not need to be the same. For example, a cache might have a smaller line size than memory line size. If memory provides data in chunks of 64 bytes, and the cache stores data in chunks of 32 bytes, the cache will allocate two cache lines to store the data from memory. The data cache on the UltraSPARC III family of processors is implemented in this way. The first-level, on-chip, cache line size is 32 bytes, but the line size for the second-level cache is 64 bytes. The advantage of having a smaller line size is that a line fetched into the cache will contain a higher proportion of useful data. As an example, consider a load of 4 bytes. This is 1/8 of a 32-byte cache line, but 1/16 of a 64-byte cache line. In the worst case, 7/8 of a 32-byte cache line, or 15/16 of a 64-byte cache line, is wasted.

Alternatively, the cache can have a line size that is bigger than memory. For example, the cache may hold lines of 128 bytes, whereas memory might return lines of 64 bytes. Rather than requesting that memory return an additional 64 bytes (which may or may not be used), the cache can be *subblocked*. Subblocking is when each cache line, in a cache with a particular line size, contains a number of smaller-size subblocks; each subblock can hold contiguous data or be empty. So, in this example, the cache might have a 128-byte line size, with two 64-byte subblocks. When a new line (of 64 bytes) is fetched from memory, the cache will clear a line of 128 bytes and place those new 64 bytes into one-half of it. If the other adjacent 64 bytes are fetched later, the cache will add those to the other half of the cache line. The advantage of using subblocks is that they can increase the capacity of the cache without adding too much complexity. The disadvantage is that the cache may not end up being used to its full capacity (some of the subblocks may not end up containing data).

1.8 Interacting with the System

1.8.1 Bandwidth and Latency

Two critical concepts apply to memory. The first is called *latency*, and the second is called *bandwidth*. Latency is the time it takes to get data onto the chip from memory (usually measured in nanoseconds or processor clock cycles), and bandwidth is the amount of data that can be fetched from memory per second (measured in bytes or gigabytes[3] per second).

These two definitions might sound confusingly similar, so consider as an example a train that takes four hours to travel from London to Edinburgh. The "latency" of the train journey is four hours. However, one train might carry 400 people, so the bandwidth would be 400 people in four hours, or 100 people per hour.

Now, if the train could go twice as fast, the journey would take two hours. In this case, the latency would be halved, and the train would still carry 400 people, so the "bandwidth" would have doubled, to 200 people per hour.

Instead of making the train twice as fast, the train could be made to carry twice the number of people. In this case, the train could get 800 people there in four hours, or 200 people per hour; twice the bandwidth, but still the same four-hour latency.

---

3. A gigabyte is 2^{20} bytes, or very close to 1 billion bytes. In some instances, such as disk drive capacity, 10^9 is used as the definition of a gigabyte.

In some way, the train works as a good analogy, because data does arrive at the processor in batches, rather like the train loads of passengers. But in this case, the batches are the cache lines. On the processor, multiple packets travel from memory to the processor. The total bandwidth is the cumulative effect of all these packets arriving, not the effect of just a single packet arriving.

Obviously, both bandwidth and latency change depending on how far the data has to travel. If the data is already in the on-chip caches, the bandwidth is going to be significantly higher and the latency lower than if it has to be fetched from memory.

One important point is to be aware of *data density*, that is, how much of the data that is fetched from memory will end up being using by the application. Think of it as how many people actually want to take the train. If the train can carry 400 people, but only four people actually *want* to take it, although the potential bandwidth is 100 people per hour, the useful bandwidth is one person every hour. In computing terms, if there are data structures in a program, it is important to ensure that they do not have unused space in them.

Bandwidth is a resource that is consumed by both loads and stores. Stores can potentially consume twice the bandwidth of loads, as mentioned in Section 1.6.2. When a processor changes part of a cache line, the first thing it has to do is to fetch the entire cache line from memory, then modify the part of the line that has changed, and finally write the entire line back to memory.

1.8.2 System Buses

When processors are configured in a system, typically a system bus connects all the processors and the memory. This bus will have a clock speed and a width (measured by the number of bits that can be carried every cycle). You can calculate the bandwidth of this bus by multiplying the width of the data by the frequency of the bus. It is important to realize that neither number on its own is sufficient to determine the performance of the bus. For example a bus that runs at 100MHz delivering 32 bytes per cycle will have a bandwidth of 3.2GB/s, which is much more bandwidth than a 400MHz bus that delivers only four bytes per cycle (1.6GB/s).

The other point to observe about the bandwidth is that it is normally delivered at some granularity—the cache line size discussed earlier. So, although an application may request 1MB of data, the bus may end up transporting 64MB of data if one byte of data is used from each 64-byte cache line.

As processors are linked together, it becomes vital to ensure that data is kept synchronized. Examples of this happening might be multiple processors calculating different parts of a matrix calculation, or two processors using a "lock" to ensure that only one of them at a time accesses a shared variable.

One synchronization method is called *snooping*. Each processor will watch the traffic on the bus and check that no other processor is attempting to access a memory location of which it currently has a copy. If one processor detects another processor trying to modify memory that it has a copy of, it immediately releases that copy.

A way to improve the hardware's capability to use snooping is to use a directory mechanism. In this case, a directory is maintained showing which processor is accessing which part of memory; a processor needs to send out messages to other processors only if the memory that it is accessing is actually shared with other processors.

In some situations, it is necessary to use instructions to ensure consistency of data across multiple processors. These situations usually occur in operating system or library code, so it is uncommon to encounter them in user-written code. The requirement to use these instructions also depends on the processor; some processors may provide the necessary synchronization in hardware. In the SPARC architecture, these instructions are called MEMBAR instructions. MEMBAR instructions and memory ordering are discussed further in Section 2.5.6. On x64 processors, these instructions are called fences, and are discussed in more detail in Section 3.8.

1.9 Virtual Memory

1.9.1 Overview

Physical memory refers to the memory chips that hold the programs and their data. Each chip, and every location within each chip, has a physical address. The processor uses the physical address to fetch the data from the chip. The idea of virtual memory is that an application does not get to see where the data is physically located; the program sees a *virtual address*, and the processor translates the program's virtual addresses into physical memory addresses.

This might seem like a more complex way of doing things, but there are two big advantages to using virtual memory.

First, it allows the processor to write some data that it is not currently using to disk (a cheaper medium than RAM), and reuse the physical memory for some current data. The page containing the data gets marked as being stored on disk. When an access to this data takes place the data has to first be loaded back from disk, probably to a different physical address, but to the same virtual address. This means that more data can be held in memory than there is actual physical memory (i.e., RAM chips) on the system.

The process of storing data on disk and then reading it back later when it is needed is called *paging*. There is a severe performance penalty from paging data out to disk; disk read and write speeds are orders of magnitude slower than memory chips. However, although it does mean that the computer will slow down from this disk activity, it also means that the work will eventually complete—which is, in many cases, much better than hitting an out-of-memory error condition and crashing.

Second, it enables the processor to have multiple applications resident in memory, all thinking that they have the same layout in memory, but actually having different locations in physical memory. It is useful to have applications laid out the same way; for example, the operating system can always start an application by jumping to exactly the same virtual address. There is also an advantage in sharing information between processes. For example, the same library might be shared between multiple applications and each application could see the library at a different virtual memory address, even though only one copy of the library is loaded into physical memory.

1.9.2 TLBs and Page Size

The processor needs some way to map between virtual and physical memory. The structure that does this is called the Translation Lookaside Buffer (TLB). The processor will get a virtual address, look up that virtual address in the TLB, and obtain a physical address where it will find the data.

Virtual memory is used for both data and instructions, so typically there is one TLB for data and a separate TLB for instructions, just as there are normally separate caches for data and for instructions.

The TLBs are usually on-chip data structures, and as such they are constrained in size and can hold only a limited number of translations from virtual to physical memory. If the required translation is not in the TLB, it is necessary to retrieve the mapping from an in-memory structure sometimes referred to as a Translation Storage Buffer (TSB). Some processors have hardware dedicated to "walking" the TSB to retrieve the mapping, whereas other processors trap and pass control into the operating system where the walk is handled in software. Either way, some performance penalty is associated with accessing memory which does not have the virtual-to-physical mapping resident in the TLB. It is also possible for mappings not to be present in the TSB. The handling of this eventuality is usually relegated to software and can incur a significant performance penalty.

Each TLB entry contains mapping information for an entire "page" of memory. The size of this page depends on the sizes available in the hardware and the way the program was set up. The default page size for SPARC is 8KB, and for x64 it is 4KB.

On SPARC, the largest page size supported is 256MB. The larger the page size, the fewer TLB entries are required to map the program and data. However, allocating a large page size requires contiguous memory, and unused portions of that memory cannot be used to support other applications. Consequently, the memory footprint of the application may increase. Also, with each application having a larger footprint, fewer applications may simultaneously fit into physical memory.

1.10 Indexing and Tagging of Memory

When data is held in the cache, each line of data has to be tagged with the memory address it came from. The processor uses the tag to determine whether a particular line is a match for the memory address that it is seeking. The tags can contain either the virtual or the physical address of the data. The physical address is an ideal way of tagging the cached data, because there is a single physical address, whereas the same physical address might map onto several virtual addresses (e.g., if one copy of a library is shared among multiple applications).

Because a performance penalty is associated with accessing the TLB, the on-chip caches often use the data's virtual address as the tag. This allows rapid retrieval of data from the on-chip caches because a TLB access is not needed (it is needed only if the processor requires the physical address). The off-chip caches, which have a longer access latency, can tolerate the additional cost of doing the virtual-to-physical translation, so the data in those caches is often stored tagged by the physical address.

The line in the cache where the data is stored is also determined by the memory address; this line is referred to as the *index*. Again, either the physical or the virtual address can be used to determine the index. Hence, caches can be described as being physically or virtually indexed and physically or virtually tagged.

1.11 Instruction Set Architecture

Modern processors can execute billions of instructions every second. Typically, these instructions are very simple operations—for example, "Add one to the value held in this register" or "Load the data from this memory location into this register." When programming using a high-level language (such as C, C++, etc.) each line of source code will get broken down into many low-level instructions for the processor to execute. The low-level instructions are sometimes referred to as *machine code* (because they are what the machine executes). The term *assembly language* is also used to describe these instructions. The assembly language provides a slightly more human-readable version of the machine code.

The set of all possible low-level instructions that a processor can execute is often referred to as the processor's instruction set architecture, or ISA. Processors within the same family will share the same ISA, although different generations of processors might have minor differences in the instructions that they implement. For example, a SPARC processor must implement the SPARC ISA; however, one processor might have some implementation-dependent instructions that another SPARC processor lacks. Similarly, the x86-compatible family has processors that implement different generations of the x86 ISA, and more recent additions that support the AMD64/EMT64 64-bit instruction set extensions.

Processors in different families will have different ISAs. This is apparent when comparing the SPARC and x64 ISAs. The SPARC assembly language has a reduced instruction set computing (RISC) heritage, meaning there are relatively few machine language instructions, and these instructions are simple operations to be used as building blocks for more complex computation. Contrast this with complex instruction set computing (CISC) machines, such as the x86, where there are a large number of available instructions and many of the instructions represent complex or multistep operations. To illustrate the difference between the two, consider filling an area of memory with zero values; on a RISC machine could be achieved using a loop of about three instructions; on a CISC machine this task might be represented as a single complex instruction.

One of the more useful aspects of the RISC nature of the SPARC instruction set is that each instruction is a fixed size of four bytes. Therefore, the processor only needs to fetch instructions from 4-byte aligned addresses. A second useful feature is that given a starting address, it is possible to read instructions both backward and forward from that address, correctly interpreting the machine code. In contrast, the CISC architecture has variable-length instructions, and as a consequence of this, the processor needs to fetch instructions from any alignment. Given the address of an instruction in memory, it is often not possible to determine the previous instruction.

This book will not dwell on assembly language, or require the reader to write assembly language. However, many of the effects that impact performance can be best observed at the level of assembly language. Hence, the following chapters on SPARC and x64 processors contain simple guides to reading assembly language.

2

The SPARC Family

2.1 Chapter Objectives

This chapter discusses the SPARC architecture developed by Sun Microsystems, Inc., and the characteristics of the various processors that implement that architecture. The chapter describes features of the architecture and assembly language. By the end of the chapter, the reader will understand how to read SPARC assembly language, and the characteristics of the various SPARC-compliant processors that are available.

2.2 The UltraSPARC Family

2.2.1 History of the SPARC Architecture

Sun Microsystems, Inc., initially shipped systems based on Motorola processors, but quickly developed the Scalable Processor Architecture (SPARC). Sun developed the SPARC architecture from 1983–1985, resulting in the 32-bit SPARC Version 7 (V7) architecture. Sun shipped the first SPARC processor in 1987 in workstation and server products. Shortly thereafter, Sun evolved the V7 architecture slightly into the better-known SPARC V8 architecture, primarily by adding hardware integer multiply and divide instructions and changing its highest-precision floating-point format from 80-bit Extended Precision to 128-bit Quad Precision.

In 1989, the SPARC International industry consortium was formed, to allow the SPARC trademark to be controlled independently of Sun and to allow the SPARC architecture to evolve through the joint efforts of multiple companies. Sun donated the SPARC architecture and the SPARC trademark to SPARC International, which continues to handle licensing of both. Anyone can produce a processor based on the SPARC architecture without owing royalties to SPARC International, although there is a nominal one-time license fee. However, for it to be commercially referred to as a SPARC processor, it has to pass compliance tests.

SPARC International allowed SPARC V8 to be used as the basis for the only open-standard 32-bit Microprocessor Architecture, which was ratified in 1994 and is known as IEEE Standard 1754-1994.

In the early 1990s, the Architecture Committee of SPARC International extended SPARC V8 to support 64-bit data and 64-bit addressing, and added some instructions. The resulting architecture, SPARC V9, is the basis for all 64-bit SPARC processors. The SPARC V9 architecture specification covers the processor's instruction set and software-observable behavior, but it does not cover its physical characteristics or how it communicates with the system. It also leaves room for many implementation-dependent characteristics.

2.2.2 UltraSPARC Processors

Sun designed the UltraSPARC I processor and its successor, the UltraSPARC II processor, and first launched them in 1995. These two processors conformed to the SPARC V9 architecture. The processors could run both the old 32-bit V8 binaries and the new 64-bit V9 binaries. There were "i" and "e" versions of the processors optimized for the price-sensitive and embedded markets.

The V9 architecture also introduced instructions that are useful for 32-bit as well as 64-bit applications. These instructions operated on 64-bit data but did not rely on 64-bit addresses. This fact leads to the hybrid "v8plus" and "v8plusa" architectures. These are for 32-bit applications that use some instructions from the V9 architecture. Older V8 machines, prior to the UltraSPARC I processor, that do not support the V9 architecture will be unable to run v8plus binaries.

Whereas UltraSPARC II was an enhancement of the UltraSPARC I processor, UltraSPARC III, which was launched in 2000, boasted a completely new design. The UltraSPARC III also forms the basis for the UltraSPARC IIIi series of processors and the follow-on UltraSPARC IV processors.

In 2006, the UltraSPARC T1 processor was launched with a new design implementing the SPARC V9 architecture. The design for the UltraSPARC T1 was also made available under the GNU public license (GPL), making it the first open source 64-bit processor. In 2007, the UltraSPARC T2, the follow-on processor to the UltraSPARC T1, was launched together with systems using the SPARC64 VI processor.

2.3 The SPARC Instruction Set

2.3.1 A Guide to the SPARC Instruction Set

The SPARC processor is an example of a reduced instruction set computer (RISC). The procesor can execute a small set of simple instructions. Complex operations are completed using many of these simple instructions. The fundamental template of a machine instruction in assembly language instruction is shown in Example 2.1.

Example 2.1 Basic Template for the SPARC Assembly Language

```
Instruction <source>,<destination>
```

In its simplest form, a SPARC assembly language instruction takes something from a source (or sources) and puts it in a destination. The parameters read from left to right; the source parameter is on the left and the destination parameter is on the right. Example 2.2 shows an example of a simple instruction, the add instruction, which adds the value from one register to that from another register and places the result in a third register. In this case, the instruction adds the value from register %i1 to the value from register %i2, and places result in register %i3.

Example 2.2 The add Instruction

```
add %i1,%i2,%i3
```

Notice that the names of the registers in SPARC assembly language are denoted by a percentage sign. The integer registers on SPARC are named the global registers %g0 to %g7, the local registers %10 to %17, the input registers %i0 to %i7, and the output registers %o0 to %o7, and can hold 64-bit values. This gives a total of 32 registers, but several of the registers are reserved for particular use by the hardware, and some others are reserved for system software and therefore cannot be used freely. The registers with specific uses are detailed in Table 2.1. A few of the registers have special purposes that are worth mentioning at this point.

- Register %g0 always contains the value 0 and writes to register %g0 are discarded.

- Registers %i0 to %i7 and %o0 to %o7 have a special behavior. When a function is called, the inputs to the function are passed in the %i registers; when the function ends, the values are returned in the %o0 (and possibly %o1) registers.

A set of single-precision floating-point registers is also available, denoted %f0 to %f31. Double-precision results are stored by using two adjacent single-precision registers or by using additional double-precision registers available from %f32 to %f62. These additional double-precision registers cannot be used in single-precision calculations. The double-precision registers are addressed as the even-numbered floating-point registers.

Example 2.3 shows the floating-point double-precision addition instruction. In this case, it adds the contents of floating-point register pairs (%f0,%f1) and (%f2,%f3), and places the result in register pair (%f6,%f7). The names of all SPARC floating-point instructions start with the letter *f*. If the floating-point instructions operate on double-precision registers, the instruction ends with the letter *d*; if they use single-precision registers, it ends with the letter *s*. Consequently, there is an fadds instruction for single-precision floating-point and an faddd instruction for double-precision floating-point.

Example 2.3 Example of Floating-Point Double-Precision Addition

```
faddd %f0, %f2, %f6
```

Load and store instructions are used to load data from memory into the registers, or to store data from the registers into memory. It is necessary to specify the address of the location in memory that should be accessed. SPARC supports three *addressing modes* (ways of calculating the address of the memory location): register, register plus register, and register plus constant offset.

Example 2.4 shows various load and store operations. For the loads, the final parameter is the register that receives the data from memory; for the stores, the destination memory address is the final parameter. Notice that the memory address is enclosed in square brackets. For loads and stores, the final letter indicates the size of the data loaded or stored. If the ld or st is unadorned with a letter, it is a load or store of a 4-byte integer value or a 4-byte floating-point value—the destination register indicates whether it is integer or floating-point. A last letter of *x* indicates an "extended" 8-byte integer. If the ld or st ends with the letter *d*, it is a load or store of a double-precision floating-point value.

Example 2.4 Examples of Various Load and Store Instructions

```
ld      [%i4],%g2
ldd     [%i5+%o7],%f0
ldd     [%i1-16],%f6
stx     %o4,[%i1]
std     %f6,[%g2+%i1]
st      %f0,[%g1-64]
```

The code in Example 2.4 show all three addressing modes. The first load is from a memory location whose address is stored in a register. The second load uses the register plus register addressing mode. The third load uses the register plus constant offset addressing mode.

There are two types of control transfer instructions: branches and calls. They differ only in that a call instruction places the address of the current instruction into a register so that a later return instruction can return to this point. The SPARC instruction set has an interesting feature called the *branch delay slot*. A delay slot contains the instruction immediately following a branch, or other control transfer instruction, and this instruction gets executed with the branch. The idea was to give the processor something to do while it was completing the branch.

Example 2.5 shows an example of a branch and the instruction in its delay slot. This is a branch less than or equal to (ble) instruction, and it uses the integer condition code register (%icc) to decide whether to take the branch. The integer condition code register is set by the compare (cmp) synthetic instruction which compares the value in register %i0 with that in register %i2. The combined effect of the compare and branch instructions is to branch if the value held in %i0 is less than or equal to the value in %i2.

Example 2.5 Comparison, Branch Instruction, and Instruction in Delay Slot

```
cmp         %i0,%i2
ble,a,pt    %icc, 0x10b48
faddd       %f30, %f62, %f30
```

There are a couple of adornments to the branch. The first is the modifier ,a, which means that the following instruction should be executed only if the branch is actually taken (if the branch is not taken, the following instruction should be "annulled"). In this case, the floating-point addition will be performed only if the branch is taken. The second adornment is ,pt, which tells the processor that the compiler expected this branch to be taken most of the time; it stands for "predicted taken." A corresponding ,nt means "predicted not taken."

A `call` instruction causes a jump to a particular address, and places the address of the call instruction into the `%o7` register so that the corresponding return (`ret`) synthetic instruction can return to that point.

2.3.2 Integer Registers

Thirty-two integer registers are directly accessible at any given time on a SPARC processor. These are split into four groups: *global registers* (`%g`), which are shared across function calls; *in registers* (`%i`), which contain the parameters passed into functions; *local registers* (`%l`), which can be used to hold values that are local to a routine; and *out registers* (`%o`), which contain values to be passed on to other called routines. The integer registers are shown in Figure 2.1.

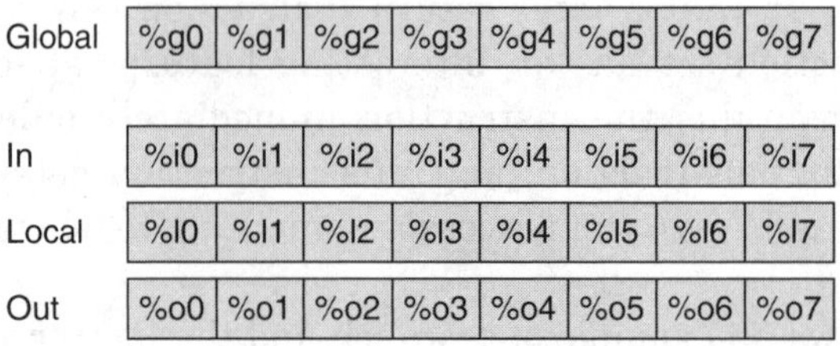

| Global | %g0 | %g1 | %g2 | %g3 | %g4 | %g5 | %g6 | %g7 |

| In | %i0 | %i1 | %i2 | %i3 | %i4 | %i5 | %i6 | %i7 |

| Local | %l0 | %l1 | %l2 | %l3 | %l4 | %l5 | %l6 | %l7 |

| Out | %o0 | %o1 | %o2 | %o3 | %o4 | %o5 | %o6 | %o7 |

Figure 2.1 Integer Registers

Several of the 32 integer registers are reserved for particular tasks. You should be careful when developing libraries not to use the registers that are reserved for application use. Table 2.1 lists the registers and their uses. Sometimes the documention refers to the registers by index number: `r[0]` is equivalent to `%g0`, `r[8]` is `%o0`, `%r[16]` is `%l0`, and `%r[24]` is `%i0`.

Table 2.1 Register Usage Conventions

Register Number	General (%g0–%g7) (%r[0]–%r[7])	Out (%o0–%o7) (%r[8]–%r[15])	Local (%l0–%l7) (%r[16]–%r[23])	In (%i0–%i7) (%r[24]–%r[31])
0	Always zero	Call parameter 1/ Returned value 1		Callee parameter 1/Return value 1
1		Call parameter 2		Callee parameter 2
2	Reserved for application	Call parameter 3		Callee parameter 3

Table 2.1 Register Usage Conventions (*continued*)

Register Number	General (%g0–%g7) (%r[0]–%r[7])	Out (%o0–%o7) (%r[8]–%r[15])	Local (%l0–%l7) (%r[16]–%r[23])	In (%i0–%i7) (%r[24]–%r[31])
3	Reserved for application	Call parameter 4		Callee parameter 4
4	Reserved for application. General use in V9 SPARC architecture.	Call parameter 5		Callee parameter 5
5	Reserved for system (only in V8 SPARC architecture)	Call parameter 6		Callee parameter 6
6	Reserved for system (e.g., DBX)	Stack pointer		Frame pointer
7	Reserved for system (current thread pointer)	Used by hardware to hold address of call instructions		Used by hardware to hold return address for callee

2.3.3 Register Windows

The processor uses what are called *register windows* to provide registers for a function that is called. When a function is called, the address of the call instruction is placed into the register %o7. Then the processor jumps to the address of the callee routine. If the callee routine needs registers with which to work, it can save the registers from the caller routine by executing the SAVE instruction. This provides a fresh "window" of registers for the routine to work with.

A register window comprises the %out registers, the %local registers, and the %in registers. When the SAVE instruction is executed, the %out registers become the %in registers, and a fresh set of %out and %local registers are given to the routine. Values that are to be passed into a routine are placed into the %out registers by the calling routine. When the called routine executes the SAVE instruction, it finds that the %in registers contain the parameters that were passed to it. If there are more than six parameters to be passed to the routine, the other parameters are passed through the stack in memory. The use of register windows is shown in Figure 2.2.

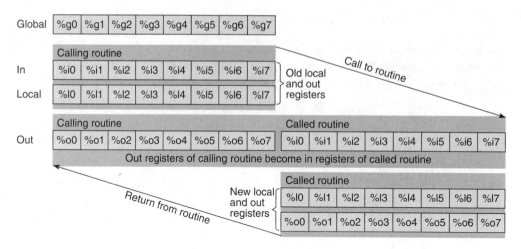

Figure 2.2 Register Windows

In the hardware, there are a number of overlapping sets of registers, and the SAVE instruction just moves to using the next set. When the routine completes, a RESTORE instruction will move the register window back up to the previous set of registers; the %in registers for the called routine become the %out registers for the calling routine; the calling routine gets back the values that it had in the %local and %in registers.

The hardware has space for only a limited number of register windows to be held on the chip. If an empty set of registers is not available, the processor traps to the operating system. The operating system then writes the oldest set of registers to memory (this is called *spilling the registers to memory*), and then this newly emptied set is presented for the routine to use. Conversely, if the RESTORE instruction finds that the previous register window has been stored in memory, the processor will trap to the operating system and the operating system will load the registers back into memory (this is called *filling the registers*).

The net result of this is that in many cases, routines are able to get fresh sets of registers to work with, without having to spill or fill anything to/from memory. A downside to this approach is that if a spill (or fill) trap does occur, sixteen 64-bit registers have to be stored to (or loaded from) memory, even if the routine requires only a couple of registers.

The other use of the SAVE and RESTORE instructions is to handle the stack and frame pointers. Both of these pointers point to *stack space* (i.e., places in main memory where temporary data, such as local variables, can be held). The stack pointer holds the address of the stack for the current routine, and the frame pointer holds the address of the stack of the routine which called the current routine. Notice that the stack pointer is held in %o6, which on a save will become %i6, the frame pointer for the called routine.

At the end of a routine, a return instruction is executed, which uses the value from %i7 to determine the address to return to. This address is typically %i7+8, because %i7 contains the address of the call instruction, and the call instruction is immediately followed by another instruction in its delay slot. So, the first new instruction is eight bytes from the address of the call instruction.

An integer return value from a routine would be placed in %i0, which becomes %o0 on return to the calling routine, after the RESTORE instruction.

2.3.4 Floating-Point Registers

There are 32 double-precision (64-bit) floating-point registers, labeled as even register numbers from %f0 to %f62. The lower 16 double-precision registers can also be accessed as single-precision (32-bit) registers; for example, the double-precision register %f0 comprises two single-precision registers %f0 and %f1. Pairs of double-precision floating-point registers can also be accessed as quad-precision (128-bit). These are labeled as register indexes that are multiples of four (%f0, %f4, ... , %f60); however, quad-precision floating-point arithmetic is performed in software on current generations of processors. The floating-point registers are shown in Figure 2.3.

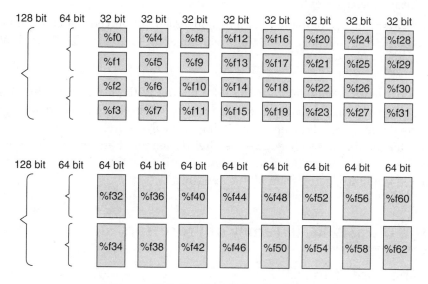

Figure 2.3 Floating-Point Registers

For 32-bit (V8) code, floating-point values are passed into routines using the integer registers; in 32-bit code, the integer registers are 32 bits wide, so double-precision floating-point values are passed in two integer registers. For 64-bit code, the calling convention is to pass floating-point values into functions using the floating-point registers.

Functions that return floating-point values place the value in %f0 for both v8 and v9 codes.

2.4 32-bit and 64-bit Code

Altough the UltraSPARC is a 64-bit processor, it has the ability to run both 32-bit and 64-bit applications. The V8 architecture represents the 32-bit instruction set; the V9 architecture has all the 64-bit instructions. Some of the instructions, the prefetch instruction, for example, from the V9 architecture can also be used in 32-bit codes.

The V9 architecture has the following differences.

- Some additional instructions (e.g., prefetch) are available.
- Floating-point numbers are passed to subroutines in floating-point registers, which can result in performance gains.
- The long data type becomes 8 bytes.
- Pointers become 8 bytes.
- A greater amount of memory can be addressed; 32-bit code can address up to 4 GB of virtual memory, and 64-bit code can address up to ~16 million terabytes of virtual memory.

There are some downsides to using 64-bit code. With the increase in data type size, the program will probably use more memory. The increase in data type size also means that more data ends up being passed around. Also, the instruction sequence for loading a 64-bit address is slightly longer than that for loading a 32-bit address. Consequently, the size of an application for both data and instructions may increase slightly going from 32-bit to 64-bit.

2.5 The UltraSPARC III Family of Processors

2.5.1 The Core of the CPU

The UltraSPARC IIII family of processors share a common core architecture, which has six execution pipes: two integer pipes, a load/store pipe, two floating-point pipes (add and multiply), and a branch pipe. A maximum of four instructions can be dispatched down these pipes in a single clock cycle.

The load/store pipe handles load, store, and *prefetch instructions*. A prefetch instruction is a request to fetch data from memory. They are issued well in advance of that data being needed in order to give time for the request to complete. Generally, only one of these three types of instructions can be dispatched per cycle. Integer divides and multiplies, being long latency instructions, are also dispatched to the load/store pipe.

There are two integer pipes, for instructions such as add, compare, and logical operations.

There is a branch pipe dedicated to handling branch instructions.

Floating-point operations get dispatched to the floating-point add (FGA) or the floating-point multiply (FGM) pipe. Floating-point square root and division are handled by the floating-point multiply pipe.

2.5.2 Communicating with Memory

The UltraSPARC III family has a number of caches that reduce both the memory traffic and the load/store latency. The first-level on-chip caches are the data cache and instruction cache. The on-chip prefetch cache is a small cache that exists to handle floating-point data. The on-chip write cache holds and coalesces stored data to reduce store bandwidth consumption. The caches where the processor first looks for data are referred to as the *first level*, or *L1 caches*. Figure 2.4 shows the caches in an UltraSPARC III family processor.

The second-level (L2) cache is accessed in parallel with the first-level cache, to reduce the latency when the data is not in the first-level cache but is in the second-level cache. This cache was off-chip on the UltraSPARC III and UltraSPARC IV processors, but on-chip for the UltraSPARC IV+ processor. The UltraSPARC IV+ processor also adds an off-chip third-level cache.

The prefetch cache is worthy of some further discussion. The prefetch cache is accessed only by floating-point loads, not integer loads. Integer loads fetch data from the data cache or from the second-level cache. Data can be prefetched into the prefetch cache by either hardware or software prefetch. Floating-point loads will load data from the prefetch cache in preference to the data cache. Hence, if there are two loads and one of them is a floating-point load that has data in the prefetch cache, it may be possible for both loads to be executed in the same cycle.

There are three methods by which to get data into the prefetch cache: a software prefetch instruction, a hardware prefetch, or a floating-point load that misses. If a floating-point load misses, the data is brought into both the data cache and the prefetch cache. If there are subsequent hits to this cache line, and

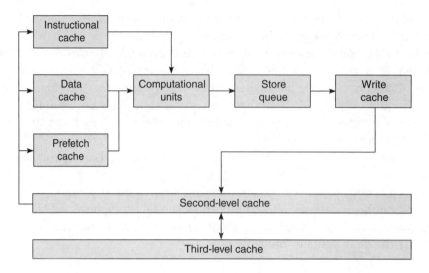

Figure 2.4 Caches in an UltraSPARC III Family Processor

the next line is present in the second-level cache, hardware prefetch will fetch the next line from the second-level cache. In this way, it is possible to do hardware streaming of floating-point data from the second-level cache into the prefetch cache and then to the registers without disturbing (or "polluting") data held in the data cache. Data in the prefetch cache will be invalidated if there is a store to that cache line.

The write cache holds data that is waiting to be flushed back to the second-level cache or to memory. When data is stored it is placed in an eight-entry store queue. This store queue drains into the write cache. When a store is written to the write cache, the rest of the cache line is fetched and merged into the cache. If the cache line to which the data is stored is also present in the data cache, that cache will be updated at the same time the store is committed to the write cache. The write cache will coalesce multiple stores to the same cache line, and therefore reduce traffic to the second-level cache.

Table 2.2 compares the cache configurations of the various members of the UltraSPARC III/IV family of processors.

2.5.3 Prefetch

One of the major benefits of the UltraSPARC III family of processors has been the introduction of more powerful software prefetch. The hardware can handle up to eight outstanding prefetches to memory. This helps with streaming data from memory, and it helps in situations where multiple data items are wanted from different

Table 2.2 Cache Configurations

Cache	UltraSPARC IIIi	UltraSPARC IIICu	UltraSPARC IV	UltraSPARC IV+
Instruction cache	64KB (four-way) 32-byte line	32KB (four-way) 32-byte line	32KB (four-way) 32-byte line	64KB (four-way) 64-byte line
Data cache	64KB (four-way) 32-byte line	64KB (four-way) 32-byte line	64KB (four-way) 32-byte line	64KB (four-way) 32-byte line
Prefetch cache	2KB (four-way) 64-byte line	2KB (four-way) 64-byte line	2KB (four-way) 64-byte line	2KB (four-way) 64-byte line
Write cache	2KB (four-way) 64-byte line	2KB (four-way) 64-byte line	2KB (four-way) 64-byte line Hashed index	2KB (four-way) 64-byte line Hashed index
Instruction translation lookaside buffer (TLB)	16-entry (16-way) 128-entry (two-way)	16-entry (16-way) 128-entry (two-way)	16-entry (16-way) 128-entry (two-way)	16-entry (4-way) 512-entry (two-way)
Data TLB	16-entry (16-way) 2x512-entry (two-way)	16-entry (16-way) 2x512-entry (two-way)	16-entry 16-way 2x512-entry (two-way)	16-entry 16-way 2x512-entry (two-way)
Second-level cache	1MB (four-way) 64-byte line	8MB (two-way) 512-byte line 64-byte subblock	8MB(two-way) 128-byte line 64-byte subblock	2MB (four-way) 64-byte line
Third-level cache	–	–	–	32MB (four-way) 64-byte line

places in memory. In most cases, the compiler is able to do a good job of inserting prefetch instructions, but it is also possible to manually insert the instructions in the instances where the compiler is suboptimal.

A number of variants of prefetch are available for different situations. The variants are summarized in Table 2.3. Data can be prefetched for reading or writing, and for single or multiple uses. This determines which caches the data is fetched into, and whether the data is fetched for shared access or for exclusive access by a single core.

There are also strong and weak variants of the prefetch instruction. On the UltraSPARC III and UltraSPARC IV, both strong and weak prefetches are interpreted as weak prefetches. Weak prefetches will be dropped on a TLB miss, or if the maximum number of outstanding prefetches is reached (the prefetch queue becomes full). If multiple prefetches are emitted to the same location in memory, the processor will drop duplicate requests. The UltraSPARC IV+ honors the strong

Table 2.3 The Four Prefetch Variants

Prefetch Variant	Used Many	Used Once
Prefetch read	Prefetch to prefetch cache and second-level cache	Prefetch to prefetch cache
Prefetch write	Prefetch to second-level cache	Prefetch to second-level cache

prefetch, which means that it will prefetch the data from memory, even if this requires handling a TLB miss. The UltraSPARC IV+ also treats the weak variant slightly differently: It will still drop a weak prefetch if it incurs a TLB miss, but it will not drop it if the prefetch queue becomes full. Instead, it will wait for an available slot.

Because prefetches are more speculative in nature, they may be assigned a lower priority than loads or stores, which may result in them taking slightly longer to fetch data from memory than a load or store might achieve.

As discussed in Section 2.5.2, the prefetch cache handles only floating-point data. Integer data cannot be prefetched into the first-level caches, but can be prefetched into the second-level cache.

2.5.4 Blocking Load on Data Cache Misses

One limitation of the UltraSPARC III family of processors is that they stall on data cache misses. So, if the data is not resident in the first-level caches, they will stall waiting for data to be returned either from the second-level caches or from memory. This was a change from the UltraSPARC II processor which stalled on the *use* of data if the data was not loaded by the time the dependent instruction was executed. This decision was made to simplify the processor pipeline. To compensate for the slight drop in average performance from this approach, the processor gained prefetch and the prefetch cache.

2.5.5 UltraSPARC III-Based Systems

The UltraSPARC IIIi processor is used in systems with up to four processors. The UltraSPARC III processor can be used in this size of system, but it can also be used in much larger systems. This is also true of the UltraSPARC IV and Ultra-SPARC IV+ processors.

A small system has the advantage of low memory latency, because the memory can be placed physically close to the processor. As the number of processors increases, the chances that the data a particular processor requires is in memory close to that processor diminishes. Solaris 9 and later have memory placement optimization (MPO) features to compensate for this by trying to colocate data with the processors that use the data.

Typically, a single board can accommodate four CPUs. The data is kept synchronized by the processors "snooping," or watching what the other processors are doing and releasing their copy of the data to which another processor wants to write.

You can use this same protocol to connect several boards, but the amount of traffic the system can handle quickly becomes limited by the amount of metadata that needs to be passed around for the data to remain synchronized (the metadata is information about which processor owns particular addresses in memory). Figure 2.5 shows two processor boards, and the route that CPU 1 would have to take to obtain data stored on the second board.

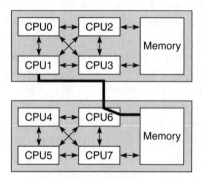

Figure 2.5 Two Boards

The time it takes to fetch data from memory depends on how the system is designed. For some systems, memory is attached to a single processor, which means that processor has low memory latency, whereas other processors have higher memory latency.

An alternative setup is that each processor has some memory, and it takes slightly longer for a processor to access the memory attached to another processor than it does to access its own memory. This is referred to as Non-Uniform Memory Access (NUMA). One way to make the memory latency more uniform under this setup is to interleave the memory. *Interleaving* is when sequential memory accesses go to memory attached to different processors. This has the advantages of presenting a memory latency that is the average over all the access times for the interleaved memory, and ensuring that memory accesses are evenly distributed across memory controllers. Interleaving is often done within a single board where the differences in memory latency between the various processors are low.

Larger systems use both directory-based and snooping protocols. The directory contains information about who owns which memory ranges. If no one is sharing a range of data, it is not necessary to use snooping to keep the data synchronized. However, if a range of data is being shared, snooping is used to maintain coherence. This means that on systems with both directory- and snoop-based coherency, processors only accessing memory that is physically located on their board have no need to tell other boards about their memory accesses. Only when a range of memory is shared between two boards is it necessary for snoop traffic to go between the boards.

Larger systems are more likely to be NUMA. The difference between memory latency for the local board and the remote board is sufficiently large that it would be inappropriate to try to "average" the memory latency through interleaving the memory accesses. The more appropriate approach is to attempt to place the data close to the processor working on it. This is achieved through MPO. The feature works by assigning each processor to a latency group or *l-group*, a set of processors with which it shares the same memory latency. Each processor within an l-group will tend to allocate memory that is also within the l-group, when it is possible to do so. The applications should run faster because more of the memory accesses are likely to be local. The other part of the MPO is to try to keep threads scheduled on processors within their home l-group. If a thread is scheduled outside of its l-group, the local memory that it was allocated will suddenly become remote memory, and the thread will suffer from increased memory latency.

2.5.6 Total Store Ordering

The SPARC architecture defines various memory ordering modes. The UltraSPARC III family of processors implements Total Store Ordering (TSO), which means that if two memory operations are issued in a particular order, the effects of the first operation will be observed by the second. For example, consider a store followed by a load. If the load is to the same address as the store, it is guaranteed that the load will see the data that the store saved.

Several other memory ordering modes define more relaxed criteria for how the processor can behave. For memory operations to be seen in the correct order on processors that implement the more relaxed modes, it is necessary to use MEMBAR instructions to maintain the ordering of memory operations. On the UltraSPARC III family of processors, it is rarely necessary to use MEMBARs; for example, it is necessary to use MEMBAR insructions in the presence of block loads and store operations. The User's Guide to the processor contains more detailed information on this. The UltraSPARC III will interpret MEMBAR instructions as NOPs if they are not required on a TSO processor.

2.6 UltraSPARC T1

The UltraSPARC T1 processor takes a different approach to providing compute power. The Throughput Computing approach is to provide many hardware threads on the processor rather than just one single thread per CPU. Each individual thread is not as fast as it could be if the processor had been designed to have just one single thread, but the fact that there are many threads means that for suitable workloads, the UltraSPARC T1 can achieve much more useful work than a processor that runs only a single thread.

The UltraSPARC T1 has between four and eight cores, depending on the system. Each core handles four threads, which means that a system can have between 16 and 32 active hardware threads. Each core has a simple design that executes a single instruction from one of its four threads every cycle. The processor is available at several different clock speeds. Assume that the processor runs at 1.2GHz. Each core will run at the same clock speed, and have four threads. This means that if each thread were always ready to execute an instruction, the threads would be running at 300MHz (300 million instructions per second); however, if only one thread is active, that thread gets the entire 1200MHz. Now, the processor's big advantage is that workloads rarely manage to run one instruction every cycle; most workloads spend a lot of time stalled, waiting for data to be returned from memory. When one thread is stalled and waiting for data from memory, the other threads share the available cycles between them. As a result, the four threads can achieve very high core utilization, which makes for very efficient use of the hardware.

Each core has a 16KB (four-way associative) instruction cache and an 8KB, four-way associative, data cache. All the cores share a single 3MB, 12-way associative L2 cache.

Another advantage of the UltraSPARC T1 is that being a single processor means it does not have to negotiate memory accesses with other processors. The memory latency, power consumption, and complexity of the system are all lower.

The UltraSPARC T1 has a single floating-point unit, which makes it unsuitable for workloads in which more than about 1% of the work comprises floating-point instructions.

2.7 UltraSPARC T2

The UltraSPARC T2 processor has a similar design to the UltraSPARC T1. However, it features two significant changes from the preceding version. The first is that each core can now handle eight threads and can issue two instructions per cycle. The eight threads are split into two groups of four instructions; one instruction from each group of four can be issued each cycle. The second change is that each core now has a dedicated floating-point unit, meaning that the processor is theoretically capable of up to 11.2 GFLOPS (when running at 1.4GHz). The processor also includes hardware acceleration for a wider range of encryption and network acceleration tasks.

2.8 SPARC64 VI

The SPARC64 VI is an out-of-order processor with two cores, each capable of executing two threads, making a total of four threads per CPU. Each core has 128KB of instruction cache and 128KB of data cache. Depending on the particular processor, either a 5MB or a 6MB on-chip second-level cache is shared between the two cores.

There are two levels of TLBs, and two 32-entry micro TLBs per core—one for data and one for instructions. There are also two data TLBs—one with 2,048 entries and the other with 32, and the same for instruction TLBs.

The processors are designed for use in systems containing between four and 64 CPUs, making a total of 16 to 256 threads.

3

The x64 Family of Processors

3.1 Chapter Objectives

This chapters gives an overview of the x64 architecture and history, covering how it has evolved, the changes to the instruction set, and the recent extensions to 64-bit. The chapter also describes the x64 assembly language and registers. By the end of the chapter, the reader will be able to comprehend simple assembly language statements, and will understand the improvements and trade-offs made in using the AMD64/EM64T instruction set.

3.2 The x64 Family of Processors

The x86 line of processors started in the late 1970s with the 16-bit 8086 processor, which was able to address up to 1MB of memory using a combination of 16-bit general registers and 16-bit segment registers that were shifted and added together to form the address. The 80286 (also called the 286) processor introduced a new mode of operation called "protected mode" (the older mode of operation was given the name "real mode"), which allowed the processor to use the values held in segment registers to address up to 16MB of memory.

The 80386, introduced in the mid 1980s, was a 32-bit x86 processor that was able to address up to 4GB of memory. Instruction set extensions, such as MMX and SSE, started to appear in the late 1990s. These extensions were initially aimed at handling media (such as video), but the later extensions included instructions to handle floating-point computation.

The x64 processor is an extension of the x86 processor with 64-bit memory addressing capabilities, additional registers, and a set of additional instructions. These extensions are also known as AMD64 or EM64T, and the original x86 instruction set is referred to as IA-32. Together with the new instructions and registers comes a new Application Binary Interface (ABI) that documents the appropriate conventions to use when writing 64-bit applications.

The processor has been extended in two ways, and it is important to consider both of these separately.

One improvement is that the processor gained the capability to handle 64-bit virtual addresses. A 32-bit processor can address up to 2^{32} bytes of memory, or 4GB. This was once an unbelievably large amount of memory, but it is now commonplace. A 64-bit processor has the capability of addressing 2^{64} bytes of memory; however, the current implementations of processors often do not have the capability to address this entire range of physical memory, using only 44 bits to address physical memory rather than the entire 64 bits. Being able to address this much memory has a lot of benefits, but the cost is that pointers and longs go from 32 bits (four bytes) to 64 bits (eight bytes), which increases the application's memory footprint. This increase in memory footprint can cause a reduction in performance as data structures become larger and more data has to be fetched from memory.

The second improvement was that the processor gained additional registers. The original x86 family of processors had very few registers. In many codes, the number of registers was insufficient to hold all the important values. The compiler would have to store (*spill*) the value in a register to memory. This would free the register to hold the next value needed by the calculation, and the original value would then have to be reloaded (called *filling*). Having more registers available means that these loads and stores can be avoided, which can lead to signficant gains in performance.

The 64-bit ABI also introduces some improvements, such as a better convention to use when passing parameters to routines, which can potentially lead to performance gains.

The important point to observe from this discussion is that there are advantages to the 64-bit processor extensions that lead to performance improvements, but there are also drawbacks to using 64-bit addressing, which can result in a loss of performance. A rule of thumb is that performance will improve unless the application makes extensive use of the pointer or long type data.

3.3 The x86 Processor: CISC and RISC

The x86 processor is a complex instruction set computer (CISC) processor. The processor has a wide range of relatively high-level instructions. For example, consider the following two snippets of code. Example 3.1 shows a memory copy loop on a SPARC processor (which is a reduced instruction set computer [RISC] processor, as discussed in Section 2.3.1 of Chapter 2).

Example 3.1 Memory Copy Loop on SPARC

```
1:    ldx   [%o1+%o3],%o4
      deccc  8, %o3
      bne  1
      stx  %o4,[%o2+%o3]
```

Example 3.2 shows an equivalent snippet of code for the x86. On the CISC processor, the entire loop has been replaced with a single instruction. Although this may look faster, typically the single instruction gets decoded within the processor to a loop of micro-instructions. So, the processor actually ends up executing micro-instructions that are broadly similar to the SPARC code, but when the disassembly is inspected only a single instruction is visible.

Example 3.2 Memory Copy Loop on x86

```
rep movsd
```

The x64 instruction set extensions are more RISC-like in nature and rely less on micro-instructions.

3.4 Byte Ordering

Another major difference between the SPARC and x86 processors is byte ordering. This refers to the order in which values are stored in memory. The SPARC processor is big-endian and the x86 processor is little-endian. The byte ordering defines whether the largest part of the values is stored lower or higher in memory. Table 3.1 shows how the 16-bit hex value 0x1234 will be stored in memory in big-endian and little-endian machines.

Table 3.1 Value 0x1234 Stored in Both Big- and Little-Endian Formats

Memory Address	Big-Endian	Little-Endian
0x2000	0x12	0x34
0x2001	0x34	0x12

A processor's *endianness* is not often important. However, there is a potential for problems in the following situations.

- When the programmer has assumed a particular order for the value in memory. Example 3.3 shows code that is sensitive to the layout of the bytes in memory. When compiled on a big-endian system the value at c[2] will be 0x14; when compiled on a little-endian system the value will be 0x13.

Example 3.3 Code That Is Sensitive to Endianness

```
#include <stdio.h>

union block
{
   int i;
   char c[4];
};

void main()
{
   union block b;
   b.i=0x12131415;
   printf("%x\n",b.c[2]);
}
```

- When reading or writing binary data to disk or over the network. If a file is to be shared between systems with two different endiannesses, care needs to be taken to either convert the file between the two systems, or program one of the two systems to convert the file as it accesses it. For example, consider a system that records 32-bit timestamps to disk every time an event occurs. The data will be ordered on disk differently depending on the system's endianness.

An example of where this problem has been solved is in the TCP/IP used in networking. In the protocol, there are a number of multibyte values. To avoid problems with endianness, these values are always defined to be big-endian. The network driver on a little-endian system has to convert these values appropriately. The byte order functions in the network library can be used to facilitate the conversion from the host endianness to the network endianness.

3.5 Instruction Template

The x64 processor has a rich instruction set. Consequently, it is outside the bounds of this book to even briefly cover all the possible instructions. However, it is necessary to have some understanding of how to interpret an x86/x64 instruction.

The x86/x64 instructions typically take two operands rather than the three found in the SPARC assembly. For example, the code shown in Example 3.4 copies a word (16 bits) from the register %ax to the register %bx. The w in the instruction mnemonic indicates that it is manipulating a word. Similar instructions exist to copy a byte (mnemonic b, eight bits), a double word (mnemonic d, 32 bits), and a quad word (mnemonic q, 64 bits). The convention I used to write the assembly language in this book is the AT&T convention, which places the destination register on the right. There is also an Intel convention which places the destination register on the left, adjacent to the instruction name.

Example 3.4 Example of an x64 Instruction

```
movw %ax, %bx
```

The calling convention for IA-32 programs is to pass parameters for function calls on the stack, not through registers. You can achieve this using push and pop instructions, which make the code look quite cluttered and involve a number of store and load operations. In comparison, the 64-bit ABI calling convention is to pass the first four parameters in registers and pass the remaining parameters on the stack. This is much closer to the SPARC calling convention. It can also be faster because, in many cases, the push and pop operations are no longer necessary.

For x86 code, the application has a stack pointer (%esp) and a base (or frame) pointer (%ebp). These two pointers perform very similar tasks—allowing programs to access parameters and local variables. It is possible to write code that does not use the base pointer (%ebp), but the cost is that it is no longer easy to identify the call stack under the debugger or performance analysis tools (or in C++ exception handling).

For x64 code, an alternative approach is to remove the need for the two pointers. This approach uses a section in the binary called .eh_frame to record, at compile time, information about the stack. The tools can use this information at runtime to gather call stack information.

3.6 Registers

One of the major changes introduced with the x64 instruction set architecture (ISA) is the increase in the number of architectural registers, from eight general-purpose registers with the IA-32 ISA to 16 with the x64 ISA. The architectural registers are the registers that you can refer to by name in instructions. Although there are a limited number of architectural registers, the processor will often have many physical registers. Each physical register can hold a value that the processor is using during current calculations, but the programmer cannot directly address the physical registers. The physical registers are necessary for out-of-order processors, because many instructions that use a given architecture register can be executing at the same time. A description of the architectural registers available on x86/x64 processors is as follows:

In 32-bit mode, there are eight 32-bit general-purpose architectural registers (%eax, %ebx, %ecx, %edx, %esi, %edi, %ebp, %esp). The lower 16 bits of these registers can be accessed as %ax, %bx, %cx, %dx, %si, %di, %bp, %sp. Finally, four of these registers can be accessed by either the lower bits (bits 0–7) or bits 8–15 as %al, %bl, %cl, %dl and %ah, %bh, %ch, %dh. Most of these registers have an assigned function: %esp is the stack pointer, %ebp is the base pointer (or frame pointer), %cx is used to hold iteration counts for the REP instruction, and %esi and %edi are the source and destination addresses for the REP MOV instruction. The 32-bit general-purpose registers are shown in Figure 3.1.

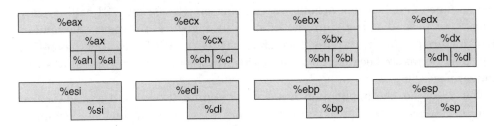

Figure 3.1 32-bit General-Purpose Registers

The segment registers (%cs, %ds, %es, %fs, %gs, %ss) remain from the original 8086 design. Most of these registers normally contain the value zero because memory is addressed as a single flat address space. However, the %fs and %gs segment registers are used to point to thread and CPU local data.

The program counter, or instruction pointer register, is named %eip (or %rip in 64-bit mode).

In 64-bit mode, the number of integer registers has been doubled to 16. The 64-bit registers are given the names %rax, %rbx, %rcx, %rdx, %rdi, %rsi, %rbp, %rsp, and %r8–%r15. The new registers are also available as 32-bit registers with the suffix *d*, and as 16-bit registers with the suffix *w*. It is possible to address the lower byte in the registers using the suffix *b*. The 64-bit general-purpose registers are shown in Figure 3.2.

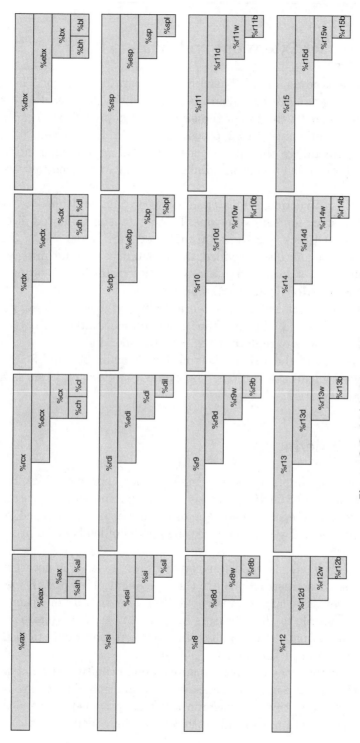

Figure 3.2 64-bit General-Purpose Registers

3.7 Instruction Set Extensions and Floating Point

The x87 was introduced as a stack-based floating-point coprocessor. The x87 used stack registers %st0–%st7 to hold floating-point values. The operations were performed on the numbers at the top of the stack. This approach has been available through many generations of IA-32 processors. Being stack-based, it has some inflexibility. One advantage that it has over most other implementations is the existence of 80-bit extended precision numbers, which can be used to provide more accurate results.

The first major instruction set extension was to add multimedia extensions, called the MMX instruction set extensions. These extensions allowed direct access to the floating-point stack registers through registers %mm0–%mm7. The MMX instruction set extensions also provided the capability of doing integer calculations on multiple items of data held in a single %mm register. This is often known as Single Instruction, Multiple Data (SIMD) processing.

Further instruction set extensions were SSE and SSE2. These added the %xmm0–%xmm7 registers and additional floating-point calculation ability. SSE2 provides sufficient operations to replace the x87 floating-point stack.

Under the 64-bit ABI, the x87 stack is no longer available, and SSE2 instructions must be used for all calculations. The number of %xmm registers is also doubled to 16 (%xmm0–%xmm15).

3.8 Memory Ordering

The x86/x64 processor implements a weaker memory ordering than Total Store Ordering (TSO) on the SPARC processor. Although individual processors will always see the results of operations in the order in which they occured, other processors on a multiple-CPU system may see the results of loads and stores in different orders.

Sometimes this behavior is important, and in these cases it is necessary to add *fence* instructions. These instructions are the equivalent of MEMBAR instructions on SPARC processors. The mfence instruction requires that all outstanding memory operations are visible to all processors before the next load or store instruction is visible. The lfence instruction applies the same constraint only to load instructions, and sfence performs the same task for stores.

The types of code that may require synchronization primitives are not within the scope of this book. They are usually necessary when multiple threads are being synchronized; normally this kind of synchronization is provided by vendor-supplied libraries, hence most programmers will not encounter these instructions.

PART II

Developer Tools

4

Informational Tools

4.1 Chapter Objectives

The objective of this chapter is to introduce the tools that are available to assist in diagnosing and determining system configuration, development, and performance problems. We will use some of these tools later in the book to examine particular situations.

By the end of the chapter, the reader will have knowledge of most commonly useful tools available both on Solaris and as part of the developer tools.

4.2 Tools That Report System Configuration

4.2.1 Introduction

This section covers tools that report static information about the system, such as the type of processor installed and so forth.

4.2.2 Reporting General System Information (`prtdiag`, `prtconf`, `prtpicl`, `prtfru`)

`prtdiag` is a purely informational tool that prints the machine's diagnostic details. The exact output depends on the system. I included it in this chapter because it can be a source of useful information about the setup of the machine. It is located in /usr/sbin. The tool is often the first place to look for information on the processors and memory that are installed in the system, as well as general system configuration.

Output from prtdiag on a two-CPU UltraSPARC IIICu system is shown in Example 4.1. The output identifies the processors and the system clock speed, together with the amount of memory installed and in which memory slots it is installed. The output refers to the UltraSPARC IIICu processor as the UltraSPARC III+, and further abbreviates this to US-3+.

Example 4.1 Sample Output from prtdiag

```
$ /usr/sbin/prtdiag
System Configuration: Sun Microsystems sun4u SUNW,Sun-Blade-1000 (2xUltraSPARC III+)
System clock frequency: 150 MHZ
Memory size: 2GB
=============================== CPUs ====================================
                    E$        CPU     CPU       Temperature
CPU    Freq         Size      Impl.   Mask     Die     Ambient
---    --------     ------    ------  ----     --------  --------
  0    900 MHz      8MB       US-III+  2.2      75 C     25 C
  1    900 MHz      8MB       US-III+  2.2      75 C     24 C
=============================== IO Devices ==============================
       Bus   Freq
Brd    Type  MHz   Slot     Name                                 Model
---    ----  ----  ----     ------------------------------       ---------------
  0    pci   33     1       SUNW,m64B (display)                  SUNW,370-4362
  0    pci   66     4       SUNW,qlc-pci1077,2200.5 (scsi-fc+
  0    pci   33     5       ebus/parallel-ns87317-ecpp (para+
  0    pci   33     5       ebus/serial-sab82532 (serial)
  0    pci   33     5       network-pci108e,1101.1 (network)     SUNW,pci-eri
  0    pci   33     5       firewire-pci108e,1102.1001 (fire+
  0    pci   33     6       scsi-pci1000,f.37 (scsi-2)
  0    pci   33     6       scsi-pci1000,f.37 (scsi-2)
======================= Memory Configuration ===========================
Segment Table:
-----------------------------------------------------------------
Base Address       Size         Interleave Factor   Contains
-----------------------------------------------------------------
0x0                2GB              4                BankIDs 0,1,2,3
Bank Table:
-----------------------------------------------------------------
              Physical Location
ID            ControllerID GroupID  Size        Interleave Way
-----------------------------------------------------------------
0             0             0        512MB       0
1             0             1        512MB       1
2             0             0        512MB       2
3             0             1        512MB       3
Memory Module Groups:
-----------------------------------------------------
ControllerID   GroupID   Labels
-----------------------------------------------------
0              0         J0100,J0202,J0304,J0406
0              1         J0101,J0203,J0305,J0407
```

Other tools exist that provide system information at various levels of detail. The tools `prtconf`, `prtpicl`, and `prtfru` produce long lists of system configuration information, the contents of which depend on the details available on the particular platform.

4.2.3 Enabling Virtual Processors (`psrinfo` and `psradm`)

`psrinfo` is a tool that will report whether the virtual processors are enabled. Sample output from `psrinfo`, run on a system with two 900MHz processors, is shown in Example 4.2. You can obtain more detailed output using `psrinfo -v`.

Example 4.2 Sample Output from `psrinfo` and `psrinfo -v`

```
$ psrinfo
0       on-line    since 11/20/2003 11:18:59
1       on-line    since 11/20/2003 11:19:00
$ psrinfo -v
Status of virtual processor 0 as of: 10/23/2006 21:47:30
  on-line since 11/20/2003 11:19:00.
  The sparcv9 processor operates at 900 MHz,
      and has a sparcv9 floating-point processor.
Status of virtual processor 1 as of: 10/23/2006 21:47:30
  on-line since 11/20/2003 11:19:00.
  The sparcv9 processor operates at 900 MHz,
      and has a sparcv9 floating-point processor.
```

Solaris 10 introduced the `-p` option to `psrinfo` that reports on the physical processors in the system. Example 4.3 shows the output from a system that has a single UltraSPARC T1 physical processor with 32 virtual processors.

Example 4.3 Output from `psrinfo -pv` from an UltraSPARC T1 System

```
$ psrinfo -pv
The physical processor has 32 virtual processors (0, 1, 2, 3, 4, 5, 6, 7, 8, 9, 10, 11,
12, 13, 14, 15, 16, 17, 18, 19, 20, 21, 22, 23, 24, 25, 26, 27, 28, 29, 30, 31)
  UltraSPARC T1 (cpuid 0 clock 1200 MHz)
```

You can enable or disable the virtual processors using the `psradm` tool. The `-f` flag will disable a processor and the `-n` flag will enable it. This tool is available only with superuser permissions.

The `-i` flag for `psradm` excludes CPUs from handling interrupts; this may be of use when partitioning the workload over multiple CPUs. Example 4.4 shows the command for excluding CPU number 1 from the CPUs that are available to handle interrupts.

Example 4.4 Excluding a CPU from Interrupt Handling

```
$ psradm -i 1
$
```

4.2.4 Controlling the Use of Processors through Processor Sets or Binding (`psrset` and `pbind`)

It is possible to configure systems so that the processors are kept in discrete sets. This will partition compute resources so that particular applications run on particular sets of processors. The command to do this is psrset, and it is available only with superuser permissions. Example 4.5 illustrates the use of processor sets.

Example 4.5 Example of the `psrset` Command

```
# psrset -c 1
created processor set 1
processor 1: was not assigned, now 1
# psrset
user processor set 1: processor 1
# psrset -e 1 sleep 1
# psrset -d 1
removed processor set 1
```

The code in Example 4.5 first shows the creation of a processor set using the psrset -c option, which takes a list of processor IDs and binds those processors into a set. The command returns the id of the set that has just been created. The command psrset with no options reports the processor sets that are currently in existence, and the processors that belong to those sets. It is possible to run a particular process on a given set using the psrset -e option, which takes both the processor set to use and the command to execute on that set. Finally, the psrset -d option deletes the processor set that is specified.

You must be careful when using processor sets (or any partitioning of the processor resources). Using processor sets, it is possible to introduce *load imbalance*, in which a set of processors is oversubscribed while another set is idle. You need to consider the allocation of processors to sets at the level of the entire machine, which is why the command requires superuser privileges.

It is a good practice to check for both the number of enabled virtual processors (using psrinfo) and the existence of processor sets whenever the system's performance is being investigated. On systems where processor sets are used regularly, or processors are often switched off, they can be a common reason for the system not providing the expected performance.

It is also possible to bind a single process to a particular processor using the pbind command, which takes the -b flag together with the pid and the processor ID as inputs when binding a process to a processor, and the -u flag together with the pid to unbind the process. Unlike processor sets that exclude other processes from running on a given group of processors, processor binding ensures that a particular process will run on a particular processor, but it does not ensure that other processes will not also run there.

4.2.5 Reporting Instruction Sets Supported by Hardware (`isalist`)

isalist is a Solaris tool that outputs the instruction sets architectures (ISAs) the processor supports. This can be useful for picking the appropriate compiler options (this will be covered in Section 5.6.5 of Chapter 5). It is also useful in determining the particular variant of CPU that the system contains. Example 4.6 shows output from the isalist command on an UltraSPARC III-based system. It shows that there is a SPARC processor in the system, and that this can handle SPARC V7, V8, and V9 binaries. The processor can also handle the VIS 2.0 instruction set extensions.

Example 4.6 Sample Output from the isalist Command

```
$ isalist
sparcv9+vis2 sparcv9+vis sparcv9 sparcv8plus+vis sparcv8plus sparcv8
sparcv8-fsmuld sparcv7 sparc
```

4.2.6 Reporting TLB Page Sizes Supported by Hardware (`pagesize`)

In Section 1.9.2 of Chapter 1 we discussed the Translation Lookaside Buffer (TLB), which the processor uses to map virtual memory addresses to physical memory addesses. Different processors are able to support different page sizes. The advantage of larger page sizes is that they let the TLB map more physical memory using a fixed number of TLB entries. For example, a TLB with 64 entries can map 8KB*64=512KB when each entry is an 8KB page, but can map 4MB*64=256MB when each entry holds a 4MB page. The number of different page sizes that can be supported simultaneously is hardware-dependent. Even if the hardware supports large page sizes, there is no guarantee that an application will recieve large pages if it requests them. The number of available large pages depends on the amount of memory in the system and the degree to which contiguous memory is available.

The pagesize command prints out the different TLB page sizes that the processor can support. If no flags are specified, the utility will print the default page size. If the flag -a is used, it will report all the available page sizes (see Example 4.7).

Example 4.7 Sample Output from the `pagesize` Command

```
$ pagesize -a
8192
65536
524288
4194304
```

The `pmap` command (covered in Section 4.4.7) reports the page sizes that an application has been allocated.

It is possible to change the page sizes that an application requests. You can do this in several ways.

- At compile time, you can use the `-xpagesize` compiler flag documented in Section 5.8.6 of Chapter 5.
- You can preload the Multiple PageSize Selection (`mpss.so.1`) library, which uses environment variables to set the page sizes. We will cover preloading in more detail in Section 7.2.10 of Chapter 7. An example of using preloading to set the page size for an application appears in Example 4.8. In this example, the environment is being set up to request 4MB pages for both the application stack and the heap.

Example 4.8 Using `mpss.so.1` to Set the Page Size for an Application

```
$ setenv MPSSHEAP 4M
$ setenv MPSSSTACK 4M
$ setenv LD_PRELOAD mpss.so.1
$ a.out
```

- You can set the preferred page size for a command or for an already running application through the `ppgsz` utility. This utility takes a set of page sizes plus either a command to be run with those page sizes, or a `pid` for those page sizes to be applied to. Example 4.9 shows examples of using the `ppgsz` command.

Example 4.9 Using the `ppgsz` Command

```
% ppgsz -o heap=4M a.out
% ppgsz -o heap=64K -p <pid>
```

Table 4.1 shows the supported page sizes for various processors.

Table 4.1 Page Sizes Supported by Various Processor Types

Processor	4KB	8KB	64KB	512KB	2MB	4MB	32MB	256MB
UltraSPARC IIICu		✓	✓	✓		✓		
UltraSPARC IV		✓	✓	✓		✓		
UltraSPARC IV+		✓	✓	✓		✓	✓	✓
UltraSPARC T1		✓	✓			✓		✓
UltraSPARC T2		✓	✓			✓		✓
SPARC64 VI		✓	✓	✓		✓	✓	✓
x64	✓				✓			

4.2.7 Reporting a Summary of SPARC Hardware Characteristics (`fpversion`)

`fpversion` is a tool that ships with the SPARC compiler and is not available on x86 architectures. The tool will output a summary of the processor's capabilities. The most important part of the output from `fpversion` is that it displays the options the compiler will use when it is told to optimize for the native platform (see `-xtarget=native` in Section 5.6.4 of Chapter 5).

Example 4.10 shows output from `fpversion` from an UltraSPARC IIICu-based system.

Example 4.10 Output from `fpversion` on an UltraSPARC IIICu Based System

```
$ fpversion
A SPARC-based CPU is available.
Kernel says CPU's clock rate is 1050.0 MHz.
Kernel says main memory's clock rate is 150.0 MHz.

Sun-4 floating-point controller version 0 found.
An UltraSPARC chip is available.

Use "-xtarget=ultra3cu -xcache=64/32/4:8192/512/2" code-generation option.

Hostid = 0x83xxxxxx.
```

4.3 Tools That Report Current System Status

4.3.1 Introduction

This section covers tools that report system-wide information, such as what processes are being run and how much the disk is being utilized.

4.3.2 Reporting Virtual Memory Utilization (vmstat)

vmstat is a very useful tool that ships with Solaris and reports the system's virtual memory and processor utilization. The information is aggregated over all the tasks of all the users of the system. Example 4.11 shows sample output from vmstat.

Example 4.11 Sample Output from vmstat

```
$ vmstat 1
 procs     memory              page              disk          faults      cpu
 r b w   swap    free    re mf pi po fr de sr f0 sd sd --   in   sy   cs us sy id
 0 0 0 5798208 1784568 25 61  1  1  1  0  0  0  1  0  0  120  170   94  9  6 85
 0 0 0 5684752 1720704  0 15  0  0  0  0  0  0  0  0  0  155   35  135 50  0 50
 0 0 0 5684752 1720688  0  0  0  0  0  0  0  0  0  0  0  117   10   98 50  0 50
 0 0 0 5684560 1720496  0 493 0  0  0  0  0  0  0  0  0  114  260   91 49  1 50
 0 0 0 5680816 1716744  2  2  0  0  0  0  0  0  0  0  0  118  196  103 50  0 50
 0 0 0 5680816 1716648 18 18  0  0  0  0  0  0  0  0  0  148   23  116 50  0 50
 0 0 0 5680816 1716584  0  0  0  0  0  0  0  0  0  0  0  115   19  100 50  0 50
 0 0 0 5680752 1716520  0 40  0  0  0  0  0 22  0  0  0  129   14   99 50  4 46
 0 0 0 5680496 1716264  0  0  0  0  0  0  0  0  0  0  0  109   24  100 50  0 50
 0 0 0 5680496 1716184 11 11  0  0  0  0  0  0  0  0  0  140   23  107 50  0 50
```

Each column of the output shown in Example 4.11 represents a different metric; the command-line argument of 1 requested that vmstat report status at one-second intervals. The first row is the average of the machine since it was switched on; subsequent rows are the results at one-second intervals.

The columns that vmstat reports are as follows.

- procs: The first three columns report the status of processes on the system. The r column lists the number of processes in the run queue (i.e., waiting for CPU resources to run on), the b column lists the number of processes blocked (e.g., waiting on I/O, or waiting for memory to be paged in from disk), and the w column lists the number of processes swapped out to disk. If the number of processes in the run queue is greater than the number of virtual processors, the system may have too many active tasks or too few CPUs.

- memory: The two columns referring to memory show the amount of swap space available and the amount of memory on the free list, both reported in kilobytes. The swap space corresponds to how much data the processor can map before it runs out of virtual memory to hold it. The free list corresponds to how much data can fit into physical memory at one time. A low value for remaining swap space may cause processes to report out-of-memory errors. You can get additional information about the available swap space through the swap command (covered in Section 4.3.3).

- `page`: The columns labeled `re` to `sr` refer to paging information. The `re` column lists the number of pages containing data from files, either executables or data, that have been accessed again and therefore reclaimed from the list of free pages. The `mf` column lists the number of minor page faults, in which a page was mapped into the process that needed it. The `pi` column lists the number of kilobytes paged in from disk and the `po` column lists the number of kilobytes paged out to disk. The `de` column lists the anticipated short-term memory shortfall in kilobytes, which gives the page scanner a target number of pages to free up. The `sr` column lists the number of pages scanned per second. A high scan rate (`sr`) is also an indication of low memory, and that the machine is having to search through memory to find pages to send to disk. The solution is to either run fewer applications or put more memory into the machine. Continuously high values of `pi` and `po` indicate significant disk activity, due to either a high volume of I/O or to paging of data to and from disk when the system runs low on memory.

- `disk`: There is space to report on up to four disk drives, and these columns show the number of disk operations per second for each of the four drives.

- `faults`: There are three columns on faults (i.e., traps and interrupts). The `in` column lists the number of interrupts; these are used for tasks such as handling a packet of data from the network interface card. The `sy` column lists the number of system calls; these are calls into the kernel for the system to perform a task. The `cs` column lists the number of context switches, whereby one thread leaves the CPU and another is placed on the CPU.

- `cpu`: The final three columns are the percentage of user, system, and idle time. This is an aggregate over all the processors. Example 4.11 shows output from a two-CPU machine. With an idle time of 50%, this can mean that both CPUs are busy, but each only half the time, or that only one of the two CPUs is busy. In an ideal world, most of the time should be spent in user code, performing computations, rather than in the system, managing resources. Of course, this does not mean that the time in user code is being spent efficiently, just that the time isn't spent in the kernel or being idle. High levels of system time mean something is wrong, or the application is making many system calls. Investigating the cause of high system time is always worthwhile.

4.3.3 Reporting Swap File Usage (`swap`)

Swap space is disk space reserved for anonymous data (data that is not otherwise held on a filesystem). You can use the `swap` command to add and delete swap space from a system. It can also list the locations of swap space using the `-l` flag, and report a summary of swap space usage under the `-s` flag. Examples of output from both of these flags is shown in Example 4.12.

Example 4.12 Output from the `swap` Command

```
% swap -l
swapfile              dev  swaplo   blocks      free
/dev/dsk/c1t0d0s1   118,33      16 25175408  25175408
% swap -s
total: 2062392k bytes allocated + 1655952k reserved = 3718344k used, 36500448k avail-
able
```

4.3.4 Reporting Process Resource Utilization (`prstat`)

`prstat` was a very useful addition to Solaris 8. It prints out a list of the processes that are consuming the most processor time, which can be helpful in identifying processes that are consuming excessive amounts of CPU resources. It also reports useful values, such as the amount of memory used.

Example 4.13 shows the first few lines of output from `prstat`. It reports a screen of information, each line representing a particular process. By default, the processes are listed starting with the one that is consuming the most CPU time.

Example 4.13 Sample Output from `prstat`

```
  PID USERNAME  SIZE   RSS STATE  PRI NICE      TIME  CPU PROCESS/NLWP
29013 martin   4904K 1944K cpu0    40    0   0:01:15  44% myapplication/1
  210 root     4504K 2008K sleep   59    0   0:27:34 0.1% automountd/2
29029 martin   4544K 4256K cpu1    59    0   0:00:00 0.1% prstat/1
  261 root     2072K    0K sleep   59    0   0:00:00 0.0% smcboot/1
...
```

The columns are as follows.

- `PID`: The process ID (PID), which is a unique number assigned to identify a particular process.
- `USERNAME`: The ID of the user owning the process.
- `SIZE`: The total size of the process. This is a measure of how much virtual address space has been allocated to the process. It does not measure how much physical memory the process is currently using.
- `RSS`: The resident set size (RSS) of the process, that is, how much of the process is actually in memory. The RSS of an application can fluctuate depending on how much data the application is currently using, and how much of the application has been swapped out to disk.

- STATE: The state of the process, that is, whether it is sleeping, on a CPU (as the two processes for "martin" are in the example), or waiting for a processor to run on.

- PRI: The priority of the process, which is a measure of how important it is for CPU time to be allocated to a particular process. The higher the priority, the more time the kernel will allow the process to be on a CPU.

- NICE: The nice value for the process, which allows the user to reduce the priority of an application to allow other applications to run. The higher the nice value, the less CPU time will be allocated to it.

- TIME: The CPU time that the process has accumulated since it started.

- CPU: The percentage of the CPU that the process has recently consumed.

- PROCESS/NLWP: The name of the executable, together with the number of lightweight processes (LWPs) in the process. From Solaris 9 onward, LWPs are equivalent to threads. prstat can also report activity on a per-thread basis using the -L flag.

You can obtain a more accurate view of system utilization by using the prstat command with the -m flag. This flag reports processor utilization using microstate accounting information. Microstate accounting is a more accurate breakdown of where the process spends its time. Solaris 10 collects microstate accounting data by default. Example 4.14 shows example output from this command.

Example 4.14 Output from prstat -m

```
  PID USERNAME USR SYS TRP TFL DFL LCK SLP LAT VCX ICX SCL SIG PROCESS/NLWP
 1946 martin   0.1 0.3 0.0 0.0 0.0 0.0 100 0.0  23   0 280   0 prstat/1
 5063 martin   0.2 0.0 0.0 0.0 0.0 0.0 100 0.0  24   0  95   0 gnome-panel/1
 5065 martin   0.2 0.0 0.0 0.0 0.0 0.0 100 0.0  13   0  22   0 nautilus/3
 7743 martin   0.1 0.0 0.0 0.0 0.0 0.0 100 0.0  61   0  76   0 soffice1.bin/6
 5202 martin   0.0 0.0 0.0 0.0 0.0 0.0 100 0.0  24   2  40   0 gnome-termin/1
...
Total: 115 processes, 207 lwps, load averages: 0.00, 0.01, 0.02
```

The columns in Example 4.14 are as follows.

- PID: The PID of the process.
- USERNAME: The User ID of the process owner.
- USR to LAT: The percentage of time spent by the process in the various modes: user mode (USR), system mode (SYS), system traps (TRP), text (i.e., program instruction) page faults (TFL), data page faults (DFL), user locks (LCK), sleeping (SLP), and waiting for the CPU (LAT).

- VCX and ICX: The number of context switches, voluntary (VCX) and involuntary (ICX). A voluntary context switch is one in which the process either completes its task and yields the CPU, or enters a wait state (such as waiting for data from disk). An involuntary context switch is one in which another higher-priority task is assigned to the CPU, or the process uses up its allocation of time on the CPU.
- SCL: The number of system calls.
- SIG: The number of signals received.
- PROCESS/NLWP: The name of the process (PROCESS) and the number of LWPs (NLWP).

It is possible to use the <column> flag -s to sort by a particular column. In Example 4.15, this is used to sort the processes by RSS.

Example 4.15 Output from prstat Sorted by RSS

```
$ prstat -s rss
   PID USERNAME  SIZE   RSS STATE  PRI NICE      TIME  CPU PROCESS/NLWP
  8453 root      403M  222M sleep   49    0  13:17:50 0.0% Xsun/1
 28059 robin     218M  133M sleep   49    0   0:06:04 0.1% soffice2.bin/5
 28182 robin     193M   88M sleep   49    0   0:00:54 0.0% soffice1.bin/7
 26704 robin      87M   72M sleep   49    0   0:06:35 0.0% firefox-bin/4
...
```

4.3.5 Listing Processes (ps)

ps displays a list of all the processes in the system. It is a very flexible tool and has many options. The output in Example 4.16 shows one example of what ps can report.

Example 4.16 Sample Output from ps

```
$ ps -ef
   UID   PID  PPID  C    STIME TTY      TIME CMD
  root     0     0  0   Jul 06 ?        0:00 sched
  root     1     0  0   Jul 06 ?        0:01 /etc/init -
  root     2     0  0   Jul 06 ?        0:13 pageout
...
```

The options passed to the ps command in Example 4.16 are -e, to list all the processes; and -f, to give a "full" listing, which is a particular set of columns (in particular, it gives more information about how the application was invoked than the alternative -l "long" listing).

The columns in the output are as follows.

- UID: The UID of the user who owns the process. A large number of processes are going to be owned by root.
- PID: The PID of the process.
- PPID: The PID of the parent process.
- C: This column is obsolete. It used to report processor utilization used in scheduling.
- STIME: The start date/time of the application.
- TTY: The controlling terminal for the process (where the commands that go to the process are being typed). A question mark indicates that the process does not have a controlling terminal.
- TIME: The accumulated CPU time of the process.
- CMD: The command being executed (truncated to 80 characters). Under the -f flag, the arguments are printed as well, which can be useful for distinguishing between two processes of the same name.

One of the most useful columns is the total accumulated CPU time for a process, which is the amount of time it has been running on a CPU since it started. This column is worth watching to check that the critical programs are not being starved of time by the noncritical programs.

Most of the time it is best to pipe the output of ps to some other utility (e.g., grep), because even on an idle system there can be many processes.

4.3.6 Locating the Process ID of an Application (pgrep)

It is often necessary to find out the PID of a process to examine the process further. It is possible to do this using the ps command, but it is often more convenient to use the pgrep command. This command returns processes with names that match a given text string, or processes that are owned by a given user. Example 4.17 shows two examples of the use of this command. The first example shows the tool being used to match the name of an executable. In the example, the -l flag specifies that the long output format should be generated, which includes the name of the program. The second example shows the -U flag, which takes a username and returns a list of processes owned by that particular user—in this case, the processes owned by root.

Example 4.17 Output from `pgrep`

```
% pgrep -l soff
28059 soffice2.bin
28182 soffice1.bin
% pgrep -lU root
    0 sched
    1 init
    2 pageout
    3 fsflush
  760 sac
...
```

4.3.7 Reporting Activity for All Processors (`mpstat`)

The `mpstat` tool reports activity on a per-processor basis. It reports a number of useful measures of activity that may indicate issues at the system level. Like `vmstat`, `mpstat` takes an interval parameter that specifies how frequently the data should be reported. The first lines of output reported give the data since boot time; the rates are reported in events per second. Sample output from `mpstat` is shown in Example 4.18.

Example 4.18 Sample Output from `mpstat`

```
$ mpstat 1
CPU minf mjf xcal  intr ithr  csw icsw migr smtx  srw syscl  usr sys  wt idl
  0   29   1   38   214  108  288   10    6   14    0   562   36   2   0  62
  1   27   1   27    44   29  177    9    6   67    0   516   33   2   0  65
CPU minf mjf xcal  intr ithr  csw icsw migr smtx  srw syscl  usr sys  wt idl
  0    7   0   11   207  103   64    9   10    0    0     7   39   1   0  60
  1    0   0    4    14    2   54   11   11    0    0     5   61   0   0  39
CPU minf mjf xcal  intr ithr  csw icsw migr smtx  srw syscl  usr sys  wt idl
  0    0   0    6   208  106   60    7    8    0    0    14   47   0   0  53
  1    0   0   65    16    9   46    6    7    0    0     4   53   2   0  45
CPU minf mjf xcal  intr ithr  csw icsw migr smtx  srw syscl  usr sys  wt idl
  0    0   0    6   204  103   36    6    3    0    0     5   68   0   0  32
  1    0   0    1     9    2   64    6    7    0    0     5   32   0   0  68
CPU minf mjf xcal  intr ithr  csw icsw migr smtx  srw syscl  usr sys  wt idl
  0    0   0    2   205  104   14   10    2    0    0     4   98   0   0   2
  1    0   0    1    34   31   93    2    2    0    0    15    2   0   0  98
CPU minf mjf xcal  intr ithr  csw icsw migr smtx  srw syscl  usr sys  wt idl
  0    0   0    8   204  104   40    2    6    0    0     5   51   0   0  49
  1    0   0    0    11    2   58    8    6    0    0     5   49   0   0  51
....
```

Each line of output corresponds to a particular CPU for the previous second. The columns in the `mpstat` output are as follows.

- CPU: The ID of the CPU to which the data belongs. Data is reported on a per-CPU basis.

- `minf`: The number of minor page faults per second. These occur when a page of memory is mapped into a process.

- `mjf`: The number of major page faults per second. These occur when the requested page of data has to be brought in from disk.

- `xcal`: The number of interprocess cross-calls per second. This occurs when a process on one CPU requests action from another. An example of this is where memory is unmapped through a call to `munmap`. The `munmap` call will use a cross call to ensure that other CPUs also remove the mapping to the target memory range from their TLB.

- `intr`: The number of interrupts per second.

- `ithr`: The number of interrupt threads per second, not counting the clock interrupt. These are lower-priority interrupts that are handled by threads that are scheduled onto the processor to handle the interrupt event.

- `csw`: The number of context switches per second, where the process either voluntarily yields its time on the processor before the end of its allocated slot or is involuntarily displaced by a higher-priority process.

- `icsw`: The number of involuntary context switches per second, where the process is removed from the processor either to make way for a higher-priority thread or because it has fully utilized its time slot.

- `migr`: The number of thread migrations to another processor per second. Usually, best performance is obtained if the operating system keeps the process on the same CPU. In some instances, this may not be possible and the process is migrated to a different CPU.

- `smtx`: The number of times a mutex lock was not acquired on the first try.

- `srw`: The number of times a read/write lock was not acquired on the first try.

- `syscl`: The number of system calls per second.

- `usr`: The percentage of time spent in user code.

- `sys`: The percentage of time spent in system code.

- `wt`: The percentage of time spent waiting on I/O. From Solaris 10 onward, this will report zero because the method of calculating wait time has changed.

- `idl`: The percentage of time spent idle.

In the code in Example 4.18, the two processors are spending about 50% of their time in user code and 50% of their time idle. In fact, just a single process is running. What is interesting is that this process is migrating between the two processors (you can see this in the migrations per second). It is also apparent that processor 0 is handling most of the interrupts.

4.3.8 Reporting Kernel Statistics (`kstat`)

`kstat` is a very powerful tool for returning information about the kernel. The counts it produces are the number of events since the processor was switched on. So, to determine the number of events that an application causes, it is necessary to run `kstat` before and after the application, and determine the difference between the two values. Of course, this is accurate only if just one process is running on the system. Otherwise, the other processes can change the numbers.

One of the metrics that `kstat` reports is the number of emulated floating-point instructions. Not all floating-point operations are performed in hardware; some have been left to software. Obviously, software is more flexible, but it is slower than hardware, so determining whether an application is doing any floating-point operations in software can be useful. An example of checking for unfinished floating-point traps is shown in Example 4.19. The `-p` option tells `kstat` to report statistics in a parsable format; the `-s` option selects the statistic of interest.

Example 4.19 Using `kstat` to Check for Unfinished Floating-Point Traps

```
$ kstat -p -s 'fpu_unfinished_traps'
unix:0:fpu_traps:fpu_unfinished_traps          32044940
$ a.out
$ kstat -p -s 'fpu_unfinished_traps'
unix:0:fpu_traps:fpu_unfinished_traps          32044991
```

Example 4.19 shows the number of unfinished floating-point operations reported by `kstat` before the application ran, and the number afterward. The difference between the two values is 51, which means that 51 unfinished floating-point operations were handled by trapping to software between the two calls to `kstat`. It is likely that these traps were caused by the application `a.out`, but if there was other activity on the system, these traps cannot be confidently attributed to any one particular process. To have some degree of confidence in the number of traps on a busy system, it is best to repeat the measurement several times, and to measure the number of traps that occur when the application is not running.

4.3.9 Generating a Report of System Activity (`sar`)

The `sar` utility records system activity over a period of time into an archive for later analysis. It is possible to select which aspects of system performance are recorded. Once an archive of data has been recorded, `sar` is also used to extract the particular activities of interest.

To record a `sar` data file it is necessary to specify which system events should be recorded, the name of the file in which to record the events, the interval between samples, and the number of samples you want. An example command line for sar is shown in Example 4.20.

Example 4.20 Example Command Line for sar

```
$ sar -A -o /tmp/sar.dat 5 10
```

This instructs sar to do the following.

1. Record all types of events (-A).
2. Store the events in the file /tmp/sar.dat.
3. Record a sample at 5-second intervals.
4. Record a total of 10 samples.

When sar runs it will output data to the screen as well as to the data file, as shown in Example 4.21.

Example 4.21 Output from sar as It Runs

```
$ sar -A -o /tmp/sar.dat 5 10

SunOS machinename 5.9 Generic_112233-01 sun4u    08/26/2003

21:07:39    %usr    %sys    %wio    %idle
            device  %busy   avque   r+w/s   blks/s  avwait  avserv
            runq-sz %runocc swpq-sz %swpocc
            bread/s lread/s %rcache bwrit/s lwrit/s %wcache pread/s      pwrit/s
            swpin/s bswin/s swpot/s bswot/s pswch/s
            scall/s sread/s swrit/s fork/s  exec/s  rchar/s wchar/s
            iget/s  namei/s dirbk/s
            rawch/s canch/s outch/s rcvin/s xmtin/s mdmin/s
            proc-sz ov      inod-sz ov      file-sz ov      lock-sz
            msg/s   sema/s
            atch/s  pgin/s  ppgin/s pflt/s  vflt/s  slock/s
            pgout/s ppgout/s pgfree/s pgscan/s %ufs_ipf
            freemem freeswap
            sml_mem alloc   fail    lg_mem  alloc   fail    ovsz_alloc fail

21:07:44      50      1         0      50
              fd0       0            0.0      0      0     0.0       0.0
              ssd0      0            0.0      0      0     0.0       0.0
              ssd0,a    0            0.0      0      0     0.0       0.0
              ssd0,b    0            0.0      0      0     0.0       0.0
              ssd0,c    0            0.0      0      0     0.0       0.0
              ssd0,h    0            0.0      0      0     0.0       0.0
              ssd1      0            0.0      0      0     0.0       0.0
              ssd1,a    0            0.0      0      0     0.0       0.0
```

continues

Example 4.21 Output from `sar` as It Runs (*continued*)

```
    ssd1,b        0          0.0        0        0     0.0      0.0
    ssd1,c        0          0.0        0        0     0.0      0.0
    ssd1,h        0          0.0        0        0     0.0      0.0
      0.0         0          0.0        0
        0         0          100        0        0     100        0        0
     0.00       0.0         0.00      0.0       99
       76         6           14     0.00     0.00    1550     2850
        0         0            0
        0         0          161        0        0       0
  65/30000        0  157574/157574      0      0/0       0      0/0
     0.00      0.00
     0.00      0.00         0.00     0.60     2.20    0.00
     0.00      0.00         0.00     0.00     0.00
   247682  17041644
        0         0            0        0        0       0  17858560        0
```

Example 4.21 presents a lot of information. The text at the beginning supplies a template that indicates what the counters represent. The information is as follows.

- First it reports the time the system spent in user (`%usr`), system (`%sys`), waiting for block I/O (`%wio`), and idle (`%idle`).

- Next is a section for each device that reports the device name, percentage of time busy (`%busy`), average queue length while the device was busy (`avque`), number of reads and writes per second (`r+w/s`), number of 512-byte blocks transferred per second (`blk/s`), average wait time in ms (`avwait`), and average service time in ms (`avserv`).

- The length of the queue of runnable processes (`runq_sz`) and the percentage of time occupied (`%runocc`) are listed next. The fields `swpq-sz` and `%swpocc` no longer have values reported for them.

- Next is the number of transfers per second of buffers to disk or other block devices. Read transfers per second (`bread/s`), reads of system buffers (`lread/s`), cache hit rate for reads (`%rcache`), write transfers per second (`bwrit/s`), writes of system buffers (`lwrit/s`), cache hit rate for writes (`%wcache`), raw physical device reads (`pread/s`), and raw physical device writes (`pwrit/s`) are included.

- Swapping activity is recorded as the number of swap-ins per second (`swpin/s`), number of blocks of 512 bytes swapped in (`bswin/s`), number of swap-outs per second (`swpot/s`), number of 512-byte blocks swapped out (`bswot/s`), and number of process switches per second (`pswch/s`). The number of 512-byte blocks transfered includes the loading of programs.

- System calls are reported as the total number of system calls per second (`scall/s`), number of read calls per second (`sread/s`), number of write calls per second (swrit/s), number of forks per second (fork/s), number of execs per second (exec/s), number of characters transferred by read (rchar/s), and number of characters transferred by write (wchar/s).

- Next is a report of file access system routines called per second. The number of files located by inode entry (iget/s), number of file system pathname searchs (namei/s), and number of directory block reads (dirbk/s) are included.

- TTY I/O reports stats on character I/O to the controlling terminal. This includes raw character rate (rawch/s), processed character rate (canch/s), output character rate (outch/s), receive rate (rcvin/s), transmit rate (xmtin/s), and modem interrupts per second (mdmin/s).

- Process, inode, file, and lock table sizes are reported as proc-sz, inod-sz, file-sz, and lock_sz. The associated overflow (ov) fields report the overflows that occur between samples for each table.

- The number of messages and semaphores per second is reported as msg/s and sema/s.

- Paging to memory is reported as the number of page faults per second that were satisfied by reclaiming a page from memory (atch/s), the number of page-in requests per second (pgin/s), the number of page-ins per second (ppgin/s), the number of copy on write page faults per second (pflt/s), the number of page not in memory faults per second (vflt/s), and the number of faults per second caused by software locks requiring physical I/O (slock/s).

- Paging to disk is reported as the number of requested page-outs per second (pgout/s), the number of page-outs per second (ppgout/s), the number of pages placed on the free list per second (pgfree/s), the number of pages scanned per second (pgscan/s), and the percentage of igets that required a page flush (%ufs_ipf).

- Free memory is reported as the average number of pages available to user processes (freemem), and the number of disk blocks available for swapping (freeswap).

- Kernel memory allocation is reported as a small memory pool of free memory (sml_mem), the number of bytes allocated from the small memory pool (alloc), and the number of requests for small memory that failed (fail). Similar counters exist for the large pool (lg_mem, alloc, fail). The amount of memory allocated for oversize requests is reported as ovsz_alloc, and the number of times this failed as fail.

The command to read an existing `sar` output file is shown in Example 4.22.

Example 4.22 Command Line to Instruct `sar` to Read an Existing Data File

```
$ sar -A -f /tmp/sar.dat
```

This asks `sar` to output all (-A) the information from the `sar` archive (/tmp/sar.dat). It is possible to request that `sar` output only a subset of counters.

In the `sar` output shown in Example 4.21, it is apparent that the CPU is 50% busy (in fact, it is a two-CPU system, and one CPU is busy compiling an application), and that there is some character output and some read and write system calls. It is reasonably apparent that the system is CPU-bound, although it has additional CPU resources which could potentially be used to do more work.

4.3.10 Reporting I/O Activity (`iostat`)

The `iostat` utility is very similar to `vmstat`, except that it reports I/O activity rather than memory statistics.

The first line of output from `iostat` is the activity since boot. Subsequent lines represent the activity over the time interval between reports. Example output from `iostat` is shown in Example 4.23.

Example 4.23 Example of `iostat` Output

```
% iostat 1
      tty          ssd0           ssd1           nfs1           nfs58          cpu
  tin tout kps tps serv  kps tps serv  kps tps serv  kps tps serv  us sy wt id
    0    2  17   1   90   22   1   45    0   0    0    0   0   27  20  1  0 79
    0  234   0   0    0    8   1    6    0   0    0    0   0    0  50  2  0 48
    0   80   0   0    0    0   0    0    0   0    0    0   0    0  50  0  0 50
    0   80   0   0    0  560   4   16    0   0    0    0   0    0  46  2  1 50
    0   80   0   0    0  352   4   13    0   0    0    0   0    0  48  8  0 44
    0   80   0   0    0  560  15   13    0   0    0    0   0    0  42  6  2 50
```

The information is as follows.

- The first two columns give the number of characters read (`tin`) and written (`tout`) for the tty devices.

- The next four sets of three columns give information for four disks. The `kps` column lists the number of kilobytes per second, `tps` the number of transfers per second, and `serv` the average service time in ms.

- CPU time is reported as a percentage in user (`us`), system (`sy`), waiting for I/O (`wt`), and idle (`id`).

Another view of I/O statistics is provided by passing the `-Cnx` option to `iostat`. Output from this is shown in Example 4.24.

Example 4.24 Output from `iostat -Cnx 1`

```
$ iostat -Cnx 1
....
                    extended device statistics
    r/s    w/s   kr/s    kw/s wait actv wsvc_t  asvc_t  %w  %b device
    0.0   25.0    0.0   594.0  0.0  0.3    0.0    12.7   0   4 c0
    0.0    0.0    0.0     0.0  0.0  0.0    0.0     0.0   0   0 c1
    0.0    0.0    0.0     0.0  0.0  0.0    0.0     0.0   0   0 c0t0d0
    0.0   25.0    0.0   594.0  0.0  0.3    0.0    12.7   0   8 c0t1d0
    0.0    0.0    0.0     0.0  0.0  0.0    0.0     0.0   0   0 c1t2d0
...
```

In Example 4.24, each disk gets a separate row in the output. The output comprises the following columns:

- `r/s`: Reads per second
- `w/s`: Writes per second
- `kr/s`: Kilobytes read per second
- `kw/s`: Kilobytes written per second
- `wait`: Average number of transactions waiting for service
- `actv`: Average number of transactions actively being serviced
- `wsvc_t`: Average service time in wait queue, in milliseconds
- `asvc_t`: Average time actively being serviced, in milliseconds
- `%w`: Percentage of time the waiting queue is nonempty
- `%b`: Percentage of time the disk is busy
- `device`: The device that this applies to

In the example shown in Example 4.24, the busy device is `c0t1d0`, which is writing out about 600KB/s from 25 writes (about 24KB/write), each write taking about 13 ms. The device is busy about 8% of the time and has an average of about 0.3 writes going on at any one time.

If a disk is continuously busy more than about 20% of the time, it is worth checking the average service time, or the time spent waiting in the queue, to ensure that these are low. Once the disk starts to become busy, the service times may increase significantly. If this is the case, it may be worth investigating whether to spread file activity over multiple disks. The `iostat` options `-e` and `-E` will report the errors that have occurred for each device since boot.

4.3.11 Reporting Network Activity (`netstat`)

`netstat` can provide a variety of different reports. The `-s` flag shows statistics per protocol. A sample of the output showing the statistics for the IPv4 protocol is shown in Example 4.25.

Example 4.25 Example of `netstat -s` Output

```
% netstat -s
...
IPv4    ipForwarding        =        2    ipDefaultTTL        =      255
        ipInReceives        =8332869      ipInHdrErrors       =        0
        ipInAddrErrors      =        0    ipInCksumErrs       =        0
        ipForwDatagrams     =        0    ipForwProhibits     =        0
        ipInUnknownProtos   =        2    ipInDiscards        =        0
        ipInDelivers        =8316558      ipOutRequests       =13089344
        ipOutDiscards       =        0    ipOutNoRoutes       =        0
        ipReasmTimeout      =       60    ipReasmReqds        =        0
        ipReasmOKs          =        0    ipReasmFails        =        0
        ipReasmDuplicates   =        0    ipReasmPartDups     =        0
        ipFragOKs           =        0    ipFragFails         =        0
        ipFragCreates       =        0    ipRoutingDiscards   =        0
        tcpInErrs           =        0    udpNoPorts          =    17125
        udpInCksumErrs      =        0    udpInOverflows      =        0
        rawipInOverflows    =        0    ipsecInSucceeded    =        0
        ipsecInFailed       =        0    ipInIPv6            =        0
        ipOutIPv6           =        0    ipOutSwitchIPv6     =      213
...
```

You can obtain a report showing input and output from `netstat -i`; an example is shown in Example 4.26. This output shows the number of packets sent and received, the number of errors, and finally the number of collisions.

Example 4.26 Example of `netstat -i` Output

```
% netstat -i 1
input    eri0  output                    input  (Total) output
packets errs  packets errs   colls   packets errs   packets errs  colls
486408174 5   499073054 3       0   530744745 5   543409625 3       0
        5 0           9 0       0          12 0          16 0        0
        6 0          10 0       0          13 0          17 0        0
        6 0          10 0       0          14 0          18 0        0
```

The collision rate is the number of collisions divided by the number of output packets. A value greater than about 5% to 10% may indicate a problem. Similarly, you can calculate error rates by dividing the number of errors by the total input or output packets. An error rate greater than about one-fourth of a percent may indicate a problem.

4.3.12 The snoop command

The snoop command, which you must run with superuser privileges, gathers information on the packets that are passed over the network. It is a very powerful way of examining what the network is doing, and consequently the command has a large number of options. In "promiscuous" mode, it gathers all packets that the local machine can see. In nonpromiscuous mode (enabled using the -P flag), it only gathers information on packages that are addressed to the local machine. It is also possible to gather a trace of the packets (using the -o flag) for later processing by the snoop command (using the -i flag). The packets collected (or examined) can be filtered in various ways, perhaps most usefully by the machines communicating, alternatively individual packets can be printed out. An example of the output from the snoop command is shown in Example 4.27.

Example 4.27 Output from the snoop Command

```
$ snoop
Using device /dev/eri (promiscuous mode)
here -> mc1 TCP D=1460 S=5901 Ack=2068723218 Seq=3477475694 Len=0 Win=50400
here -> mc2 TCP D=2049 S=809  Ack=3715747853 Seq=3916150345 Len=0 Win=49640
mc1 -> here TCP D=22   S=1451 Ack=3432082168 Seq=2253017191 Len=0 Win=33078
...
```

Note that snoop can capture and display unencrypted data being passed over the network. As such, use of this tool may have privacy, policy, or legal issues in some domains.

4.3.13 Reporting Disk Space Utilization (df)

The df command reports the amount of space used on the disk drives. Example output from the df command in shown in Example 4.28.

Example 4.28 Example Output from the df Command

```
% df -kl
Filesystem            kbytes     used    avail capacity  Mounted on
/dev/dsk/c0t1d0s0    3096423  1172450  1862045    39%    /
/proc                      0        0        0     0%    /proc
mnttab                     0        0        0     0%    /etc/mnttab
fd                         0        0        0     0%    /dev/fd
swap                 9475568       48  9475520     1%    /var/run
swap                 9738072   262552  9475520     3%    /tmp
/dev/dsk/c0t1d0s7   28358357 26823065  1251709    96%    /data
/dev/dsk/c0t2d0s7   28814842 23970250  4556444    85%    /export/home
```

The `-kl` option tells `df` to report disk space in kilobytes (rather than as the number of 512-byte blocks), and to only report data for local drives. The columns are reasonably self-explanatory and include the name of the disk, the size, the amount used, the amount remaining, and the percentage amount used. The final column shows the mount point. In this example, both the `/data` and the `/export/home` file systems are running low on available space. On Solaris 9 and later there is a `-h` option to produce the output in a more human-readable format.

4.3.14 Reporting Disk Space Used by Files (`du`)

The `du` utility reports the disk space used by a given directory and its subdirectories. Once again, there is a `-k` option to report usage in kilobytes. On Solaris 9 and later, there is also a `-h` option to report in a human-readable format. Example output from the `du` command is shown in Example 4.29.

Example 4.29 Example of Output from the `du` Command

```
% du -k
8         ./.X11-unix
8         ./.X11-pipe
3704      .
% du -h
   8K     ./.X11-unix
   8K     ./.X11-pipe
 3.6M     .
```

The `du` command in Example 4.29 reported that two directories consume 8KB each, and there is about 3.6MB of other data in the current directory.

4.4 Process- and Processor-Specific Tools

4.4.1 Introduction

This section covers tools that report the status of a particular process, or the events encountered by a particular processor.

4.4.2 Timing Process Execution (`time`, `timex`, and `ptime`)

The commands `time`, `timex`, and `ptime` all report the amount of time that a process uses. They all have the same syntax, as shown in Example 4.30. All three tools produce output showing the time a process spends in user code and system code, as well as reporting the elapsed time, or wall time, for the process. The wall time is the time between when the process started and when it completed. A multi-threaded process will typically report a combined user and system time that is greater than the wall time. The tools do differ in output format. The tool `timex` can be passed additional options that will cause it to report more information.

Example 4.30 Syntax of the `time` Command

```
% time <app> <params>
```

4.4.3 Reporting System-Wide Hardware Counter Activity (`cpustat`)

`cpustat` first shipped with Solaris 8. It is a tool for inspecting the hardware performance counters on all the processors in a system. The performance counters report events that occur to the processor. For example, one counter may be incremented every time data is fetched from memory, and another counter may be incremented every time an instruction is executed. The events that can be counted, and the number of events that can be counted simultaneously, are hardware-dependent. Opteron processors can typically count four different event types at the same time, whereas UltraSPARC processors typically only count two. We will discuss hardware performance counters in greater depth in Chapter 10.

`cpustat` reports the number of performance counter events on a system-wide basis, hence it requires superuser permissions to run. So, if multiple programs are running, the reported values will represent the events encountered by all programs. If the system is running a mix of workloads, this information may not be of great value, but if the system is performing a single job, it is quite possible that this level of aggregation of data will provide useful information.

Assume that the system is dedicated to a single task—the program of interest—and the program is in some kind of steady state (e.g., it is a Web server that is dealing with many incoming requests). The command line for `cpustat`, shown in Example 4.31, is appropriate for an UltraSPARC IIICu-based system. The output is a way of determining which performance counters are worth further investigation.

Example 4.31 Sample Command Line for `cpustat` to Collect System-Wide Stats

```
$ cpustat  -c pic0=Dispatch0_IC_miss,pic1=Dispatch0_mispred,sys \
           -c pic0=Rstall_storeQ,pic1=Re_DC_miss,sys \
           -c pic0=EC_rd_miss,pic1=Re_EC_miss,sys \
           -c pic0=Rstall_IU_use,pic1=Rstall_FP_use,sys \
           -c pic0=Cycle_cnt,pic1=Re_PC_miss,sys \
           -c pic0=Instr_cnt,pic1=DTLB_miss,sys \
           -c pic0=Cycle_cnt,pic1=Re_RAW_miss,sys
```

When the -c flag is passed to cpustat (and cputrack) it provides a pair of
counters on which to collect. These are referred to as pic0 and pic1. More than 60
event types are available to select from on the UltraSPARC IIICu processor, and
two can be selected at once. Some of the event types are available on only one of
the counters, so not every pairing is possible. The ,sys appended at the end of the
pair of counter descriptions indicates that the counters should also be collected
during system time. The counters are collected in rotation, so each pair of counters
is collected for a short period of time. The default interval is five seconds.

If the program is not in a steady state—suppose it reads some data from memory and then spends the next few seconds in intensive floating-point operations—it
is quite possible that the coarse sampling used earlier will miss the interesting
points (e.g., looking for cache misses during the floating-point-intensive code, and
looking for floating-point operations when the data is being fetched from memory).
Example 4.32 shows the command line for cputrack to rotate through a selection
of performance counters, and partial output from the command.

Example 4.32 Example of cpustat Output

```
$ cpustat     -c pic0=Rstall_storeQ,pic1=Re_DC_miss,sys \
>             -c pic0=EC_rd_miss,pic1=Re_EC_miss,sys \
>             -c pic0=Rstall_IU_use,pic1=Rstall_FP_use,sys \
>             -c pic0=Cycle_cnt,pic1=Re_PC_miss,sys \
>             -c pic0=Instr_cnt,pic1=DTLB_miss,sys \
>             -c pic0=Cycle_cnt,pic1=Re_RAW_miss,sys
  time cpu event   pic0       pic1
 5.005 0   tick 294199   1036736 # pic0=Rstall_storeQ,pic1=Re_DC_miss,sys
 5.005 1   tick 163596  12604317 # pic0=Rstall_storeQ,pic1=Re_DC_miss,sys
10.005 0   tick   5485    965974 # pic0=EC_rd_miss,pic1=Re_EC_miss,sys
10.005 1   tick  76669  11598139 # pic0=EC_rd_miss,pic1=Re_EC_miss,sys
...
```

The columns of cpustat output shown in Example 4.32 are as follows.

- The first column reports the time of the sample. In this example, the samples
  are being taken every five seconds.

- The next column lists the CPU identifier. The samples are taken and reported
  for each CPU.

- The next column lists the type of event. For cpustat, the type of event is
  only going to be a tick.

- The next two columns list the counts for performance counters pic0 and
  pic1 since the last tick event.

- Finally, if cpustat is rotating through counters, the names of the counters
  are reported after the # sign.

4.4.4 Reporting Hardware Performance Counter Activity for a Single Process (cputrack)

cputrack first shipped with Solaris 8. It is another tool that reports the number of performance counter events. However, cputrack has the advantages of collecting events only for the process of interest and reporting the total number of such events at the end of the run. This makes it very useful for situations in which the application starts, does something, and then exits.

The script in Example 4.33 shows one way that cputrack might be invoked on a process.

Example 4.33 Script for Invoking cputrack on an Application

```
$ cputrack -c pic0=Dispatch0_IC_miss,pic1=Dispatch0_mispred,sys \
          -c pic0=Rstall_storeQ,pic1=Re_DC_miss,sys \
          -c pic0=EC_rd_miss,pic1=Re_EC_miss,sys \
          -c pic0=Rstall_IU_use,pic1=Rstall_FP_use,sys \
          -c pic0=Cycle_cnt,pic1=Re_PC_miss,sys \
          -c pic0=Instr_cnt,pic1=DTLB_miss,sys \
          -c pic0=Cycle_cnt,pic1=Re_RAW_miss,sys \
          -o <desired location of results file> \
          <application>
```

The script in Example 4.33 demonstrates how to use cputrack to rotate through the counters and capture data about the run of an application. The same caveat applies as for cpustat: Rotating through counters may miss the events of interest. An alternative way to invoke cputrack is to give it just a single pair of counters. The example in Example 4.34 shows this.

Example 4.34 Example of cputrack on a Single Pair of Counters

```
$ cputrack -c pic0=Cycle_cnt,pic1=Re_DC_miss testcode
  time lwp      event       pic0       pic1
 1.118  1        tick   663243149   14353162
 2.128  1        tick   899742583    9706444
 3.118  1        tick   885525398    7786122
 3.440  1        exit  2735203660   33964190
```

The output in Example 4.34 shows a short program that runs for three seconds. cputrack has counted the number of processor cycles consumed by the application using counter 0, and the number of data-cache miss events using counter 1; both numbers are per second, except for the line marked "exit," which contains the total counts over the entire run. The columns in the output are as follows.

- `time`: The time at which the sample was taken. In this case, the samples were taken at one-second intervals.

- `lwp`: The LWP that is being sampled. If the `-f` option is passed to `cputrack`, it will follow child processes. In this mode, data from other LWPs will be interleaved.

- `event`: The event type, such as `ticks` or the `exit` line. Each tick event is the number of events since the last tick. The exit line occurs when a process exits, and it reports the total number of events that occurred over the duration of the run. The event line also reports data at points where the process forks or joins.

- `pic0` and `pic1`: The last two columns report the number of events for the two performance counters. If `cputrack` were rotating through performance counters, the names of the performance counters would be reported after a # sign.

It is also possible to attach `cputrack` to a running process. The option for this is `-p <pid_id>`, and `cputrack` will report the events for that process.

4.4.5 Reporting Bus Activity (`busstat`)

The `busstat` tool reports performance counter events for the system bus. The available performance counters are system-dependent. The `-l` option lists the devices that have performance counter statistics available. The `-e` option will query what events are available on a particular device.

The currently set performance counters can be read using the `-r` option. To select particular performance counters it is necessary to use the `-w` option, but this requires superuser privileges. An example of using `busstat` to measure memory activity on an UltraSPARC T1-based system is shown in Example 4.35.

Example 4.35 Using `busstat` to Query Memory Activity on an UltraSPARC T1

```
# busstat -l
Busstat Device(s):
dram0 dram1 dram2 dram3 jbus0
# busstat -e dram0
pic0
mem_reads
mem_writes

....
pic1
mem_reads
mem_writes

...
# busstat -w dram0,pic0=mem_reads,pic1=mem_writes
time dev    event0           pic0    event1          pic1
1    dram0  mem_reads        45697   mem_writes      8775
2    dram0  mem_reads        37827   mem_writes      3767
```

4.4.6 Reporting on Trap Activity (`trapstat`)

`trapstat` is a SPARC-only tool that first shipped with Solaris 9 and enables you to look at the number of traps the kernel is handling. It counts the number of traps on a system-wide basis, hence it requires superuser privileges. For example, it is a very useful tool for looking at TLB misses on the UltraSPARC II. Example 4.36 shows output from `trapstat`.

Example 4.36 Sample Output from `trapstat`

```
vct name                   |     cpu0
---------------------------+----------
 20 fp-disabled            |        6
 24 cleanwin               |       31
 41 level-1                |        4
 44 level-4                |        0
 46 level-6                |        2
 49 level-9                |        1
 4a level-10               |      100
 4e level-14               |      101
 60 int-vec                |        3
 64 itlb-miss              |        3
 68 dtlb-miss              |   144621
 6c dtlb-prot              |        0
 84 spill-user-32          |        0
 8c spill-user-32-cln      |        0
 98 spill-kern-64          |      612
 a4 spill-asuser-32        |        0
 ac spill-asuser-32-cln    |      199
 c4 fill-user-32           |        0
 cc fill-user-32-cln       |       70
 d8 fill-kern-64           |      604
108 syscall-32             |       26
```

In the output shown in Example 4.36, a number of data TLB traps are occurring. This is the number per second, and 144,000 per second is not an unusually high number. Each trap takes perhaps 100 ns, so this corresponds to a few milliseconds of real time. We discussed TLB misses in greater detail in Section 4.2.6.

A high rate of any trap is a cause for concern. The traps that most often have high rates are TLB misses (either instruction [itlb-miss] or data [dtlb-miss]), and spill and fill traps.

Spill and fill traps indicate that the code is making many calls to routines, and each call may make further subcalls before returning (think of the program having to run up and then down a flight of stairs for each function call and its corresponding return). Each time the processor makes a call, it needs a fresh register window. When no register window is available, the processor will trap so that the operating system can provide one. I discussed register windows in Section 2.3.3 of Chapter 2. It may be possible to avoid this by either compiling with crossfile optimizations enabled (as discussed in Section 5.7.2 of Chapter 5), or restructuring the code so that each call will do more work.

It is possible to make `trapstat` run on a single process. The command line for this is shown in Example 4.37.

Example 4.37 Command Line to Run `trapstat` on a Single Program

```
# trapstat <program> <args>
```

At the end of the run of the process, this will report the number of traps that the single process caused. The figures will be reported (by default) as the number of traps per second.

4.4.7 Reporting Virtual Memory Mapping Information for a Process (`pmap`)

The `pmap` utility returns information about the address space of a given process. Possibly the most useful information the utility returns is information about the page size mapping returned under the -s option.

Example 4.38 shows a sample of output from the `pmap` utility under the -s option. The output is useful in that it shows where the code and data are located in memory, as well as where the libraries are located in memory. For each memory range, a page size is listed in the Pgsz column. In this case, all the memory has been allocated on 8KB pages (I discussed page sizes in Section 1.9.2 of Chapter 1). Output from `pmap` is the best way to determine whether an application has successfully obtained large pages.

Example 4.38 `pmap -s` Output

```
% pmap -s 7962
7962:   ./myapp params
 Address   Kbytes Pgsz Mode   Mapped File
00010000     272K  8K  r-x--  /export/home/myapp
00054000      80K   -  r-x--  /export/home/myapp
00068000      32K  8K  r-x--  /export/home/myapp
0007E000      48K  8K  rwx--  /export/home/myapp
...
000D2000    2952K  8K  rwx--   [ heap ]
...
004D4000    1984K  8K  rwx--   [ heap ]
006C4000       8K   -  rwx--   [ heap ]
006C6000   50944K  8K  rwx--   [ heap ]
...
FF210000       8K  8K  r-x--  /usr/platform/sun4u-us3/lib/libc_psr.so.1
FF220000      32K  8K  r-x--  /opt/SUNWspro/prod/usr/lib/libCrun.so.1
...
```

The page size for an application can be controlled at runtime (see Section 4.2.6) or at compile time (see Section 5.8.6 of Chapter 5).

4.4.8 Examining Command-Line Arguments Passed to Process (`pargs`)

The `pargs` command reports the arguments passed to a process. The command takes either a `pid` or a core file. An example of this command is shown in Example 4.39.

Example 4.39 Example of `pargs`

```
$ sleep 60&
[1] 18267
$ pargs 18267
18267:  sleep 60
argv[0]: sleep
argv[1]: 60
```

4.4.9 Reporting the Files Held Open by a Process (`pfiles`)

The `pfiles` utility reports the files that a given `pid` has currently opened, together with information about the file's attributes. An example of the output from this command is shown in Example 4.40.

Example 4.40 Output from `pfiles`

```
% pfiles 7093
7093:   -csh
  Current rlimit: 256 file descriptors
   0: S_IFCHR mode:0666 dev:118,32 ino:3422 uid:0 gid:3 rdev:13,2
      O_RDONLY|O_LARGEFILE
   1: S_IFCHR mode:0666 dev:118,32 ino:3422 uid:0 gid:3 rdev:13,2
      O_RDONLY|O_LARGEFILE
   2: S_IFCHR mode:0666 dev:118,32 ino:3422 uid:0 gid:3 rdev:13,2
      O_RDONLY|O_LARGEFILE
...
```

4.4.10 Examining the Current Stack of Process (`pstack`)

The `pstack` tool prints out the stack dump from either a running process or a core file. An example of using this tool to print the stack of the `sleep` command is shown in Example 4.41. This tool is often useful in determining whether an application is still doing useful computation or whether it has hit a point where it is making no further progress.

Example 4.41 Output from `pstack`

```
% sleep 10 &
[1] 4556
% pstack 4556
4556:   sleep 10
 ff31f448 sigsuspend (ffbffaa8)
 00010a28 main     (2, ffbffbdc, ffbffbe8, 20c00, 0, 0) + 120
 000108f0 _start   (0, 0, 0, 0, 0, 0) + 108
```

4.4.11 Tracing Application Execution (`truss`)

`truss` is a useful utility for looking at the calls from an application to the operating system, calls to libraries, or even calls within an application. Example 4.42 shows an example of running the application `ls` under the `truss` command.

Example 4.42 Output of the `truss` Command Running on `ls`

```
$ truss ls
execve("/usr/bin/ls", 0xFFBFFBE4, 0xFFBFFBEC)  argc = 1
mmap(0x00000000, 8192, PROT_READ|PROT_WRITE|PROT_EXEC,
    MAP_PRIVATE|MAP_ANON, -1, 0) = 0xFF3B0000
resolvepath("/usr/bin/ls", "/usr/bin/ls", 1023) = 11
resolvepath("/usr/lib/ld.so.1", "/usr/lib/ld.so.1", 1023) = 16
stat("/usr/bin/ls", 0xFFBFF9C8)          = 0
open("/var/ld/ld.config", O_RDONLY)      Err#2 ENOENT
open("/usr/lib/libc.so.1", O_RDONLY)     = 3
fstat(3, 0xFFBFF304)                     = 0
....
```

When an application is run under `truss` the tool reports every call the operating system made. This can be very useful when trying to determine what an application is doing. The `-f` flag will cause `truss` to follow forked processes.

When `truss` is run with the `-c` flag it will provide a count of the number of calls made, as well as the total time accounted for by these calls. Example 4.43 shows the same `ls` command run, but this time only the count of the number of calls is collected.

Example 4.43 Call Count for the `ls` Command Using `truss`

```
$ truss -c ls
syscall            seconds   calls   errors
_exit               .000       1
write               .000      35
open                .000       7       3
close               .000       4
time                .000       1
brk                 .000      10
```

Example 4.43 Call Count for the `ls` Command Using `truss` (*continued*)

```
stat              .000        1
fstat             .000        3
ioctl             .000        3
execve            .000        1
fcntl             .000        1
mmap              .000        7
munmap            .000        1
memcntl           .000        1
resolvepath       .000        5
getdents64        .000        3
lstat64           .000        1
fstat64           .000        2
                --------   ------   ----
sys totals:       .002       87        3
usr time:         .001
elapsed:          .020
```

It is also possible to run `truss` on an existing process. This will generate the same output as invoking `truss` on the process initially. This is useful for checking whether a process is still doing something. Example 4.44 shows the command line to do this.

Example 4.44 Attaching `truss` to an Existing Process

```
$ truss -p <pid>
```

It is also possible to use `truss` to print out the calls within an application. The `-u` flag takes the names of the libraries of interest, or `a.out` to represent the application. The tool will then report calls made by these modules, as shown in Example 4.45.

Example 4.45 `truss` Used to Show Calls Made within an Application

```
% truss -u a.out bzip2
execve("bzip2", 0xFFBFFB84, 0xFFBFFB8C)  argc = 1
-> atexit(0x2be04, 0x44800, 0x0, 0x0)
  -> mutex_lock(0x456e8, 0x0, 0x0, 0x0)
  -> _return_zero(0x456e8, 0x0, 0x0, 0x0)
  <- mutex_lock() = 0
  -> mutex_unlock(0x456e8, 0x1, 0x0, 0x0)
  -> _return_zero(0x456e8, 0x1, 0x0, 0x0)
  <- mutex_unlock() = 0
<- atexit() = 0
-> _init(0x0, 0x44800, 0x0, 0x0)
  -> _check_threaded(0x44a68, 0x0, 0x0, 0x0)
    -> thr_main(0x0, 0x0, 0x0, 0x0)
    -> _return_negone(0x0, 0x0, 0x0, 0x0)
    <- thr_main() = -1
  <- _check_threaded() = 0x44a68
<- _init() = 0
-> main(0x1, 0xffbffb84, 0xffbffb8c, 0x44800)
  -> signal(0x2, 0x1724c, 0x0, 0x0)
....
```

4.4.12 Exploring User Code and Kernel Activity with dtrace

The dtrace utility is part of Solaris 10, and it offers an unprecedented view into the behavior of user code and system code. Using dtrace, it is possible to count the number of times a routine gets called, time how long a routine takes, examine the parameters that are passed into a routine, and even find out what a routine was doing when a given event happened. All of this makes it a very powerful tool, but to describe it in sufficient detail is beyond the scope of this book. A simple example of the use of dtrace is shown in Example 4.46. This script counts the number of calls to malloc, and for each call it records the size of the memory requested.

Example 4.46 dtrace Script to Count the Calls to malloc

```
#!/usr/sbin/dtrace -s
pid$target:libc.so:malloc:entry
{
  @proc[probefunc]=count();
  @array[probefunc]=quantize(arg0);
}

END
{
  printa(@proc);
  printa(@array);
}
```

The output from this script, when run on the command ls, is shown in Example 4.47. The output shows that malloc is called 15 times, and displays a histogram of the requested memory sizes.

Example 4.47 Number and Size of Calls to malloc by ls

```
# ./malloc.d -c ls
dtrace: script './malloc.d' matched 2 probes
...
dtrace: pid 3645 has exited
CPU     ID                      FUNCTION:NAME
 16      2                              :END
  malloc                                                              15

  malloc
          value  ------------- Distribution ------------- count
              4 |                                          0
              8 |@@@@@                                     2
             16 |@@@@@@@@@@@@@@@@                          6
             32 |@@@                                       1
             64 |@@@@@@@@                                  3
            128 |                                          0
```

Example 4.47 Number and Size of Calls to `malloc` by `ls` *(continued)*

```
          256 |@@@@@                                        2
          512 |                                             0
         1024 |                                             0
         2048 |                                             0
         4096 |                                             0
         8192 |                                             0
        16384 |                                             0
        32768 |@@@                                          1
        65536 |                                             0
```

Once the sizes of the memory requests have been determined, it may also be interesting to find out where the memory requests are being made. The script shown in Example 4.48 captures the call stack for the calls to `malloc`.

Example 4.48 Capturing the User Call Stack for Calls to `malloc`

```
#!/usr/sbin/dtrace -s
pid$target:libc.so:malloc:entry
{
  @stack[ustack(5)]=count();
  @array[probefunc]=quantize(arg0);
}

END
{
  printa(@stack);
  printa(@array);
}
```

An example of running the script to capture the call stack of calls to `malloc` is shown in Example 4.49.

Example 4.49 Call Stack for `malloc` Requests Made by the Compiler

```
# ./malloc_stack.d -c "cc -O an.c"
dtrace: script './malloc_stack.d' matched 2 probes
dtrace: pid 4063 has exited
CPU     ID                    FUNCTION:NAME
  6      2                          :END
...
            cc`malloc
            libc.so.1`calloc+0x58
            cc`stralloc+0x8
            cc`str_newcopy+0xc
            cc`addopt+0x88
            154
```

continues

Example 4.49 Call Stack for `malloc` Requests Made by the Compiler (*continued*)

```
malloc
          value  ------------- Distribution ------------- count
              0 |                                            0
              1 |                                            2
              2 |@@@                                         21
              4 |@@@@@@                                      52
              8 |@@@@@@@@@@                                  88
             16 |@@@@@@@@                                    65
             32 |@@@@@@                                      52
             64 |@@@@@                                       44
            128 |@                                           5
            256 |                                            2
            512 |                                            1
           1024 |                                            0
```

4.5 Information about Applications

4.5.1 Reporting Library Linkage (`ldd`)

The `ldd` utility reports the shared libraries that are linked into an application. This is useful for acquiring information, but it should not have any effect on performance (unless the wrong version of a library is selected somehow).

The output in Example 4.50 shows the library the application is searching for on the left, and the library that has been located on the right.

Example 4.50 Output from `ldd` Showing the Linking of a Particular Application

```
$ ldd ap27
      libm.so.1 =>     /usr/lib/libm.so.1
      libc.so.1 =>     /usr/lib/libc.so.1
      /usr/platform/SUNW,Sun-Blade-2500/lib/libc_psr.so.1
```

Passing the `-r` option to `ldd` will cause it to check both the objects that are linked into the application and the particular function calls that are required. It will report whether the application is missing a library, and it will report the functions that are missing.

The output shown in Example 4.51 is from the `-r` option passed to `ldd`. There are two items of interest. First, `ldd` reports that it is unable to locate the `libsunmath` library, which is Sun's library of additional mathematical functions. Under this option, `ldd` reports the two function calls that it is unable to locate, and these function calls correspond to square root calls for single-precision floating-point, and for long integers.

Example 4.51 The `-r` Option for `ldd`

```
$ ldd -r someapp
        libdl.so.1 =>      /usr/lib/libdl.so.1
        libnsl.so.1 =>     /usr/lib/libnsl.so.1
        libgen.so.1 =>     /usr/lib/libgen.so.1
        libm.so.1 =>       /usr/lib/libm.so.1
        libc.so.1 =>       /usr/lib/libc.so.1
        libsocket.so.1 =>      /usr/lib/libsocket.so.1
        libsunmath.so.1 =>     (file not found)
        libelf.so.1 =>     /usr/lib/libelf.so.1
        libmp.so.2 =>      /usr/lib/libmp.so.2
        /usr/platform/SUNW,Sun-Blade-1000/lib/libc_psr.so.1
        symbol not found: sqrtf
(someapp)
        symbol not found: sqrtl
(someapp)
```

The paths where libraries are located are hard-coded into the application at link time. I will cover the procedure for doing this in more detail in Section 7.2.6 of Chapter 7. At runtime, it is possible to use the LD_LIBRARY_PATH environment variable to override where the application finds libraries, or to assist the application in locating a particular library. So, for the case in Example 4.51, if the LD_LIBRARY_PATH variable were set to point to a directory containing libsunmath.so, ldd would report that the application used that version of the library. Example 4.52 shows an example of setting the LD_LIBRARY_PATH environment variable under csh. Of course, you can use the same environment variable to change where the application loads all its libraries from, so be careful when setting it and do not rely on it as the default mechanism to enable an application locating its libraries at deployment.

Example 4.52 Example of Setting the LD_LIBRARY_PATH Variable

```
$ setenv LD_LIBRARY_PATH /export/home/my_libraries/
```

The LD_LIBRARY_PATH environment variable will override the search path for both 32-bit and 64-bit applications. To explicitly set search paths for these two application types you can use the environment variables LD_LIBRARY_PATH_32 and LD_LIBRARY_PATH_64.

It is also possible to set the LD_PRELOAD environment variable to specify a library that is to be loaded before the application. This enables the use of a different library in addition to the one shipped with the application. This can be a useful way to debug the application's interactions with libraries. I will cover this in more detail in Section 7.2.10 of Chapter 7.

The -u option will request that ldd report any libraries that are linked to the application but not used. In Example 4.53, both libm (the math library) and libsocket (the sockets library) are linked into the application but not actually used.

Example 4.53 Example of ldd -u to Check for Unused Libraries

```
$ ldd -u ./myapp
        libdl.so.1 =>     /usr/lib/libdl.so.1
        libnsl.so.1 =>    /usr/lib/libnsl.so.1
        libm.so.1 =>      /usr/lib/libm.so.1
        libc.so.1 =>      /usr/lib/libc.so.1
        libsocket.so.1 =>      /usr/lib/libsocket.so.1
        /usr/platform/SUNW,Sun-Blade-1000/lib/libc_psr.so.1

    unused object=/usr/lib/libm.so.1
    unused object=/usr/lib/libsocket.so.1
```

Another useful option for ldd is the -i flag. This requests that ldd report the order in which the libraries will be initialized. The output from ldd shown in Example 4.54 indicates that libc is initialized first, and libsocket is initialized last.

Example 4.54 Example of ldd -i Output

```
$ ldd -i ./thisapp
        libdl.so.1 =>     /usr/lib/libdl.so.1
        libnsl.so.1 =>    /usr/lib/libnsl.so.1
        libm.so.1 =>      /usr/lib/libm.so.1
        libc.so.1 =>      /usr/lib/libc.so.1
        libsocket.so.1 =>      /usr/lib/libsocket.so.1
        libmp.so.2 =>     /usr/lib/libmp.so.2
        /usr/platform/SUNW,Sun-Blade-1000/lib/libc_psr.so.1

    init object=/usr/lib/libc.so.1
    init object=/usr/lib/libmp.so.2
    init object=/usr/lib/libnsl.so.1
    init object=/usr/lib/libsocket.so.1
```

4.5.2 Reporting the Type of Contents Held in a File (file)

The file tool reports on the type of a particular file. It can be useful for situations when it is necessary to check whether a particular application is a script wrapper for the actual real application, or the real application. Another way this tool can help is in determining on what type of processor a given application will run. Recall that the isalist tool from Section 4.2.5 reported the processor's architecture; the file tool will report the architecture an application requires. For a given application to run on a particular machine, the processor needs to support the application's architecture.

Example 4.55 shows `file` being run on an application. The binary is 32-bit and requires at least a v8plus architecture to run.

Example 4.55 Example of Running `file` on an Application

```
$ file a.out
a.out:          ELF 32-bit MSB executable SPARC32PLUS Version 1, V8+ Required, dynami-
cally linked, not stripped
```

The `file` command is often useful when examining files or libraries to determine why linking failed with an error reporting an attempt to link 32-bit and 64-bit objects.

4.5.3 Reporting Symbols in a File (nm)

The nm tool reports the symbols defined inside a library, object file, or executable. Typically, this tool will dump out a lot of information. The useful information is usually the names of routines defined in the file, and the names of routines the file requires. If the file has been stripped (using the `strip` utility), no information is reported. A snippet of example output from nm is shown in Example 4.56.

Example 4.56 Short Sample of Output from nm

```
$ nm a.out
a.out:
[Index]    Value      Size     Type   Bind  Other Shndx   Name
[45]    |    133144|       4|OBJT |WEAK |0    |15     |environ
[60]    |    132880|       0|FUNC |GLOB |0    |UNDEF  |exit
[37]    |     67164|      40|FUNC |LOCL |0    |8      |foo
[53]    |     67204|      48|FUNC |GLOB |0    |8      |main
[42]    |    132904|       0|FUNC |GLOB |0    |UNDEF  |printf
...
```

The output from nm shown in Example 4.56 indicates that a.out defines a couple of routines, such as main and foo, but depends on libraries to provide the routines exit and printf.

4.5.4 Reporting Library Version Information (pvs)

It is possible to define multiple versions of a library in a single library file. This is an important mechanism to allow older applications to run with newer versions of a library. The older library API is still available, and the older applications will link to these versions. The newer API is also present, and the newer applications will link to this.

The pvs utility prints out information about the functions and versions of those functions that a library exports, or the library versions that a library or executable requires. By default, pvs will report both the definitions in the library and the requirements of the library.

Example 4.57 shows pvs reporting the versions of the libraries that the ls executable requires.

Example 4.57 Libraries Required by the ls Command

```
% pvs /bin/ls
        libc.so.1 (SUNW_1.19, SUNWprivate_1.1);
```

The -r option, for displaying only the requirements of the file, can be used to show that libc.so.1 requires libdl.so.1, as demonstrated in Example 4.58.

Example 4.58 Requirements of libc.so.1

```
% pvs -r /usr/lib/libc.so.1
        libdl.so.1 (SUNW_1.4, SUNWprivate_1.1);
```

The -d option shows the versions defined in the library. Example 4.59 shows part of the output of the versions defined in libc.so.1.

Example 4.59 Versions Defined in libc.so.1

```
% pvs -d /usr/lib/libc.so.1
        libc.so.1;
        SUNW_1.21.2;
        SUNW_1.21.1;
        SUNW_1.21;
        SUNW_1.20.4;
....
```

It is also possible to list the symbols defined in a library using the -s flag. Part of the output of this for libdl.so.1 is shown in Example 4.60.

Example 4.60 Versions of Functions Exported by libdl.so.1

```
$ pvs -ds /usr/lib/libdl.so.1
        libdl.so.1:
                _DYNAMIC;
                _edata;
                _etext;
                _end;
                _PROCEDURE_LINKAGE_TABLE_;
        SUNW_1.4:
                dladdr1;
        SUNW_1.3:
        SUNW_1.2:
        SUNW_1.1:
                dlmopen;
                dldump;
                dlinfo;
...
```

4.5.5 Examining the Disassembly of an Application, Library, or Object (dis)

The dis utility will disassemble libraries, applications, and object files. An example of this is shown in Example 4.61.

Example 4.61 Example of Using dis

```
$ /usr/ccs/bin/dis a.out
                ****    DISASSEMBLER   ****


disassembly for a.out

section .text
_start()
        10694:  bc 10 20 00       clr       %fp
        10698:  e0 03 a0 40       ld        [%sp + 0x40], %l0
        1069c:  13 00 00 83       sethi     %hi(0x20c00), %o1
        106a0:  e0 22 61 8c       st        %l0, [%o1 + 0x18c]
        106a4:  a2 03 a0 44       add       %sp, 0x44, %l1
...
```

4.5.6 Reporting the Size of the Various Segments in an Application, Library, or Object (`size`)

The `size` utility prints the size in bytes of the various segments in an application, library, or object file. When used without parameters the command reports the size of the `text` (executable code), `data` (initialized data), and `bss` (uninitialized data). The `-f` flag reports the name of each allocatable segment together with its size in bytes. The `-n` flag also reports the nonloadable segments (these segments contain metadata such as debug information). An example is shown in Example 4.62.

Example 4.62 Using the `size` Command

```
% size a.out
3104 + 360 + 8 = 3472
% size -fn a.out
17(.interp) + 304(.hash) + 592(.dynsym) + 423(.dynstr) + 48(.SUNW_version) +
12(.rela.data) + 72(.rela.plt) + 1388(.text) + 16(.init) + 12(.fini) + 4(.rodata) +
4(.got) + 124(.plt) + 184(.dynamic) + 48(.data) + 8(.bss) + 1152(.symtab) +
525(.strtab) + 248(.debug_info) + 53(.debug_line) + 26(.debug_abbrev) + 650(.comment) +
184(.shstrtab) = 6094
```

4.5.7 Reporting Metadata Held in a File (`dumpstabs`, `dwarfdump`, `elfdump`, `dump`, and `mcs`)

It is possible to extract information about how an application was built using the `dumpstabs` utility, which is shipped with the compiler. This utility reports a lot of information, but the most useful is the command line that was passed to the compiler. Two other utilities serve a similar purpose: `dwarfdump`, which reports the data for applications built with the dwarf debug format, and `elfdump` which reports similar information for object files. All three utilities can take various flags to specify the level of detail, but by default, `dumpstabs` and `elfdump` print out all information, whereas `dwarfdump` does not report anything for versions earlier than Sun Studio 11 (in these cases, use the `-a` flag to print all the information). Applications built with the Sun Studio 10 compiler (and earlier) default to the stabs format, so `dumpstabs` is the appropriate command to use. In Sun Studio 11, the C compiler switched to using dwarf format. In Sun Studio 12, all the compilers default to using dwarf format.

Example 4.63 shows an example of building a file using Sun Studio 10, and then using `dumpstabs` and `grep` to extract the compile line used to build the file. In general, a lot of information is reported by `dumpstabs`, so passing the output through `grep` and searching for either the name of the file or the CMDLINE marker will reduce the output substantially.

Example 4.63 Example of Searching for the Command Line for a Compiler Using Sun Studio 10

```
$ cc -fast -o test test.c
$ dumpstabs test | grep test.c
  36:                   test.c  00000000  00000000  LOCAL    FILE  ABS
   0:  .stabs "test.c",N_UNDF,0x0,0x3,0xb8
   2:  .stabs "/export/home; /opt/SUNWspro/prod/bin/cc -fast -c test.c",N_CMD-
LINE,0x0,0x0,0x0
```

A similar set of actions for Sun Studio 11 and `dwarfdump` is shown in Example 4.64.

Example 4.64 Example of Searching for the Command Line for a Compiler Using Sun Studio 11

```
$ cc -fast -o test test.c
$ dwarfdump test | grep command_line
      DW_AT_SUN_command_line  /opt/SUNWspro/prod/bin/cc -fast -c  test.c
< 13>  DW_AT_SUN_command_line  DW_FORM_string
```

It is also possible to use the `dump` command with the `-sv` option to extract most of the information from an executable. This will dump all the sections in an executable, printing those that are text in text format and the other sections as hexadecimal. An example of the output from `dump` is shown in Example 4.65. The actual output from the command runs to a number of pages, and Example 4.65 shows only a small part of this output.

Example 4.65 Example of Output from `dump`

```
$ dump -sv a.out

a.out:

.interp:
        2f 75 73 72 2f 6c 69 62 2f 6c 64 2e 73 6f 2e 31 00

.hash:
        00 00 00 95 00 00 00 8e 00 00 00 00 00 00 00 00 00 00 00
....
    **** STRING TABLE INFORMATION ****
```

continues

Example 4.65 Example of Output from `dump` (*continued*)

```
.strtab:
   <offset>      Name
   <0>
   <1>           a.out
   <7>           crti.s
   <14>          crt1.s
   <21>          __get_exit_frame_monitor_ptr
...
.stab.indexstr:
   <offset>      Name
   <115>         /tmp/;/opt/SUNWspro/prod/bin/f90 -g -qoption f90comp -
h.XAzwWCA01y4\$DCK. test.f90
...
```

The `mcs` tool, which is shipped with Solaris, manipulates the comments section in `elf` files. The `-p` option will print the comments. It is possible to delete the comments section using `-d`, or append more strings using `-a`. The comments section often holds details of the compiler version used and the header files included. An example of manipulating the comments section is shown in Example 4.66. The initial comments section shows the version information for the compiler, together with details of the header files included at compile time. Using the `mcs` flag `-a`, it is possible to append another comment to the file.

Example 4.66 Manipulating the Comments Section Using `mcs`

```
$ cc -O code.c
$ mcs -p a.out
a.out:

cg: Sun Compiler Common 11 2005/10/13
cg: Sun Compiler Common 11 2005/10/13
@(#)stdio.h      1.84    04/09/28 SMI
@(#)feature_tests.h    1.25    07/02/02 SMI
...
ld: Software Generation Utilities - Solaris Link Editors: 5.10-1.486
$ mcs -a "Hello" a.out
$ mcs -p a.out
a.out:


...
ld: Software Generation Utilities - Solaris Link Editors: 5.10-1.486
Hello
```

5

Using the Compiler

5.1 Chapter Objectives

The objective of this chapter is to introduce the Sun Studio compiler and explain how to use it to get the best performance out of an application. The first part of the chapter discusses basic compiler options. This is followed by a section on more advanced compiler options. The chapter closes with a discussion of compiler pragmas, which are statements that you can insert into the source code to assist the compiler. By the end of the chapter, the reader will have a broad understanding of the ways compiler can be used to improve application performance.

5.2 Three Sets of Compiler Options

One way to think about compiler options is to imagine three different sets of options, for three different requirements. These three sets are as follows.

- Debug. During application development, typically you need a set of flags that enable full application debugging and rapid compile time.
- Optimized code. Usually you want to have an optimized version of the application for development work (as the code becomes more stable) and for release.

- Aggressively optimized code. Depending on the project's performance requirements, it may be necessary to use aggressive optimizations to get the best out
  of the code, or it may be useful to test aggressive optimizations to see whether
  they provide significant performance improvements.

There are some simple rules to follow when building sets of compiler flags.

- Always include debug information, because it is impossible to know when it
  will be necessary to debug or profile the application. The debug information
  can track individual instructions back to lines of source, even at high optimization.
- Explicitly target the appropriate hardware architecture to ensure that the
  machine used to build the application can have no impact on the generated
  code. I discuss this is further in Section 5.4.4.
- Use only the flags that improve application performance, and are safe for the
  application.

There are three things to consider when selecting compiler flags.

- Using more aggressive optimizations will typically cause the compile time to
  increase. Therefore, you should use only optimizations that provide performance gains.
- As more aggressive optimizations are used, the chance of them exposing a
  bug in the source code of the application increases. This is because as the
  optimization levels increase, the compiler will use less-forgiving assumptions
  about the application. Examples of this are variables that the programmer
  assumes are volatile but not marked as such; or places where two pointers
  alias, but the application has been compiled with the compiler flag to assume
  no such aliasing.
- Some aggressive optimizations may cause differences in the results of floating-
  point computations.

For all these reasons, a comprehensive test suite is always recommended when
experimenting with alternative choices of compiler options.

There is no such thing as a single set of flags that will work for all applications.
It is always worth reviewing and revising the flags that are used. Table 5.1 lists a
set of starting-point flags for the three levels of optimization suitable for compilers
before Sun Studio 12.

The Sun Studio 12 compiler can use a slightly different set of flags, as shown in
Table 5.2.

Table 5.1 Optimization Flags for Compiler Versions Prior to Sun Studio 12

Optimization Level	Optimization Flags	Debug	Target Architecture
Debug	None	-g	-xtarget=generic [32-bit SPARC] -xtarget=generic -xarch=sse2 [32-bit x64] -xtarget=generic64 [64-bit]
Optimized	-O	-g [C/Fortran] -g0 [C++]	-xtarget=generic -xtarget=generic -xarch=sse2 -xtarget=generic64
High optimization	-fast -xipo	-g [C/Fortran] -g0 [C++]	-xtarget=generic -xtarget=generic -xarch=sse2 -xtarget=generic64

Table 5.2 Optimization Flags for Compiler Versions of Sun Studio 12 and Later

Optimization Level	Optimization Flags	Debug	Target Architecture
Debug	None	-g	-xtarget=generic [32-bit SPARC] -xtarget=generic -xarch=sse2 [32-bit x64] -xtarget=generic -m64 [64-bit]
Optimized	-O	-g	-xtarget=generic -xtarget=generic -xarch=sse2 -xtarget=generic -m64
High optimization	-fast -xipo	-g [C/Fortran] -g0 [C++]	-xtarget=generic -xtarget=generic -xarch=sse2 -xtarget=generic -m64

There are three parts to these settings: the debug flags, the optimization flags, and the flags to specify the target hardware. I will discuss these in more detail in the following sections.

5.3 Using -xtarget=generic on x86

Sun Studio will target a 386 processor when given the -xtarget=generic option on x86 platforms. For many codes this may not be the best processor to select. For example, this processor does not have the SSE instruction set extensions. The option -xarch=sse2 will allow the compiler to use SSE2 instructions. These instructions first appeared in the Pentium 4 processor, so most commonly available x86 machines will support them. Binaries that use SSE or SSE2 instructions will not behave correctly when run on platforms without the hardware support for these instruction set extensions.

Use of these instructions requires at least Solaris 9 update 6; earlier versions of the operating system do not support them. If the application needs to run on an earlier operating system version, `-xtarget=386` will generate code that does not use these instruction set extensions.

5.4 Optimization

5.4.1 Optimization Levels

The optimization-level flags represent a trade-off between compile time and runtime. A lower optimization level tells the compiler to spend less time compiling the code, and consequently often leads to a longer runtime. A number of optimization levels are available, and these permit the compiler to do different degrees of optimization.

For many codes the `-O` flag represents a good trade-off between runtime and compile time. At the other end of the spectrum, the `-fast` flag represents a more aggressive set of optimizations, and you can use it in the process of estimating the best performance that the application can achieve. I will discuss the `-fast` compiler flag further in Section 5.4.3.

There are a range of optimization levels, and although it is not expected that a particular set of levels needs to be determined for any application, it is useful to see the progression from local optimizations at `-xO1` to more global optimizations at `-xO5`. Table 5.3 lists the type of optimization performed at the various optimization levels.

Table 5.3 Optimization Levels

Optimization Level	Comment
None specified	No significant optimization performed. Shortest compile time. Will generate code with roughly `-xO2` performance if debug information is not requested. Code will slow down if debug information is requested.
-xO1	Minimal optimization
-xO2	Global variables are assumed volatile (I cover this in more detail shortly)
-xO3	Code is optimized at a function level. Variables are assumed not to be volatile unless declared as such. Typically `-xO3` represents a good trade-off between compile time and runtime. Equivalent to `-O` for the Sun Studio 9 and later compilers.

Table 5.3 Optimization Levels (*continued*)

Optimization Level	Comment
-xO4	Code is optimized at the file level. Functions are inlined if appropriate.
-xO5	Equivalent to -xO4 in the absence of profile information. With profile information the compiler will investigate a number of potential feedback-guided optimizations.
-fast	A macro that contains a number of aggressive optimization flags, which may give improved application performance

The other consequence of increasing the optimization level is that the compiler will have a lower tolerance for ambiguity in the source code. For example, at -xO2, all variables are assumed to be volatile, whereas at -xO3, only variables marked as being volatile are treated as such.

A *volatile variable* is a variable that may have its value changed by something other than the code that is referencing it. Typically, volatile variables occur when the value is being read from hardware and the state of the hardware may change over time, or when a variable is shared by multiple threads and another thread may change its value. The consequence of a variable being volatile is that the compiler has to store its value back to memory every time the value is changed and read its value from memory every time it is required, which introduces a large overhead on variable accesses. A nonvolatile variable can be held in a register, which means that operations on it are much cheaper. This means code that functions correctly at -xO2 may not function correctly at -xO3 if the behavior depends on a variable being treated as volatile, but the variable is not declared as such.

Many of the more advanced optimizations (such as cross-file inlining) require a level of optimization greater than -xO2. When the compiler encounters this requirement, it may either increase the level of optimization to do the necessary analysis, or ignore the option. In either case, it will emit a warning. Example 5.1 shows an example of this behavior.

Example 5.1 Example of Compiler Behavior When an Insufficient Optimization Level Is Specified

```
% cc -xdepend test.c
cc: Warning: Optimizer level changed from 0 to 3 to support dependence based transfor-
mations.
% cc -xipo test.c
cc: Warning: -xO4 or above is needed for -xipo; -xipo ignored.
```

A final point to observe is that if no optimization level is specified, no optimization is performed, unless one of the flags causes the compiler to increase the optimization level. So, it is critical to at least specify -O to ensure some degree of optimization.

5.4.2 Using the -o Optimization Flag

The -O optimization flag represents a good trade-off between compile time and performance. Since the Sun ONE Studio 9 release of the compiler, it has corresponded to an optimization level of -xO3.

5.4.3 Using the -fast Compiler Flag

The -fast compiler flag is a *macro option*, that is, it enables a set of options designed to give best performance on a range of codes. There are three items to be aware of when using the -fast macro flag:.

- -fast includes the -xtarget=native option, which tells the compiler to assume that the platform being used to generate the application is also the type that will run the application. This may be an issue if the application is compiled on a platform with a more modern CPU than the platform, which it is to be deployed. To avoid this issue, always specify the target platform when compiling. Often, this will be the -xtarget=generic flag, as discussed in Section 5.4.4.

- Because -fast provides a general set of options, it is important to be aware that it may not turn out to be the best set of options for a particular code. In particular, -fast contains optimizations that simplify floating-point mathematical operations. These optimizations are very general, and most compilers do them, but in some circumstances they may not be appropriate. Another assumption that -fast makes for C is that pointers to different basic types do not alias (i.e., a pointer to an integer would never point to the same location in memory as a pointer to a floating-point value).

- The definition of -fast may evolve from release to release. A new optimization will be introduced into -fast in one compiler release and the optimization will eventually percolate down to less-aggressive levels of optimization.

Because of these considerations, you can use -fast as a first stop when optimizing applications, before exploring the options that it enables in more detail. Be aware of what -fast means, and consider whether it is appropriate to continue using the whole macro or whether it would be better to hand-pick a selection of the options that -fast enables.

You should use the -fast flag when compiling and when linking the program. Some of the optimizations enabled (e.g., -dalign in Fortran) alter data alignment, and as such they require all the modules to be aware of the new layout.

5.4.4 Specifying Architecture with `-fast`

The -fast compiler flag includes the -xtarget=native flag, which specifies that the type of machine used to compile the program is also the type of machine which will run the program. Obviously, this is not always the case, so it is recommended that you specify the target architecture when using -fast.

Example 5.2 shows the compile line to be used with -fast to specify that 32-bit code should be generated. It is essential to notice the order in which the flags have been used. The compiler evaluates flags from left to right, so the -xtarget setting overrides the setting applied by -fast. If the options were specified in the opposite order, -fast would override the -xtarget setting specified earlier on the command line.

Example 5.2 Compile Line for -fast and 32-bit Code

```
-fast -xtarget=generic
```

Example 5.3 shows the compile line that you should use with -fast to specify that 64-bit code should be generated. With Sun Studio 12, the user also has the equivalent option of appending the -m64 flag to the command line shown in Example 5.3 to generate a 64-bit binary.

Example 5.3 Compile Line for -fast and 64-bit Code

```
-fast -xtarget=generic64
```

The objective of the "generic" target is to pick a blended SPARC or x64 target that provides good performance over the widest range of processors. When a generic target is requested, the compiler will produce code that requires at least an UltraSPARC-I on SPARC systems, or a 386 for x86 systems. On x86 systems, it may be appropriate to select a more recent architecture than 386 to utilize the SSE and SSE2 instruction set extensions. The generic keyword works for both x64 and SPARC systems, and is consequently a good flag to select when one Makefile has to target the two architectures. Although the compiler flag has the same name for both architectures, the generated binaries will of course be specific to the architecture doing the compilation. There is no facility to cross-compile (e.g., build a SPARC binary on an x64 system).

5.4.5 Deconstructing -fast

The definition of -fast may not be constant from release to release. It will gradually evolve to include new optimizations. Consequently, it is useful to be aware of what the -fast macro expands into. The optimizations that -fast enables are documented, but it is often easier to gather this information from the compiler. Fortunately, the compiler provides a way to extract the flags comprising -fast. The compiler has a flag that enables verbose output. For the C compiler it is the -# flag, and for the C++ and Fortran compilers it is the -v (lowercase *v*) flag.

The compiler is actually a collection of programs that get invoked by a driver. The cc, CC, or f90 command is a call to the driver, which translates the compiler flags into the appropriate command lines for the components that comprise the compiler. The output of the verbose flag (-# or -v) shows the details of these calls to these various stages, together with the expanded set of flags that are passed to the stages. Example 5.4 is the transcript of a session showing the output from the C compiler when invoked on a file with -# and -fast.

Example 5.4 Verbose Output from Compiler

```
$ cc -# -fast test.c
cc: Warning: -xarch=native has been explicitly specified, or implicitly specified by a
macro option, -xarch=native on this architecture implies -xarch=v8plusb which generates
code that does not run on pre UltraSPARC III processors
...
###     command line files and options (expanded):
### -D__MATHERR_ERRNO_DONTCARE -fns -fsimple=2 -fsingle -ftrap=%none -xalias_
level=basic -xarch=v8plusb -xbuiltin=%all -xcache=64/32/4:8192/512/1 -xchip=ultra3
-xdepend -xlibmil -xmemalign=8s -xO5 -xprefetch=auto,explicit test.c
/opt/SUNWspro/prod/bin/acomp ...
/opt/SUNWspro/prod/bin/iropt ...
/usr/ccs/bin/ld ...
```

In the transcript in Example 5.4, most of the output has been edited out, because it is not relevant. The compiler's components invocations have been left in, but the critical line is the one following the comment ### command line files and options (expanded). This line shows exactly what -fast was expanded to.

5.4.6 Performance Optimizations in -fast (for the Sun Studio 12 Compiler)

Table 5.4 lists the optimizations that -fast enables for the Sun Studio 12 compiler. These optimizations may have an impact on all codes. They target the integer instructions used in the application—the loads, stores, and so on as well as the layout of and the assumptions the compiler makes about the data held in memory.

Table 5.4 General Compiler Optimizations Included in `-fast`

Flag	C	C++	Fortran	Comment
`-xO5`	Y	Y	Y	Set highest level of optimization
`-xtarget=native`	Y	Y	Y	Optimize for system being used to compile
`-xalias_level=basic`	Y			Assert that different basic C types do not alias each other
`-xbuiltin=%all`	Y	Y		Recognize standard library calls
`-xdepend`	Y	Y	Y	Perform dependency analysis
`-xmemalign=8s`	Y	Y	Y	Assume 8-byte memory alignment (SPARC only)
`-aligncommon=16`			Y	Align common block data to 16-byte boundaries
`-xprefetch_level=2`			Y	Select aggressiveness of prefetch insertion
`-pad=local`			Y	Optimize padding for local variables
`-xregs=frameptr`	Y	Y	Y	Use frame pointer register (x86 only)

Table 5.5 lists the compiler optimizations included in `-fast` that specifically target floating-point applications. Chapter 6 discusses floating-point optimization flags in detail.

Table 5.5 Floating-Point Optimizations Included in `-fast`

Flag	C	C++	Fortran	Comments
`-fsimple=2`	Y	Y	Y	Perform aggressive floating-point optimizations
`-ftrap=%none`	Y	Y		Do not trap on IEEE exceptions
`-ftrap=common`			Y	Trap only on common IEEE exceptions
`-xlibmil`	Y	Y	Y	Use inline templates for math functions
`-xlibmopt`	Y	Y	Y	Use optimized math library
`-fns`	Y	Y	Y	Enable floating-point nonstandard mode
`-xvector=lib`			Y	Convert loops to vector calls (SPARC only)
`-fsingle`	Y			Do not promote single-precision variables to double
`-nofstore`	Y	Y	Y	Do not convert floating-point values to assigned size (x86 only)

Tables 5.4 and 5.5 cover the set of generally useful performance flags. Even if -fast does not turn out to be the ideal flag for an application, it can be worth picking out one or more of the flags in -fast and using them. Flags in -fast normally perform optimizations on a broad range of applications, and it would not be surprising to find that only a few of the flags improve the performance of any particular application. Later sections on compiler flags will deal with these optimizations in greater detail.

5.5 Generating Debug Information

5.5.1 Debug Information Flags

The compiler will include debug information if the -g flag (or -g0 for C++) is used. There are a number of good reasons for including debug information.

- If the application requires debugging, it is essential to have the compiler generate this data.
- When performance analysis is performed (using Analyzer; see Section 8.2 of Chapter 8), having the debug information allows the tool to report time spent on a per-source-line basis.
- The compiler generates commentary that describes what optimizations it performed and why, as well as including a range of other useful information. This commentary is shown in the Performance Analyzer and in the er_src tool, as discussed in Section 8.20 of Chapter 8. Example 5.5 shows an example of compiler commentary.

Example 5.5 Example of Compiler Commentary

```
Loop below pipelined with steady-state cycle count = 6 before unrolling
Loop below unrolled 3 times
Loop below has 1 loads, 5 stores, 0 prefetches, 1 FPadds, 1 FPmuls,
        and 0 FPdivs per iteration
   7.    for (i=0; i<SIZE; i++) {a[i]=(double)i*i;b[i]=0;}
```

The -g0 flag tells the C++ compiler to generate debug information without disabling these optimizations. The -g flag disables some optimizations for C++, hence it is recommended to use -g0 instead.

5.5.2 Debug and Optimization

There is some interplay between the debug information available and the optimization level selected. With no optimization flags, the compiler will provide considerable debug information, but this does incur a runtime performance penalty. At higher levels of optimization, the amount of debug information available is reduced. At optimization levels greater than -xO3, performance is considered a higher priority than debug information. You can find more details on the interaction between debug and optimization in Section 9.4.2 of Chapter 9.

In general, it is very useful to include debug information when building an application, because it has little or no impact on performance (for binaries compiled with optimization), and it is extremely helpful for both debugging and performance analysis.

5.6 Selecting the Target Machine Type for an Application

5.6.1 Choosing between 32-bit and 64-bit Applications

The compiler has some default assumptions about the type of machine on which the application it is building will run. By default, the compiler will build an application that runs well on a wide range of hardware, not taking advantage of any hardware features that are limited to only a few processors. The compiler will also generate a 32-bit application. The defaults may not be optimal choices for any given application. One of the key decisions to make is whether to target a 32-bit or a 64-bit application.

The major advantage of specifying a 64-bit architecture is that it will support a much larger address space than the 4GB limit for a 32-bit application.

When an application is compiled for 64-bit, various data structures increase in size. Long integers and pointers become 64 bits in size rather than 32 bits. Hence, the memory footprint for the application will increase, and this will often lead to a drop in performance. If the data is mainly pointers or long integers, the memory footprint can nearly double and the difference in performance can be significant.

On x64-based systems, the 64-bit instruction set is significantly improved over the 32-bit instruction set. In particular, more registers are available for the compiler to use. These additional registers can lead to a significant gain in performance, despite the increased memory footprint.

On SPARC-based systems, a 64-bit version of an application will typically run slightly slower than a 32-bit version of the same application. On x64-based systems, the 64-bit version of an application may well run faster.

5.6.2 The Generic Target

By default, the compiler will select a generic 32-bit model for the processor on which the application will run. The idea of a generic model is that the compiler will favor code that runs well on all platforms over code that exploits features of a single platform. The generic target is the one to use when it is necessary to produce a single binary that runs over a wide range of processors. (Binaries targeted for generic targets are not cross-platform. A generic targeted binary compiled on a SPARC system will run only on SPARC-based systems, and will not run on an x86 system.)

A corresponding `generic64` target will produce a 64-bit binary that has good performance over a wide range of processors.

The `-xtarget` flag is a macro flag that sets three parameters that control the type of code that is generated. It is also possible to set these parameters independently of the `-xtarget` flag. The three parameters are as follows.

- The cache size. You can explicitly set cache configuration using the `-xcache` flag.

- The instruction selection and scheduling, which you can also set using the `-xchip` flag.

- The instruction set, which you can explicitly set using the `-xarch` flag.

In many cases the generic target is the best choice, but that does not necessarily exploit all the features of recent processors. It is possible to use the `-xtarget` compiler flag to specify a particular processor. This will favor performance on that processor over performance on other compatible processors. In some cases, it can result in a binary that does not run on some processors because they lack the instructions the compiler has assumed are present.

There are two reasons to specify an architecture other than generic.

- The developer knows deployment of the application is restricted to a certain range of processors. This might be the case if, for example, the application will be deployed on only one particular machine. Even in this situation, it is appropriate to test the hypothesis that setting the specific target does lead to better performance than using the generic target.

- The application uses features that are available on only a subset of processors; for example, if the application uses a specific instruction. However, it may be appropriate to implement the processor-specific part of the application as a library that is loaded at runtime depending on the processor's characteristics. I discuss machine-specific libraries in Section 7.2.6 of Chapter 7.

For Sun Studio 12 and earlier, the generic option for x86 processors is equivalent to 386. Best performance for a more recent AMD64 or EMT64 processor is to use -xtarget=opteron, which builds a 32-bit application using features included in the SSE2 instruction set extensions.

The -fast compiler flag includes the -xtarget=native flag, which tells the compiler that the build machine is the same type of machine as the machine on which the code will be run. Consequently, it is best to always specify the desired build target for the application, to avoid the possibility that the choice may be made implicitly by the build machine.

5.6.3 Specifying Cache Configuration Using the -xcache Flag

The -xcache option tells the compiler the characteristics of the cache. This information is part of the information reported by the SPARC tool fpversion discussed in Section 4.2.7 of Chapter 4. Example 5.6 shows an example of the output from fpversion.

Example 5.6 Output from fpversion on an UltraSPARC IIICu-Based System

```
$ fpversion
A SPARC-based CPU is available.
Kernel says CPU's clock rate is 1050.0 MHz.
Kernel says main memory's clock rate is 150.0 MHz.

Sun-4 floating-point controller version 0 found.
An UltraSPARC chip is available.

Use "-xtarget=ultra3cu -xcache=64/32/4:8192/512/2" code-generation option.

Hostid = 0x83xxxxxx.
```

The first three parameters the -xcache flag uses describe the first-level data cache (size in kilobytes, line size in bytes, associativity), and the next three parameters describe the second-level cache (size in kilobytes, line size in bytes, associativity). The example describes a 64KB first-level data cache with 32-byte line sizes that is four-way associative, and an 8MB second-level data cache with 512-byte line sizes that is two-way associative.

The compiler uses this information when it is trying to arrange data access patterns so that all the data that is reused between loop iterations fits into the cache. In general, this option will not have any effect on performance, because most code is not amenable to cache-size optimizations. However, for some code, typically floating-point loop-intensive code, this option does demonstrate a significant performance gain.

5.6.4 Specifying Code Scheduling Using the `-xchip` Flag

The `-xchip` option controls the scheduling of the instructions, and which instructions the compiler picks if alternative instruction sequences are equivalent in functionality. In particular, this flag controls the instruction latencies the compiler assumes for the target processor. For example, consider the floating-point multiply instruction. On the UltraSPARC II, this instruction has a three-cycle latency, whereas on the UltraSPARC III, this instruction takes four cycles. A binary scheduled for the UltraSPARC II would ideally have an instruction that uses the results of a floating-point multiply placed two cycles after the multiply upon which it depends. When this binary is run on an UltraSPARC III processor, the processor may sit idle for a single cycle waiting for the initial floating-point multiply to complete before the dependent instruction can be issued.

5.6.5 The `-xarch` Flag and `-m32`/`-m64`

The `-xarch=<architecture>` flag specifies the architecture (or instruction set) of the target machine. The instruction set represents all the instructions that are available on the machine. A binary that uses instructions that are unavailable on a particular processor may not run (if it does run, the missing instructions will have to be emulated in software, which results in a slower-running application). The available options for this flag significantly change in Sun Studio 12. In compiler versions prior to Sun Studio 12, one of the purposes of this flag was to specify whether a 32-bit or 64-bit application should be generated.

In Sun Studio 12, the architecture has been separated from whether the application is 32-bit or 64-bit. The two new flags, `-m32` and `-m64`, control whether a 32-bit or 64-bit application should be generated. The `-xarch` flag now only has to specify the instruction set that is to be used in generating the binary. For SPARC processors, the generic architecture is often a good choice; for x64 processors, selecting SSE2 as a target architecture will get the best performance and a reasonable coverage of commonly encountered systems.

Table 5.6 specifies some of the common architectures using the Sun Studio 11 options and the new Sun Studio 12 options.

Table 5.6 Common Architecture Options

Sun Studio 11 Options	Comment	Sun Studio 12 Options
`-xtarget=generic`	Default option, 32-bit application	`-m32`
`-xtarget=generic64`	64-bit application	`-m64`

Table 5.6 Common Architecture Options (*continued*)

Sun Studio 11 Options	Comment	Sun Studio 12 Options
-xtarget=opteron	32-bit application, AMD64-based system	-m32 -xtarget=opteron
-xtarget=opteron -xarch=amd64	64-bit application, AMD64-based system	-m64 -xtarget=opteron
-xarch=v8plusa	32-bit application, SPARC V9-based system with instruction set extensions	-m32 -xarch=sparcvis
-xarch=v9a	64-bit application, SPARC V9-based system with instruction set extensions	-m64 -xarch=sparcvis
Not available	32-bit application, SPARC V9-based system with floating-point multiply accumulate instructions	-m32 -xarch=sparcfmaf
Not available	64-bit application, SPARC V9-based system with floating-point multiply accumulate instructions	-m64 -xarch=sparcfmaf

5.7 Code Layout Optimizations

5.7.1 Introduction

A number of optimizations lead to better code layout. These optimizations do not really change the instructions that are used, but they do change the way they are laid out in memory. These optimizations target the following things.

- Branch mispredictions. The code can be laid out so that the branches that are probably taken are the straight path, and branch instructions represent "unusual" or "infrequent" events. This reduces branch misprediction rates, and the corresponding stalls in the flow of instructions.

- Instruction cache or instruction translation lookaside buffer (TLB) layout. The code can be laid out in memory so that hot instructions are grouped together and cold instructions are put elsewhere. This means that when a page is mapped into the instruction TLB or a line is brought into the instruction cache, it will mainly contain instructions that will be used. This reduces instruction cache misses and instruction TLB misses.

- Inlining of routines. When the compiler can determine that a particular
  routine is called frequently and that the overhead of calling the routine is
  significant when compared to the time spent doing useful work in the routine, that routine is a candidate for being inlined. This means the code
  from the routine is placed at the point at which the routine is called,
  replacing the call instruction. This removes the cost of calling the code, but
  does increase the size of the code.

One way to think about the options for code layout improvements is to consider
them as a number of complementary techniques.

- Crossfile optimization (discussed in Section 5.7.2) examines the code and
  locates routines which are small and frequently called. These routines get
  inlined into their call sites, removing the overhead of the call and potentially
  exposing other opportunities for optimization. Crossfile optimization will
  work without profile feedback information, but the presence of profile feedback information will help the compiler to make better decisions.
- Mapfiles (discussed in Section 5.7.3) improve the layout of the code in memory, grouping all the hot (frequently executed) parts of the code together and
  placing the cold (infrequently executed) parts out of the way. This optimization improves code's footprint density in memory.
- Profile feedback (discussed in Section 5.7.4) is a mechanism that gives the
  compiler more information about the code's runtime behavior. This helps the
  compiler make the correct decisions about which branches are usually taken,
  and which routines are good candidates for inlining.
- Finally, on SPARC, link-time optimization (discussed in Section 5.7.5) can
  look at the whole program and, using profile feedback information, can perform the same optimizations as the mapfiles, as well as additional optimizations to reduce instruction count using information about how the code is
  laid out in memory. Link-time optimization renders the use of mapfiles
  unnecessary.

5.7.2 Crossfile Optimization

Crossfile optimization can be extremely important. At -xO4, the compiler starts to
inline within the same source file, but not across source files. Using crossfile optimization, the compiler is able to inline across the source files.

The advantages of doing this are as follows.

- The call overhead is removed. There are no call and return instructions, which means less branching and fewer instructions executed. Similarly, removing calls also removes stores and loads of function parameters to the stack.

- The code is laid out in straighter blocks, which can improve instruction-cache locality and performance.

- Inlining the code can expose opportunities for further performance gains.

Example 5.7 shows an example of a program that will benefit from inlining. In fact, there are a number of benefits from performing the inlining.

Example 5.7 Example of an Inlining Opportunity

```
void set(int* bitmap, int x, int width, int y, int height,int colour)
{
  bitmap[y*width + x]=colour;
}

void main()
{
  int x,y,height=1000,width=1000,colour=0;
  int bitmap[height*width];
  for (x=0; x<width; x++)
    for (y=0; y<height; y++)
      set(bitmap,x,width,y,height,colour);
}
```

- The `set` routine will be called `height*width` times—in this case, 1 million times. Given that the routine contains little code, the overhead of the call is going to represent a large proportion of the time spent in the routine.

- Every time the routine is entered, the `y` variable has to be multiplied by the `width`, to calculate the correct position in the array. The integer multiplication operation will take a few cycles, so a large number of cycles will be spent repeatedly doing this calculation.

- Finally, the inner loop is over the `y` variable, and this means the memory in the `bitmap` is not accessed contiguously, but rather at intervals of `width`. This striding through memory will also cost in terms of performance. Once the compiler inlines the routine, it can also determine that the memory access pattern is inefficient and perform the necessary loop reordering.

If the `set` and `main` routines are located in the same source file, compiling at -x04 will cause the compiler to inline `set` and perform the optimizations suggested earlier. If they are located in separate source files, the compiler will need to be told to do crossfile optimization, using the -xipo flag, to get the performance. When the compiler optimizes the routine, it will produce code is similar to that shown in Example 5.8.

Example 5.8 Equivalent Code after Inlining and Optimization

```
void main()
{
  int i,height=1000,width=1000,colour=0;
  int bitmap[height*width];
  for (i=0; i<height*width; i++) bitmap[i]=colour;
}
```

Two flags perform crossfile optimization: -xcrossfile and -xipo. -xcross-file is the old flag that requires that all the files be presented to the compiler at the same time; in most circumstances, this is a severe restriction. -xipo enables the compiler to perform crossfile optimization at link time. This is normally much more convenient for build processes. The constraint with -xipo is that the compiler, and not the linker, must be invoked to do the linking. The flag also needs to be specified for both the compile and the link passes.

A further level of crossfile optimization is enabled with -xipo=2. At this level, the compiler attempts to improve data layout in memory. I discuss the types of memory optimizations the compiler attempts to improve in Section 11.4 of Chapter 11.

5.7.3 Mapfiles

Mapfiles are a very easy way of telling the linker how to arrange the code in an application to place it most efficiently in memory. A mapfile works at the routine level, so the linker can sort the routines in a particular order but cannot specify the way the code is laid out within the routine. Two flags are necessary to enable the compiler to use mapfiles: the -M <name of mapfile> flag, which eventually gets passed to the linker, and the -xF flag, which tells the compiler to place every function in its own section. Example 5.9 shows an example command line.

Example 5.9 Linking Using a Mapfile

```
$ cc -O a.c b.c c.c main.c -xF -M mapfile.txt -o test
```

Mapfiles are very easy to use. You can prepare them manually by editing a text file, or the Analyzer can output them (as shown in Section 8.12 of Chapter 8). Example 5.10 shows an example of a mapfile.

Example 5.10 Example of a Mapfile

```
section1=LOAD ?RXO;
section1: .text%c: c.o;
section1: .text%a: a.o;
section1: .text%b: b.o;
section1: .text%main: main.o;
```

The structure of the mapfile, shown in Example 5.10, is relatively easy to understand. In this example, each file defines a function of the same name as the file (i.e., a.c contains the function a). The resulting executable will have the routines in the order c, a, b, and finally main. The structure of the mapfile is as follows.

- The first line defines a section for the executable (called section1). It is a LOAD segment, which means that it has a location in memory. The segment also has the following flags: read-only (R), executable (X), and ordered (O). Being an ordered segment means that the mapfile defines the order in which the routines appear in the final binary.

- The next lines define the order of the routines for the named section. Each line starts with the name of the section to which the line applies. Because the functions are being ordered, each function is specified as .text%<function name>. If there are multiple functions of the same name within the executable, the object file that contains the function can also be specified, as shown in the example.

Mapfiles become more useful as the size of the program increases. This is because a small program may fit entirely in the instruction cache, or the second-level cache, and will be mapped by the instruction TLB. However, some programs are sufficiently large that they no longer fit into the caches, or incur instruction TLB misses. In either case, mapfiles can be an effective way to ensure that the critical code has as small a footprint in memory as possible.

5.7.4 Profile Feedback

Profile feedback gives the compiler a great deal of information about the probabilities and frequency with which a given branch is taken or untaken. This allows it to make sensible decisions about how to structure the code.

To use profile feedback, the program must be initially compiled with -xprofile=collect. Under the -xprofile=collect flag, the compiler produces an "instrumented" version of the binary, meaning that every branch instruction has code surrounding it that counts the number of times the branch was taken. The next step is to run this version of the program on data similar to the kind of data on which the program will typically be used. This can be a single run of the program, or multiple runs; the results will be aggregated. The data that is collected as a result of these runs is stored in the location specified. The program is then recompiled with the -xprofile=use flag, which tells the compiler to use the profile data that has been collected.

The -xprofile=[use|collect] flag can take a further specifier, which is the name and location of the directory that will contain the profile information. If this specifier is omitted, the compiler will place the profile information in the same place as the binary, and give the profile directory the same name as the binary but with ".profile" appended. If the name is omitted from the -xprofile=use flag, the compiler will default to using a.out (even if a name for the binary is specified using a -o flag). Therefore, it is best to specify a path to the profile directory when using profile feedback. This makes it easier to know during the -xprofile=use phase where the profile is located.

Example 5.11 shows the sequence of instructions for using profile feedback. It is important to keep the other compiler flags the same for both the collect and use runs, because changing the flags may result in a different ordering of the instructions, and it would no longer be possible for the compiler to determine which branches correspond in the two builds.

Example 5.11 Using Profile Feedback

```
% cc -xO3 -xtarget=ultra3 -xprofile=collect:/tmp/profile test.c
% a.out
% cc -xO3 -xtarget=ultra3 -xprofile=use:/tmp/profile  test.c
```

Profile feedback is useful for the following kinds of optimizations.

- Laying out the application code so that branch statements are rarely taken. This allows the processor to "fall through" the branches without incurring the cost of fetching new instructions from a different address in memory.

- Inlining routines that are called many times. This optimization eliminates the cost of calling the routine.

- Moving code that is executed infrequently out of the hot part of the routine. This leads to fewer unused instructions in the caches, which means they are more effective in storing code that is likely to be reused.

- Many other optimizations—for example, knowing which variables to hold in registers—also benefit from more detailed knowledge of frequently executed code paths.

The code shown in Example 5.12 has branches with predictable behavior. However, the compiler is unlikely to be able to statically determine the branch pattern (although this particular instance is sufficiently simple that it could in the future). The computation on the usually taken path is a multiplication. If this computation were a simple addition or set operation, the compiler might be able to use conditional moves to replace the branch altogether.

Example 5.12 Code with Branches Predictable at Runtime

```
#include <stdlib.h>
#include <stdio.h>

void main()
{
  int i=0;
  int t=0;
  for (i=0; i<100; i++)
  {
    if (i*i>=0)
    { t=t*t; }
    else
    { t--; }
  }
  printf("Total = %d\n",t);
}
```

Example 5.13 shows the disassembly from the code compiled without profile feedback. The compiler has no information to go on, so it has decided that each part of the if condition is equally likely. So, for each case, one branch is taken.

Example 5.13 Code Compiled with No Profile Information

```
10bb0:   96 4b 00 0c   mulx    %o4, %o4, %o3
10bb4:   80 a2 e0 00   cmp     %o3, 0
10bb8:   06 40 00 05   bl,pn   %icc, 0x10bcc
10bbc:   9b 3a 60 00   sra     %o1, 0, %o5
10bc0:   92 4b 40 0d   mulx    %o5, %o5, %o1
10bc4:   10 80 00 04   ba      0x10bd4
10bc8:   94 02 a0 01   inc     %o2

10bcc:   92 02 7f ff   inc     -1, %o1
10bd0:   94 02 a0 01   inc     %o2

10bd4:   80 a2 a0 63   cmp     %o2, 99
10bd8:   04 4f ff f6   ble,pt  %icc, 0x10bb0
10bdc:   99 3a a0 00   sra     %o2, 0, %o4
```

When compiled with profile feedback, the compiler has information that indicates which code path is most likely, and it is able to structure the code so that the common case has the shortest code path. Example 5.14 shows this code. In this rearrangement of the code, the frequently executed path has taken one branch back to the top of the loop, but the infrequently executed code has taken two branches.

Example 5.14 Code Compiled with Profile Information

```
10bb0:   96 4b 00 0c   mulx    %o4, %o4, %o3
10bb4:   80 a2 e0 00   cmp     %o3, 0
10bb8:   06 40 00 0c   bl,pn   %icc, 0x10be8
10bbc:   9b 3a 60 00   sra     %o1, 0, %o5
10bc0:   92 4b 40 0d   mulx    %o5, %o5, %o1
10bc4:   94 02 a0 01   inc     %o2
10bc8:   80 a2 a0 63   cmp     %o2, 99
10bcc:   04 4f ff f9   ble,pt  %icc, 0x10bb0
10bd0:   99 3a a0 00   sra     %o2, 0, %o4

...

10be8:   92 02 7f ff   inc     -1, %o1
10bec:   10 bf ff f7   ba      0x10bc8
10bf0:   94 02 a0 01   inc     %o2
```

Obviously, when using profile feedback, there is a concern that the program will end up "overoptimized" for the case used for the training—and consequently perform badly on other cases. A couple of points should be considered.

- Always use a representative case for the training run. If the training data is not representative or if it does not cover all the common cases, it is possible to not get the best performance. You can use multiple training workloads to increase code coverage. Branches where the training data was inconclusive will be optimized as equally likely to be taken or untaken.

- A lot of codes have tests in them to check for corner cases. Profile feedback allows the compiler to identify these kinds of tests, and work on the assumption that they will remain corner cases in the actual run of the program. This is often where the performance comes from—the fact that the compiler can take a block of if statements and determine that one particular path through the code is likely to be executed many more times than other paths.

Consequently, it is very likely that using profile feedback will result in improvements in performance for the general case, because the profile will eliminate the obvious "unlikely code" and leave the "likely" code as the hot path.

One way to evaluate whether the data used for the training run is similar to the data used during real workloads is to use coverage tools (such as tcov, covered in Section 8.18 of Chapter 8, or BIT, covered in Section 8.17 of Chapter 8) to determine how much of the code has been exercised, and adding appropriate test cases to reach 100% coverage. Although coverage does not guarantee that the training code is taking the same pattern of branches as the real application would, it will at least indicate that the training run is executing the same parts of the code.

5.7.5 Link-Time Optimization

Another phase of the SPARC compiler is the link-time optimization phase. At link time, the compiler has seen all the code and produced the object files, but because it cannot see the entire application, it has to guess at the best thing to do. Here are some examples of things that cannot be determined until link time.

- Global variables in programs are accessed using a combination of a base address plus an offset. At compile time, it is not possible to know how many global variables are going to be present in the program, and consequently, whether two variables are sufficiently close in memory that they can be accessed using the same base address.

- In general, most branches in programs are short, but occasionally there are some long branches. The instructions to perform a long branch have a higher cost than the normal branch instructions. At compile time, it is not possible to tell whether the code might just fit into the range of a normal branch instruction. However, at link time it may be possible to replace a long-range branch with a lower-cost shorter-range branch instruction.

- It is possible to improve instruction cache utilization by laying out the code better. However, you can do this only at link time, when all the code is known. This is similar to what you can achieve with mapfiles. However, link-time optimization has a big advantage over mapfiles. Mapfiles work at the level of laying out routines in memory, whereas link-time optimization can actually work within routines. Figure 5.1 shows two routines, A and B, each having a hot part and a cold part. With link-time optimization, the hot part of routine A can be placed with the hot part of routine B, and their cold parts can also be placed together. This leads to much higher efficiency when packing the instruction cache.

It is very easy to use link-time optimization: Just append the `-xlinkopt[=2]` flag to the compile line and link lines (see Example 5.15). It relies heavily on execution frequency information, so it will work most effectively in the presence of profile feedback information.

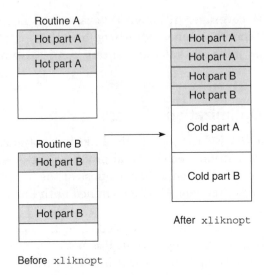

Figure 5.1 Improving Instruction Cache Layout with Link-Time Optimization

Example 5.15 Using Link-Time Optimization

```
% cc -xO3 -xtarget=ultra3 -xprofile=collect test.c
% a.out
% cc -xO3 -xtarget=ultra3 -xprofile=use test.c -xlinkopt=2
```

There are two levels for -xlinkopt. Level one, the default, just rearranges the code to use the instruction cache more effectively; level two does optimizations on the code to take advantage of the linker's knowledge of the addresses of variables or other blocks of code.

5.8 General Compiler Optimizations

5.8.1 Prefetch Instructions

Prefetch instructions are requests to the processor to fetch the data held at a memory address before the processor needs that data. Prefetch instructions can have a significant impact on an application's performance. Consider a simple example in which all the data an application needs to use is resident in memory, and it takes 200 cycles for the data to get from memory to the CPU. When the processor needs an item of data it has to wait 200 cycles for the data to arrive from memory. You can use a single, well-placed prefetch instruction to fetch that data. In this case, the prefetch instruction will cost one cycle (to issue the instruction), but will save 200 cycles.

The -xprefetch flag controls whether the compiler generates prefetch instructions. Since Sun Studio 9, the compiler has defaulted to generating prefetch instructions on SPARC hardware when an appropriate target instruction set has been selected. On x64 processors it is necessary to specify a target architecture of at least SSE (e.g., using the -xarch=sse flag) to cause the compiler to generate prefetch instructions.

It can be difficult for the compiler to insert prefetch instructions for all situations in which they will improve performance. The x64 processors typically have a hardware prefetch unit that speculatively prefetches the address the processor expects to access next, given the previous addresses accessed. In simple cases, the memory access pattern is readily apparent, and a hardware prefetch unit can often predict these patterns with a high degree of accuracy. In more complex access patterns, the compiler cannot determine from the code exactly which memory operations would benefit from being prefetched, and hardware prefetch will struggle to predict these accesses. Given the potential gains from a successful prefetch instruction, it is often helpful for the compiler to generate more speculative prefetches. Speculative prefetches can useful in a number of situations.

- Situations in which the compiler has difficulty predicting the exact address of the next memory reference—for example, where an array is strided through using an uneven stride.

- Places where the compiler cannot determine whether a memory access is likely to be resident in the caches or whether it must be fetched from memory. This is common in cases where multiple streams of data are being fetched, some from memory and some that are short enough to fit into the caches.

- Parts of the code where it is helpful to prefetch a memory location for a second time. For example, the data may have been knocked out of the on-chip caches before it was used, or the prefetch instruction may not have been issued due to resource constraints.

The -xprefetch_level flag increases the number of speculative prefetch instructions that are issued. For codes where the data mainly resides in memory, increasing the prefetch level will also improve performance. For codes where the data is rarely resident in memory, the benefits of issuing prefetch instructions are less clear.

If the data is mainly resident in the on-chip caches, including prefetch instructions can lead to a reduction in performance. The prefetch instructions do not provide any benefit, because the data is already available to the processor. Also, each prefetch instruction takes up an instruction issue slot that could have been used for other work. Finally, the prefetch instructions typically have some "book-keeping" instructions, such as calculating the next address to be prefetched, and these instructions also take up some issue slots that could have used for useful work.

The compiler typically does a good job determining the appropriate trade-offs and puts prefetch instructions in the places where they will benefit the application's performance. The `-xprefetch_level` flag provides some control in situations where the application has a large memory-resident data set that will benefit from more speculative use of prefetch instructions.

5.8.2 Enabling Prefetch Generation (`-xprefetch`)

The code shown in Example 5.16 calculates a vector product. Both vectors need to be streamed through, so this is a natural place where prefetch can be useful.

Example 5.16 Example Code That Streams Data from Memory

```
float total(float *a, float *b,int n)
{
  int i;
  float total=0.0;
  for (i=0; i<n; i++)
  {
    total += a[i]*b[i];
  }
  return total;
}
```

Example 5.17 shows the flags necessary to enable prefetch generation for versions of the compiler prior to Sun Studio 9 on an UltraSPARC system. Sun Studio 9 and later compilers have prefetch generation enabled by default.

Example 5.17 Compiling to Include Prefetches

```
$ cc -xO3 -xtarget=ultra3 -xprefetch ex5.16.c
```

Example 5.18 shows the command line to build the same file on x64 with prefetch enabled.

Example 5.18 Compiling with Prefetch on x64

```
$ cc -O -xarch=sse ex5.16.c
```

Example 5.19 shows the disassembly code from the SPARC verison of the routine, and includes the two prefetches that the compiler generates to improve performance.

Example 5.19 SPARC Assembly Code with Prefetches Inserted

```
                          .L900000108:
/* 0x0074        7 */     add       %o3,8,%o3
/* 0x0078        */       ld        [%o2],%f20
/* 0x007c        */       add       %o2,32,%o2
/* 0x0080        */       prefetch      [%o0+272],0
/* 0x0084        */       cmp       %o3,%o5
/* 0x0088        */       add       %o0,32,%o0
/* 0x008c        */       fmuls     %f0,%f20,%f28
/* 0x0090        */       fadds     %f2,%f4,%f26
/* 0x0094        */       ld        [%o0-32],%f24
/* 0x0098        */       ld        [%o2-28],%f22
/* 0x009c        */       prefetch      [%o2+244],0
/* 0x00a0        */       fmuls     %f24,%f22,%f7
/* 0x00a4        */       fadds     %f26,%f28,%f5
/* 0x00a8        */       ld        [%o0-28],%f1
...
/* 0x0104        */       fadds     %f10,%f12,%f2
/* 0x0108        */       ble,pt    %icc,.L900000108
/* 0x010c        */       ld        [%o0-4],%f0
```

Example 5.20 shows part of the equivalent disassembly for x64.

Example 5.20 x64 Assembly Code with Prefetches Inserted

```
.CG3.15:
        prefetcht0 128(%esi)                    ;/ line : 8
        fldl       (%esi)                       ;/ line : 8
        fmull      (%ebx)                       ;/ line : 8
        fstpl      (%esi)                       ;/ line : 8
        fwait
        prefetcht0 136(%ebx)                    ;/ line : 8
        fldl       8(%esi)                      ;/ line : 8
        fmull      8(%ebx)                      ;/ line : 8
        fstpl      8(%esi)                      ;/ line : 8
        fldl       16(%esi)                     ;/ line : 8
        fmull      16(%ebx)                     ;/ line : 8
        fstpl      16(%esi)                     ;/ line : 8
        fldl       24(%esi)                     ;/ line : 8
        fmull      24(%ebx)                     ;/ line : 8
        fstpl      24(%esi)                     ;/ line : 8
        fwait
        addl       $32,%ebx                     ;/ line : 8
        addl       $32,%esi                     ;/ line : 8
        addl       $4,%edx                      ;/ line : 8
.LU2.47:
        cmpl       $1023,%edx                   ;/ line : 8
        jle        .CG3.15                      ;/ line : 8
```

5.8.3 Controlling the Aggressiveness of Prefetch Insertion (`-xprefetch_level`)

The `-xprefetch_level` flag provides a degree of control over the aggressiveness of prefetch insertion. By default, the compiler will attempt to place prefetches into loops which look sufficiently predictable that prefetch will work. Increasing the prefetch level allows the insertion of prefetches into codes where the loops are not quite so predictable. Therefore, the prefetches become more speculative in nature (the compiler expects the data to be used, but is not certain of this).

Example 5.21 shows the number of prefetch instructions in the binary when the code from Example 5.16 is compiled with various levels of optimization.

Example 5.21 The Impact of `-xprefetch_level` on the Number of Prefetches

```
$ cc -xtarget=ultra3 -xprefetch -xO3 -S ex5.16.c
$ grep -c prefetch ex5.16.s
13
$ cc -xtarget=ultra3 -xprefetch -xO3 -S -xprefetch_level=2 ex5.16.c
$ grep -c prefetch ex5.16.s
16
$ cc -xtarget=ultra3 -xprefetch -xO3 -S -xprefetch_level=3 ex5.16.c
$ grep -c prefetch ex5.16.s
18
```

The `-xprefetch_level` flag controls the number of prefetch instructions generated. For some codes this will help performance, for other codes there will be no effect, and for still other codes the performance can decrease. The behavior depends on both the application and the workload run.

5.8.4 Enabling Dependence Analysis (`-xdepend`)

The `-xdepend` flag for C, C++, and Fortran switches on improved loop dependence analysis. (`-xdepend` is included in `-fast` for C, but appears in `-fast` for C++ only in Sun Studio 12. For Fortran, `-xdepend` is enabled at optimization levels of `-xO3` and above.) With this flag, the compiler will perform array subscript analysis and loop nest transformations, and will try to reduce the number of loads and stores.

The code in Example 5.22 shows a hot inner loop that benefits from dependence analysis. The code is a calculation of a matrix d which has a number of "layers" of 3x3 elements. The calculation of d for each iteration depends on the calculation of d for a previous layer; there is some reuse of the d variable within each iteration.

Example 5.23 shows the effect of compiling with and without dependence analysis. The effect for this loop is quite pronounced.

Example 5.22 Loop with Dependencies

```
totald=0;
starttime();
for (count=0;count<RPT;count++)
for (i1=2; i1<SIZE; i1++)
{
  for (i2=0;i2<3;i2++)
  {
    for (i3=0;i3<3;i3++)
    {
      d[i1][i2][i3]+=d[i1-2][i2][i3];
      d[i1][i3][i2]-=d[i1][i2][i3];
    }
    totald+=d[i1][3][3];
  }
}
endtime(SIZE*RPT*9);
```

Example 5.23 Compiling with and without Dependence Analysis

```
$ cc -xO5 -xtarget=ultra3 -xprefetch ex5.22.c
$ a.out
Time per iteration 18.03 ns
$ cc -xO5 -xtarget=ultra3 -xprefetch -xdepend ex5.22.c
$ a.out
Time per iteration 13.15 ns
```

In this situation, dependence analysis enables the compiler to do a number of optimizations. First, the compiler can look at identifying variables which are reused, and so can avoid some memory operations. It can also look at unrolling the loops, or otherwise changing the loops, to maximize the potential reuse of variables. The changing of the loops allows the compiler to better determine streams of data that can be prefetched.

5.8.5 Handling Misaligned Memory Accesses on SPARC (-xmemalign/-dalign)

The current UltraSPARC processors do not handle misaligned memory accesses in hardware. For example, an 8-byte value has to be aligned on an 8-byte boundary. If an attempt is made to load misaligned data, the program will either generate a SIGBUS error or trap to the operating system so that the misaligned load can be emulated. In contrast, the x64 family of processors handle misalignment in hardware.

Consequently, the compiler has a SPARC-specific flag, -xmemalign, which specifies the default alignment that the compiler should assume, as well as what behavior should occur when the data is misaligned. For 32-bit applications, since Sun Studio 9, the default is for the compiler to assume 8-byte alignment and to trap and correct any misaligned data accesses. For 64-bit applications, the compiler assumes 8-byte alignment, but the application will SIGBUS on a misaligned access.

Using the -xmemalign flag, it is possible to specify that the compiler should assume a lesser degree of alignment. If this is specified, the compiler will emit multiple loads so that the data can be safely loaded without causing either a SIGBUS or a trap.

If the application makes regular access to misaligned data, it is usually preferable to use the -xmemalign flag to specify a lower assumed alignment, because adding a few load instructions will be significantly faster than trapping to the operating system. If the data is rarely misaligned, it is more efficient to specify the highest alignment, and to take a rare trap when the data is found to be misaligned. Most applications do not have misaligned data, so the default will work adequately. Table 5.7 shows a subset of the available settings for -xmemalign, and summarizes the reasons to use them.

Table 5.7 Common Settings for -xmemalign

-xmemalign	Assumed Alignment	Will Correct Misaligned Data	Comment
8s	8-byte	No	Use when the application does not access misaligned data
8i	8-byte	Yes	Use when the application may have occasional misaligned accesses
4s	4-byte	No	Use when all memory operations are at least 4-byte aligned
4i	4-byte	Yes	Use when most accesses are 4-byte aligned, but there is still some access that is misaligned
1s	1-byte	No	Use when there are frequent accesses to misaligned data, and that data may even be misaligned at a byte level. Equivalent to -xmisalign.

The -dalign flag is an alternative way to specify 8-byte alignment. In C and C++, the -dalign flag is equivalent to -xmemalign=8s; in Fortran, -dalign expands to -xmemalign=8s -xaligncommon=16. The -xaligncommon=16 flag will cause the Fortran common block elements to be aligned up to a 16-byte boundary for 64-bit applications and an 8-byte boundary for 32-bit applications. In Fortran, if one module is compiled with `-dalign` or `-xaligncommon`, all modules have to be compiled with the same flag.

5.8.6 Setting Page Size Using `-xpagesize=<size>`

The default page size for SPARC systems is 8KB, which means virtual memory is mapped in chunks of 8KB in the TLB (see Section 1.9.2 of Chapter 1). The page size for x64 systems is 4KB. You can change the page size to a larger value so that more memory can be mapped using the same number of TLB entries. However, changing the page size does not guarantee that the application will get that page size at runtime. The operating system will honor the request if there are sufficient pages of contiguous physical memory.

The page sizes that are available depend on the processor; the flag will have no effect at runtime if the page size is not available on the processor. The common page size settings are 4KB, 8KB, 64KB, 512KB, 2MB, 4MB, and 256MB. Table 4.1 in Chapter 4 lists the page sizes for various processors. The `pagesize` command, discussed in Section 4.2.6 of Chapter 4, will print out the page sizes that are supported on the hardware.

The `-xpagesize` compiler flag will cause the application to request a particular page size at runtime. Example 5.24 shows an example of using this flag. The flag needs to be used at both compile time and link time. Two other related flags, `-xpagesize_heap` and `-xpagesize_stack`, allow the user to independently specify the page size used to map the heap and the stack.

Example 5.24 Specifying Page Size at Compile Time

```
$ cc -O -xpagesize=64K -o app app.c
```

5.9 Pointer Aliasing in C and C++

5.9.1 The Problem with Pointers

There is a problem with pointers in that often the compiler is unable to tell from the context exactly what the pointers point to. In practical terms, this means the compiler must make the safest assumption possible: that different pointers may point to the same region of memory. Example 5.25 shows an example of a routine into which three pointers are passed.

Example 5.25 Example of Pointer Aliasing Problem

```
void test(int n, float *a, float *b, float *c)
{
  int i;
  float carry=0.0f;
  for (i=1; i<n; i++)
  {
    a[i]=a[i]*b[i]+c[i]*carry;
    carry = a[i]+b[i]*c[i];
  }
}
```

Example 5.26 shows the results of disassembling the compiled code. For clarity, the loads and stores have been annotated with the structures being loaded or stored. The disassembly shows the entire loop. By counting the number of floating-point operations, it is easy to determine that this is a single iteration of the loop. For each iteration of the loop there should be three loads, of a[i], b[i], and c[i], and one store of c[i]. However, there are two additional loads in the disassembly shown in Example 5.26. These correspond to reloads of the variables b[i] and c[i]. The problem here is that there is a store to a[i] between the first use of b[i] and c[i] and their subsequent reuse. The compiler is unable to know at compile time whether this store to a[i] will change the value of b[i] or c[i], so it has to make the safe assumption that it will change their values.

Example 5.26 Compiling Code and Examining with Aliasing Problem

```
% cc -xO3 -S ex5.25.c
% more ex5.25.s
...
                        .L900000110:
/* 0x00a4      8 */     ld      [%o3],%f25      ! load c[i]
/* 0x00a8      9 */     add     %g3,1,%g3
/* 0x00ac        */     add     %o1,4,%o1
/* 0x00b0        */     cmp     %g3,%o5
/* 0x00b4        */     add     %o2,4,%o2
/* 0x00b8      8 */     fmuls   %f0,%f2,%f29
/* 0x00bc      9 */     add     %o3,4,%o3
/* 0x00c0      8 */     fmuls   %f25,%f4,%f27
/* 0x00c4        */     fadds   %f29,%f27,%f6
/* 0x00c8        */     st      %f6,[%o1-8]     ! store a[i]
/* 0x00cc      9 */     ld      [%o3-4],%f31    ! reload c[i]
/* 0x00d0        */     ld      [%o2-8],%f2     ! reload b[i]
/* 0x00d4        */     fmuls   %f2,%f31,%f4
/* 0x00d8      8 */     ld      [%o1-4],%f0     ! load a[i+1]
/* 0x00dc        */     ld      [%o2-4],%f2     ! load b[i+1]
/* 0x00e0      9 */     bl      .L900000110
/* 0x00e4        */     fadds   %f6,%f4,%f4
....
```

It is hard for the compiler to resolve aliasing issues at compile time. Often, insufficient information is available. Suppose that for a given value of i, the address of a[i] is different from the addresses of b[i] and c[i]. This would allow the compiler to avoid reloading b[i] and c[i] after the store of a[i]. However, the code snippet is a loop, and really the compiler would like to unroll and pipeline the loop. Unrolling and pipelining refer to the optimization of performing multiple iterations of the loop at the same time, much like a manufacturing pipeline. I discuss unrolling and pipelining further in Section 11.2.2 of Chapter 11. After performing this optimization, the store to a[i] might happen after the load of b[i+1] or c[i+2]. So, it is not sufficient to know that just one particular index in the arrays does not alias. The compiler has to be certain that it is true for a range of values of the index variable.

The basic rule is that if the code has pointers in it, the compiler has to be very cautious about how it treats those pointers, and how it treats other variables after a store to a pointer variable. As an example, consider the case where instead of passing the length of the array to the function by value, it is available to the routine as a global variable, as Example 5.27 shows.

Example 5.27 Global Variables and Pointers

```
extern int n;

void test(float *a, float *b, float *c)
{
  int i;
  float carry=0.0f;

  for (i=1; i<n; i++)
  {
    a[i]=a[i]*b[i]+c[i]*carry;
    carry = a[i]+b[i]*c[i];
  }
}
...
/* 0x0030      11 */    ld      [%o4],%f0      ! load b[i]
/* 0x0034      12 */    add     %g3,1,%g3
/* 0x0038      11 */    ld      [%g4],%f4      ! load c[i]
/* 0x003c         */    fmuls   %f2,%f0,%f12
/* 0x0040         */    fmuls   %f4,%f18,%f6
/* 0x0044         */    fadds   %f12,%f6,%f16
/* 0x0048         */    st      %f16,[%o3]     ! store a[i]
/* 0x004c      12 */    add     %o3,4,%o3
/* 0x0050         */    ld      [%o4],%f10     ! reload b[i]
/* 0x0054         */    add     %o4,4,%o4
/* 0x0058         */    ld      [%g4],%f8      ! reload c[i]
/* 0x005c         */    add     %g4,4,%g4
/* 0x0060         */    ld      [%g2],%g1      ! reload n
/* 0x0064         */    fmuls   %f10,%f8,%f14
/* 0x0068         */    cmp     %g3,%g1
/* 0x006c         */    fadds   %f16,%f14,%f18
/* 0x0070         */    bl,a    .L900000111
/* 0x0074      11 */    ld      [%o3],%f2      ! load a[i+1]
```

In this case, the compiler cannot tell whether the store to the a[i] array will change the value of n (the variable holding the upper bound for the loop) and cause the bounds of the loop to change. Consequently, with every iteration the loop bounds have to be reloaded. The situation would be worse if the index variable, i, were also a global. In this case, i would have to be stored before the loads of the values held in the arrays, and reloaded after the store of a[i].

The programmer will often know that a[i] does not point to the same memory as b[i] and c[i]. The remainder of this section discusses how to look for aliasing problems, and how to tell the compiler to avoid them.

5.9.2 Diagnosing Aliasing Problems

One way to diagnose aliasing problems is to count the number of load operations in the disassembly, and compare it with the expected number of load operations. Unfortunately, this may not be an exact science, because some of the loads and stores might be required to free up or reload a register to make more efficient use of the available registers. For the code shown in Example 5.27, the source shows three loads and one store per iteration, whereas the disassembly shows six loads and one store—many more memory operations than would be expected.

An similar approach is to look for repeated memory accesses to the same address. In the code shown in Example 5.27, the load of the loop bound at 0x0060 is from memory pointed to by the loop-invariant register %g2. Similarly, the loads at 0x0050 and 0x0058 are reloading the same data as the loads at 0x0030 and 0x0038. The loads are before and after the store statement, which makes it very clear that the store statement has a potential aliasing problem with the loads.

A heuristic for identifying aliasing problems is to look for load operations hard up against store operations. Example 5.27 shows a very good example of this. Three load operations immediately follow the store at 0x0048. A better way to schedule the code would be to place these loads among the floating-point instructions at 0x003c-0x0044. This would allow the processor to start the memory operations while the floating-point operations completed. Because the compiler did not do this optimization, it indicates that either the code was compiled without optimization, or there was some kind of aliasing problem.

5.9.3 Using Restricted Pointers in C and C++ to Reduce Aliasing Issues

One way to make it easier for the compiler to optimize code containing pointers is to use *restricted* pointers. A restricted pointer is a pointer to an area of memory that no other pointers point to. There is support in the C and C++ compilers to declare a single pointer as being restricted, or to specify that pointers passed as function parameters are restricted.

In the example code shown in Example 5.27, the store to a[i] causes the compiler to have to reload b[i] and c[i]. If the pointer to a is recast as a restricted pointer, the compiler knows that a points to its own area of memory that is not shared with either b or c; hence, b and c do not need to be reloaded after the store to a. Example 5.28 shows the change to the function prototype. In this case, the number of loads per iteration is reduced to three—no variables are reloaded.

Example 5.28 Use of Restricted Specifier

```
      void test(float *restrict a, float *b, float *c)
      ...
                            .L900000111:
      /* 0x0070        12 */        add      %o3,1,%o3
      /* 0x0074         */          add      %o2,4,%o2
      /* 0x0078        11 */        ld       [%g5],%f30        ! load b[i]
      /* 0x007c        12 */        cmp      %o3,%o5
      /* 0x0080         */          add      %g5,4,%g5
      /* 0x0084        11 */        ld       [%o2-4],%f28      ! load c[i]
      /* 0x0088         */          fmuls    %f0,%f30,%f1
      /* 0x008c        12 */        add      %o0,4,%o0
      /* 0x0090        11 */        fmuls    %f28,%f2,%f3
      /* 0x0094        12 */        fmuls    %f30,%f28,%f5
      /* 0x0098        11 */        fadds    %f1,%f3,%f7
      /* 0x009c         */          ld       [%o0-4],%f0       | load a[i+1]
      /* 0x00a0         */          st       %f7,[%o0-8]       ! store a[i]
      /* 0x00a4        12 */        ble,pt   %icc,.L900000111
      /* 0x00a8         */          fadds    %f7,%f5,%f2
```

An alternative solution would be to define the b or c pointer as being restricted. In this situation, both b and c would have to be declared as restricted so that neither is reloaded.

It is also possible to use the -xrestrict compiler flag, which will specify that for the file being compiled, all pointer-type formal parameters are treated as restricted pointers.

Restricted pointers can be a very useful way to inform the compiler that memory regions do not overlap. However, if the compiler flag or the keyword is used incorrectly (i.e., the pointers do overlap), the application's behavior is undefined.

5.9.4 Using the -xalias_level Flag to Specify the Degree of Pointer Aliasing

The -xalias_level compiler flag is available in both C and C++. The flag specifies the degree of aliasing that occurs in the code between different types of pointers. The options in C and C++ are very similar, but the settings have different names.

As with the -xrestrict compiler flag, the -xalias_level flag represents an agreement between the developer and the compiler, which tells the compiler how pointers are used within the application. If the flag is used inappropriately, the resulting application will have undefined behavior.

5.9.5 -xalias_level for C

Table 5.8 summarizes the various options for the -xalias_level flag for C.

Table 5.8 -xalias_levels for C

-xalias_level	Comment
any	Any pointer can point to anything (default)
basic	Basic types do not alias each other, except char*, which can point to anything (included in -fast)
weak	Structure pointers alias by offset in bytes
layout	Structure pointers may alias by field index
strict	Structure pointers to structures with the same field types can alias
std	Structure pointers to structures with the same field names can alias
strong	Pointers do not alias with structure fields. char* is a pointer to a char.

5.9.6 -xalias_level=any in C

-xalias_level=any is the default setting, which tells the compiler that any pointer can potentially alias any other pointer. This is the simplest level of aliasing—the compiler has to treat any pointer as being "wild"—and it could point to anything. Inevitably, this means that when there are pointers, the compiler is unable to do much (if any) optimization.

As an example of this consider the disassembly shown in Example 5.29. This is based on the code shown in Example 5.27, but this time one of the vectors is defined as type integer. To perform calculations on the integer values, they are loaded into floating-point registers and then converted from integer values into single-precision floating-point values using the fitos instruction.

Once again, the compiler has to reload both the vectors and the loop boundary variable, because it cannot tell whether the store to a[i] has changed them. The code has six load instructions and one store; optimally, the code would have three load instructions and one store.

Example 5.29 Example of Possible Aliasing between `ints` and `floats`

```
void test(float *a, int *b, float *c)
...
/* 0x0030    11 */    ld      [%g5],%f0    !load b[i] (integer)
/* 0x0034    12 */    add     %g3,1,%g3
/* 0x0038    11 */    ld      [%g4],%f6    !load a[i] (float)
/* 0x003c       */    fitos   %f0,%f2
/* 0x0040       */    fmuls   %f4,%f2,%f14
/* 0x0044       */    fmuls   %f6,%f22,%f12
/* 0x0048       */    fadds   %f14,%f12,%f20
/* 0x004c       */    st      %f20,[%g1]   ! store a[i]
/* 0x0050    12 */    add     %g1,4,%g1
/* 0x0054       */    ld      [%g5],%f8    ! reload b[i] (integer)
/* 0x0058       */    add     %g5,4,%g5
/* 0x005c       */    ld      [%g4],%f10   ! reload c[i] (float)
/* 0x0060       */    add     %g4,4,%g4
/* 0x0064       */    ld      [%g2],%o3    ! reload n
/* 0x0068       */    fitos   %f8,%f16
/* 0x006c       */    cmp     %g3,%o3
/* 0x0070       */    fmuls   %f16,%f10,%f18
/* 0x0074       */    fadds   %f20,%f18,%f22
/* 0x0078       */    bl,a,pt %icc,.L900000111
/* 0x007c    11 */    ld      [%g1],%f4    ! load c[i] (float)
```

5.9.7 `-xalias_level=basic` in C

`-xalias_level=basic` is the default level for `-fast`. This tells the compiler to assume that pointers to different basic types do not alias. So, taking the example in Example 5.29, a pointer to an integer and a pointer to a float never point to the same address.

However, the pointer to a character (`char*`) is assumed to be able to point to anything. The rationale for this is that in some programs, the `char*` pointer is used to extract data from other objects on a byte-by-byte basis.

Example 5.30 shows the code generated when the source code from Example 5.29 is recompiled with the `-xalias_level=basic` compiler flag. The store is of a floating-point value; by the aliasing assertion used, it is not necessary to reload the integer values. This eliminates the need to reload n, the loop boundary value, and it eliminates the need to reload the integer array b (even though the integer array is actually loaded into a floating-point register to perform the calculation). This reduces the number of loads to four as only the array c is reloaded; this is a floating-point array and could potentially alias with the floating-point array a.

Example 5.30 Pointers to `ints` and `floats` under `-xalias_level=basic`

```
                         .L900000111:
/* 0x007c     12 */      add      %g3,1,%g3
/* 0x0080      */        add      %o2,4,%o2
/* 0x0084     11 */      ld       [%o0],%f11      ! load a[i]
/* 0x0088     12 */      cmp      %g3,%o5
/* 0x008c      */        add      %o1,4,%o1
/* 0x0090     11 */      ld       [%o2-4],%f5     ! load c[i]
/* 0x0094      */        fmuls    %f11,%f8,%f9
/* 0x0098     12 */      add      %o0,4,%o0
/* 0x009c     11 */      fmuls    %f5,%f0,%f7
/* 0x00a0      */        fadds    %f9,%f7,%f19
/* 0x00a4      */        st       %f19,[%o0-4]    ! store a[i]
/* 0x00a8     12 */      ld       [%o2-4],%f13    ! reload c[i]
/* 0x00ac      */        fmuls    %f8,%f13,%f17
/* 0x00b0     11 */      ld       [%o1-4],%f15    ! load b[i+1]
/* 0x00b4      */        fitos    %f15,%f8
/* 0x00b8     12 */      ble,pt   %icc,.L900000111
/* 0x00bc      */        fadds    %f19,%f17,%f0
```

5.9.8 -xalias_level=weak in C

Moving to `-xalias_level=weak`, the major difference is in structures. This enables the compiler to assume that structure members can only alias by offset in bytes. So, two pointers to structure members will alias if both structure members have the same type and the same offset in bytes from the base of the structure.

For the purposes of discussing the remaining `-xalias_levels`, consider the two structures shown in Example 5.31. Both are the same size and start with common fields, but one has two shorts, whereas the other has a single integer occupying the same position in the structure.

Example 5.31 Two Structures

```
struct s1 {
  int s1i1;
  float s1f1;
  short s1s1;
  short s1s2;
  int s1i2;
} *sp1;

struct s2 {
  int s2i1;
  float s2f1;
  int s2i2;
  int s2i3;
} *sp2;
```

Under `-xalias_level=weak`, the first integer fields (`s1i1` and `s2i1`), the floating-point fields (`s1f1` and `s2f1`), and the final integer fields (`s1i2` and `s2i3`) might alias because they are of the same type and all occupy the same offsets into the structures. However, the first integer field of one structure (s1i1) will not alias with the last integer field of the other structure (s2i3) because they occupy different offsets from the base of the structure. Although the two shorts (s1s1 and s1s2) occupy the same offset as the integer field in the other structure (s2i2), they do not alias because they are of different types. Figure 5.2 shows the aliasing between the two structures.

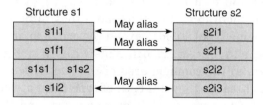

Figure 5.2 All Possible Aliasing between the Structures s1 and s2 under -xalias_level=weak

Example 5.32 shows some example code that uses the two structures and illustrates the kinds of aliasing issues that might be present. Under -xalias_level=any, all the variables in structure s2 need to be reloaded after every store because they could have been impacted by the store. Under -xalias_level=basic, the integer variables need to be reloaded after an integer store, and the floating-point variables need to be reloaded after a floating-point store.

Example 5.32 Potential Aliasing Problems Using Two Structures

```
void test( struct s1 *s1, struct s2 *s2)
{
  s1->s1i1 += s2->s2i1 + s2->s2f1 + s2->s2i2 + s2->s2i3;
  s1->s1f1 += s2->s2i1 + s2->s2f1 + s2->s2i2 + s2->s2i3;
  s1->s1s1 += s2->s2i1 + s2->s2f1 + s2->s2i2 + s2->s2i3;
  s1->s1i2 += s2->s2i1 + s2->s2f1 + s2->s2i2 + s2->s2i3;
}
```

Under -xalias_level=weak, the compiler will assume that aliasing might occur by offset and type. For the store to s1i1, this is an integer at offset zero in the structure, so it might have aliased with s2i1, and therefore the compiler will reload that variable. Similarly, the store to s1f1 might have aliased with the variable s2f1, so that needs to be reloaded. The store to s1s1 matches the variable s2i2 by offset but not by type, so s2i2 does not need to be reloaded. Finally, the store to s1i2 might alias with the variable s2i3, but given that this store is the last statement, there is no need to reload s2i3.

5.9.9 -xalias_level=layout in C

For -xalias_level=layout, the idea of a *common area* of the structure is introduced. The common area comprises the fields at the start of the structure that are the same in both structures. For the structures in Example 5.31, the common fields are the initial integer and float fields. For -xalias_level=layout, fields at the same offset in the common area may alias (note that to be in the common area, they must share the same type). Fields beyond the common area do not alias.

At -xalias_level=layout, s1i1 can alias with s2i1 because they both are the same type and are in the common area of the two structures. Similarly, s1f1 and s1f2 might alias because they are both of type float, at the same index of the common area. However, because s1s1 is of type short, and the variable s2i2 at the corresponding offset in the other structure is of type integer, this indicates the end of the common area, so they do not alias. Similarly, although s1i2 and s2i3 share both the same offset and the same type, they are no longer in the common area, so they do not alias. This is shown in Figure 5.3.

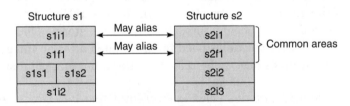

Figure 5.3 Aliasing under -xalias_level=layout

5.9.10 -xalias_level=strict in C

Under -xalias_level=strict, pointers to structures containing different field types do not alias. The structures shown in Example 5.31 would be considered as not aliasing because they do not contain an identical set of types in an identical order.

5.9.11 -xalias_level=std in C

The difference between -xalias_level=std and -xalias_level=strict is that for -xalias_level=std the names of the fields are also considered. So, even if both structures have identical fields in them, pointers to them will be considered as not aliasing if the names of the fields are different. This is the degree of aliasing assumed possible in programs that adhere to the C99 standard.

5.9.12 -xalias_level=strong in C

Two additional changes come in at -xalias_level=strong. First, pointers are assumed not to point to fields in structures. Second, it is the only level where char* is treated as a pointer that can only point to characters and not to other types.

5.9.13 -xalias_level in C++

Table 5.9 shows the available settings for -xalias_level in C++.

Table 5.9 -xalias_levels for C++

-xalias_level	Comment
any	Any pointer can point to anything
simple	Basic types do not alias each other, except char*, which can point to anything
compatible	Structure pointers may alias by field index

5.9.14 -xalias_level=simple in C++

For C++, the -xalias_level=simple level corresponds to -xalias_level=basic in C, that is, the pointers to different basic types do not alias.

5.9.15 -xalias_level=compatible in C++

For C++, the -xalias_level=compatible flag is equivalent to -xalias_level=layout in C. So, two pointers could alias if they point to the common section of two structures.

5.10 Other C- and C++-Specific Compiler Optimizations

5.10.1 Enabling the Recognition of Standard Library Routines (-xbuiltin)

-xbuiltin allows the compiler to recognize standard library functions and either replace them with faster inline versions or know whether the function could modify

global data. The exact functions that the compiler is able to recognize and replace
evolves with the compiler version. Example 5.33 shows an example.

Example 5.33 Example of Code That Can Be Optimized with `-xbuiltin`

```
#include <stdlib.h>

extern int n;

int test(int a)
{
  int c = a*n;
  int d = abs(a);
  return c + d *n;
}
```

In Example 5.33, the program uses a global variable n before and after a function call to `abs`. Because n is global, a call to another function might alter its
value—in particular, the function `abs` might cause n to be modified. Hence, the
compiler needs to reload n after the function call, as shown in Example 5.34.

Example 5.34 Code Compiled without `-xbuiltin`

```
$ cc -xO3 -S ex5.33.c
$ more ex5.33.s
...
/* 0x0008       9 */     sethi   %hi(n),%i4
/* 0x000c       7 */     ld      [%i5+%lo(n)],%i5 ! load n
/* 0x0010        */      smul    %i0,%i5,%i2
/* 0x0014       8 */     call    abs
/* 0x0018       6 */     or      %g0,%i0,%o0
/* 0x001c       9 */     ld      [%i4+%lo(n)],%i3 ! load n
/* 0x0020        */      smul    %o0,%i3,%i1
```

When compiled with `-xbuiltin`, the compiler recognizes `abs` as a library function and knows that the function cannot change the value of the variable n. Hence,
the compiler does not need to reload the variable after the call. This is shown in
Example 5.35.

Example 5.35 Code Compiled with `-xbuiltin`

```
$ cc -xO3 -S -xbuiltin ex5.33.c
$ more ex5.33.s
...
/* 0x0004        */      sethi   %hi(n),%i5
/* 0x0008        */      ld      [%i5+%lo(n)],%i5 ! load n
/* 0x000c       7 */     smul    %i0,%i5,%i4
/* 0x0010       8 */     call    abs
/* 0x0014       6 */     or      %g0,%i0,%o0
/* 0x0018       9 */     smul    %o0,%i5,%i3
```

There are a few things to consider when using `-xbuiltin`.

- If the application were to include its own function `abs`, the definition of this function `abs` would override the definition in the header files, and the compiler would reload the variable `n`.

- If the compiler uses an inline template to replace a library function call, it is no longer possible to use a different library at runtime to handle that call.

- This works only if the appropriate header files are included. In many cases, the `-xbuiltin` flag only provides the compiler with additional information about the behavior of functions (such as whether they might modify global variables). This is achieved by having pragmas in the header files which contain this information.

- The `-xlibmil` compiler flag, which is discussed in Section 6.2.19 of Chapter 6, may provide inline templates for some of the routines `-xbuiltin` recognizes.

5.11 Fortran-Specific Compiler Optimizations

5.11.1 Aligning Variables for Optimal Layout (`-xpad`)

There are two settings for `-xpad`: `local` and `common`. These affect the padding used for the local variables and for the common block in Fortran. Fortran specifies very tightly how the variables should be lined up in the common blocks, and to save space, it does not pad local variables; but this may not be optimal when performance is considered. For example, it may be necessary to load a floating-point double with two floating-point single loads, because the double is not correctly aligned. Telling the compiler to insert padding allows it to move the variables around to maximize performance. You can also use the flag to improve data layout in memory and avoid data thrashing in the caches.

Note that if there are multiple files, it is necessary to use the same `-xpad` flag setting to compile all the files. Otherwise, it is possible that one file may anticipate a different layout than another file, and the program will either crash or give incorrect results.

5.11.2 Placing Local Variables on the Stack (`-xstackvar`)

The `-xstackvar` flag places local variables on the stack. One advantage of doing this is that it makes writing recursive code significantly easier, because new copies of the variables get allocated for every level of recursion. Use of this flag is encouraged when writing parallel code, because each thread will end up with its own copy of local variables.

A downside of using -xstackvar is that it will increase the amount of stack space that the program requires, and it is possible that the stack may overflow and cause a segmentation fault. The default stack size is 8MB for the main stack. You can increase this using the `limit stacksize` command as shown in Example 5.36.

Example 5.36 Setting the Stack Size

```
$ limit stacksize 65536
```

5.12 Compiler Pragmas

5.12.1 Introduction

Pragmas are compiler directives that are inserted into source code. They make assertions about the code; they tell the compiler additional information that it can use to improve the optimization of the code.

When a pragma refers to variables, the pragma must occur before the variables are declared. However, when a pragma refers to functions, it must occur after the prototypes of the functions have been declared. When the pragma refers to a loop, the next loop the compiler encounters has the assertion.

You insert pragmas into code using #pragma in C/C++ and c$pragma in Fortran.

5.12.2 Specifying Alignment of Variables

`#pragma align <1,2,4,8,16,32,64,128> (<list of variable names>)` specifies that the variables be aligned on a particular alignment. The code in Example 5.37 shows an example of the use of the pragma.

Example 5.37 Example of the `align` Pragma

```
#include <stdio.h>
#pragma align 128 (a,b)
int a,b;
void main()
{
    printf("&a=%p &b=%p\n",&a,&b);
}
```

Example 5.38 shows the results of compiling and running code with the pragma. Variables a and b align on 128-byte boundaries (the addresses are printed as hex values).

Example 5.38 Results of Running Code with Aligned Variables

```
$ cc -O ex5.37.c
$ a.out
&a=20880 &b=20900
```

5.12.3 Specifying a Function's Access to Global Data

`#pragma does_not_read_global_data` (<list of function names>) and `#pragma does_not_write_global_data` (<list of function names>) assert that a given function does not read or write (depending on the pragma) global data. This means the compiler can assume at the calling site that registers do not need to be saved before the call or do not need to be loaded after the call, or that the saving of registers can be deferred. Example 5.39 shows an example of these pragmas.

Example 5.39 Example of Global Data Pragmas

```
#include <stdio.h>
int a;
void test1(){}
void test2(){}
void test3(){}
#pragma does_not_read_global_data(test3)
#pragma does_not_write_global_data(test2,test3)
void main()
{
  int i;
  a=1;
  test1();
  a+=1;
  test2();
  for(i=0; i<10; i++)
  {
    a+=1;
    test3();
  }
  printf("a=%d\n",a);
}
```

Example 5.40 shows the results of compiling the code shown in Example 5.39.

Before the call to test1, the a variable is stored in case it is read by the test1 routine. After the call to test1, the a variable is reloaded in case the test1 routine has changed the a variable.

Example 5.40 Example of Optimizations around Function Calls with Pragmas

```
$ cc -xO3 -S ex5.39.c
...
/* 0x0004         0 */    sethi   %hi(a),%i5
/* 0x0008        11 */    or      %g0,1,%i4
/* 0x000c        12 */    call    test1
/* 0x0010        11 */    st      %i4,[%i5+%lo(a)] ! store a before call
/* 0x0014         0 */    add     %i5,%lo(a),%i2
/* 0x0018        15 */    or      %g0,0,%i0
/* 0x001c        13 */    ld      [%i2],%i5        ! load a after call
/* 0x0020           */    add     %i5,1,%i1
/* 0x0024        14 */    call    test2
/* 0x0028        13 */    st      %i1,[%i2]        ! store a before call
/* 0x002c        17 */    add     %i1,1,%i1
                        .L900000409:
/* 0x0030        18 */    call    test3
/* 0x0034           */    add     %i0,1,%i0
/* 0x0038           */    cmp     %i0,10
/* 0x003c           */    bl,a    .L900000409
/* 0x0040        17 */    add     %i1,1,%i1
```

The pragma informs the compiler that the test2 routine does not write global data, but it may read global data, so the compiler has to store a before test2 is called. However, it knows its value is not changed by the routine, so the variable does not have to be reloaded afterward. For test3, the compiler knows the routine neither reads nor writes the a variable, so the a variable does not need to be stored before the call to test3, or reloaded afterward.

5.12.4 Specifying That a Function Has No Side Effects

#pragma no_side_effect (<list of function names>) tells the compiler that the function has no side effects—its return value depends only on the input parameters, and it does not access or modify any other data. Example 5.41 shows an example of this pragma.

The effects of this pragma are interesting. The compiler is now able to eliminate the calls to test2 and test3, because the pragma asserts that the routines only access the parameters passed in and do not cause changes to global state. For test2, there is no return value, so the call can be eliminated. For test3, a parameter is passed in, but there is no return value, so the call can be eliminated. For test4, however, the call has to remain because there is a return value. The a variable is stored before the call to test4, but it does not need to be reloaded afterward because the routine cannot have changed it. You can see this in the assembly code in Example 5.42, where the variable a is stored before the call to test1, reloaded, stored again before the call to test4 (having eliminated test2 and test3), and not reloaded after the call to test4.

Example 5.41 Example of the `no_side_effect` Pragma

```
#include <stdio.h>
int a;
void test1(){}
void test2(){}
void test3(int a){}
int test4(int a){return a;}
#pragma no_side_effect(test2,test3,test4)
void main()
{
  int i;
  a=1;
  test1();
  a+=1;
  test2();
  a+=1;
  test3(a);
  a+=1;
  a+=test4(a);
  printf("a=%d\n",a);
}
```

Example 5.42 Assembly Code of Calls with the `no_side_effect` Pragma Asserted

```
/* 0x0004     11 */    sethi   %hi(a),%i5
/* 0x0008        */    or      %g0,1,%i4
/* 0x000c     12 */    call    test1
/* 0x0010     11 */    st      %i4,[%i5+%lo(a)] ! store a
/* 0x0014     13 */    sethi   %hi(a),%i3
/* 0x0018     18 */    sethi   %hi(a),%i0
/* 0x001c     13 */    ld      [%i3+%lo(a)],%i5 ! load a
/* 0x0020     19 */    sethi   %hi(.L121),%17
/* 0x0024     17 */    add     %i5,3,%i2
/* 0x0028        */    st      %i2,[%i3+%lo(a)] ! store a
/* 0x002c     18 */    call    test4
/* 0x0030        */    or      %g0,%i2,%o0
/* 0x0034        */    add     %i2,%o0,%i1
/* 0x0038        */    st      %i1,[%i0+%lo(a)] ! store a
/* 0x003c     19 */    add     %17,%lo(.L121),%i0
```

5.12.5 Specifying That a Function Is Infrequently Called

`#pragma rarely_called (<list of function names>)` tells the compiler that the functions are rarely called, and provides what amounts to static profile-feedback-type information. If a function is rarely called, the compiler will (probably) not inline it, and will assume that conditional calls to it are generally untaken. Example 5.43 shows an example of this pragma. The code shown has two similar statements, but the location of the call to the rarely called location is changed.

Example 5.44 shows the output from the compiler for this code. You can see that the compiler has arranged the code so that the call to the rarely executed routine

Example 5.43 Example of `rarely_called` Pragma

```
void infrequent();
#pragma rarely_called (infrequent)
int test(int i, int* x, int* y)
{
  if (x[i]>0) {infrequent();} else {x[i]++;}
  if (y[i]>0) {y[i]++;} else {infrequent();}
}
```

is not the fall-through. To achieve this it had to invert the condition test on the second branch from a "greater than" comparison to a "less than or equal to" comparison. The calls to the `infrequent` function are not shown in this code snippet.

Example 5.44 Disassembly Code Resulting from the `rarely_called` Pragma

```
/* 0x0004      5 */      sll      %i0,2,%i3
/* 0x0008        */      ld       [%i1+%i3],%i0 ! load x[i]
/* 0x000c        */      cmp      %i0,0
/* 0x0010        */      bg,pn    %icc,.L77000020 ! branch on x[i]
/* 0x0014        */      add      %i0,1,%i6
                  .L77000021:
/* 0x0018      5 */      st       %i6,[%i1+%i3]
/* 0x001c      6 */      ld       [%i2+%i3],%i1 ! load y[i]
                  .L900000109:
/* 0x0020      6 */      cmp      %i1,0
/* 0x0024        */      ble,pn   %icc,.L77000024 ! branch on y[i]
/* 0x0028        */      add      %i1,1,%i4
                  .L77000023:
/* 0x002c      6 */      st       %i4,[%i2+%i3]
/* 0x0030        */      ret      ! Result =
/* 0x0034        */      restore  %g0,%g0,%g0
```

5.12.6 Specifying a Safe Degree of Pipelining for a Particular Loop

Pipelining is where the compiler overlaps operations from different iterations of the loop to improve performance. Figure 5.4 shows an illustration of this. In the figure, both loops complete four iterations of the original loop in a single iteration of the modified loop. When the loop is unrolled, these four iterations are performed sequentially. This optimization improves performance because it reduces the instruction count of the loop. When the compiler is also able to pipeline the loop, it interleaves instructions from the different iterations. This allows it to better schedule the instructions such that fewer cycles are needed for the four iterations.

`#pragma pipeloop (N)` tells the compiler that the following loop has a dependency at N iterations, so up to N iterations of the loop can be pipelined. The most useful form of this pragma is `pipeloop(0)`, which tells the compiler that there is no cross-iteration data dependancy, so the compiler is free to pipeline the loop as it sees fit.

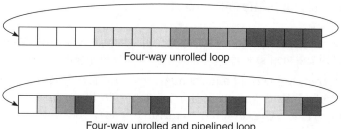

Figure 5.4 Unrolling and Pipelining

In the example shown in Example 5.45 the pragma is used to assert that there is no dependence between iterations of the loop. This allows the compiler to assume that stores to the a array will not impact values in either the b or the indexa array. Under this pragma, the compiler is able to both unroll and pipeline the loop.

Example 5.45 Example of Using the `pipeloop` Pragma

```
double calc(int * indexa, double *a, double *b)
{
  #pragma pipeloop(0)
  for (int i=0; i<10000; i++)
  {
     a[indexa[i]]+=a[indexa[i]]*b[i];
  }
}
```

5.12.7 Specifying That a Loop Has No Memory Dependencies within a Single Iteration

`#pragma nomemorydepend` tells the compiler that there are no memory dependancies (i.e., aliasing) within a single interation of the following loop. This allows the compiler to move the instructions within a single loop iteration to improve the schedule, but it will not allow the compiler to mix instructions from different loop iterations.

5.12.8 Specifying the Degree of Loop Unrolling

`#pragma unroll (N)` suggests to the compiler that the loop following the pragma should be unrolled N times. This can be useful in situations where the developer has some information about the loop that the compiler is unable to derive.

This might be useful in the following situations:

- When the compiler will aggressively unroll a loop, but the developer knows the trip count of the loop is very low, so the unrolled loop will never get executed
- When the compiler could be more aggressive in unrolling a loop, or the exact trip count of a loop is known to the developer; in these cases, the developer may want to cause the compiler to unroll a loop more times

Example 5.46 shows an example of the use of this pragma.

Example 5.46 unroll Pragma

```
#pragma unroll(2)
for (int i=0; i<N; i++)
{
  ....
}
```

5.13 Using Pragmas in C for Finer Aliasing Control

In C, it is possible to insert pragmas into the source code to achieve a finer degree of control over the use of aliasing information by the compiler. For the compiler to take advantage of these pragmas it must be using at least -xalias_level=basic.

Example 5.47 shows code that has the potential for aliasing problems. In this code, the a array might alias with the b or c array, or might even alias with the externally declared variable n. As such, in the absence of any aliasing information, the compiler has to assume that the b and c arrays, and the n variable, have to be reloaded after every store to the a array.

Example 5.47 Code with Potential Aliasing

```
extern int n;

void test(float *a, float *b, float *c)
{
  int i;
  float carry=0.0f;
  for (i=1; i<n; i++)
  {
    a[i]=a[i]*b[i]+c[i]*carry;
    carry = a[i]+b[i]*c[i];
  }
}
```

Example 5.48 shows part of the assembly code generated by the compiler from the source code in Example 5.47. Recent compilers may produce multiple versions of this loop, each version making different aliasing assumptions. This version assumes that all the pointers may alias.

Example 5.48 Disassembly Code in the Absence of Aliasing Information

```
                   .L900000111:
/* 0x0030    10 */    ld      [%g5],%f0     ! load b[]
/* 0x0034    11 */    add     %g3,1,%g3
/* 0x0038    10 */    ld      [%g4],%f4     ! load c[]
/* 0x003c     */    fmuls   %f2,%f0,%f12
/* 0x0040     */    fmuls   %f4,%f18,%f6
/* 0x0044     */    fadds   %f12,%f6,%f16
/* 0x0048     */    st      %f16,[%g1]    ! store a[]
/* 0x004c    11 */    add     %g1,4,%g1
/* 0x0050     */    ld      [%g5],%f10    ! reload b[]
/* 0x0054     */    add     %g5,4,%g5
/* 0x0058     */    ld      [%g4],%f8     ! reload c[]
/* 0x005c     */    add     %g4,4,%g4
/* 0x0060     */    ld      [%g2],%o3     ! reload n
/* 0x0064     */    fmuls   %f10,%f8,%f14
/* 0x0068     */    cmp     %g3,%o3
/* 0x006c     */    fadds   %f16,%f14,%f18
/* 0x0070     */    bl,a,pt %icc,.L900000111
/* 0x0074    10 */    ld      [%g1],%f2     ! load a[]
```

Recompiling the code in Example 5.47 with the -xalias_level=basic compiler flag enables the compiler to eliminate the reload of the n variable, because n is an integer and the store is of a floating-point value.

Alternatively, the -xrestrict compiler flag would tell the compiler that each pointer passed into the function pointed to its own area of memory, so the reloads of the b and c arrays and the n variable would be unnecessary. Similarly, declaring pointer a as being restricted would tell the compiler that it pointed to its own area of memory and would avoid the reload of the other variables.

5.13.1 Asserting the Degree of Aliasing between Variables

#pragma alias_level <level> (<list of types>) and #pragma alias_level <level> (<list of variables>) tell the compiler that for the current file, the variables or types listed behave as specified by the alias level; the same levels are used as those defined in Section 5.9.

This is useful for adjusting the alias level for a single file where the variables are either well behaved or badly behaved. For example, if two pointers are known to (potentially) alias, they can be pragma'd as having an alias level of any.

You can inform the compiler that the int type can be aliased by any pointer by modifying the code as shown in Example 5.49.

Example 5.49 Use of the `alias_level` Pragma for the `int` Type

```
#pragma alias_level any (int)
extern int n;

void test(float *a, float *b, float *c)
{
  int i;
  float carry=0.0f;
  for (i=1; i<n; i++)
  {
    a[i]=a[i]*b[i]+c[i]*carry;
    carry = a[i]+b[i]*c[i];
  }
}
```

It is also possible to specify the alias level for a single variable for the scope of the file. The variable has to have file-level scope. Example 5.50 shows an example of this; in this example, the a variable has file-level scope, and the pragma tells the compiler that it may alias with anything. As a consequence, the external n variable will need to be reloaded after every store to a.

Example 5.50 Use of the `alias_level` Pragma to Specify Aliasing for a Single Variable

```
extern float *a;
#pragma alias_level any (a)

extern int n;

void test(float *b, float *c)
{
  int i;
  float carry=0.0f;
  for (i=1; i<n; i++)
  {
    a[i]=a[i]*b[i]+c[i]*carry;
    carry = a[i]+b[i]*c[i];
  }
}
```

5.13.2 Asserting That Variables Do Alias

#pragma alias (<list of types>) and #pragma alias (<list of pointers>) tell the compiler that either the types or the variables will alias each other within the current scope. Example 5.51 shows an example of the use of this pragma. In this case, the compiler is told that integer and floating-point variables do alias. Under this pragma, the compiler will need to reload n after every store to a[].

Example 5.51 Use of the `alias` Pragma

```
extern int n;

void test(float *a, float *b, float *c)
{
  int i;
  float carry=0.0f;
#pragma alias (int,float)
  for (i=1; i<n; i++)
  {
    a[i]=a[i]*b[i]+c[i]*carry;
    carry = a[i]+b[i]*c[i];
  }
}
```

If there are multiple pointers of different types, you can use the `alias` pragma to tell the compiler that the different pointer types do alias (even when the `-xalias_level=basic` flag is used). Example 5.52 shows an example of this. In this case, the `c` pointer is of type integer, and the alias pragma is used to specify that this particular pointer will `alias` with the pointer a. This means that stores to a will cause the compiler to have to reload c, which would not have been the case normally under `-xalias_level=basic`.

Example 5.52 Example of the `alias` Pragma Used for Pointers

```
extern int n;

void test(float *a, float *b, int *c)
{
  int i;
  float carry=0.0f;
#pragma alias (a,c)
  for (i=1; i<n; i++)
  {
    a[i]=a[i]*b[i]+c[i]*carry;
    carry = a[i]+b[i]*c[i];
  }
}
```

5.13.3 Asserting Aliasing with Nonpointer Variables

`#pragma may_point_to (<pointer>,<list of variables>)` informs the compiler that a pointer may point to any one of a list of variables. Example 5.53 shows an example of this. This pragma tells the compiler that the a pointer may point to (and therefore change) the n variable. As a result, each store to a[] causes the compiler to reload n.

Example 5.53 Example of the `may_point_to` Pragma

```
extern int n;

void test(float *a, float *b, float *c)
{
  int i;
  float carry=0.0f;
#pragma may_point_to(a,n)
  for (i=1; i<n; i++)
  {
    a[i]=a[i]*b[i]+c[i]*carry;
    carry = a[i]+b[i]*c[i];
  }
}
```

5.13.4 Asserting That Variables Do Not Alias

`#pragma noalias (<list of types>)` and `#pragma noalias (<list of variables>)` tell the compiler that the variables or types do not alias each other within the current scope. The code in Example 5.54 shows the use of this pragma. With this pragma inserted into the code, the compiler is able to assume that the arrays a, b, and c do not alias; consequently, b and c do not need to be reloaded after every store to a.

Example 5.54 Example of the `noalias` Pragma

```
extern int n;

void test(float *a, float *b, float *c)
{
  int i;
  float carry=0.0f;
#pragma noalias (a,b,c)
  for (i=1; i<n; i++)
  {
    a[i]=a[i]*b[i]+c[i]*carry;
    carry = a[i]+b[i]*c[i];
  }
}
```

5.13.5 Asserting No Aliasing with Nonpointer Variables

`#pragma may_not_point_to (<pointer>,<list of variables>)` tell the compiler that the pointer does not point to any of the listed variables within the current scope. Example 5.55 shows an example of this pragma. In this case, `carry` is defined as an external variable of type float, which means that under `-xalias_level=basic`, stores to the a array might alias to to the `carry` variable. Hence, the `carry` variable will have to be reloaded after every store to the a array. Under the pragma, the compiler knows that stores to a do not impact the variable `carry`, so it is not necessary to reload `carry` after every store to the a array. There is an interesting twist here, in that the `carry` variable may be aliased by either array b or array c, which means that the assignment to `carry` must result in a store to memory, in case it changes a value in the b or c array.

Example 5.55 Example of the `may_not_point_to` Pragma

```
extern int n;
extern float carry;

void test(float *a, float *b, float *c)
{
  int i;
  carry=0.0;
#pragma may_not_point_to(a,carry)
  for (i=1; i<n; i++)
  {
    a[i]=a[i]*b[i]+c[i]*carry;
    carry = a[i]+b[i]*c[i];
  }
}
```

5.14 Compatibility with GCC

The Sun Studio compiler handles an expanding subset of the GCC extensions. However, it is always possible that the particular idiom used in an application is not supported. For compilations on SPARC-based systems, it is possible to use the GCC for SPARC Systems compiler, which you can freely download from http://cool-tools.sunsource.net/gcc/. This compiler uses the GCC frontend to parse the source files, together with the code generator from the Sun Studio compiler, to actually produce the object files.

The potential benefits of using the GCC for SPARC Systems compiler are as follows:

- Compatibility with GCC
- Improved code generation from the Sun Studio code generator
- Support for additional optimizations, such as crossfile optimizations

Floating-Point Optimization

6.1 Chapter Objectives

It would seem intuitive that computers are machines for handling numbers, so therefore, they should excel at handling floating-point arithmetic. Floating-point optimization is an interesting topic because it actually turns out to be more complex than you might expect. Floating-point mathematics is covered by the IEEE-754 standard, and optimization of floating-point arithmetic relaxes the constraint on the compiler to conform to this standard (the Sun compiler adheres to the standard unless flags are used that relax this constraint).

By the end of this chapter, the reader will understand the optimizations that can be applied to floating-point computation and the impact these optimizations will have on the accuracy of the generated results.

6.2 Floating-Point Optimization Flags

6.2.1 Mathematical Optimizations in `-fast`

Table 6.1 shows the floating-point optimization flags that are included in the `-fast` compiler flag for the C, C++, and Fortran languages. These flags represent optimizations that have been found to be generally useful for floating-point applications. In this section, I will describe the flags and present the trade-offs that you need to consider when using the flags.

Table 6.1 Floating-Point Optimization Flags Included in `-fast`

Flag	Comment	C	C++	Fortran
`-fns`	Floating-point nonstandard mode	Y	Y	Y
`-fsimple=2`	Aggressive floating-point optimizations	Y	Y	Y
`-ftrap=%none`	Don't trap on IEEE exceptions	Y	Y	
`-ftrap=common`	Trap only on "common" IEEE exceptions			Y
`-xlibmil`	Use inline templates for math functions	Y	Y	Y
`-fsingle`	Float expressions are evaluated in single-precision	Y		
`-xlibmopt`	Use optimized math library	Y	Y	Y
`-xvector`	Generate calls to vector math library			Y
`-fnostore`	Do not convert temporary values into shorter formats (x86 only)	Y	Y	Y

The other option enabled in `-fast` for C is `-D__MATHERR_ERRNO_DONTCARE`, which tells the compiler to assume that the math functions defined in `math.h` have no side effects (such as setting the error reporting variable `errno`). I discuss this in more detail in Section 6.2.15.

6.2.2 IEEE-754 and Floating Point

The IEEE-754 standard determines how floating-point arithmetic should function on a "standard" computer, which is the default mode for the compiler. Adherence to the standard means calculations have to be performed in a particular order, and the compiler cannot take shortcuts. This may mean that the calculations take longer. Using the `-fns` and `-fsimple` compiler flags allows the compiler to produce code that might obtain results faster; however, using the flags means the resulting code no longer adheres to the standard.

Even using IEEE-754 mathematics does not guarantee "correct" results. The intention of the standard is to make code portable so that you can run the code on different platforms, and expect the same support and conventions. It does not guarantee that the results will be identical on the two platforms.

The IEEE-754 standard describes two commonly occurring storage formats for numbers: single- and double-precision. These take four and eight bytes, respectively. It is important to realize that precision does not mean accuracy; accuracy is whether a number is correct, whereas precision is how many decimal places are specified in the number. It is worth observing that using double precision can, in many cases, improve accuracy. Single precision holds about 6–9 significant figures, and double precision holds about 15–17.

When floating-point numbers are stored, they are stored as the nearest number that can be represented in binary format. So, some numbers (such as 1/3) cannot be exactly represented in this format. As such, by its very nature, floating-point arithmetic on a computer has some degree of inaccuracy, and in this section, I will provide examples of how this manifests itself.

Given that storage of floating-point numbers is an approximation, there will always be some error for any application. One technique that improves this situation is the use of interval arithmetic. Briefly, intervals are a way for the computer to calculate the lower and upper bounds for a value. When a calculation is performed on an interval, the output is also an interval. If the calculation is well behaved, the output will have an upper and lower bound that are in close agreement. If the algorithm is less well behaved, the difference between the upper and lower bounds could be substantial. Although the Sun Studio compilers do support interval arithmetic, further discussion of the topic is beyond the scope of this book.

6.2.3 Vectorizing Floating-Point Computation (`-xvector`)

The `-xvector` flag asks the compiler to recognize situations in which multiple calls to a mathematical function (e.g., `log`, `sin`, `cos`, etc.) can be replaced with a single call to a function that works on a vector of values.

Because the calculation of the values of these functions involves many steps, and all the steps have to be completed serially, it turns out that in some cases doing several calculations at once actually takes about the same time as doing one. Consequently, it is possible to see a speed increase just using this flag.

Example 6.1 shows a code snippet that could be vectorized; one array is produced by calculating the sine of every element in another array. If this code is compiled with both the `-xvector` and `-xbuiltin` flags, the call to `sin` will be replaced by a call to the vector `sin` routine, contained in the vector math library. This is demonstrated in Example 6.2.

Example 6.1 Example of Vectorizable Code

```
#include <math.h>
extern double x[100],y[100];
void calc()
{
  int i;
  for (i=0; i<100; i++)
    x[i]=sin(y[i]);
}
```

Example 6.2 Enabling Compiler to Insert Calls to Vector Library

```
$ cc -xO3 -S ex6.1.c
$ grep sin ex6.1.s
/* 0x001c          7 */         call    sin
$ cc -xO3 -xbuiltin -xvector -S ex6.1.c
$ grep sin ex6.1.s
/* 0x0020          */           call    __vsin_
```

Example 6.3 shows an example of code that calls the vector library directly. You can find further details about the vector library under `man libmvec`, and details of a similar library for complex vector operations under `man clibmvec`.

Example 6.3 Calling the Vector Library Directly

```
#include <math.h>
extern double x[100],y[100];
void vsin_(int *n, double *x, int *stridex, double  *y,  int *stridey);

void calc()
{
  int i;
  int stride=1;
  int length=100;
  vsin_(&length,x,&stride,y,&stride);
}
```

There are a few things to observe about calling `libmvec`.

- No header files for the vector math library are included with the compiler, so it is necessary to extract the required headers from the man pages.
- To call the vector routine, it is also necessary to link in the vector library. You van do this by including -xvector on the compile line.
- The vectors passed into the library must not alias or overlap.

6.2.4 Vectorizing Computation Using SIMD Instructions (-xvector=simd) (x64 Only)

On x64 platforms, the -xvector flag also has support for recognizing opportunities to use Single Instruction, Multiple Data (SIMD) instructions. These instructions simultaneously perform the same operation on multiple items of data, reducing the total number of instructions needed and increasing performance. To do this the compiler needs the -xvector=simd flag and the appropriate architecture setting of -xarch=sse2.

Example 6.4 shows an example of this optimization. In the example, the `mulps` instruction is used to multiply four single-precision pairs of numbers; the surrounding move instructions are responsible for loading the SSE2 registers with the data, and then storing the result back to memory.

Example 6.4 Generating SIMD Instructions

```
% more ex6.4.c
void calc (float * restrict a, float * restrict b, int count)
{
  for (int i=0; i<count; i++) {a[i]=a[i]*b[i];}
}
$ cc -fast -xarch=sse2 -xvector=simd -S ex6.4.c
$ more ex6.4.s
...
.LU16.124:
        movlps      (%edx),%xmm0                      ;/ line : 3
        movhps      8(%edx),%xmm0                     ;/ line : 3
        movlps      (%ecx),%xmm1                      ;/ line : 3
        movhps      8(%ecx),%xmm1                     ;/ line : 3
        mulps       %xmm1,%xmm0                       ;/ line : 3
        movlps      %xmm0,(%edx)                      ;/ line : 3
        movhps      %xmm0,8(%edx)                     ;/ line : 3
        addl        $16,%edx                          ;/ line : 3
        addl        $16,%ecx                          ;/ line : 3
        addl        $4,%eax                           ;/ line : 3
        cmpl        %edi,%eax                         ;/ line : 3
        jle         .LU16.124                         ;/ line : 3
....
```

6.2.5 Subnormal Numbers

Subnormal numbers are floating-point numbers that are very close to zero. The idea of supporting them is that they form a gradual underflow between the smallest floating-point number that can be represented in the "normal" way, and zero.

Floating-point numbers are represented as $x*2^y$, where x is called the mantissa and y is called the exponent. Using this notation, it is possible to represent some values in multiple ways. For example, consider representing a half in base 10. A half can be represented as $0.5*10^0$ or as $5.0*10^{-1}$. A way to normalize this is to say that all numbers should have a single nonzero digit before the decimal point. This would make the second representation of a half the appropriate one in decimal. In binary, this translates to always storing numbers with the first bit set to 1.

A floating-point number has a certain number of bits to represent the mantissa and a certain number of bits to represent the exponent. If the first bit of the mantissa is always set to be one, the only way to make a number smaller is to make the exponent more negative. Subnormal numbers fill the range between the value zero, and the smallest number that can be represented by the largest negative exponent and a mantissa with a leading one. For subnormal numbers, rather than representing the number using a leading one, the mantissa has a leading zero. Subnormal numbers have a reduced precision (because fewer bits are available to hold the mantissa), so they are trading precision for smoothing the transition between small nonzero numbers and zero.

Calculations on subnormal numbers usually have a longer latency than operations on normal numbers. The UltraSPARC family of processors handle subnormal numbers by trapping to software to complete the calculation. The Opteron processors handle operations on subnormal numbers using microcoded instructions; these take significantly longer to execute, but less time than taking a trap. If there are significant numbers of calculations on subnormal numbers, the processor might spend a considerable amount of time handling them. If a program encounters significant numbers of subnormal numbers, it indicates that it is performing many reduced-accuracy calculations on numbers close to zero. This indicates that the program is performing calculations at the limit of the range of numbers that can be represented in floating-point registers, and consequently the output from the program may be inaccurate.

Example 6.5 shows some code that generates subnormal numbers. The program takes a floating-point number and keeps dividing by two until it becomes zero. The value starts at 1.0, in the range of the "normal" floating-point numbers, and then goes into the subnormal numbers.

Example 6.5 Example of Code That Generates Subnormal Numbers

```
#include <stdio.h>
#include <sys/time.h>

void main ()
{
  double f=(double)1.0;
  hrtime_t start,end;
  while (f>0)
  {
    start = gethrtime();
    f=f * (double)0.5;
    end = gethrtime();
    printf("f=%e time=%lld\n",f,end-start);
  }
}
```

Example 6.6 shows this code being run (the call to gethrtime seems to be accurate only to within 200ns on this system). The critical things to note are that initially each calculation is taking <200ns, but at the end each calculation is taking about 6,000ns. Also notice that the program keeps running until the f variable is about $4*10^{-324}$, at which point the value becomes zero when divided by two.

Example 6.6 Timing of Subnormal Numbers

```
$ cc -xO3 ex6.5.c
$ a.out
...
f=5.000000e-01 time=600
f=2.500000e-01 time=200
f=1.250000e-01 time=200
f=6.250000e-02 time=200
f=3.125000e-02 time=0
f=1.562500e-02 time=200
...
f=1.976263e-323 time=6400
f=9.881313e-324 time=6200
f=4.940656e-324 time=6200
f=0.000000e+00 time=7400
```

6.2.6 Flushing Subnormal Numbers to Zero (-fns)

The -fns flag enables floating-point nonstandard mode. In this mode, subnormal numbers may be flushed to zero. Doing this flush to zero will mean that the computation in the program no longer meets the IEEE-754 standard, but for some codes it may result in a speed increase and for many codes there may be no difference in the output. Example 6.7 shows the same code as in Example 6.5, but this time compiled with the -fns flag.

Example 6.7 Tail of Output of Program Compiled with -fns

```
$ cc -xO3 -fns ex6.5.c
$ a.out
...
f=1.780059e-307 time=200
f=8.900295e-308 time=0
f=4.450148e-308 time=200
f=2.225074e-308 time=200
f=0.000000e+00 time=0
```

Example 6.7 shows that the performance of the program remains <200ns for all iterations, but that the value at the final iteration is at about $2*10^{-308}$ rather than $4*10^{-324}$.

The -fns flag causes the compiler to include code that changes the behavior of the processor so that it may flush subnormal numbers to zero. This means the flag is effective only when compiling the main program.

6.2.7 Handling Values That Are Not-a-Number

Under IEEE-754, a value for Not-a-Number (NaN) is defined. Calculations that would normally produce errors (e.g., zero divided by zero) can produce the result

NaN (because the answer is not representable as a number) instead of causing the program to terminate. Such an operation would also raise an exception. Handling this exception enables a program to handle such calculations gracefully, rather than dumping core.

It is also the case that NaN *propagate*, meaning that a calculation where one operand is a NaN produces NaN as a result. This way, a calculation will produce either a "valid" (i.e., numerical) result, or a NaN, meaning that some part of the calculation was invalid. Example 6.8 shows an example in which a NaN is generated as output.

Example 6.8 Example of a Calculation Generating a NaN

```
$ cat ex6.8.c
#include <stdio.h>
void main()
{
   double a=0;
   double b=a/a;
   printf("b=%f\n",b);
}
$ cc ex6.8.c
$ a.out
b=NaN
```

One interesting property of NaNs is that they fail the equality test—they are unorderable, they are neither bigger nor smaller than numbers, and one NaN does not equal another NaN. The code in Example 6.9 illustrates that NaNs fail the equality test: A NaN is generated when zero is divided by zero. Even though the NaN is compared to itself, the test fails. In fact, this is the test for NaNs; they are values that are not equal to themselves.

Example 6.9 NaNs Fail the Equality Test

```
$ cat ex6.9.c
#include <stdio.h>
void main()
{
   double a=0;
   double b=a/a;
   if (b==b) printf("Equal\n");
   if (b!=b) printf("Not equal\n");
}
$ cc ex6.9.c
$ a.out
Not equal
```

One further classification of NaNs is that they have two types: signaling NaNs and quiet NaNs. Operations on signaling NaNs will generate a floating-point exception (which can then be caught), whereas operations on quiet NaNs do not generate exceptions (except when they are used in ordered comparisons).

6.2.8 Enabling Floating-Point Expression Simplification (`-fsimple`)

The `-fsimple` flag enables floating-point simplification. It allows the compiler to reorder floating-point expressions, replace long-latency floating-point operations with algebraically equivalent but faster versions, or omit some kinds of operations. One way to imagine what the flag can do is to think of it as allowing the compiler to assume that the rules of algebra carry over into floating-point arithmetic performed on a computer. In fact, floating-point math has more complex rules than normal algebra. Here are a couple of examples of situations in which algebra and floating-point computation do not agree.

- A floating-point variable may not always equal itself. Consider the statement (x==x). Normally this would be expected to always be true. However, as described in Section 6.2.7, this is not true for NaNs.

- In algebra, division by a value is equivalent to multiplication by the reciprocal of the value. In other words, a/b is equal to a*(1/b). Unfortunately, because the multiplication by the reciprocal involves two floating-point operations, whereas the division is only a single operation, the results of the two are rarely identical (in the least significant bits). Also, calculating the reciprocal of b may generate floating-point overflow, which would not occur in the calculation of a/b.

Generally, these kinds of simplifications can have a performance impact on floating-point applications, because they enable the compiler to do things such as reorder additions or replace divides with multiplication by the reciprocal.

Table 6.2 shows the three settings for `-fsimple`.

Table 6.2 Settings for `-fsimple`

`-fsimple` Setting	Comment
0	No floating-point simplification allowed
1	There are no NaNs in the data, so tests such as (x==x) can be replaced with TRUE. Allow generally appropriate floating-point optimizations.
2	Allow aggressive floating-point optimizations, such as hoisting of divides, and reordering of floating-point expressions.

The default setting for -fsimple is zero, which means that the compiler adheres to the IEEE-754 standard. However, -fast includes the -fsimple=2 flag, which allows aggressive floating-point reordering (and hence, potentially higher performance), but no longer adheres to IEEE-754. Aside from adherence to the standard, you should use -fsimple=0 in calculations in which operations on NaNs are important, and when interval arithmetic is used.

The next few sections will look at various transformations that are possible under the -fsimple flag.

6.2.9 Elimination of Comparisons

In the code in Example 6.9, the comparison of a NaN with itself produces the result that it is not equal. In Example 6.10, the code is recompiled with the -fsimple=2 flag (although the same behavior would result with -fsimple=1). The flag enables the compiler to assume that b variable is always equal to itself; hence, the program always prints "Equal".

Example 6.10 Equality Testing Under -fsimple=2

```
$ cat ex6.10.c
#include <stdio.h>
void main()
{
  double a=0;
  double b=a/a;
  if (b==b) printf("Equal\n");
  if (b!=b) printf("Not equal\n");
}
$ cc -xO3 ex6.10.c
$ a.out
Not equal
$ cc -xO3 -fsimple=2 ex6.10.c
$ a.out
Equal
```

6.2.10 Elimination of Unnecessary Calculation

For floating-point math, it is sometimes important to perform calculations to observe their side effects. For example, you might perform a calculation to check for overflow; the results of the calculation might not be useful, but the fact that the calculation succeeded without generating an overflow might be important.

As a consequence of this, it is not possible for the compiler to remove floating-point calculations, even when the results of the calculations are not used, except under the control of the -fsimple=1 flag.

Example 6.11 shows a floating-point calculation in which the result is stored in a local variable, but never used. Even though the variable is never used, the compiler will still have to perform the calculation. If this code is compiled without

-fsimple, the divide operation is performed. If -fsimple=1 is specified, the compiler has the freedom to eliminate the unused divide operation.

Example 6.11 Example of Redundant Floating-Point Calculation

```
void test(float a, float b)
{
    float c=a/b;
}
```

6.2.11 Reordering of Calculations

The language standards dictate that operations are completed in the order specified. This has two parts to it. First, parentheses are honored, and second, that calculations are carried out in the order that the program specifies. Consider the code shown in Example 6.12. In this code, a sum is calculated.

Example 6.12 Calculation of a Sum of a Vector

```
int i;
double a[LEN];
double total = 0;
for (i=0; i<LEN; i++)
    total += a[i];
```

There is a performance issue with this code in that each addition to the variable total has to complete before the next addition can start. This means that each iteration of the loop takes at least as long as a single addition takes.

There is a faster way to do this summation, and that is to have multiple summation variables, with each variable totaling part of the final result. Example 6.13 shows the transformed code.

Example 6.13 Summation Code Restructured to Use Four Temporary Variables

```
int i;
double a[LEN];
double total = 0, total1 = 0, total2 = 0, total3 = 0, total4 = 0;
for (i=0; i<LEN-4; i+=4)
{
    total1 += a[i];
    total2 += a[i+1];
    total3 += a[i+2];
    total4 += a[i+3];
}
for ( ; i<LEN; i++)
    total += a[i];

total = total + total1 + total2 + total3 + total4;
```

Obviously, it is very painful to manually do this kind of transformation for all the places in the code where summations occur, and in fact, this is the kind of transformation the -fsimple=2 flag enables the compiler to do. Example 6.14 shows a full example of the two code snippets. I discuss the timing harness, defined in timing.h and used for all the examples in this book, in Section 7.4.1 of Chapter 7.

Example 6.14 Timing Loop Unrolling

```
#include "timing.h"

#define SIZE 6000
#define RPT 100
static float f[SIZE],g[SIZE];

int main()
{
  int index,count;
  float totalf=0.0,tf1,tf2,tf3,tf4;
  for (index=0; index<SIZE; index++) f[index]=g[index]=1.0;
  printf("(a+b)                ");
  starttime();
  for (count=0; count<RPT; count++)
    {
    for (index=0;index<SIZE;index++)
      totalf+=(f[index]+g[index]);
    totalf=totalf*1.7;
    }
  endtime(SIZE*RPT);
  printf("(a+b) unrolled         ");
  starttime();
  for (count=0; count<RPT; count++)
    {
    tf1=tf2=tf3=tf4=0;
    for (index=0;index<SIZE-4;index+=4)
      {
      tf1+=(g[index]   +f[index]  );
      tf2+=(g[index+1]+f[index+1]);
      tf3+=(g[index+2]+f[index+2]);
      tf4+=(g[index+3]+f[index+3]);
      }
    totalf+=tf1+tf2+tf3+tf4;
    totalf=totalf*1.7;
    }
  endtime(SIZE*RPT);
}
```

Running the code shown in Example 6.14 with and without -fsimple=2 produces the results shown in Table 6.3.

Table 6.3 Performance Gains from Using -fsimple=2 on Vector Summation

Code	Single-Precision	Single-Precision with **-fsimple=2**
(a+b)	5.45ns	3.40ns
(a+b) unrolled	3.09ns	2.96ns

There are some possible problems with doing this kind of optimization. Consider the sequence shown in Example 6.15.

Example 6.15 Problem Number Sequence for Summation

```
10000, -10000, 20000, -20000, 30000, -30000 ....
```

In Example 6.15, the summation will produce the value zero, because each term is canceled by the next one. However, if the summation is split into four (each summation dealing with every fourth value in the vector), the individual summations will not cancel out, and there is a chance that precision will be lost as the numbers grow larger. On the other hand, look at the sequence shown in Example 6.16; in this case, using four temporary variables may well increase the precision of the result, because all the small numbers will be added together in one total and all the large values in another.

Example 6.16 Different Problem Sequence for Summations

```
10000, 0.1, 20000, 0.2, 30000, 0.3, ...
```

It may appear that adding a sequence of numbers is very hard to do. Of course, the examples shown in Examples 6.15 and 6.16 represent extremes, and most code falls between these two. Some algorithms, such as the Kahan Summation Formula, reduce these kinds of problems. It is also useful to always use double precision, which will also increase the number of decimal places and the range of numbers that can be held in a variable.

On the other hand, it is conceivable that the mix of numbers that occur in the code does not have the mix of small and large, or positive and negative, which amplifies this kind of issue. It is also possible that the difference in results that are obtained from the program is only in the least significant bits, and this may well be dwarfed by the accuracy of the data that is fed into the program.

6.2.12 Kahan Summation Formula

Section 6.2.11 introduces the issues with reordering floating-point calculations. The Kahan Summation Formula represents one way to produce more accurate results in a given precision (e.g., single or double precision). Example 6.17 shows four methods of computing a summation: two "traditional" ways of summing a series of numbers, one using single precision and one using double precision; and the Kahan formulation both in single and double precision.

Example 6.17 Summation Formulae

```
float fsum(float * array, int n)
{
  float total=0.0;
  for (int i=0; i<n; i++) {total+=array[i];}
  return total;
}

float kfsum(float * array, int n)
{
  float total, temp1, temp2 , carry;
  carry=0.0;
  total = array[0];
  for (int i=1; i<n; i++)
  {
    temp1 =array[i] - carry;
    temp2 =total + temp1;
    carry = (temp2 - total) - temp1;
    total = temp2;
  }
  return total;
}
double dsum(float * array, int n)
{
  double total=0.0;
  for (int i=0; i<n; i++) {total+=array[i];}
  return total;
}

double kdsum(float * array, int n)
{
  double  total, temp1, temp2 , carry;
  carry=0.0;
  total = array[0];
  for (int i=1; i<n; i++)
  {
    temp1 =array[i] - carry;
    temp2 =total + temp1;
    carry = (temp2 - total) - temp1;
    total = temp2;
  }
  return total;
}
```

You can test the various approaches using the test harness shown in Example 6.18. This test harness prepares an array with alternating large and small values.

Example 6.19 shows the results of compiling and running this test program without floating-point simplification enabled.

The single-precision summation provides a result that is correct to about four significant figures. The Kahan formula improves this to seven significant figures, still using just single-precision variables. Double precision obtains 12 significant figures, whereas double precision using the Kahan formula provides the most accurate result with about 15 significant figures.

Example 6.18 Summation Test Harness

```
void setarray(float * array,int n)
{
  for (int i=0; i<n; i+=2)
  {
    array[i]=1/100001.0;
  }
  for (int i=1; i<n; i+=2)
  {
    array[i]=100001.0;
  }
}

void main()
{
  float array[100000];
  setarray(array,100000);
  printf(" fsum = %12.8f\n", fsum(array,100000));
  printf("kfsum = %12.8f\n",kfsum(array,100000));
  printf(" dsum = %12.8f\n", dsum(array,100000));
  printf("kdsum = %12.8f\n",kdsum(array,100000));
}
```

Example 6.19 Results of Summation Code

```
% cc -O ex6.17.c
% a.out
 fsum = 5000756736.00000000
kfsum = 5000050176.00000000
 dsum = 5000050000.49729729
kdsum = 5000050000.49999523
```

6.2.13 Hoisting of Divides

Division is an operation that takes a processor a large number of cycles to complete. Consider that addition and multiplication each might take about four cycles, whereas division might take 20 or more cycles. Given this fact, it is a good plan to avoid divisions wherever possible. Under -fsimple=2, the compiler will, where possible, replace divisions with multiplication by the reciprocal, or even delay them until later in program execution.

Often, divides by a constant value appear within a loop, and under this optimization, the divide can be done once before the loop (called *hoisting* the divide out of the loop), and the loop can progress with the much cheaper multiply operation. Example 6.20 shows code that demonstrates the potential for this optimization.

Example 6.20 Code in Which the Divide Can Be Hoisted

```
for (i=0; i<LEN; i++)
  total += a[i]/b;
```

You can transform the code shown in Example 6.20 into the faster-running code shown in Example 6.21.

Example 6.21 Alternative Sequence of Faster Running Code

```
for (i=0; i<LEN; i++)
  total += a[i];
total = total /b;
```

Note that for the code shown in Example 6.21, the compiler also would split the total variable into four components, but for clarity this optimization is not shown here.

Example 6.22 shows some code that can demonstrate the performance gains you can obtain by hoisting the division operation out of the critical loop.

Example 6.22 Timing Code for Divide Operations

```
#include <stdio.h>
#include "timing.h"

#define SIZE 6000
#define RPT 100
static float f[SIZE],g[SIZE];

int main()
{
  int index,count;
  float totalf=0.0;
  for (index=0; index<SIZE; index++) f[index]=g[index]=1.0;
  printf("(a+b)/const            ");
  starttime();
  for (count=0; count<RPT; count++)
    {
    for (index=0;index<SIZE;index++)
      totalf+=(f[index]+g[index])/3.88;
    totalf=totalf*1.7;
    }
  endtime(SIZE*RPT);
}
```

Example 6.23 shows the performance gains from running the code in Example 6.22 with and without -fsimple=2.

Example 6.23 Timing Running with and without -fsimple=2

```
$ cc -xO3  ex6.22.c
$ a.out
(a+b)/const            Time per iteration 23.01 ns
$ cc -xO3 -fsimple=2 ex6.22.c
$ a.out
(a+b)/const            Time per iteration 16.23 ns
```

The hoisting of division operations has similar problems to the summation seen in Section 6.2.10. The summation may overflow before the divide operation is performed. It also has the rounding problems associated with replacing a one-step division by a two-step process.

6.2.14 Honoring of Parentheses at Levels of Floating-Point Simplification

At -fsimple=0, the compiler will honor the parentheses placed around calculations; at -fsimple=2, the compiler will maintain the same algebraic formula, but may replace it with something that can be executed more efficiently.

For example, Example 6.24 shows two algebraically equivalent floating-point expressions.

Example 6.24 Example of Simplification of a Floating-Point Expression

```
(a+b)*c - b*c = a*c
```

The Kahan Summation Formula shown in Example 6.17 is sensitive to the order in which expressions are calculated. Examination of the formula indicates that by removing parentheses, much of the calculation can be eliminated, and it essentially resolves to a straightforward summation of all the values in an array. Hence, compiling the Kahan Summation Formula is one situation that is incompatible with the use of the -fsimple flag.

6.2.15 Effect of -fast on errno

The expansion of -fast for C includes the definition of the preprocessor variable _ _MATHERR_ERRNO_DONTCARE. This variable changes the way some of the functions in the math.h header file are defined. Example 6.25 shows a snippet from the header file.

Example 6.25 Snippet of math.h

```
#if defined(__MATHERR_ERRNO_DONTCARE)
#pragma does_not_read_global_data(erf, erfc, hypot)
#pragma does_not_write_global_data(erf, erfc, hypot)
#pragma no_side_effect(erf, erfc, hypot)
#endif
```

The pragmas that are enabled are does_not_read_global_data, which means the compiler does not have to store variables back to memory before the call to the function (see Section 5.12.3 of Chapter 5), does_not_write_global_data, which means variables do not need to be reloaded after the function call, and no_side_effect, which allows the compiler to eliminate the call if the result of the call is not used (see Section 5.12.4 of Chapter 5). The presence of these pragmas gives the compiler the freedom to ignore changes to the errno variable for these mathematical routines, but does not force the compiler to do so.

The errno variable is also disrupted by the use of the -xbuiltin flag, which enables the compiler to replace calls to known library routines defined in math.h and stdio.h with intrinsic functions; -xlibmil, which replaces some mathematical function calls with equivalent inline templates (e.g., fabs and sqrt); and -xlibmopt, which uses optimized versions of some mathematical functions.

When the -mt compiler flag is specified to generate a multithreaded application, errno becomes a function call that manipulates a thread-local copy of the errno variable.

6.2.16 Specifying Which Floating-Point Events Cause Traps (-ftrap)

The -ftrap flag specifies which IEEE floating-point events will cause a trap. The default depends on language. Table 6.4 lists the various trapping modes.

Table 6.4 Options for the -ftrap Flag

Trapping Mode	Comment
%all	Enable all trapping modes
%none	Disable all trapping modes
common	Invalid, division by zero, and overflow enabled
[no%]invalid	Trap if the invalid operation exception is raised
[no%]overflow	Trap if the number is too large to fit into the size of variable used to hold the result
[no%]underflow	Trap if the result of an operation is too small to fit into the size of variable used to hold the result
[no%]division	Enable division-by-zero trap
[no%]inexact	Trap if the value of an operation is different from the exact result of the same operation. Most operations raise this exception.

Note that all files in a program must be compiled with the same trapping mode for the program to give the correct behavior.

6.2.17 The Floating-Point Exception Flags

When a floating-point exception occurs—for example, a division by zero is encountered during the run of the program—this event is recorded in a set of floating-point exception flags. You can query the state of the flags through the `ieee_flags` function, as shown in Example 6.26.

Example 6.26 Accessing the Floating-Point Exception Flags

```
int i=ieee_flags(char* action, char* mode, char* in, char* out);
```

The `action` parameter is a string containing one of `get`, `set`, `clear`, or `clearall`. The `mode` parameter will typically be a string containing the word `exception`. The `in` parameter is either the name of a particular exception, or empty. If the `in` parameter names an exception, the `out` parameter will be written with the name of the exception if that exception has occurred. If the `in` parameter is empty, the `out` parameter will contain the name of the highest-priority exception that has occured. Example 6.27 shows code that demonstrates how to clear and read the exception flags.

Example 6.27 Reading the Floating-Point Exception Flags

```
#include <sunmath.h>

void main()
{
  char *text;
  double a=5.55;
  ieee_flags("clear","exception","inexact",&text);
  ieee_flags("get","exception","inexact",&text);
  printf("Inexact flag %s\n",text);
  a=a*1.77;
  ieee_flags("get","exception","inexact",&text);
  printf("Inexact flag %s\n",text);
}
```

Example 6.28 shows the results of compiling and running the program from Example 6.27. The program needs to be linked with the Sun Math Library (`-lsunmath`).

Example 6.28 Compiling and Running Program to Read Floating-Point
Exception Flags

```
% cc -O ex6.27.c -lsunmath
% a.out
Inexact flag
Inexact flag inexact
```

If the program is compiled so that traps are taken on floating-point exceptions, the application will call handlers for the exceptions. These handlers are installed using the `ieee_handler` function, as shown in Example 6.29.

Example 6.29 Function to Install a Floating-Point Exception Handler

```
ieee_handler(char* action, char* exception, sig_fpe_handler_type handler);
```

Depending on whether the action is `get`, `clear`, or `set`, this function will either return the current handler for a given type of exception, remove the current handler and disable the trap, or install a new handler for that type of exception. Example 6.30 shows an example of setting a handler.

Example 6.30 Handler for Division-by-Zero Exception

```
#include <sunmath.h>
#include <stdlib.h>
void handler(int signal)
{
  printf("Division by zero error\n");
  exit(1);
}

void main()
{
  char *text;
  double a=0.0;
  ieee_handler("set","division",&handler);
  a=1/a;
}
```

Example 6.31 shows the results of compiling and running the code that has a handler for division-by-zero exceptions.

Example 6.31 Compiling and Running Code Containing Floating-Point
Exception Handler

```
% cc -O ex6.30.c -lsunmath
% a.out
Division by zero error
```

6.2.18 Floating-Point Exceptions in C99

C99 defines an improved set of routines to manipulate the exception flags. You
should not mix these routines with the routines outlined in Section 6.2.17. These
routines, together with Sun-specific extensions, provide a much richer interface.
For example, it is easily possible for the exception-handling routine to determine
what operation caused the exception and what the values were, and even to write
a new result back into the calculation.

To use these routines on Solaris 9 it is necessary to link with the C99 floating-
point library, using the -lm9x compiler flag. You also need to specify the path to
the libraries. On Solaris 10, the functionality is included in the default math
library (-lm). Example 6.32 shows example code that uses this interface to set and
read the exception flags.

Example 6.32 C99 Functions to Access Floating-Point Exception Flags

```
#include <fenv.h>
#include <stdio.h>
void handler (int ex, fex_info_t *info)
{
  printf("In handler\n");
}

void main()
{
  double a=5.55;
  feclearexcept(FE_INEXACT);
  fex_set_handling(FEX_INEXACT,FEX_CUSTOM, &handler);
  if (fetestexcept(FE_INEXACT) & FE_INEXACT) {printf("Inexact flag set\n");}
  else {printf("Inexact flag clear\n");}
  a=a*1.77;
  if (fetestexcept(FE_INEXACT) & FE_INEXACT) {printf("Inexact flag set\n");}
  else {printf("Inexact flag clear\n");}
}
```

Example 6.33 shows the results of compiling and running this code.

Example 6.33 Compiling and Running C99 Floating-Point Exception Code

```
$ cc -O ex6.32.c -L/opt/SUNWspro/lib -R/opt/SUNWspro/lib -lm9x
$ a.out
Inexact flag clear
In handler
Inexact flag set
```

6.2.19 Using Inline Template Versions of Floating-Point Functions (`-xlibmil`)

The `-xlibmil` option specifies that the compiler should use inline templates for some common mathematical functions. The inline template versions of the code do not set `errno` or respect user-specified `matherr`, but will raise the appropriate floating-point exceptions, and the results do conform to IEEE-754. The advantage of using inline templates is that the call overhead is avoided, and the code can probably be better scheduled.

Example 6.34 shows some source code that has the potential to replace the call to the function `fabs` with an equivalent inline template. In fact, in this case SPARC assembly already has `fabs` primative, so the inline template is a single function. Example 6.35 shows the result of compiling with the `-xlibmil` flag.

Example 6.34 Source Code with Potential for Inlining a Math Function

```
#include <math.h>

float test(float a)
{
  return fabs(a);
}
```

Example 6.35 Inline Template for `fabs` Used with `-xlibmil`

```
$ cc -O -xlibmil -S ex6.34.c
$ more ex6.34.s
...
/* 000000        4 */     st     %o0,[%sp+68]
/* 0x0004        5 */     ld     [%sp+68],%f2
/* 0x0008          */     retl          ! Result =  %f0
/* 0x000c          */     fabss  %f2,%f0
```

The `-xlibmil` flag is closely linked to the `-xbuiltin` compiler flag discussed in Section 5.10.1 of Chapter 5. Often, the two flags will be used together to ensure that the compiler substitutes higher-performing versions of all the routines that it is able to.

6.2.20 Using the Optimized Math Library (-xlibmopt)

The optimized math library (libmopt) contains versions of the common mathematical functions that have improved speed, while raising floating-point exceptions and producing results that conform to IEEE-754. However, they do not set errno or respect user-specified matherr. Example 6.36 shows an example program.

Example 6.36 Program That Calls Sin and Cosine Functions

```
#include "timing.h"
#include <math.h>

void main()
{
  int i;
  double d;
  starttime();
  for (i=0; i<100000; i++)
  {
    d=sin(1.5)+cos(1.5);
  }
  endtime(100000);
}
```

Example 6.37 shows the results of compiling the program with and without the optimized math library.

Example 6.37 Difference in Performance When Compiled with libmopt

```
% cc -O ex6.36.c -lm
% a.out
Time per iteration 492.94 ns
% cc -O ex6.36.c -xlibmopt
% a.out
Time per iteration 148.12 ns
```

6.2.21 Do Not Promote Single-Precision Values to Double Precision (-fsingle for C)

The -fsingle flag allows the compiler to keep single-precision floating-point values as single precision and not promote them to double precision. This is important only for -Xt and -Xs compiler modes (which are not the default). These modes favor the K&R standard rather than the ISO C standard, and as a result, in these modes a float variable would normally be promoted to a double. Usually, double-precision mathematics is used because it is more accurate, but avoiding the conversion improves performance.

6.2.22 Storing Floating-Point Constants in Single Precision (-xsfpconst for C)

The reason for the -xsfpconst flag is that the C standard specifies that floating-point values that are not explicitly cast are to be considered as doubles. Example 6.38 shows some code samples that demonstrate this.

Example 6.38 Sample Code to Demonstrate Promotion of Constants to Double Precision

```
float test1(float i){return 1.3*i;}
float test2(float i){return (double)1.5*i;}
float test3(float i){return (float)1.7*i;}
double test4(double i) {return 1.9*i;}
```

Example 6.39 shows the assembly code generated by the compiler for the important part of the test1 routine. After the i variable is loaded, it is converted to a double-precision value (by the instruction fstod) to be multiplied by the double-precision value 1.3, and then converted back into a single-precision value (by the instruciton fdtos) to be returned by the function.

Example 6.39 Assembly Code for Critical Part of test1 Routine

```
/* 0x000c         */      ld      [%sp+68],%f2
/* 0x0010         */      fstod   %f2,%f0
/* 0x0014         */      fmuld   %f0,%f4,%f6
/* 0x0018         */      retl    ! Result =  %f0
/* 0x001c         */      fdtos   %f6,%f0
```

If the code were compiled with the -xsfpconst flag, the 1.3 would be considered a single-precision value, and the conversions of the i variable and the result would be avoided. You can see the downside of compiling with the -xsfpconst flag in the disassembly for the test4 routine, when compiled with the flag.

Example 6.40 shows the disassembly code for the test4 routine, when compiled with the -xsfpconst flag. In this case, the constant is stored as a single-precision value and has to be converted to double precision before it can be used in the multiplication. The other issue here is that the constant has been stored with less precision, and this may impact the result of the calculation. Notice also that the code shown has been compiled without -dalign, so it takes two loads to load the double-precision value of i.

Example 6.40 Assembly Code for the test4 Routine, Compiled with -xsfpconst

```
/* 0x000c          */        ld       [%o5+%lo(___const_val_1.3)],%f2
/* 0x0010          */        fstod    %f2,%f6
/* 0x0014          */        ld       [%sp+68],%f4
/* 0x0018          */        ld       [%sp+72],%f5
/* 0x001c          */        retl     ! Result =   %f0
/* 0x0020          */        fmuld    %f6,%f4,%f0
```

A recommendation is to always specify whether a constant is double-precision or single-precision. Obviously, this can be very tedious on a large program, and the -xsfpconst flag may help in these situations. However, it is really only necessary to specify the precision for the critical (in terms of performance or functionality) regions of code.

6.3 Floating-Point Multiply Accumulate Instructions

The SPARC64 VI processor has the capability to execute fused floating-point multiply accumulate instructions (support for these instructions was first available in the Sun Studio 12 compiler). These instructions complete the operation

$$d = (a \times b) + c$$

in the same time it takes to complete either a multiply or an addition. The fused instruction also, theoretically, has greater accuracy.

When a floating-point instruction is executed, the computation is typically completed with more bits of precision than can be held in a register. At the end of the operation, the result is rounded so that it fits into a register. When a multiply instruction is followed by an addition instruction there are two rounding operations. If the multiply and addition are combined into a single instruction, there is only a single rounding operation at the end of the computation. When the multiply and addition are combined in this way, avoiding the intermediate rounding operation, the instruction is called a *fused* multiply accumulate. It is also possible to have unfused multiply accumulate instructions which provide the same result as performing the two operations separately.

Performing only a single rounding operation may cause applications to produce different results when compiled to use fused multiply accumulates than if the same application were compiled to use two instructions, and have two rounding operations. Hence, the compiler does not use these by default. To use the operations two compiler flags are necessary; first the appropriate architecture must be specified using -xarch=sparcfmaf, and second the compiler needs permission to generate the fused instruction using the -fma=fused flag. The flags necessary for this are shown in Example 6.41, together with the assembly language that results from using these instructions.

Example 6.41 Compiler Flags Necessary to Generate Floating-Point
Multiple Accumulates

```
$ more ex6.41.c
double add_mul(double a, double b)
{
  return a+a*b;
}
$ cc -S -O -xarch=sparcfmaf -fma=fused ex6.41.c
$ more ex6.41.s
...
/* 0x0020          */          retl     ! Result =  %f0
/* 0x0024          */          fmaddd   %f4,%f2,%f4,%f0
...
```

On Solaris 10, which supports C99, it is also possible to call the C99 fmaf function to calculate a fused floating-point multiply accumulate, as shown in Example 6.42.

Example 6.42 Calling the C99 fmaf Function

```
#include <math.h>
void main ()
{
  printf("%f\n",fmaf(1.0,2.0,3.0));
}
```

6.4 Integer Math

Integer math is not affected by the use of the -fsimple compiler flag, but that does not mean that it is any less important. Both integer multiplication and division are long latency instructions, and you should avoid them if at all possible. Example 6.43 shows code that demonstrates the performance difference between integer and floating-point division.

Example 6.43 Code to Demonstrate the Performance of Integer and
Floating-Point Divides

```
#include "timing.h"

#define SIZE 6000
#define RPT 100
static float f[SIZE],g[SIZE];
static int fi[SIZE],gi[SIZE];

int main()
{
  int index,count,total=0;
  float totalf=0.0;
  for (index=0; index<SIZE; index++)
  {
    f[index]=g[index]=(float)1.0;
    fi[index]=gi[index]=1;
  }
  printf("fp                ");
  starttime();
  for (count=0; count<RPT; count++)
  {
    for (index=0;index<SIZE;index++)
      totalf+=(f[index]/g[index]);
    totalf=totalf*2;
  }
  endtime(SIZE*RPT);
  printf("int               ");
  starttime();
  for (count=0; count<RPT; count++)
  {
    for (index=0;index<SIZE;index++)
      total+=(fi[index]/gi[index]);
    total=total*2;
  }
  endtime(SIZE*RPT);
  if ((total==0)||(totalf==0.0)) return 1;
}
```

Example 6.44 shows the results of compiling and running the code in Example 6.43.

Example 6.44 Performance of Integer and Floating-Point Divides

```
% cc -O ex6.43.c
% a.out
fp              Time per iteration 18.96 ns
int             Time per iteration 57.86 ns
```

Note that integer divide is much longer latency than integer multiply, so if it is possible to restructure the code to avoid the divide, performance may be improved.

Example 6.45 shows some code that tests the ratio of two numbers. This code will result in an integer divide operation. However, it is possible to replace the divide with a multiply. This has two general benefits. Principally, the multiply operation is faster than the divide operation, but in this case, the multiply is by a constant of three, and the compiler can replace the multiply by three with a faster sequence of operations.

Example 6.45 Example of Integer Divide

```
int test(int a, int b)
{
  if (a/b==3) return 1;
  return 0;
}
```

The alternative coding shown in Example 6.46 will not work for all values of b. In some cases, it is possible that multiplying b by three will cause an overflow, whereas the divide operation would work. More seriously, the code will not work for many situations where both a and b are negative.

Example 6.46 Alternative Coding Avoiding the Divide Operation

```
int test(int a, int b)
{
  if ((a>=3*b) && (a<3*b+b) ) return 1;
  return 0;
}
```

It is possible (in most cases) to replace integer divide with floating-point divide, but it is not permissible (due to rounding) to replace integer division with a floating-point multiplication by a reciprocal. The code in Example 6.47 shows such a situation.

Example 6.47 Example of Code That Is Sensitive to `-fsimple`

```
void main()
{
  int i,j;
  for (j=1;j<100; j++)
   for (i=1; i<100; i++)
    if (i/j != (int)((float)i/(float)j) )
      printf("i=%d j=%d i/j=%d fi/fj=%d\n",i,j,
             i/j,(int)((float)i/(float)j) );
}
```

The code in Example 6.47 will not indicate any problem values when compiled without `-fsimple=2`; this indicates that it is a legitimate optimization to replace the integer divide with the floating-point divide. However, if this code is recompiled with `-fsimple=2`, the compiler will observe that, for the inner loop, the j variable is invariant. So, it is possible to calculate the reciprocal of the j variable before the inner loop, and multiply by that inside the inner loop. Compiling with -fsimple=2 produces the output shown in Example 6.48. The output shows a number of (i,j) pairs where the floating-point division produces a different result to the integer division.

Example 6.48 Output of Code When Compiled with -fsimple=2

```
% cc -O -fsimple=2 -xtarget=ultra3 ex6.47.c
% a.out
i=41 j=41 i/j=1 fi/fj=0
i=82 j=41 i/j=2 fi/fj=1
i=47 j=47 i/j=1 fi/fj=0
i=94 j=47 i/j=2 fi/fj=1
i=55 j=55 i/j=1 fi/fj=0
i=61 j=61 i/j=1 fi/fj=0
i=82 j=82 i/j=1 fi/fj=0
i=83 j=83 i/j=1 fi/fj=0
i=94 j=94 i/j=1 fi/fj=0
i=97 j=97 i/j=1 fi/fj=0
```

6.4.1 Other Integer Math Opportunities

Calculations can often be performed more quickly if one of the operands is a power of two. Example 6.49 shows an example of this. The modulo operation can be greatly simplified, to an AND operation, if the divisor is a power of two.

Example 6.49 Example of Powers of Two Improving Performance

```
#include "timing.h"

void test1(int a)
{
  if (a%100==0) {printf("Index 0");}
}

void test2(int a)
{
  if (a%128==0) {printf("Index 0");}
}

void main()
{
  int i;
  starttime();
  for (i=0; i<100000; i++) {test1(5);}
  endtime(100000);
  starttime();
  for (i=0; i<100000; i++) {test2(5);}
  endtime(100000);
}
```

Example 6.50 shows the results of compiling and running the code from Example 6.49.

Example 6.50 Performance Difference with Careful Choice of Divisor

```
$ cc -O ex6.49.c
$ a.out
Time per iteration 25.82 ns
Time per iteration 14.49 ns
```

Note that it is relatively easy to inadvertently include integer math into code. The code in Example 6.51 looks correct at first glance, but the abs function takes an integer value, so the compiler has to convert the array variable into an integer, call the abs function on that integer to get the absolute value of it, and finally convert that integer back into a floating-point number to add it onto total. In this case, the function that should be called is fabs.

Example 6.51 Using an Integer Function on Floating-Point Data

```
float total,array[SIZE];
for (index=0; index<SIZE;index++)
  total+=abs(array[index]);
```

6.5 Floating-Point Parameter Passing with SPARC V8 Code

When an application is compiled for SPARC V8 (32-bit code), floating-point function parameters are passed in the integer registers if they occur in the first six 32-bit parameters passed to the function (note that passing a 64-bit value requires two 32-bit registers). In the V9 instruction set architecture (ISA), the floating-point parameters are passed through the floating-point registers. Example 6.52 shows an example of where a double-precision parameter is passed into a routine using the V8 calling convention.

To do the V8 parameter passing, it is necessary for the values to be moved from the floating-point registers into the integer registers, to be passed to the function, and then back again inside the body of the function. Moving from the integer to the floating-point registers (and back) necessitates storing and loading the values to and from the stack.

However, you can avoid some of these stores and loads if the floating-point parameters are placed after six 32-bit parameters have been passed into the function. In this situation, the values are passed in the stack, so the calling code has to store them into the stack, and the called code just has to reload them from the

Example 6.52 Passing Floating-Point Parameters in V8 Code

```
! FILE ex6.52.c

!    1                  !double fp(double a)
!    2                  !{
!    3                  !  return a*2.0;
!    4                  !}
!
! SUBROUTINE fp
!
! OFFSET    SOURCE LINE LABEL   INSTRUCTION
                             fp:
/* 000000        2 */     st      %o0,[%sp+68]
/* 0x0004        3 */     sethi   %hi(___const_seg_900000102),%o5
/* 0x0008        2 */     st      %o1,[%sp+72]
/* 0x000c        3 */     ldd     [%o5+%lo(___const_seg_900000102)],%f4
/* 0x0010          */     ld      [%sp+68],%f2
/* 0x0014          */     ld      [%sp+72],%f3
/* 0x0018          */     retl    ! Result = %f0
/* 0x001c          */     fmuld   %f2,%f4,%f0
```

stack. Although this is still not as fast as passing them in registers, it does cut down the number of stores and loads that are necessary.

The code shown in Example 6.53 is an example of the differences between the two ways of passing parameters.

Example 6.53 Two Different Ways of Passing Floating-Point Parameters in V8 Code

```
#include "timing.h"

double f1(double fp1, double fp2, double fp3,
         double fp4, double fp5, double fp6)
{ return fp1+fp2+fp3; }

double f2(double fp1, double fp2, double fp3,
         double fp4, double fp5, double fp6)
{ return fp4+fp5+fp6; }

void main()
{
  int count;
  double value;

  starttime();
  for(count=0; count<1024*1024; count++)
  { value=f1(1.0,1.0,1.0,1.0,1.0,1.0); }
  endtime(1024*1024);

  starttime();
  for(count=0; count<1024*1024; count++)
  { value=f2(1.0,1.0,1.0,1.0,1.0,1.0); }
  endtime(1024*1024);
}
```

Example 6.54 shows the performance difference between the two approaches. In the f1 routine the first three parameters are used. These parameters are double-precision floating-point values, so they are passed in the first six integer registers. To get the values into the floating-point registers, they need to be stored to the stack and then reloaded. The f2 routine uses parameters that are passed after the six integer registers have been used, so the values are stored to the stack by the calling routine, and then loaded by the called routine. Because the first three double-precision parameters are not used, the compiler does not have to generate code that moves them into the floating-point registers. The only cost of obtaining the floating-point values is that of loading them from the stack, hence the second routine runs substantially faster.

Example 6.54 Performance Difference from Different Ordering of Floating-Point Parameters

```
$ cc -O ex6.53.c
$ a.out
Time per iteration 44.26 ns
Time per iteration 25.48 ns
```

7

Libraries and Linking

7.1 Introduction

Linking is the final step in generating an application. This chapter discusses how to link to existing libraries and how to develop new libraries. There are two types of libraries: static and dynamic. Static libraries are typically used as part of the build process, whereas dynamic libraries are usually shipped as part of the final product. When dynamic libraries are used as part of an application it is necessary to specify how those libraries are to be located at runtime. Another useful type of library is an interposing library. These libraries fit between an application and its original libraries and provide replacement code to be called instead of the code in the original libraries. By the end of the chapter, the reader will know how to generate and use both static and dynamic libraries as well as use interposition and auditing to examine the runtime use of libraries. The reader will also know some of the features of the libraries shipped as part of Solaris and the compiler suite.

7.2 Linking

7.2.1 Overview of Linking

Linking is the process of combining all the object files produced by the compiler with any libraries that are required to produce an executable, shared object, or even other object files. It is performed by the linker, `ld`. You can invoke the linker directly, but this can involve knowing some details of the compilation system. Therefore, it is strongly recommended that you perform the linking process by invoking the compiler on the object files, and allowing the compiler to call the linker with the appropriate linker options.

7.2.2 Dynamic and Static Linking

In general, you can link libraries either as part of the executable (static linking), or dynamically at runtime. It is usually preferable to use dynamic linking, because doing so provides a number of benefits.

- Dynamic linking enables libraries (and their code) to be shared among multiple applications. The libraries can even be loaded only when needed.
- Dynamic linking allows the system to pick the appropriate version of a library at runtime, depending on the characteristics of the platform upon which it is running. For example, an application run on an UltraSPARC II-based system can pick up libraries optimized for the UltraSPARC II, and the same application run on an UltraSPARC III-based system can pick up a version of the libraries optimized for the UltraSPARC III. The operating system uses this method to provide versions of the C runtime library that are optimized for the hardware running them.
- With dynamic linking, you can use an interposing library to examine function calls, and to gain knowledge of the application's runtime behavior (as demonstrated in Section 7.2.10).
- You can replace dynamic libraries with new or debug versions without having to change the application.

Of course, there are also advantages for statically linking libraries into an application.

- It is slightly faster to call a statically linked library than a dynamically linked library.
- It is possible to know exactly what code will be called. With dynamically linked libraries, the code that gets run depends on what is installed on the system.

A static library is given the postfix `.a`, meaning "archive"—for example, `libtest.a`. The library will become part of the executable; the `.a` file will not need to be distributed or be present on the system at runtime. A dynamic library is given the postfix `.so`, meaning "shared object"—for example, `libtest.so`. The library will be loaded at runtime, so it must be available on the target system.

One of the most important libraries on the system is the C runtime library (`libc`). For 64-bit applications, this has always been solely available as a dynamic library. For versions of Solaris earlier than Solaris 10, this library and a number of other system libraries were provided for 32-bit applications, as both a static and a dynamic library. Unfortunately, using the static library turned out to be a source of problems. The role of the library is to provide an interface between user code and the kernel; hence, kernel changes could require changes in the system libraries. Once a static version of the library is linked into an application, it is impossible to patch the library; hence, use of the static version of the system libraries has been strongly discouraged. Starting with Solaris 10, the system libraries (including `libc`) are available only as dynamic versions for both 32-bit and 64-bit applications.

7.2.3 Linking Libraries

To link a library into an application, you must at least specify which library is required, using the `-l<library>` flag. A few other flags are useful as well.

- The `-L<path>` flag tells the compiler where to search for the following libraries at link time.

- The `-R<path>` flag tells the application where to search for the following libraries at runtime.

- The `-l<library>` flag tells the compiler which library to link in. The linker will search for a library with a prefix of `lib`, so the `-lmylib` flag would look for a library named `libmylib.so` or `libmylib.a` (you can use the flags `-Bstatic` and `-Bdynamic` before the library appears on the command line to specify which version to use if both are available).

Example 7.1 shows an example of linking a library into an application. The `-L` flag tells the compiler that the `mylib` library is located in the current directory. The `-R` flag tells the application that the library will be located in the current directory at runtime. This is a poor way to specify the runtime location of the library, because the application would fail to locate the library if it were invoked from a different directory. I describe a better approach in Section 7.2.6.

Example 7.1 Example of Linking a Library into an Application

```
$ cc -O -o myapp -R. -L. -lmylib myapp.c
```

7.2.4 Creating a Static Library

The process of creating a static library is relatively straightforward. A static library is nothing more than a collection of object files. It is referred to as an archive and given the suffix .a. The tool to create an archive for C and Fortran objects is ar. Example 7.2 shows the syntax for creating an archive.

Example 7.2 Syntax for Creating an Archive

```
$ ar -r <archive> <object files>
```

For C++ object files, it is necessary to invoke the compiler to generate the archive files. The compiler needs to add more information to the object files, particularly to support templates. The C++ compiler option to generate an archive is -xar, an example of which is shown in Example 7.3.

Example 7.3 Example of Making an Archive of C++ Object Files

```
% CC -xar -o myapp.a myapp.cc
```

At link time, the linker will search any archives specified on the link line and pull in code from them as needed.

7.2.5 Creating a Dynamic Library

The flag to tell the linker to generate a dynamic library is -G. A dynamic library is also referred to as a shared object, and is given the suffix .so to reflect this.

By default, the compiler will produce code that is designed to reside at a fixed position in memory. When it is loaded, the library has to be updated with its actual location in memory. This is known as a position-dependent library. This can cause a significant performance hit when the library is loaded. If the test in Example 7.4 returns a result for a given library, that library is position dependent.

Example 7.4 Testing a Library for Position Dependence

```
$ dump -L libtest.so|grep TEXTREL
[9]      TEXTREL        0
```

The linker can report objects containing position-dependent code at link time using the -ztext flag, as shown in Example 7.5.

Example 7.5 Detecting Position-Dependent Code at Link Time

```
% cc -g -o libtest.so -G test.c -ztext
Text relocation remains                        referenced
   against symbol                offset        in file
$XB5wWCA9MdrF3xS.r.c             0x18          test.o
$XB5wWCA9MdrF3xS.r.c             0x1c          test.o
$XB5wWCA9MdrF3xS.r.c             0x28          test.o
```

To avoid this startup cost, you can compile libraries in a position independent way. On SPARC, two flags enable this: -xcode=pic13 and -xcode=pic32 (these flags are equivalent to the obsolete SPARC flags -Kpic and -KPIC). The difference between the two flags is the number of relocatable symbols (variables and routines) that the library can contain; -xcode=pic13 provides fewer (2^{11} symbols versus 2^{30} symbols). There is also a performance difference between the two flags. -xcode=pic13 requires one instruction to load the address of a symbol, whereas -xcode=pic32 requires three. If the compile-time error too many symbols require 'small' PIC references is reported, it is necessary to build the library with -xcode=pic32. On x86, the flags -Kpic and -KPIC generate position-independent code and have the same constraint of 2^{11} symbols.

Example 7.6 shows an example of a command line to build a position-independent shared library.

Example 7.6 Example Command Line to Generate a Library

```
$ cc -G -xcode=pic13 -o libtest.so test.c
```

7.2.6 Specifying the Location of Libraries

At runtime, when an application is loaded, it is necessary to load the required libraries. The program that does this is called the *runtime linker*. The runtime linker will, by default, look for 32-bit libraries in /lib and /usr/lib and 64-bit libraries in /lib/64 and /usr/lib/64. If the libraries that an application requires are not to be found there, it is necessary for the application to describe where those libraries are to be found.

You can specify two flags at compile time to tell the compiler and application where to find libraries. The -L flag tells the compiler where to look for libraries when it is generating the application. The -R flag tells the compiler to include a runtime path to the libraries. The application will use this path to locate the libraries at runtime.

Example 7.7 shows an example of specifying where a library is to be found at runtime and at compile time. In the example, the location of the library is set to be the current directory, which can be correct at compile time but is unlikely to be correct at runtime. It is also possible to specify a hardcoded path where the libraries will be installed. This approach enables the application to locate the libraries, but at the expense of flexibility in terms of how the application can be installed, and often whether multiple versions of the application can coexist.

Example 7.7 Example of Specifying a Compile-Time and a Runtime Library Path

```
$ cc -o myapp -L. -R. -lmylib myapp.c
```

Other similar issues need to be resolved as well. For example, how do you specify different versions of libraries for different processors?

To resolve these issues, the linker defines some symbols that simplify this task. The $ORIGIN symbol tells the linker to make the path relative to the location of the application. Example 7.8 shows an example of using the $ORIGIN symbol to specify a relative location for the library.

Example 7.8 Using $ORIGIN to Specify a Relative Path to a Library

```
$ cc -o myapp -L. -R$ORIGIN/../lib -lmylib myapp.c
```

Using the $ORIGIN symbol specifies that at runtime, the application should look for the appropriate libraries in a directory path relative to the location of the application. This is a convenient approach because the application and its libraries can be relocated anywhere, as long as the relative path from the application to the libraries remains the same.

You can use the $ISALIST symbol to search for instruction-set-specific versions of a library. The runtime linker will expand this symbol into a set of paths that include the various instruction set architectures (ISAs) returned by the isalist command (discussed in Section 4.2.5 of Chapter 4). Each ISA-specific version of the library is placed in a separate subdirectory. In this way, the application can exploit specific features of the hardware, while still having a default version of the library. An alternative way to achieve the same result is to use the $HWCAP symbol. This symbol tells the linker to inspect all the matching libraries in a given directory and find the library version that is most appropriate for the current hardware.

It is possible to use the LD_LIBRARY_PATH environment flag to specify the directories where the libraries might be located. The environment flags LD_LIBRARY_PATH_32 and LD_LIBRARY_PATH_64 exist for specifying the library search path for 32-bit and 64-bit applications, respectively. However, this approach means that the environment variable must be correctly set for the application to run; hence, its use is strongly discouraged.

7.2.7 Lazy Loading of Libraries

One way to improve the startup time of an application is to use lazy loading. By default, libraries are loaded into memory as soon as the application starts. However, for many applications the code in the library is not required as part of the application startup. Hence, loading the libraries can be delayed until the routines in them are required; this is called *lazy loading*. To specify that an application or library should use lazy loading you should pass the -zlazyload flag to the linker before the libraries that are to be lazy loaded. You can use the -znolazyload flag to return to the default behavior.

7.2.8 Initialization and Finalization Code in Libraries

Some libraries and applications will need to set up state before the library or application is executed. The easiest way to set up these sections is to use the compiler pragmas init and fini, which define the routines that should be called before and after the application or library executes, as shown in Example 7.9.

Example 7.9 Initialization and Finalization Code

```
% more init.c
#include <stdio.h>

#pragma init (start)
#pragma fini (end)

void start()
{
  printf("Started\n");
}

void end()
{
  printf("Ended\n");
}

void main()
{
  printf("Executing\n");
}
% cc -O init.c
% a.out
Started
Executing
Ended
```

7.2.9 Symbol Scoping

By default, almost all symbols are visible outside an object file (exceptions are symbols such as static variables). However, sometimes it is useful to keep functions (or variables) local to a module. You can do this using the scoping specifier __hidden (the default is __global). It is also possible to use mapfiles to achieve the same result. Example 7.10 shows an example of this. In this example, the count variable and the calc and display routines are declared with __hidden scope. The nm tool (discussed in Section 4.5.3 of Chapter 4) shows that the __hidden symbols are still defined in the library, but they are given local scope rather than the routines declared without scoping information, which have global scope. As you might expect, an application that attempts to use these local symbols is unable to link.

Example 7.10 Limiting Symbol Scope

```
% more ex7.10a.c
#include <stdio.h>

__hidden int count=0;
__hidden void calc(int value) { count+=value; }
__hidden void display() { printf("Value = %i\n",count); }
void inc() { calc(1); display();}
void dec() { calc(-1); display();}
% more ex7.10b.c
extern int count;
extern void calc(int);
extern void inc();

void main()
{
  count=5;
  calc(7);
  inc();
}
% cc -O -G -Kpic -o libscope.so ex7.10a.c
% nm libscope.so
...
[24]    |0x00000280|0x00000030|FUNC  |LOCL |0x2  |6    |calc
[26]    |0x00010428|0x00000004|OBJT  |LOCL |0x2  |14   |count
...
[38]    |0x00000308|0x00000014|FUNC  |GLOB |0    |6    |dec
[28]    |0x000002c0|0x00000034|FUNC  |LOCL |0x2  |6    |display
[45]    |0x000002f4|0x00000014|FUNC  |GLOB |0    |6    |inc
...
% cc -O -o scopetest ex7.10b.c -L. -R. -lscope
Undefined                       first referenced
 symbol                             in file
calc                               ex7.10b.o
count                              ex7.10b.o
ld: fatal: Symbol referencing errors. No output written to scopetest
```

It is also possible to use mapfiles to achieve the same result, but you need to specify mapfiles on the compile line rather than as part of the source code. Example 7.11 shows an example of this.

Example 7.11 Using Mapfiles to Specify Symbol Scope

```
% more ex7.11.map
libscope.so
{
  global:
          inc;
          dec;
  local:
          count;
          calc;
          display;
};
% cc -O -G -Kpic -o libscope.so -M ex7.11.map ex7.11.c
```

7.2.10 Library Interposition

Library interposition is a technique for finding out more information about how a program is using routines located in libraries. The big advantage is that it doesn't need the program to be modified. The interposition library is loaded before the application is loaded, and consequently the application calls the interposition library, which can then either handle the call or pass the call on to the original library.

Using this approach, the developer can discover exactly what calls are being made and what the parameters to these calls are. For example, this can be useful in determining whether there is some pattern to the calls that can be exploited to improve the application's performance.

As an example, consider the application shown in Example 7.12. This application makes a call to the `sin` function, and displays the results.

Example 7.12 Simple Application That Calls the `sin` Function

```
#include <stdio.h>
#include <math.h>
int main()
{
  double j=sin(50);
  printf("sin(50)=%5.3f\n",j);
}
```

This application is compiled with a low level of optimization as shown in Example 7.13. Note that it is necessary to pass the -lm flag to link in the math library.

Example 7.13 Compiling the Simple Application

```
$ cc -O -o sin_test ex7.12.c -lm
```

Suppose it would be useful to know the number of times the `sin` function gets called by the test program in Example 7.12. One way to achieve this is to interpose on the call to the `sin` routine that the application makes, and count the number of times it happens. Example 7.14 shows code that does this.

Example 7.14 Example Library Interposition Code

```
#include <dlfcn.h>
#include <memory.h>
#include <assert.h>
#include <thread.h>
#include <stdio.h>
#include <procfs.h>
#include <fcntl.h>

static long long count=0;

void exit(int status)
{
    printf("Calls to sin = %lld\n",count);
    (*((void (*)())dlsym(RTLD_NEXT, "exit")))(status); } double sin(double x) {
    static double (*func)()=0;
    double ret;
    if (!func) { func = (double(*)()) dlsym(RTLD_NEXT, "sin"); }
    ret = func(x);
    count++;
    return(ret);
}
```

In the code in Example 7.14, there are two function calls, `exit` and `sin`. They interpose on the existing `exit` and `sin` functions that reside in other libraries.

In the interposing function, the `dlsym` routine is called to locate the function that would have been called if this library was not there (this is necessary only if the original behavior is to be preserved). A counter is incremented every time the interposing `sin` function is called. The interposing function calls the original function to return the value of the original function call. Note that the code as written is not thread safe.

The `exit` function will be called when the library is unloaded. In the `exit` routine, it is important to call the `exit` routine of the next library so that all libraries can execute their cleanup code. In the `exit` routine for this example, the value of the `count` variable is printed before calling the original `exit` function.

The interposing library needs to be loaded before the application is loaded. This enables the interposing library to get between the application and the library that is to be inspected. The `LD_PRELOAD` environment setting is used for this purpose. This environment variable tells the operating system to insert the interposing library between the application and the libraries that the application depends on.

There are also `LD_PRELOAD_32` and `LD_PRELOAD_64` environment variables that allow different libraries to be preloaded for 32-bit and 64-bit applications.

Example 7.15 shows this interposing library being built and used to count the number of times the application calls the `sin` function.

Example 7.15 Building and Running with the Interpose Library

```
$ cc -O -G -Kpic -o mylib.so ex7.14.c
$ LD_PRELOAD=./mylib.so; export LD_PRELOAD; sin_test
sin(50)=-0.262
Calls to sin = 1
```

7.2.11 Using the Debug Interface

The `LD_DEBUG` environment setting generates debug information about the run-time linking of an application. You can use the `LD_OPTIONS` environment variable, which specifies additional flags to be used by the linker, to obtain debug information when an executable is linked.

These environment variables are useful when checking whether an application is picking up the correct libraries, or to determine which libraries an application is selecting. Various settings show different amounts of detail about the process. One of the more useful settings is `libs`, which shows how the paths to the various libraries are resolved. Example 7.16 shows an example of using `LD_DEBUG` with the `libs` option to obtain runtime linking information for the `sleep` command.

Example 7.16 Using `LD_DEBUG` to Identify Loaded Libraries

```
% setenv LD_DEBUG libs
% sleep 5
06306:
06306: configuration file=/var/ld/ld.config: unable to process file
06306:
06306: find object=libc.so.1; searching
06306:   search path=/usr/lib  (default)
06306:   trying path=/usr/lib/libc.so.1
06306:
06306: find object=libdl.so.1; searching
06306:   search path=/usr/lib  (default)
06306:   trying path=/usr/lib/libdl.so.1
06306:   trying path=/usr/platform/SUNW,Sun-Blade-21000/lib/libc_psr.so.1
06306:
06306: calling .init (from sorted order): /usr/lib/libc.so.1
06306:
06306: calling .init (done): /usr/lib/libc.so.1
06306:
06306: transferring control: sleep
06306:
06306: calling .fini: /usr/lib/libc.so.1
```

Example 7.17 shows an example of using the LD_OPTIONS environment variable to observe the linking process. The environment variable is used to pass the -D<option> flag to the linker. In this example, setting LD_OPTIONS to -Dfiles provides more information about the files used in the linking process.

Example 7.17 Using LD_OPTIONS to Observe Linking

```
$ LD_OPTIONS=-Dfiles cc -O -o scopetest ex7.10b.c -L. -R. -lscope
debug:
debug: file=/opt/SUNWspro/prod/lib/crti.o  [ ET_REL ]
debug:
debug: file=/opt/SUNWspro/prod/lib/crt1.o  [ ET_REL ]
debug:
debug: file=/opt/SUNWspro/prod/lib/misalign.o  [ ET_REL ]
debug:
debug: file=/opt/SUNWspro/prod/lib/values-xa.o  [ ET_REL ]
debug:
debug: file=ex7.10b.o  [ ET_REL ]
...
```

7.2.12 Using the Audit Interface

The audit interface exists so that a library can watch as other libraries are loaded, determine how symbols are resolved, and even change the bindings of symbols. Example 7.18 shows source code for a simple audit library. The la_version function is required to identify the library as an audit library, and to ensure that the version numbers match the target platform. The la_objopen function gets called every time a library is loaded. The code in the routine selects only the libraries that are loaded as part of the base application, and prints a message for each one.

Example 7.18 Simple Audit Library

```
#include <link.h>
#include <stdio.h>

uint_t la_version(uint_t version)
{
  return (LAV_CURRENT);
}

uint_t la_objopen(Link_map * lmp, Lmid_t lmid, uintptr_t * cookie)
{
  if (lmid == LM_ID_BASE) {printf("file %s loaded\n", lmp->l_name);}
  return 0;
}
```

Example 7.19 shows the library being built and used. It is necessary to link the audit library with the mapmalloc library as well as libc. The -z defs flag will cause the linker to report an error if the linked libraries fail to satisfy all the dependencies (this is the default for applications, but not for libraries).

Example 7.19 Building and Using the Audit Library

```
$ cc -G -Kpic -O -o audit.so.1 ex7.18.c -z defs -lmapmalloc -lc
$ LD_AUDIT=./audit.so.1; export LD_AUDIT
$ sleep 5
file sleep loaded
file /usr/lib/libc.so.1 loaded
file /usr/lib/libdl.so.1 loaded
file /usr/platform/SUNW,Sun-Blade-1000/lib/libc_psr.so.1 loaded
```

Using LD_AUDIT enables the library to have some insight into the linking and use of a library. For example, this interface could be used to return the number of calls to functions in a library, or even between libraries.

7.3 Libraries of Interest

7.3.1 The C Runtime Library (`libc` and `libc_psr`)

The `libc` library contains most of the routines an application will require at runtime. In fact, it is really two libraries: `libc.so` and `libc_psr.so`. The `libc_psr.so` library contains optimized routines for specific processors; the appropriate version of the library is selected at runtime depending on the hardware the application is run on. For example, `memcpy` and `memset` both reside in `libc_psr.so` so that these routines exploit different architectural features on different processors.

7.3.2 Memory Management Libraries

Memory management is often a bottleneck for programs. The default memory allocation routines may not give the best performance for all applications. A variety of memory managment libraries are provided. `libfast`, discussed in Section 7.3.3, is a static library option for 32-bit single threaded code. An alternative that is available in a 64-bit version but is not thread-safe is `bsdmalloc` (link using the `-lbsdmalloc` compiler flag).

Several others are provided as part of Solaris. An alternative `malloc` optimized for multithreaded applications is the multithreaded `malloc` (link using the `-lmtmalloc` compiler flag). The `libumem` library (link with `-lumem`) provides an extensive debug library for investigating memory allocation problems.

There are two parts to `malloc` performance. The first part is the speed of the `malloc` and `free` operations. The second part is the performance given by the resulting layout of data in memory. `libfast` and `bsdmalloc` have very similar `malloc` routines which give data out in power-of-two-size chunks. Hence, these `malloc`s are typically quite quick to give out memory, but have a larger memory footprint. This larger memory footprint may cause data to become aligned on power-of-two boundaries in memory, which can lead to poor utilization of the caches and the Translation Lookaside Buffer (TLB).

In general, if an application relies heavily on `malloc`, it is probably worth benchmarking the application under a range of the available `malloc`s to determine which gives the best performance. Example 7.20 shows an example snippet of code that calls `malloc` and `free`.

Example 7.20 Code That Calls `malloc` and `free`

```
#include <stdlib.h>
#include "timing.h"

void main()
{
  int i;
  char* array;
  starttime();
  #pragma omp parallel for private(array)
  for (i=0; i<100000;i++)
  {
    array=(char*)malloc(1023);
    free(array);
  }
  endtime(100000);
}
```

Various memory management libraries are available, and each offers a different trade-off between performance, debug capability, memory footprint, and thread safety. Runtimes from the simple code shown in Example 7.20 using a number of different libraries are shown in Example 7.21.

The code in Example 7.20 also contains an OpenMP directive to enable it to be run as a multithreaded application. The number of threads that the application will use is controlled by the environment OMP_NUM_THREADS variable. I discuss OpenMP in greater detail in Section 12.8 of Chapter 12. The compiler will recognize the OpenMP directive when the -xopenmp flag is specified. Example 7.22 shows the results of running this parallel application on a Solaris 9 UltraSPARC IIICu-based

Example 7.21 Single-Threaded Performance of Various `malloc` and
`free` Implementations

```
% cc -O ex7.20.c; a.out
Time per iteration 217.01 ns
% cc -O ex7.20.c -lfast; a.out
Time per iteration 45.25 ns
% cc -O ex7.20.c -lbsdmalloc; a.out
Time per iteration 118.70 ns
% cc -O ex7.20.c -lumem; a.out
Time per iteration 444.38 ns
% cc -O ex7.20.c -lmtmalloc; a.out
Time per iteration 392.52 ns
```

machine utilizing one and two threads. Ideally, when two threads execute the code, it should take half the time it takes a single thread, so the time per iteration should halve. This demonstrates that for Solaris 9, the default `malloc` in `libc` takes about three times longer when several threads are contending for it. On the other hand, `mtmalloc` and `libumem` show some performance improvement with increasing the number of threads. It is worth observing that the presence of the `-mt` compiler flag on a Solaris 9 system causes the `malloc` and `free` calls to take longer.

Example 7.22 Performance of `malloc` and `free` When Run with
Multiple Threads

```
$ OMP_NUM_THREADS=1; export OMP_NUM_THREADS
$ cc -O -xopenmp -mt ex7.20.c; a.out
Time per iteration 363.19 ns
$ cc -O -xopenmp -mt ex7.20.c -lumem; a.out
Time per iteration 522.30 ns
$ cc -O -xopenmp -mt ex7.20.c -lmtmalloc; a.out
Time per iteration 593.85 ns
$ OMP_NUM_THREADS=2; export OMP_NUM_THREADS
$ cc -O -xopenmp -mt ex7.20.c; a.out
Time per iteration 1090.08 ns
$ cc -O -xopenmp -mt ex7.20.c -lumem; a.out
Time per iteration 408.13 ns
$ cc -O -xopenmp -mt ex7.20.c -lmtmalloc; a.out
Time per iteration 303.88 ns
```

On Solaris 10, all applications are potentially multithreaded by default, and there is no penalty for adding the `-mt` flag. The performance of the `mtmalloc` and `libumem` libraries has been improved for the single-threaded case, but the scaling is worse. Example 7.23 shows results from similar hardware running Solaris 10.

Example 7.23 `malloc` Performance on Solaris 10

```
$ cc -O ex7.20.c; a.out
Time per iteration 223.28 ns
$ cc -O ex7.20.c -lfast; a.out
Time per iteration 45.88 ns
$ cc -O ex7.20.c -lbsdmalloc; a.out
Time per iteration 120.47 ns
$ cc -O ex7.20.c -lumem; a.out
Time per iteration 301.13 ns
$ cc -O ex7.20.c -lmtmalloc; a.out
Time per iteration 333.14 ns
$ OMP_NUM_THREADS=1; export OMP_NUM_THREADS
$ cc -O -xopenmp -mt ex7.20.c; a.out
Time per iteration 222.11 ns
$ cc -O -xopenmp -mt ex7.20.c -lumem; a.out
Time per iteration 293.76 ns
$ cc -O -xopenmp -mt ex7.20.c -lmtmalloc; a.out
Time per iteration 336.22 ns
$ OMP_NUM_THREADS=2; export OMP_NUM_THREADS
$ cc -O -xopenmp -mt ex7.20.c; a.out
Time per iteration 1206.96 ns
$ cc -O -xopenmp -mt ex7.20.c -lumem; a.out
Time per iteration 243.44 ns
$ cc -O -xopenmp -mt ex7.20.c -lmtmalloc; a.out
Time per iteration 313.24 ns
```

7.3.3 libfast

A static library for SPARC processors, called `libfast`, ships with the compiler. It contains some optimized string library routines, and an optimized `malloc` routine. The `-lfast` compiler flag will cause `libfast` to be linked in. This flag should be presented after the source files so that the library be linked in appropriately (because the order of linkage is important).

There are several points to observe when using `libfast`. It is not thread-safe, so you should use the library only in single-threaded applications. It is a static library, which means the routines in the library are the ones that will be used—and the benefits of using the platform-tuned versions of the routines are unavailable. Lastly, the library is available only for 32-bit applications.

In general, it should not be necessary to use `libfast`. The processor-specific library routines are typically of comparable performance. However, on some occasions the `malloc` routines may be faster, because they are simpler implementations and do not have the overhead of being thread-safe.

7.3.4 The Performance Library

The performance library contains a large number of routines that are optimized for the various SPARC and x64 processors. Consequently, you can realize significant performance gains from using these routines. Use of these libraries can also reduce application development time because fewer lines of code need to be written. To link the performance library into the application use the compiler flag `-xlic_lib=sunperf`, as shown in Example 7.24.

Example 7.24 Linking the Performance Library into an Application

```
$ cc -fast -o matvec ex7.25.c -xlic_lib=sunperf
```

The matrix-vector multiply code shown in Example 7.25 demonstrates the benefits of using the routines provided by the performance library.

Example 7.25 Example Matrix-Vector Multiply Code

```
#include <sunperf.h>
#include "timing.h"

#define LENGTH 10000
static double vector[LENGTH], matrix[LENGTH][LENGTH], vector2[LENGTH];

void main()
{
  starttime();
  for (int i=0; i<LENGTH; i++)
  {
   vector2[i]=0;
   for (int j=0; j<LENGTH; j++)
    vector2[i]+=matrix[i][j]*vector[j];
  }
  endtime(LENGTH);

  starttime();
  dgemv('N',LENGTH,LENGTH,1.0,&matrix[0][0],LENGTH,vector,1,0.0,vector2,1);
  endtime(LENGTH);
}
```

Example 7.26 shows the output from this snippet of code. It is apparent that the performance library code is about four times faster than the manually coded version of the calculation.

Example 7.26 Timing of Matrix-Vector Multiply Code

```
$ matvec
Time per iteration 212962.98 ns
Time per iteration 57400.56 ns
```

The reason for the large difference in performance is that the compiler (in this case) has not performed a loop tiling optimization which could improve data reuse, and thereby improve performance. The performance library contains hand-optimized code, which will often outperform versions of the same algorithm coded in a high-level language.

7.3.5 STLport4

The default Standard Template Library (STL) for C++ is Rogue Wave. This library is used for Application Binary Interface (ABI) compatibility reasons. However, often the STLport version of the template library is faster.

The STLport library will be used if the `-library=stlport4` compiler option is used. It is important to note the following issues regarding STLport.

- Using STLport increases the degree of standards compliance expected by the compiler. As a consequence, code that previously compiled might need additional namespace specifiers to be compiled with STLport. In general, this requires simply specifying the `std::` namespace for various functions.
- It is not possible to use STLport if the code being developed is going to be linked with other libraries or applications that use the Rogue Wave library, or some other STL library.

Example 7.27 shows code that benchmarks the performance of the `push_back` method of the `vector` template.

Example 7.27 Benchmark for `push_back` Method

```
#include <vector>
#include "timing.h"

int main()
{
  int i;
  std::vector<int> vec;
  starttime();
  for (i=0; i<100000; i++)
  {
   vec.push_back(i);
  }
  endtime(100000);
}
```

You can compile the code to use the default (Rogue Wave) or STLport4 library, as shown in Example 7.28. The STLport4 library shows nearly double the performance of the Rogue Wave library for this particular method.

Example 7.28 Performance Difference of Two STL Implementations

```
% CC -O ex7.27.cpp; a.out
Time per iteration 144.18 ns
% CC -O ex7.27.cpp -library=stlport4; a.out
Time per iteration 79.45 ns
```

7.4 Library Calls

Often, a number of different library calls are required to achieve the same results. Consequently, it is important to consider what work needs to be done and the cost of the library call to do that work.

7.4.1 Library Routines for Timing

The most obvious place where timing is important is in timing the duration of function calls. Example 7.29 shows sample code that times a number of the alternative calls for obtaining timing information.

Example 7.29 Timing Various Calls

```
#include <stdio.h>
#include <sys/time.h>
#include <sys/timeb.h>
#include <sys/types.h>
#include <time.h>

#define RPT 1000000
#include "timing.h"

unsigned long long get_tick();

int main()
{
  long count;
  struct timeb tb;
  struct timeval tp;
  time_t tloc;

  starttime();
  for (count=0; count<RPT; count++) { ftime(&tb);}
  endtime(RPT);

  starttime();
  for (count=0; count<RPT; count++) { gettimeofday(&tp,(void*)0); }
  endtime(RPT);

  starttime();
  for (count=0; count<RPT; count++) { gethrtime(); }
  endtime(RPT);

  starttime();
  for (count=0; count<RPT; count++) { time(&tloc); }
  endtime(RPT);

  starttime();
  for (count=0; count<RPT; count++) { get_tick(); }
  endtime(RPT);

  return 0;
}
```

The call to `get_tick` is actually an inline template shown in Example 7.30, which reads the hardware tick counter on the SPARC processor.

Example 7.30 Inline Template for Reading Tick Counter

```
!
! unsigned long long get_tick();
!
        .inline get_tick,0
        rd      %tick,%o0
        .end
```

Example 7.31 shows the results from building and running the program.

Example 7.31 Results of Various Timing Functions

```
$ cc -O ex7.29.c ex7.30.il -o calls
$ calls
Time per iteration 958.56 ns
Time per iteration 188.84 ns
Time per iteration 145.93 ns
Time per iteration 992.62 ns
Time per iteration 10.71 ns
```

Inlined reading of the tick counter on the processor is the fastest way to obtain a count of elapsed time, but even that takes about 10ns. The other tested routines take significantly longer, but have return values that are related to the real time in seconds. In some cases, having the time returned in seconds might be worth the additional cost.

The use of these various timing routines demonstrates that it is important to pick the appropriate routine to use. Some routines will return more information than is necessary, and consequently they take a long time to return. Other routines may return less information, but still may not be the fastest.

Example 7.32 shows the timing harness (`timing.h`) used in this book. The harness uses the `gethrtime` call, which returns time in nanoseconds since some arbitrary point in the past. As demonstrated, it is a relatively quick call, so it should be sufficient for timing most tasks that run for a reasonable number of iterations. It is not a good timer for measuring the duration of a task that completes in a few cycles, however.

Example 7.32 Timing Test Harness: `timing.h`

```
#include <stdio.h>
#include <sys/time.h>

static double s_time;

void starttime()
{
  s_time=1.0*gethrtime();
}

void endtime(long its)
{
  double e_time=1.0*gethrtime();
  printf("Time per iteration %5.2f ns\n", (e_time-s_time)/(1.0*its));
  s_time=1.0*gethrtime();
}
```

7.4.2 Picking the Most Appropriate Library Routines

Timing is one consideration when selecting the most appropriate library calls to use. It's also possible that other calls exist which return a more complete set of results in a single call. For example, the Sun Math Library (-lsunmath) contains the `sincos()` function which returns both the sine and cosine of an angle in one call. This call takes the same time as the calculation of a single one of them. Example 7.33 shows code that demonstrates using this function.

Example 7.33 Code for Testing `sincos` Function

```
#include <math.h>
#include <sunmath.h>

#include "timing.h"
#define RPT 1000000

void main()
{
  double a=1.3;
  double b,c;

  starttime();
  for (int i=0; i<RPT; i++) { b=sin(a);c=cos(a);}
  endtime(RPT);

  starttime();
  for (int i=0; i<RPT; i++) {sincos(a,&b,&c);}
  endtime(RPT);
}
```

Example 7.34 shows the results of building and running this code. The sincos function is more than twice as fast as performing both the sin and cos functions. This is to be expected as the two values rely on similar calculations, and as such can be computed in parallel. It should be noted that this is not really a perfect test, because the trigonometric functions typically have some lookup tables, and these will get cached under this test harness because the test uses only a single input value and repeatedly computes a single result.

Example 7.34 Building and Running sincos Test Code

```
% cc -O ex7.33.c -lm -lsunmath
% a.out
Time per iteration 801.13 ns
Time per iteration 286.73 ns
```

So, it is important to know what calls are available in the various libraries available with the compiler. The Sun Math library (-lsunmath) is one that contains a number of useful routines for mathematical code.

7.4.3 SIMD Instructions and the Media Library

Single Instruction, Multiple Data (SIMD) instructions are single instructions that act on multiple items of data at the same time. On SPARC, these are called the Visual Instruction Set (VIS) instructions, and on x86 these are the SSE extensions. For example, a single 8-byte register could hold eight byte-size items of data or four short-size items of data. SIMD instructions can offer a performance advantage because of their ability to parallel-process multiple items of data. The problem people often face with SIMD instructions is the overhead of converting the data into the appropriate structure for the instructions to manipulate; the cost of the conversion can easily outweigh the benefit of being able to perform multiple operations at once.

On the UltraSPARC III/IV family of processors, the VIS instructions have another performance advantage. The instructions act on the floating-point registers so that the data can be prefetched into the prefetch cache on the processor, which eliminates the cost of fetching data from the second-level cache.

One way to use routines that have been optimized using SIMD instructions is to call MediaLib. This library is available for both SPARC and x86 processors and provides a wide range of routines that handle tasks commonly found when handling media (video, images, or audio) data, or other types of data (e.g., matrix manipulation). The MediaLib library is provided as part of Solaris 10, and is available as a download for previous Solaris versions.

7.4.4 Searching Arrays Using VIS Instructions

SIMD instructions can be useful in areas other than the manipulation of media-type data. An example of using VIS instructions might be to determine the length of a string. The code shown in Example 7.35 is string-length code written in C, together with a harness that checks for correctness of the result.

Example 7.35 Test Harness for `strlen` Code (`char_search.c`)

```
#include <stdio.h>
#include <string.h>
#include "timing.h"
#define RPT 30*1024
int vis_length(char *a);
int c_length(char * a)
{
  int len=0;
  while (*a!=0){a++;len++;}
  return len;
}

void main ()
{
  char string[1024*1024];
  int index;
  for (index=0;index<1024*1024;index++){string[index]='\0';}
  starttime();
  for (index=1;index<RPT;index++)
  {
    string[index-1]='a';
    string[index]='\0';
    if (c_length(string)!=index) {printf("Error at length %i\n",index);}
  }
  endtime(RPT);
  starttime();
  for (index=1;index<RPT;index++)
  {
    string[index-1]='a';
    string[index]='\0';
    if (vis_length(string)!=index)
      {printf("Error at length %i (%i)\n",index,vis_length(string));}
  }
  endtime(RPT);
  starttime();
  for (index=1;index<RPT;index++)
  {
    string[index-1]='a';
    string[index]='\0';
    if (strlen(string)!=index)
      {printf("Error at length %i (%i)\n",index,strlen(string));}
  }
  endtime(RPT);
}
```

A VIS implementation of the code is slightly more complex, and an example is shown in Example 7.36.

Example 7.36 VIS Implementation of `strlen` (`char_search.il`)

```
/* Routine vis_length(char * string); */
/* %o0 = address of string */

.inline vis_length,4
  and %o0,3,%o2        /* check for 4-byte aligned*/
  cmp %o2,%g0          /* aligned so go to VIS code*/
  be 1f
  clr %o3              /* clear counter */
                       /* next block to handle misaligned data */
2:
  ldub  [%o0],%o1      /* load byte */
  cmp %o1,%g0          /* check if zero */
  be 4f                /* found */
  add %o0,1,%o0        /* dealt with misaligned byte */
  sub %o2,1,%o2        /* count down misaligned bytes */
  cmp %o2,%g0
  bne 2b
  add %o3,1,%o3        /* compared first character */

1:
  fzero %f0            /* clear comparison word */
  ld [%o0],%f2         /* load 4 bytes */

3:
  add %o0,4,%o0        /* move pointer 4 bytes  */
  fexpand %f2,%f4      /* expand 4 bytes into 4 shorts */
  fcmpeq16 %f0,%f4,%o1 /* compare 4 shorts */
  lda [%o0]%asi,%f2    /* speculative load of 4 bytes */
  prefetch [%o0+256],0 /* Prefetch four lines ahead */
  cmp %o1,0            /* check result of compare */
  be,a 3b             /* branch if not found */
  add %o3,4,%o3        /* increment count by four; annulled if found*/

                       /* At this point %o1 contains a bit pattern */
                       /* indicating which byte was zero */
  mov 2,%o4            /* set up mask for 2nd bit */
  andcc %o1,12,%g0     /* check upper 2 bits of return value from compare*/
  bz,a 5f
  add %o3,2,%o3        /* add two if the upper half did not contain zero */
  mov 8,%o4            /* set mask for first bit in upper half */
5:
  andcc %o1,%o4,%g0    /* mask uppermost bit set */
  bz,a 4f             /* if it is not set skip increment */
  add %o3,1,%o3        /* upper bit set, so increment counter */
4:
  or %o3,%g0,%o0       /* Copy counter to output */
.end
```

The VIS algorithm is not the most efficient possible. In particular, there are many lost cycles in the innermost loop, which could be optimized out at the expense of an increase in code size and complexity.

Here are the steps in the algorithm.

1. Ensure that the string is aligned for 4-byte access. This is done by reading one character at a time until the alignment is correct.

2. Once the correct alignment is achieved, you can use VIS instructions in the inner loop to fetch the data from memory. One unfortunate complexity is that the VIS instruction set does not have instructions that perform a comparison of bytes. The workaround is to expand the bytes into short ints, and do a comparison on these instead.

3. Once the comparison determines that there is a zero byte in the four bytes that have been loaded, it is necessary to locate the particular byte and increment the string length accordingly. The approach used in this example is to check whether there is a zero in either of the two upper bits. If there is no zero there, the zero must be in the lower bits. Having determined which pair of bits contains the zero, the next step is to mask off the upper bit of the pair and see whether that is the zero byte.

Example 7.37 shows the runtime of this example. The VIS code is about twice as fast as the C-language version, but the version of `strlen` provided by the operating system is about 30% faster than that.

Example 7.37 Performance of VIS `strlen` Code

```
$ cc -O -xarch=v8plusa ex7.35.c ex7.36.il
$ a.out
Time per iteration 59983.66 ns
Time per iteration 34316.24 ns
Time per iteration 21401.47 ns
```

The purpose of the exercise was to show that it is possible to produce inline templates that use VIS instructions. It also demonstrates that even a relatively simple loop in C ends up with some initialization and cleanup code, which adds to the overhead of using VIS.

8

Performance Profiling Tools

8.1 Introduction

Several tools are available to determine where the time is being spent in an application. Traditional approachs include gprof, which gives time-based profiles, and tcov, which gives frequencies of execution. Also, the Performance Analyzer ships as part of the developer bundle. On Solaris 10 and later, there is the option of collecting data using dtrace.

8.2 The Sun Studio Performance Analyzer

The Sun Studio Performance Analyzer is probably the most useful tool available for detailed performance analysis. It is able to show at a source line level, or at a disassembly level, exactly what is happening to an application. It is a very powerful tool, and consequently it can appear a bit daunting to use. This objective of this section is to introduce much of the functionality of this tool.

The Performance Analyzer has two parts. The first part gathers data; this part is called collect. The second part allows the user to inspect the data, and in this part two frontends are available: analyzer, which is a GUI, and er_print, which is a command-line tool. Both frontends have the same functionality; this book has examples from both.

For time-based profiling, the program is inspected a number of times per second (100 by default), and every time the analyzer looks to see what instruction is about to be executed. It records this instruction and the program continues to execute. This gives a statistical sampling of where the time is being spent. Each sample also includes call stack information. At the end of the run, if an instruction has been sampled on many occasions, something may be slowing down the program at that point.

The data collected by profiling the application is stored in an *experiment repository*, which is a directory with an extension of .er. By default, this directory is called test.1.er and is placed in the current working directory. Subsequent experiments are stored as test.2.er, and so on. A command-line option is available for changing the name and location of the experiment.

The other way to profile a program is to look at where the program is generating the processor events (such as cache misses). This is available only on processors that have the appropriate hardware counter functionality. The hardware counters are incremented every time a selected processor event occurs. The analyzer sets the processor up so that after a large number of such events—say, 100,000—an interrupt will be generated. When the analyzer receives the interrupt it inspects the program and records the instruction that is just about to be executed, together with the call stack for the routine containing the instruction. This gives a statistical sample of where in the program the particular events occur. The sampling can also gather information about the memory location that the sampled memory operations are accessing, enabling the tool to build up a map of how the target application uses memory.

The two approaches are statistical in nature, so neither will be perfectly precise. For example, there may be a delay between an interrupt being generated and the tool being notified about it. However, for a sufficiently long run (normally a few minutes, depending on program size, CPU utilization, and number of threads), they will produce a statistical view of the application's performance, and with some interpretation it is possible to accurately identify bottlenecks in the code.

8.3 Collecting Profiles

The collect utility does the work of collecting the performance data. Example 8.1 shows how to run the collector on an application to gather performance data for that application. The application can be started under collect, or collect can be attached to a running process.

Example 8.1 Running the Collector on an Application

```
$ collect <flags> <application> <parameters>
$ collect -P <pid>
```

The most common way to invoke `collect` is to type `collect` and the command necessary to run the program. However, `collect` has some options that are very useful. Table 8.1 summarizes the common ones.

Table 8.1 Options for `collect`

Flag	Description

`-p on`
`-p hi`
`-p lo`
`-p <interval>`
	The `-p` flag specifies the interval between time-based samples. The `on` setting does profiling at the default rate of 100 samples per second, `hi` uses a faster rate (for shorter-running applications), and `lo` uses a lower rate (for longer-running applications, or applications with many threads). Higher sampling rates may cause an observable distortion in the runtime of the program. The default rate normally represents an appropriate setting.
	The default is appropriate for a runtime of up to half an hour, or up to eight concurrently active threads. You should use the `-p lo` option for higher numbers of concurrently active threads, longer runtimes, or when recording to remote disks. It is also possible to specify a numeric interval in milliseconds, if more control is needed.

`-h`
`<counter0>,<overflow>,`
`<counter1>,<overflow>`
`...`
	This specifies the performance counters to collect. The performance counter events and the number of events that can be counted simultaneously depend on the hardware platform. When `collect` is run without any parameters, it will report the counters available on the system.
	The overflow values represent the number of events which have to occur before a sample is taken. If the default values are to be used, it is still necessary to specify the comma (so the command line will end up with pairs of commas between each pair of counter names).

`-d <directory>`	The `-d` option specifies the directory location where the experiment is to be stored. The default is the current directory.
`-g <groupname.erg>`	The `-g` flag files the experiment as part of a group. The name of the group must end with the extension `.erg`. When a group is loaded in the Analyzer, all the experiments in the group will be loaded. This is a convenient way to combine multiple experiments, and is particularly useful when the group contains experiments with timing profiles, and other experiments with hardware counter profiles.
`-F on`	By default, any processes that are forked by the target process will not be profiled. The `-F on` option causes forked processes to also be profiled.

continues

Table 8.1 Options for `collect` (*continued*)

Flag	Description
`-H on`	The `-H on` option gathers data on memory allocation and deallocation, providing information about the amount of memory allocated and the size of any memory leaks.
`-M on`	The `-M on` option collects data on the MPI calls made by an MPI application—for example, the number of bytes sent or received. You can find more details on MPI programs in Section 12.6.3 of Chapter 12.
`-A copy`	The profile data recorded in the experiment is designed to be examined on the system where it was recorded. If the experiment is to be examined using another system, the `-A copy` option will archive the actual libraries used into the experiment so that disassembly will be available.
`-j on`	Profiles of Java applications can also be gathered. If the target application is a `.class` or `.jar` file the Java profiling is automatically enabled. The `-j on` option is necessary to enable Java profiling if the JVM is specified as the target application.

8.4 Compiling for the Performance Analyzer

To get the most information out of the Analyzer, you should compile the application with debug information (using the `-g` compiler flag for C and Fortran, and `-g0` for C++). However, Analyzer will still work on apps compiled without `-g`, and on apps compiled with other compilers such as `gcc`; but in these cases, features such as attributing time to lines of source code may not be available. I discuss the interaction between debug information and optimization further in Section 9.4.2 of Chapter 9.

8.5 Viewing Profiles Using the GUI

Once the profile has been collected, there are two ways to examine it: using the `analyzer` GUI, or using the `er_print` command line. The choice is a matter of personal preference and convenience. The GUI offers more information, often in a very readable format, so this is usually the best way to start. However, `er_print` can be scripted, and it works well over a plain `telnet` connection.

You start the GUI by typing `analyzer`, and optionally passing it the names of one or more experiments, or the name of a group of experiments. Example 8.2 shows these three options.

The initial window, shown in Figure 8.1, shows the time spent in the various routines in the program. The Analyzer shows the time that was spent exclusively in a

Example 8.2 Three Different Ways to Invoke the `analyzer` GUI

```
$ analyzer&
$ analyzer experimentfile.er&
$ analyzer experimentgroup.erg&
```

particular routine and the time that was spent inclusively in that routine. *Inclusive time* is time spent in that routine plus any other routines called. In this example, the `Evaluate` routine takes a little more than 40 seconds out of a total user time of nearly 140 seconds. This is the routine's *Exclusive* user time. The `Evaluate` routine calls other routines, and the total time spent in the `Evalulate` routine and the routines that it calls is a little more than 60 seconds. This is the routine's *Inclusive* user time.

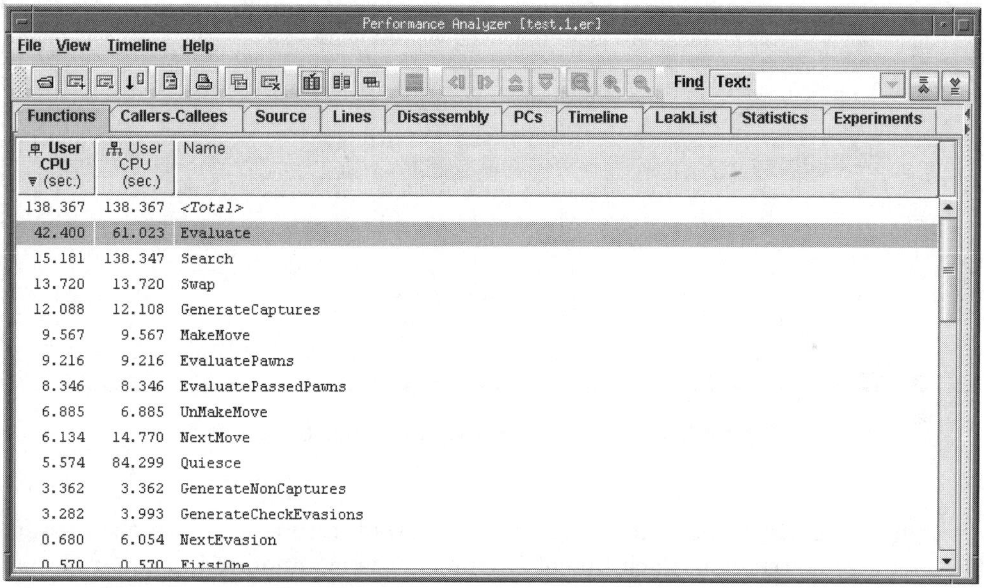

Figure 8.1 Profile of Application

In the default display, the Analyzer will normally only show the attribution of user time to functions. It is possible to display much more information than this; examples include system time, wall time, or if the heap tracing feature has been enabled, memory allocated. If an experiment containing performance counter data is loaded, that will also be displayed attributed to the listed routines.

From the function-level display, it is possible to drill down to the source and disassembly levels. The output is very similar to the profile output, in that each line of source or line of disassembly is annotated with either time or profiling events.

Figure 8.2 shows the Analyzer display of time spent on each line of source code. The line of source that contributes the most time is highlighted. In this instance, the highlighted line is showing that the `EvaluatePassedPawns` routine was called from this location, and that the routine accumulated 8 seconds of runtime from this call site. If a routine is called from multiple places in the code, each call site will show the amount of time the called routine accumulated from that particular site.

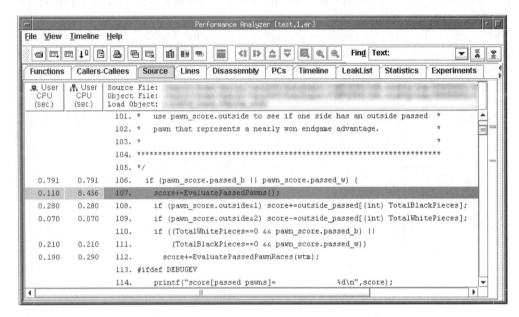

Figure 8.2 Time Spent on Various Lines of Source

Figure 8.3 is the disassembly view, which shows the time spent on each assembly language instruction. Each line of assembly code is annotated in square brackets with the line of source code that generated it. The source code timing information is generated by summing the times attributed to each line of assembly code from that source line.

8.6 Caller–Callee Information

Another useful screen is the caller–callee display. For the selected routine, it shows the functions that called it, and the functions that it called.

Figure 8.4 shows the caller–callee information for the `Evaluate` function. The `Evaluate` function is highlighted in the middle of the screen, and the two

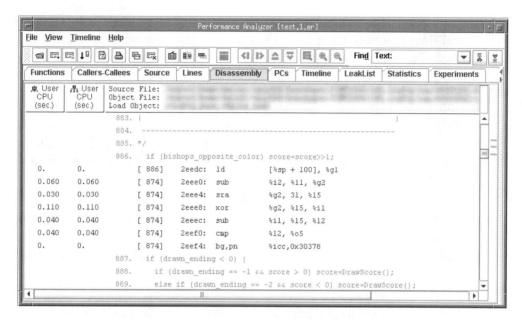

Figure 8.3 Time Spent on Disassembled Code

routines that call it are listed above it. The seven routines that `Evaluate` calls are listed below it.

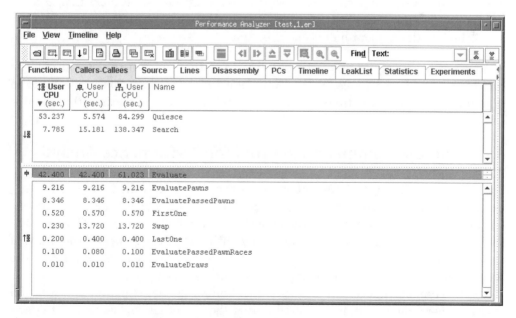

Figure 8.4 Caller–Callee Information

This display introduces the idea of *Attributed* time for a routine. This is defined as the total time that both the selected routine and the "attributed" routine are in the call stack. The easiest way to understand this is to use an example.

- The `Evaluate` routine has 61 seconds of Inclusive time. This is 61 seconds during which either the routine is executing, or a routine that it called is executing.

- The Attributed time for the `Quiesce` routine is just more than 53 seconds. This means that 53 of the 61 seconds of Inclusive user time for the selected `Evaluate` routine are due to it being called from `Quiesce`.

- Similarly, the `Search` routine gets the remaining 8 seconds or so of Attributed time, meaning that 8 seconds of the Inclusive time spent in `Evaluate` is due to it being called by the `Search` routine.

- The information indicates that it is most important to look at the calls of the `Evaluate` routine from the `Quiesce` routine, because this is where most of the time comes from.

- The Attributed time for the `Evaluate` routine is the same as its exclusive time—about 42 seconds.

- The difference between the Inclusive and Exclusive times indicates the amount of time spent calling other routines. For the `Evaluate` routine, this is 19 seconds. This time is spread among the called routines.

- The Attributed time for the `EvaluatePawns` routine is just more than 9 seconds, so of the 19 seconds of time that the `Evaluate` routine spends calling other routines, about half is spent in `EvaluatePawns`.

An alternative way to view Attributed time is that given a target routine, the sum of the Attributed times for the routines calling the target routine is equal to the sum of the Attributed times for the target routine and the routines that it calls.

8.7 Using the Command-Line Tool for Performance Analysis

There is also a command-line interface to the Analyzer, called `er_print`. `er_print` takes an experiment name as a parameter and can be run interactively, scripted, or invoked with flags that request a particular set of data. The flags follow the same syntax as the commands, only with a minus sign before the name of the command. Example 8.3 shows `er_print` being invoked to give out a list of the time spent in the top five functions from a single experiment.

The two commands used are `limit`, which limits the lines of output and is useful in cases where many routines are used during the run of an application, and `functions` (abbreviated to `func`), which reports the metric counts for all the routines.

Example 8.3 Command-Line Options to Get the Time Spent in Top Four Functions

```
$ er_print -limit 5 -func test.1.er
test.1.er: Experiment has warnings, see header for details
Functions sorted by metric: Exclusive User CPU Time

Excl.      Incl.      Name
User CPU   User CPU
  sec.       sec.
153.978    153.978    <Total>
 46.573     67.567    Evaluate
 17.112    153.948    Search
 15.281     15.281    Swap
 13.489     13.529    GenerateCaptures
```

er_print can also output the source (using the src command) and disassembly (using the dis command) for a given routine; like Analyzer, it outputs the entire source file that contains the routine, and not just the routine.

8.8 Interpreting Profiles

Section 8.3 discussed how the Analyzer works by noting the instruction is just about to be executed, rather than the instruction that is being executed. This leads to some complications in interpreting the results. The following heuristics outline how to interpret the results.

- For most instructions, the time will be attributed to the following instruction, because this is the instruction that was waiting to be executed.

- An exception to this is the case when the instruction is the target of a branch. In this case, the time will be due to a combination of the branch instruction and any instruction in the delay slot of the branch (for SPARC processors).

- If the time is caused by a trapping instruction, the time can be reported on the instruction that did the trapping, or on the next instruction. If the trapping instruction is reexecuted after the trap has completed, as is the case with Translation Lookaside Buffer (TLB) misses, the time will be reported on the instruction. If the instruction is emulated (as is the case for some floating-point operations), the time will be reported on the following instruction.

- If the event is due to a processor resource limit (such as the UltraSPARC IIICu's eight entry store queue filling up), the instruction that causes the time to be spent could be arbitrarily far away from the instruction that receives the recorded time.

This has ramifications for both the source-level view and the disassembly-level view. Because the time often gets attributed to the following instruction, the attribution of the time to exact lines of source may be incorrect (if the next line of disassembly happens to come from a different line of source). At the source-level view, this means the time spent in a loop is usually correct, but the time spent in any one line of source code within that loop may be misreported. Example 8.4 shows a short section of code to illustrate this.

Example 8.4 Code Snippet That Will Have Cache Misses

```
void main()
{
  int a[200000];
  int total=0;
  int count=0;
  for (int j=1; j<100000; j++)
  for (int i=0; i<100000; i++)
  {
    total += a[i+j];
    count+=2;
  }
  printf("%i %i\n",total,count);
}
```

Example 8.5 shows the disassembly profile of the inner loop. You can see that the time is attributed to the increment instruction at 0x10c04. The increment instruction is the target of the branch at 0x10c18, and this branch has a load instruction the delay slot. The load instruction is streaming through memory, and this is the actual instruction that is taking the time. The increment instruction just happens to be where that time is recorded, because it is the instruction executed immediately after the load.

Example 8.5 Integer Loop with Cache Misses

```
   Excl.
   User CPU
   sec.
...
                            7.    for (int i=0; i<100000; i++)
    0.              [ 7]    10bf8:  clr         %17
                            8.    {
                            9.      total += a[i+j];
...
## 37.196           [ 7]    10c04:  inc         %17
   3.723            [ 9]    10c08:  add         %o1, %i0, %o1
   7.615            [ 7]    10c0c:  inc         4, %i3
                    10.     count+=2;
   5.864            [10]    10c10:  inc         2, %o2
   8.706            [ 7]    10c14:  cmp         %17, %i4
   0.               [ 7]    10c18:  ble,a,pt    %icc,0x10c04
   0.               [ 9]    10c1c:  ld          [%i3], %i0
```

Example 8.6 shows the profile at the source level. The inc instruction at 0x10c04 was generated as part of line 7 of the source. Hence, it appears that the for statement, at line 7, is taking the majority of the time, as shown in Example 8.6. In this instance, the total time in the loop is correct, but the attribution of that time to lines of source is not perfect.

Example 8.6 Profile at the Source Level

```
Excl.
User CPU
sec.
                     1. void main()
     0.              2. {
                        <Function: main>
                     3.   int a[200000];
     0.              4.   int total=0;
     0.              5.   int count=0;
     0.              6.   for (int j=1; j<100000; j++)
##  53.517           7.   for (int i=0; i<100000; i++)
                     8.   {
     3.723           9.     total += a[i+j];
     5.864          10.     count+=2;
                    11.   }
     0.             12.   printf("%i %i\n",total,count);
                    13. }
```

8.9 Intepreting Profiles from UltraSPARC III/IV Processors

The UltraSPARC III/IV family of processors do not immediately handle interrupts if the processor is executing a floating-point instruction. Consequently, time that should have been reported on a floating-point instruction may be deferred until the first non-floating-point instruction. Example 8.7 shows a variant of the code from Example 8.4 which sums floating-point variables. In this example, roughly the same stall time is visible (it is slightly longer because the data is in double-precision numbers rather than integers). In this instance, the branch target, at 0x10c78, is a floating-point add instruction, so the time has been attributed to the first non-floating-point instruction (in this case, the increment at 0x10c7c).

Example 8.7 Floating-Point Loop with Cache Misses

```
Excl.
User CPU
sec.
...
     0.              [10]    10c78:  faddd       %f6, %f0, %f6
##  77.304          [ 8]    10c7c:  inc         %l6
     0.              [ 8]    10c80:  inc         8, %i0
                11.      count+=2;
     0.              [11]    10c84:  faddd       %f4, %f2, %f4
     6.885          [ 8]    10c88:  cmp         %l6, %l7
     0.              [ 8]    10c8c:  ble,a,pt    %icc,0x10c78
     0.              [10]    10c90:  ldd         [%i0], %f0
```

8.10 Profiling Using Performance Counters

You can also collect the profile using hardware performance counters. For example, you can profile the code using the data cache miss counter, and this profile will indicate where the data cache misses are occurring in the application. The number of counters that you can profile simultaneously is hardware-dependent. The UltraSPARC III/IV family can support a pair of performance counters; the Opteron processors can support four counters simultaneously.

It is possible to use performance counter profiling to confirm that the time in the profile shown in Example 8.7 is due to cache misses. In this case, the amount of memory being accessed is 8 bytes (for each `long long` or `double`) and 200,000 elements, for a total of ~1.6MB, which means that for this machine with an 8MB L2 cache, the data will be resident in the L2 cache. Therefore, the counter to profile is the `Re_DC_miss` counter, which counts the number of cycles spent waiting for data that is not in the first-level data cache. Example 8.8 shows the command line to collect this data.

Example 8.8 Command Line to Collect Where Cycles Are Spent on
Second-Level Cache Misses

```
$ collect -h Instr_cnt,,Re_DC_miss a.out
```

The command line uses the `-h` flag to pass information regarding which performance events to collect. Because the events of interest are available only on the second performance counter, the first performance counter is set to collect only the instruction count. Notice that the command line requires two commas (it is possible to tune the number of events that are observed before a sample is collected by putting the appropriate number in this gap). Example 8.9 shows the results of collecting this data.

The Analyzer has helpfully converted the number of stall cycles the counter reports into a number of seconds of stall time. Comparing the data presented in Example 8.8 and Example 8.9 it is apparent that the loop spends about half of the total excution time stalled on data cache misses.

Hardware counter-based profiling also suffers from the skid caused by the delay between when the event occurs and when `collect` receives the interrupt.

Example 8.9 Profiling Based on the Number of Cycles Spent Stalled
on L2 Cache Misses

```
    Excl.      Excl.
    Instr_cnt  Re_DC_miss
    Events     Events sec.
                                   <Function: main>
...
 0    0.            [10]    10c78:  faddd       %f6, %f0, %f6
## 70005454910  36.198      [ 8]   10c7c:  inc         %16
            0    0.         [ 8]   10c80:  inc         8, %i0
                      11.           count+=2;
            0    0.         [11]    10c84:  faddd       %f4, %f2, %f4
            0    8.412      [ 8]    10c88:  cmp         %16, %17
            0    0.         [ 8]    10c8c:  ble,a,pt    %icc,0x10c78
            0    0.         [10]    10c90:  ldd         [%i0], %f0
```

8.11 Interpreting Call Stacks

One of the complications with interpreting profiles is that time may be attributed
to the low-level routines that are called as part of a higher-level call. These low-
level routines appear to be the part of the code taking the time, but in fact they are
symptoms of a problem higher up the call stack. To identify this kind of problem it
is necessary to examine the call stack of the routine taking the time, and to determine which high-level routine is responsible. The code in Example 8.10 demonstrates calls to malloc, but only on closer examination of the call stack is it
apparent that malloc is causing a problem.

Example 8.10 Code for Testing malloc

```
#include <stdlib.h>
#include "timing.h"
#define RPT 10000000

void main()
{
  for (int i=0; i<RPT; i++) {malloc(48);}
}
```

Example 8.11 shows a profile of the application. The `malloc` routine has little user time directly attributed to it, and the `realfree` routine looks more responsible for the runtime.

Example 8.11 Compiling and Profiling `malloc` Testing Code

```
% cc -g -O ex8.10.c
% a.out
% collect a.out
Creating experiment database test.1.er ...
% er_print test.1.er
test.1.er: Experiment has warnings, see header for details
(er_print) func
Functions sorted by metric: Exclusive User CPU Time

Excl.     Incl.      Name
User CPU  User CPU
 sec.      sec.
6.535     6.535      <Total>
1.881     1.881      realfree
0.751     3.593      _malloc_unlocked
0.700     1.151      mutex_lock
0.660     6.004      malloc
0.530     6.535      main
...
```

By inspecting the Inclusive User time, it becomes apparent that `malloc` takes a considerable portion of the 6 seconds of runtime. It is necessary to examine the callstack to determine which routines call `malloc`, as shown in Example 8.12. The `main` routine calls `malloc`, and 6 seconds of the total runtime is attributed to `malloc` from this routine.

Example 8.12 Call Stack Showing Caller of `malloc` Routine

```
(er_print) csingle main
Callers and callees sorted by metric: Attributed User CPU Time

Attr.     Excl.     Incl.      Name
User CPU  User CPU  User CPU
 sec.      sec.      sec.
6.535     0.        6.535      _start
0.530     0.530     6.535      *main
6.004     0.660     6.004      malloc
```

If you modify the program to request 300 bytes on each iteration rather than 48 bytes, the memory footprint becomes about 3GB, and the program spends more time requesting memory from the system. The system time is not shown by default, and it is sometimes overlooked. You can use the metrics command in `er_print` to select which metrics are shown. Example 8.13 shows a profile of this revised program.

Example 8.13 Profile of Program Showing Substantial System Time

```
(er_print) metrics e.user:i.user:e.system
current: e.user:i.user:e.system:name
(er_print) limit 5
(er_print) func
Functions sorted by metric: Exclusive User CPU Time

Excl.       Incl.       Excl.       Name
User CPU    User CPU    Sys. CPU
  sec.        sec.        sec.
10.337      10.337      135.135     <Total>
 4.153       4.153        0.020     realfree
 1.711       1.711      125.378     _brk_unlocked
 1.031       2.982        9.727     _morecore
 0.881      10.307        0.        malloc
```

The same program produces a different profile on Solaris 10, as shown in Example 8.14. The system time is attributed to the take_deferred_signal routine.

Example 8.14 Profile of Code on Solaris 10

```
(er_print) metrics e.user:i.user:e.system
Current metrics: e.user:i.user:e.system:name
Current Sort Metric: Exclusive User CPU Time ( e.user )
(er_print) limit 5
(er_print) func
Functions sorted by metric: Exclusive User CPU Time

Excl.       Incl.       Excl.       Name
User CPU    User CPU    Sys. CPU
  sec.        sec.        sec.
6.004       6.004       24.177      <Total>
5.384       5.384       24.167      take_deferred_signal
0.280       5.824        0.         malloc
0.150       0.150        0.         lmutex_lock
0.150       5.974        0.010      malloc
```

The take_deferred_signal routine is called when exiting a critical region. Critical regions protect tasks such allocating memory, or aquiring mutex locks. During the critical region, signals are deferred. When the processor completes the critical code, all the signals that have been received while it was in the critical region are handled. Consequently, all the time that is recorded against the take_deferred_signal routine is actually time that was spent performing the critical task. It is necessary to examine the call stack to determine what routine is responsible for the critical region. Example 8.15 shows the process of determining that the calls to malloc are responsible for the time in the critical region. The csingle command prints out the routines that call or are called by a given routine. The caller of the take_deferred_signal routine is do_exit_critical, and this routine is called by malloc.

Example 8.15 Examing the Call Stack for `take_deferred_signal`

```
(er_print) csingle take_deferred_signal
Callers and callees sorted by metric: Attributed User CPU Time

Attr.      Excl.      Incl.      Attr.      Excl.      Name
User CPU   User CPU   User CPU   Sys. CPU   Sys. CPU
  sec.       sec.       sec.       sec.       sec.
5.384      0.         5.384      24.167     0.         do_exit_critical
5.384      5.384      5.384      24.167     24.167     *take_deferred_signal

(er_print) csingle do_exit_critical
Callers and callees sorted by metric: Attributed User CPU Time

Attr.      Excl.      Incl.      Attr.      Excl.      Name
User CPU   User CPU   User CPU   Sys. CPU   Sys. CPU
  sec.       sec.       sec.       sec.       sec.
5.384      0.280      5.824      24.167     0.         malloc
0.         0.         5.384      0.         0.         *do_exit_critical
5.384      5.384      5.384      24.167     24.167     take_deferred_signal
```

8.12 Generating Mapfiles

Section 5.7.3 of Chapter 5 discussed how to use mapfiles to improve the code layout for an application in memory. The Analyzer can generate a mapfile using the profile of an application. The optimal mapfile sorts the routines by the amount of time spent in them. That way, the hot routines are grouped together, and the cold routines are separated out. This improves the memory locality of the code and requires fewer instruction TLB entries to map the hot regions of the application. However, using mapfiles only determines the order in which the routines are placed in the binary. It does not change the order of instructions within those routines.

The option to generate a mapfile is available in both the command line and the GUI. To use this feature, it is necessary to specify the object (application or library) for which the mapfile should be generated. In the GUI, the option to generate the mapfile displays a dialog box that lists all the available objects so that the appropriate object can be selected. In `er_print`, it is necessary to use the `-objects` command-line option to display a list of objects (the application or libraries used), and then request a mapfile for that object. Example 8.16 shows an example where the executable for which the mapfile is generated is called `a.out`.

Example 8.16 Generating a Mapfile Using `er_print`

```
$ er_print -objects test.1.er
test.1.er: Experiment has warnings, see header for details
 <Unknown> (<Unknown>)
 <a.out> (/export/home/a.out)
...
$ er_print -mapfile a.out test.1.er
```

8.13 Generating Reports on Performance Using spot

The spot tool is a free add-on to Sun Studio 11 and later compilers, and you can download it from http://cooltools.sunsource.net/spot/. The Sun Studio 11 version is available only for SPARC processors; the Sun Studio 12 version is also available for x86 processors. The tool attempts to make the collection of performance data as simple and complete as possible. Example 8.17 shows the command lines for spot. The tool can be given either the entire run command for an application, or attach to an already running process (it is not recommended that you do this on a production application).

Example 8.17 Command Lines for spot

```
$ spot [-X] <app> <params>
$ spot [-X] -P <pid>
```

To generate a report spot uses multiple probes. The -X flag tells spot to use an extended set of probes. Depending on how spot is invoked, the application will be run multiple times (each time under a different probe), or if the tool is given a PID, each probe will be attached for a short period of time to sample the PID's behavior. The data gathered by spot depends on what is available, and whether the user requested the extended set of probes. The list of information types is as follows.

- Metadata, such as the date and time the report was generated, the host that the report was generated on, the build flags for the application, and the libraries linked into the application. This information is often useful in referring back to old reports.

- Performance counter metrics indicating what processor events may be responsible for contributing to the runtime of the application. I discuss performance counters in detail in Chapter 10.

- The application profile under the performance counters that contributes most events, if the extended report is requested, and if the hardware supports it. This profile indicates the points in the code where the events occur.

- The frequency of system traps over the run of the application, as well as the memory bandwidth consumed (on a system-wide basis) during the run of the application, if the hardware supports it, and if an extended report is requested.

- Execution counts at both the function and individual instruction levels, if the code has been compiled on a SPARC-based system using the Sun Studio 11 or later compiler with the -xbinopt=prepare compiler option.

▪ A time-based profile of the application. This, like the hardware counter profile, is gathered using the Performance Analyzer. For the parts of the report
containing profile data, the Analyzer experiment is converted into a set of
hyperlinked Web pages. The hyperlinks allow rapid navigation to branch targets, or from disassembly code to the line of source that generated it.

Figure 8.5 shows an example of a profile containing timing and instruction count
information. This shows a loop that is entered about 2 million times; the trip count
for the loop is about 30 billion, so on average the loop is iterated 15,000 times every
time it is entered. The hyperlinks in the figure would go back to line 92 in the source
code (shown at the top of the figure), the branch target at the top of the loop, or the
branch target out of the loop. The timing information for the loop is also shown, indicating that two of the load statements are incurring cache misses.

```
                                              92.     if (lines[i].line == line)
       0.          0        1889891       0     [ 92]    149d54:  clr       %o7
##   66.246        0      30472400400      0     [ 92]    149d58:  add       %o7, %o4, %l0
##    0.250        0      30472400400      0     [ 92]    149d5c:  prefetch  [%l0 + 128], #n_reads
##    6.785        0      30472400400      0     [ 92]    149d60:  ld        [%o7 + %o4], %o5
##  367.367        0      30472400400      0     [ 92]    149d64:  cmp       %o5, %i1
##    0.           0      30472400400      0     [ 92]    149d68:  be,pn     %icc, 0x149ec0
##    0.           0      30472400400      0     [ 92]    149d6c:  inc       %o2
##    0.           0      30471808695      0     [ 92]    149d70:  ld        [%i0 + 12], %l6
##    0.250        0      30471808695      0     [ 92]    149d74:  ld        [%i0 + 16], %l5
##  110.377       0      30471808695      0     [ 92]    149d78:  sub       %l5, %l6, %l2
##    2.552        0      30471808695      0     [ 92]    149d7c:  sra       %l2, 31, %l4
##   43.991       0      30471808695      0     [ 92]    149d80:  and       %l4, 15, %l3
##   42.440       0      30471808695      0     [ 92]    149d84:  add       %l2, %l3, %o1
##    2.382        0      30471808695      0     [ 92]    149d88:  sra       %o1, 4, %l1
##   59.382       0      30471808695      0     [ 92]    149d8c:  cmp       %o2, %l1
##    0.           0      30471808695      0     [ 92]    149d90:  bne,pt    %icc, 0x149d58
##    0.010        0      30471808695      0     [ 92]    149d94:  sll       %o2, 4, %o7
                                              93.     return;
```

Figure 8.5 Example of Profile Output from `spot`

The `BIT` tool distributed with `spot` provides the instruction count data. Once `BIT`
is installed `collect` is able to collect instruction count data using the `-c` on flag. It
is also possible to use `BIT` stand-alone to generate various reports. One report that
may be of interest is a report on the coverage of a program (how much of the program
is executed). As an example, consider the code shown in Example 8.18.

Example 8.18 Example Code for Coverage Using `BIT`

```
% more ex8.18.c
int func1(int i)
{
  return i++;
}
```

Example 8.18 Example Code for Coverage Using BIT (*continued*)

```
int func2(int i)
{
  return i--;
}

void main()
{
  int i=1;
  if (i==0) {func1(i);} else {func2(i);}
}
```

Example 8.19 shows the process of generating a report on the code coverage. The steps to using BIT to gather coverage information are first to build the binary with the compiler flag -xbinopt=prepare. Next, BIT needs to generate an instrumented version of the binary, which can then be run. The instrumented version of the binary will run several times slower than the original code. Finally, BIT can be invoked to generate the coverage report, and to generate an experiment that can be loaded into the Performance Analyzer. In this example, two of the three routines are executed, so 67% of the functions are covered.

Example 8.19 Using BIT to Generate a Report on Code Coverage

```
% cc -O -xbinopt=prepare -o cover ex8.18.c
% bit instrument cover
% cover.instr
% bit coverage cover
Creating experiment database test.1.er ...
BIT Code Coverage
Total Functions: 3
Covered Functions: 2
Function Coverage: 66.7%
Total Basic Blocks: 3
Covered Basic Blocks: 2
Basic Block Coverage: 66.7%
Total Basic Block Executions: 2
Average Executions per Basic Block: 0.67
Total Instructions: 8
Covered Instructions: 6
Instruction Coverage: 75.0%
Total Instruction Executions: 6
Average Executions per Instruction: 0.75
```

You can load the experiment into the Performance Analyzer, and it will give more detailed information on coverage, as well as give information on "uncoverage". The idea of uncoverage is to highlight the routines that are not covered by the current tests, but that would contribute the greatest increase in coverage if they were added to the test suite. Example 8.20 shows an example report showing both coverage and uncoverage for the sample program. As might be expected in this simple test case, func1 is not covered, and consequently it would contribute the most to coverage if it were included in the tests.

Example 8.20 Report Showing Coverage and Uncoverage Results from BIT

```
Excl. Bit   Excl. Bit Inst   Name
Block       Uncoverage
Covered
2           8                <Total>
1           0                func2
1           0                main
0           8                func1
```

8.14 Profiling Memory Access Patterns

Data space profiling, or *dprofiling*, is an innovative technique for looking at how time is attributed to memory locations and even structures within a program. In the Sun Studio 11 product, it is only supported for the C language.

The basic premise of dprofiling is that every time there is an event, such as a cache miss, it can be attributed to a load or store; then, information about the operation is recorded. Each load or store can be mapped back to a data structure member in the source code on which it was operating. The event also records both the physical and virtual addresses of the location in memory that was being accessed. The Analyzer can construct a map of the hot locations in memory, or even hot cache lines.

To obtain the best results from dprofiling it is necessary to build the application with the compiler flag -xhwcprof. This has two effects. First, it provides the Analyzer with annotations that indicate the names of variables and structure members that correspond to load and store instructions. Second, it changes the generated code so that it is easier for the Analyzer to determine which load or store caused a particular event. This means the code may have slightly different performance characteristics from the optimized build, but should maintain the same memory access patterns.

The code in Example 8.21 incurs cache misses on access to one member of a data structure. The code strides over a 16MB array in 64KB chunks, so not only does each access incur a data cache miss, but also each access will map to the same virtual line in the data cache.

The code can be compiled and run under collect, as shown in Example 8.22. The command line to collect requests that time profile (-p on) and performance counter (-h) data be collected for the application. The plus sign in front of the data cache read miss counter indicates that the Analyzer should attempt to correctly attribute the read miss event to the load that caused it.

Example 8.21 Code Showing Data Cache Misses

```
typedef struct a
{
  double fp;
  long long i;
} structure ;   /* Structure takes 16 bytes*/

struct a array[1024*1024];  /* array takes 16MB */
void main()
{
  for (int j=0; j<100000; j++)
  for (int i=0;i<1024*1024-16*1024; i+=4*1024)
  {
    array[i].fp += array[i+4*1024].fp + array[i+8*1024].fp
               + array[i+12*1024].fp + array[16*1024].fp;
  }
}
```

Example 8.22 Compiling and Running under `collect`

```
$ cc -O -xhwcprof -g -xdebugformat=dwarf ex8.21.c
$ collect -p on -h Instr_cnt,,+DC_rd_miss a.out
```

Having collected the experiment, it can be analyzed using er_print, as shown in Example 8.23.

Example 8.23 Disassembly under dprofile

```
$ er_print test.1.er
test.1.er: Experiment has warnings, see header for details
(er_print) metrics e.user:e.DC_rd_miss
current: e.user:e.DC_rd_miss:name
(er_print) func
Functions sorted by metric: Exclusive User CPU Time

Excl.      Excl.        Name
User CPU   DC_rd_miss
 sec.      Events
6.164      134568092    <Total>
6.164      134000532    main
0.               0      _start
0.          567560      collector_final_counters

(er_print) dis main
. . .
  Excl.      Excl.
  User CPU   DC_rd_miss
   sec.      Events
. . .
```

continues

Example 8.23 Disassembly under dprofile (*continued*)

```
   0.              0 [19] 10c08*  <branch target>          <===----<<<
## 0.050   36000170 [19] 10c08:  ldd     [%14], %f2       {structure:a -}.{double fp}
   1.491          0 [19] 10c0c:  sethi   %hi(0x60c00), %i0
   0.             0 [16] 10c10:  sethi   %hi(0x1000), %o5
## 0.040   38000150 [19] 10c14:  ldd     [%13], %f0       {structure:a -}.{double fp}
   0.180          0 [16] 10c18:  sethi   %hi(0x10000), %17
   0.             0 [16] 10c1c:  add     %15, %o5, %15
## 2.912   21000082 [19] 10c20:  ldd     [%12], %f4       {structure:a -}.{double fp}
   0.560          0 [16] 10c24:  add     %14, %17, %14
   0.             0 [16] 10c28:  add     %13, %17, %13
   0.020   15000058 [19] 10c2c:  ldd     [%i0 + 496], %f8 {structure:a -}.{double fp}
   0.330          0 [16] 10c30:  cmp     %15, %11
   0.             0 [19] 10c34:  faddd   %f2, %f0, %f6
   0.        24000072 [19] 10c38:  ldd     [%16], %f14      {structure:a -}.{double fp}
   0.010          0 [19] 10c3c:  faddd   %f6, %f4, %f10
   0.410          0 [19] 10c40:  faddd   %f10, %f8, %f12
   0.             0 [19] 10c44:  faddd   %f14, %f12, %f16
   0.140          0 [19] 10c48:  std     %f16, [%16]      {structure:a -}.{double fp}
   0.010          0 [16] 10c4c:  add     %16, %17, %16
   0.             0 [14] 10c50:  nop
   0.             0 [16] 10c54:  ble,pt  %icc,0x10c08
   0.010          0 [16] 10c58:  add     %12, %17, %12
...
```

There are three important points to observe.

- The branch target at `0x10c08` is explicitly identified by a branch target marker.

- The loads and stores are annotated with the name of the structure and member that they are using.

- The `DC_rd_miss` events (data cache read miss) have been attributed to the correct load instruction that caused them. This is different from the non-dprofile view, which would not attempt to correctly attribute the events.

Example 8.24 shows the data objects view, in which the processor events are attributed to the data objects that are present in the program.

Example 8.24 Data Objects View of Profile

```
(er_print) data_objects
Dataobjects sorted by metric: DC_rd_miss

Data.       Name
DC_rd_miss
Events
134568092   <Total>
134000532   {structure:a -}
134000532   {structure:a -}.{double fp}
   567560   (Backtracking was prevented by a jump or call instruction)
   567560   <Unknown>
```

In this view, it is apparent that most of the data cache miss events can be attributed to the a structure, and within that structure they are all attributed to the fp member.

Using dprofile, it is possible to extract further information from the experiment. In this simple example, all the array accesses map to the same cache line, but you can confirm that using dprofile.

When an application is dprofiled, the physical and virtual addresses of loads and stores are recorded (if that information is still available when the sample is taken). Using this recorded information, the cache line in the data cache that a memory reference referred to can be derived. The data cache on the UltraSPARC IIICu is 64KB in size and virtually indexed, so the variable VADDR needs to be examined (the second-level cache is physically indexed, so the appropriate variable in that case is PADDR). Each cache line is 32 bytes in size, so the lower 5 bits can be disregarded, leaving an index into the cache. The data cache is 64KB in size, so there are 2048 32-byte lines. The cache is also four-way set associative; consequently, these 2048 lines are split into 512 sets of four lines. Hence, the formula for deriving the set that was used by a particular memory operation is:

```
Set = (VADDR>>5) && 511
```

You can set up tab containing this formula in the Analyzer using the Tabs page in the Set Format dialog box, as shown in Figure 8.6.

Figure 8.6 Adding Tab Showing Data Cache Lines

Figure 8.7 shows the newly constructed tab with a text view.

It is readily apparent that all the cache misses map to the same line. If this were a real program, the next step would be to examine those misses and see where they were occurring in the source. You can do this by filtering the results. Figure 8.8 shows the new filter dialog box that can be accessed from the Filter menu option.

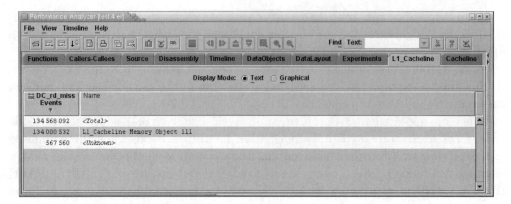

Figure 8.7 Data Cache Misses Filtered by Cache Line

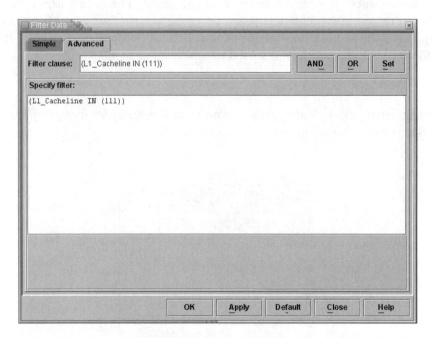

Figure 8.8 Adding Data Cache Miss Event Filter for Hottest Cache Line

In this case, the data is being filtered so that only events which map onto cache line 1 are displayed. Figure 8.9 shows the effect of this filtering on the display of events on the disassembled code.

As you might expect, all the accesses to this one set of cache lines come from the load statements in the benchmark.

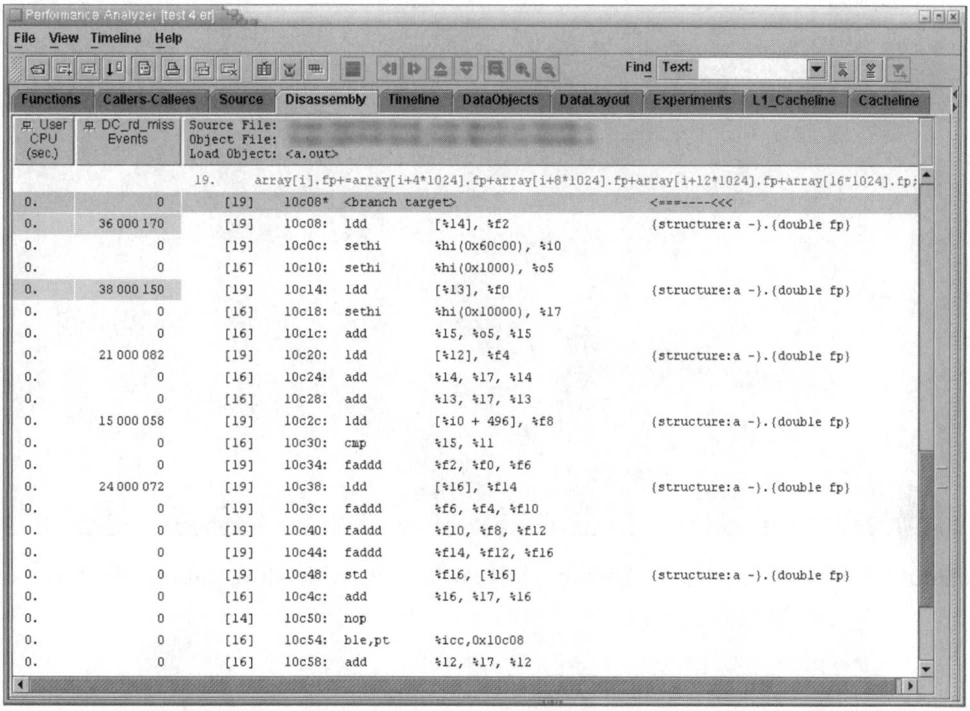

Figure 8.9 Dissassembly Showing Only the Filtered Data Cache Miss Events

You can obtain a slightly different view of the data by creating a tab that tracks the misses per virtually addressed cache line. This will show the virtual memory address that caused the most cache misses. For this case, it is necessary to use the following formula:

```
cache line = VADDR>>5
```

Figure 8.10 shows the resulting tab in graphical format.

This shows that one particular memory location is suffering most of the cache misses. Using filtering, it is possible to filter down to just these misses, and then to examine the disassembly to find out which load instructions are contributing the misses. Figure 8.11 shows the Filter Data dialog box, which selects only the data cache miss events that have this particular virtual address.

Figure 8.12 shows the results of doing this.

As you might expect, the load with the highest number of misses corresponds to the load of `array[16*1024].fp`, which is performed most frequently in the code. You can determine this by the fact that the load is indexed off `%i0`, which is

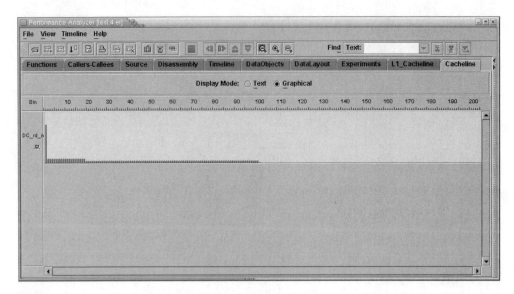

Figure 8.10 Filtered Results Showing Virtual Address with Most Data Cache Misses

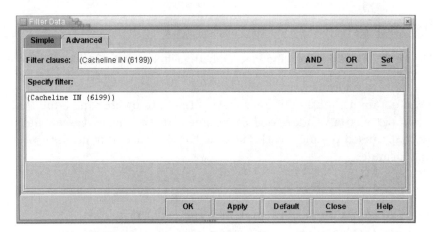

Figure 8.11 Filtering on Just the Hot Cache Line

a constant within the loop, and the reference to `array[16*1024].fp` is the only loop-invariant floating-point load that the source contains.

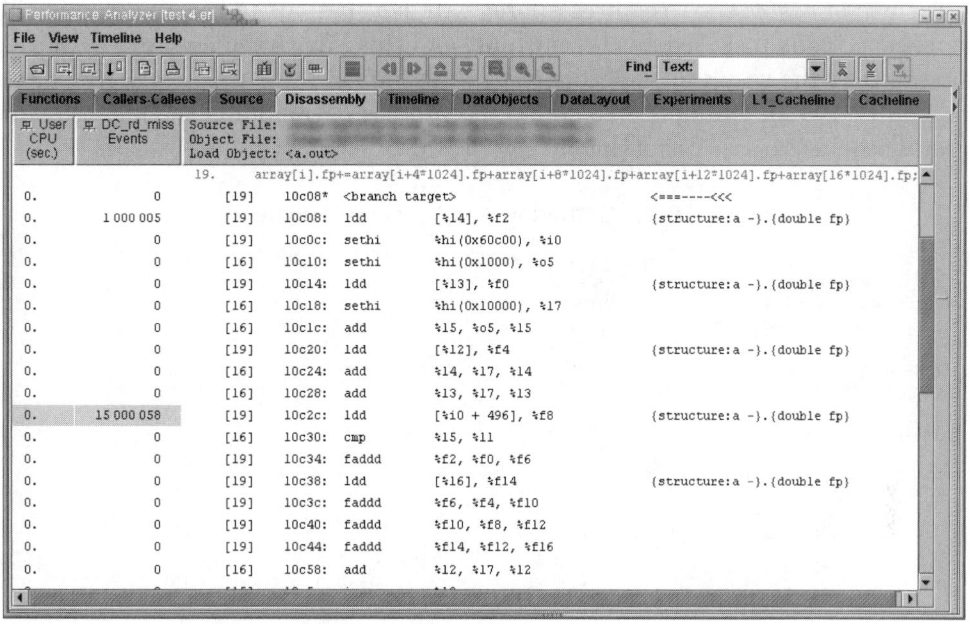

Figure 8.12 Filtered Data Showing Load Instruction

8.15 er_kernel

er_kernel is shipped as part of the Analyzer. It uses dtrace on Solaris 10 to profile an application's kernel activity. The code in Example 8.25 repeatedly calls mmap and munmap. These calls trap into the kernel to do the necessary work.

Example 8.25 Code That Calls mmap and munmap

```
#include <stdio.h>
#include <stdlib.h>
#include <sys/mman.h>
#include <sys/types.h>
#include <sys/stat.h>
#include <fcntl.h>

void main()
{
  int i,file;
  void *address;
  file = open("./test.tst", O_RDWR);

  for (i=0; i<10000000; i++)
  {
    address = mmap((caddr_t)0,1024*1024,(PROT_READ|PROT_WRITE),
              MAP_PRIVATE,file,0);
    munmap (address,1024*1024);
  }
}
```

The use of `er_kernel` requires appropriate permissions to run `dtrace`; in this instance, `sudo` is installed on the machine, and this allows the `er_kernel` to run. You can read the resulting experiment by the command-line tool `er_print`, or via the Analyzer GUI. Example 8.26 shows the process of compiling the test code and creating the `er_kernel` experiment.

Example 8.26 Gathering an `er_kernel` Experiment

```
$ cc -O ex8.25.c
$ sudo er_kernel a.out
Creating experiment database ktest.1.er ...
er_kernel: dtrace device opened
Warning: Clock profiling timer reset from 10.007 millisec. to 10.101 millisec. as
required by profiling driver

Creating experiment database ktest.1.er ...
    run until load completes or ctrl-C
er_kernel: ... begin recording kernel profile data -- pid = 27591

    sleeping 3 secs., and then running load `a.out'
    load terminated, sleeping 3 secs.

er_kernel: ... end recording kernel profile data; archiving modules
$
```

Example 8.27 shows an example of using `er_print` to analyze an `er_kernel` experiment.

Example 8.27 Using `er_print` to Examine an `er_kernel` Experiment

```
$ er_print /tmp/ktest.6.er
(er_print) limit 10
(er_print) func
Functions sorted by metric: Exclusive KCPU Cycles

Excl. KCPU  Incl. KCPU  Name
Cycles      Cycles
  sec.        sec.
45.612      45.612      <Total>
27.199      27.199      <IDLE>
 6.254       6.254      <USER_MODE>
 5.054       5.054      utl0
 1.971       2.252      syscall_mstate
 1.841       3.623      post_syscall
 1.281       6.565      syscall_trap32
 0.500       0.500      clear_stale_fd
 0.300       0.320      munmap
 0.280       0.280      gethrtime_unscaled

(er_print) csingle syscall_trap32
Callers and callees sorted by metric: Attributed KCPU Cycles
```

Example 8.27 Using `er_print` to Examine an `er_kernel` Experiment (*continued*)

```
Attr. KCPU   Excl. KCPU   Incl. KCPU   Name
Cycles       Cycles       Cycles
sec.         sec.         sec.
6.565        45.612       45.612       <Total>
1.281        1.281        6.565        *syscall_trap32
3.552        1.841        3.623        post_syscall
0.921        1.971        2.252        syscall_mstate
0.310        0.250        0.380        smmap32
0.280        0.300        0.320        munmap
0.170        0.           0.170        umount2
0.020        0.           0.020        syslwp_park
0.010        0.           0.010        close
0.010        0.           0.010        pollsys
0.010        0.           0.010        syslwp_create
```

The profile shows a substantial amount of idle time, caused by the fact that it was collected on a two-CPU system, and one of the CPUs was idle during data collection. Because `er_kernel` only has insight into kernel mode activity, the time spent in user mode cannot be appropriately attributed. It is possible to combine `collect` and `er_kernel` to gather both user and kernel mode profiles.

The `mmap` and `munmap` calls come into the kernel through `syscall_trap32`. Example 8.27 shows the callstack of this function. It is possible to obtain the disassembly code for the kernel routines. Example 8.28 shows the code for the `gethrtime_unscaled` routine, which contributes only 0.28 seconds to the total time.

Example 8.28 Disassembly of `gethrtime_unscaled` from `er_print`

```
(er_print) dis gethrtime_unscaled
Source file: (unknown)
Object file: ktest.1.er/archives/SUNW,UltraSPARC III+
Load Object: ktest.1.er/archives/SUNW,UltraSPARC III+

   Excl. KCPU   Incl. KCPU
   Cycles       Cycles
   sec.         sec.
                              <Function: gethrtime_unscaled>
## 0.140        0.140         [?]    febc:  rd      %asr24, %g1
   0.040        0.040         [?]    fec0:  retl
   0.100        0.100         [?]    fec4:  mov     %g1, %o0
```

8.16 Tail-Call Optimization and Debug

At levels of optimization below –xO4, the compiler may produce different code when the application is compiled with debug information. The difference in the code is that under debug flags, the tail-call optimization is not performed.

The code shown in Example 8.29 demonstrates an opportunity for tail-call optimization in the routine calc2.

Example 8.29 Program with Opportunity for Tail-Call Optimization

```
int calc1(int i) { return i*2;}

int calc2(int i) { return calc1(i+1); }

int calc3(int i) { return calc1(i)+1; }

void main()
{
  int i,j;
  for (j=0; j<1000; j++)
    for (i=0; i<100000; i++)
    {
      if (calc2(i)<calc3(i))
      { calc1(j);} else {calc2(j);}
    }
}
```

The return value for the calc2 routine is actually calculated by the calc1 routine. The tail-call optimization is evident in that rather than having the call to the calc1 routine return to the calc2 routine, the call returns directly to the caller of calc2 (in this case, the main routine). The result of this optimization is that it looks as though calc1 is called directly from main, when it is actually called from calc2, and this can be seen in the caller–callee data for the main routine from the code compiled without debug information shown in Example 8.30. In this call stack, main appears to call three routines directly, even though it is apparent from the source that main directly calls only callc2 and calc3.

Example 8.30 Caller–Callee Data for main with Tail-Call Optimization Enabled

```
Attr.       Excl.      Incl.      Name
User CPU    User CPU   User CPU
 sec.        sec.       sec.
3.062       0.         3.212      _start
0.821       0.821      3.062      *main
1.331       1.501      1.501      calc1
0.560       0.390      0.560      calc3
0.350       0.500      0.500      calc2
```

Example 8.31 shows the caller–callee data for the main routine when the tail-call optimization is disabled (due to debug information being generated). With the tail-call optimization disabled it is clear that main calls only calc2 and calc3.

Example 8.31 Caller–Callee Data for `main` without Tail-Call Optimization

```
Attr.      Excl.      Incl.      Name
User CPU   User CPU   User CPU
sec.       sec.       sec.
3.292      0.         3.292      _start
0.781      0.781      3.292      *main
1.631      1.261      1.631      calc2
0.881      0.731      0.881      calc3
```

8.17 Gathering Profile Information Using gprof

The traditional UNIX tool for gathering profile information is gprof. The advantage of this tool is that it provides information on both the time spent in a routine and the number of times the routine was called. However, gprof has significant disadvantages.

- The application must be recompiled with the -xpg flag to enable gprof to gather the data. Unfortunately, this recompilation means that the profiled binary may not have the same optimizations and profile as the original binary.

- The profiling adds code to the executable, and depending on the characteristics of the application, significant time may be spent in this code.

- gprof uses a heuristic to distribute time spent in a routine between all the call sites where that routine is called. gprof assumes that all calls of the routine take the same time, and therefore the time should be distributed according to the number of times the routine was called from a particular call site. For many routines, this assumption of a uniform call time is erroneous.

Example 8.32 shows an example of compiling an application for analysis with gprof.

Example 8.32 Compiling Application for Use with gprof

```
$ cc -O -xpg -o coveragepg ex8.29.c
```

There are two sections to the output from gprof. The first section shows which routines call which other routines, the number of calls, and an estimate of the time spent calling the routines. The second section is a summary of the profile of the application.

Example 8.33 shows the time attributed to the various routines using gprof. Three routines (_mcount, oldarc, and done) have time attributed to them, but they are related to the gprof instrumentation of the application rather than the original source code. Running the application to generate the profile took more than 40 seconds, more than half of this is related to the routines inserted to enable profiling.

Example 8.33 Profile from gprof

```
$ coveragepg
$ gprof coveragepg
...
    %   cumulative    self              self     total
  time    seconds   seconds   calls  ms/call  ms/call  name
  51.2      9.91      9.91                              _mcount (645)
  16.0     13.00      3.09                              oldarc [4]
   9.8     14.89      1.89 300000000     0.00     0.00  calc1 [5]
   9.5     16.72      1.83 200000000     0.00     0.00  calc2 [3]
   5.0     17.69      0.97 100000000     0.00     0.00  calc3 [6]
   4.8     18.62      0.93                              done [7]
   3.8     19.35      0.73         1   730.00  5420.00  main [1]
...
```

The output shown in Example 8.34 is the information for just the main routine. It shows that main was called only once by the _start routine; 57.4% of the total runtime was spent in the main routine and its descendants (the remainder of the runtime was spent in routines introduced to enable profiling with gprof).

The main routine called the calc2 routine 200 million times, and the calc3 routine 100 million times. Only 0.73 seconds of time is attributed to the main routine; 4.69 seconds of time is attributed to the routines it calls, referred to as its *descendents*. A total of 1.83 seconds were spent in the calc2 routine, 1.26 seconds were spent in the routines that calc2 called; similarly, 0.97 seconds were spent in the calc3 routine, and 0.63 seconds were spent in the routines that calc3 called. The attribution of time using gprof is an estimate based on the number of calls rather than an exact measurement, so you should treat it with some degree of caution.

Example 8.34 Output from gprof

```
...
                                  called/total      parents
 index  %time   self descendents  called+self      name      index
                                  called/total      children

                0.73      4.69        1/1           _start [2]
 [1]     57.4   0.73      4.69        1             main    [1]
                1.83      1.26 200000000/200000000  calc2   [3]
                0.97      0.63 100000000/100000000  calc3   [6]
...
```

Example 8.35 shows the profile gathered by collect for the same code from Example 8.36.

Example 8.35 Profile Gathered by collect

```
$ cc -g -O -o coverage ex8.29.c
$ collect coverage
Creating experiment database test.1.er ...
$ er_print -func test.1.er
Functions sorted by metric: Exclusive User CPU Time

Excl.     Incl.     Name
User CPU  User CPU
 sec.      sec.
3.292     3.292     <Total>
1.401     1.751     calc2
0.700     0.911     calc3
0.630     3.292     main
0.560     0.560     calc1
0.        3.292     _start
$ er_print -csingle main test.1.er
Callers and callees sorted by metric: Attributed User CPU Time

Attr.     Excl.     Incl.     Name
User CPU  User CPU  User CPU
 sec.      sec.      sec.
3.292     0.        3.292      _start
0.630     0.630     3.292      *main
1.751     1.401     1.751      calc2
0.911     0.700     0.911      calc3
```

The first thing to observe is that the runtime is much lower under collect. This indicates that the *probe effect* (i.e., the amount of distortion) is significantly lower. The timing information for the routines main, calc2, and calc3 appears to be similar for both gprof and collect. However, collect reports a total time of 0.56 seconds spent in calc1. In comparison, gprof reports 1.89 seconds for the same routine; a significant discrepancy.

8.18 Using tcov to Get Code Coverage Information

The tcov tool returns information about how often each line of source code is executed. This information is useful in determining whether a give workload executes all the code in an application, or just a subset. A high execution count does not necessarily mean the code takes time. It is still necessary to profile the application to tell where the time is spent. To generate the coverage information, it is necessary to recompile the application using the -xprofile=coverage compiler option to enable gathering of coverage data.

Example 8.36 shows an example program that will be used to test coverage information.

Example 8.36 Example Program for Code Coverage

```
int calc1(int i) { return i*2;}
int calc2(int i) { return calc1(i+1); }
int calc3(int i) { return calc1(i)+1; }
void main()
{
  int i,j;
  for (j=0; j<1000; j++)
   for (i=0; i<100000; i++)
   {
     if (calc2(i)<calc3(i))
      { calc1(j);} else {calc2(j);}
   }
}
```

Example 8.37 shows how to compile the example program to enable the collection of coverage information.

Example 8.37 Compiling to Enable Collection of Coverage Data

```
$ cc -O -xprofile=tcov -o coverage ex8.36.c
```

The program is then run as normal, and at the end of the run it will produce a directory containing the raw profile data (by default, this directory will be given the name of the application with the extension .profile). This data is then interpreted using the tcov utility, as shown in Example 8.38. The tcov utility will produce a text output file with the extension .tcov containing the coverage information.

Example 8.38 Collecting and Producing Coverage Data

```
$ coverage
$ ls
coverage          ex8.36.c         coverage.profile
$ tcov -x coverage.profile ex8.36.c
$ ls
coverage          ex8.36.c         ex8.36.c.tcov    coverage.profile
```

There are two parts to the coverage output. The first part is the execution frequency for each line of source code; Example 8.39 shows the output.

The second part of the output is a summary of the frequently executed basic blocks for the file; Example 8.40 shows this output. These statistics show the blocks with the

Example 8.39 Execution Counts for Each Line of Source

```
300000000 -> int calc1(int i) { return i*2;}
200000000 -> int calc2(int i) { return calc1(i+1); }
100000000 -> int calc3(int i) { return calc1(i)+1; }
            void main()
            {
                int i,j;
    1001 ->     for (j=0; j<1000; j++)
100001000 ->      for (i=0; i<100000; i++)
                {
100000000 ->        if (calc2(i)<calc3(i))
    ##### ->          { calc1(j);} else {calc2(j);}
                }
            }
```

highest execution count, the number of basic blocks in the file, the proportion of the basic blocks executed, and the average number of instructions per basic block.

Example 8.40 Summary of tcov Statistics for the File

```
            Top 10 Blocks

            Line      Count

                1   300000000
                2   200000000
                8   100001000
                3   100000000
               10   100000000
                7       1001


        7   Basic blocks in this file
        6   Basic blocks executed
    85.71   Percent of the file executed

800002001   Total basic block executions
114286000.00      Average executions per basic block
```

8.19 Using dtrace to Gather Profile and Coverage Information

It is possible to use the Solaris 10 utility dtrace to gather information about how a process spends its time, and how many times each routine is called within the process. The script shown in Example 8.41 profiles an application and displays raw data about where the application was at each sampling point. The script takes a single sample every 97ms, about 10 samples per second, so you need to multiply the results by 10 to determine time in seconds.

Example 8.41 `dtrace` Script to Profile Application

```
#!/usr/sbin/dtrace -s
profile-97
/pid==$target/
{
  @proc[ustack(1)]=count();
}

END
{
  printa(@proc);
}
```

The script has two probes: the profiling probe, `profile-97`; and the END probe. The profiling probe filters so that only the target application is profiled by checking for its `pid`. When the sample is for the target application, the count for the current address is incremented in the `@proc` array. At the exit of the application, the END probe prints out the contents of the `@proc` array.

Example 8.42 shows the results of running this `dtrace` script on the `coverageg` application.

Example 8.42 Output from Profile `dtrace` Script

```
$ ./ex8.41.d -c ./coverage
dtrace: script './ex8.41.d' matched 2 probes
dtrace: pid 3967 has exited
CPU     ID                    FUNCTION:NAME
  0      2                            :END

                coverage`calc3+0xc
                  2

                coverage`main+0x54
                  6

                coverage`main+0x18
                  8

                coverage`main+0x48
                  9

                coverage`main+0x50
                 10

                coverage`calc3+0x4
                 11

...
```

It is possible to process the output of the dtrace script and come up with the timing information comparison shown in Table 8.2. Profiles can be extracted from dtrace, collect, and gprof. The data in Table 8.2 clearly shows the distortion in the profile gathered by gprof.

Table 8.2 Estimated Profile Using dtrace Script

Routine	dtrace Estimate (Seconds)	collect Estimate (Seconds)	gprof Estimate (Seconds)
main	0.65	0.75	0.73
calc1	0.50	0.59	1.89
calc2	1.26	1.26	1.83
calc3	0.76	0.70	0.97

It is also possible to use dtrace to gather information on the number of times routines are called. Using dtrace to do this introduces a significant probe effect, so rather than count for the entire application, the script in Example 8.43 just focuses on the calc3 routine.

Example 8.43 dtrace Script to Count the Number of Invocations of the calc3 Routine

```
#!/usr/sbin/dtrace -s
pid$target::calc3:entry
{
  @proc[probefunc]=count();
}

END
{
  printa(@proc);
}
```

The dtrace script again has two probes. The first probe matches the entry point for the calc3 routine in the target pid. Each time this probe triggers, it increments a count of the number of times the function was entered. When the application exits, the END probe prints out the contents of this array.

Example 8.44 shows the output from this script.

Example 8.44 Number of Invocations of the `calc3` Routine Collected Using `dtrace`

```
# ./ex8.43.d -c ./coverage
dtrace: script './ex8.43.d' matched 2 probes
dtrace: pid 3633 has exited
CPU     ID                          FUNCTION:NAME
  2      2                                :END
  calc3                                                    100000000
```

8.20 Compiler Commentary

When the `-g` compiler flag is used, the compiler records commentary about the optimizations performed. For example, it will report the number of operations in loops, and whether the loops were unrolled or pipelined to improve performance.

The commentary is displayed when a profile of the application has been gathered and the resulting experiment has been loaded by either er_print or the Analyzer GUI. Sometimes it is helpful to be able to see the compiler commentary without first collecting a profile; the er_src utility performs this function.

The er_src utility will output the source code and compiler commentary of an application, library, or .o file that has been compiled with debug information. It can also output the disassembly for particular routines in the file. Example 8.45 shows an example program with a loop that the compiler will transform.

Example 8.45 Simple Program with Transformable Loop

```
double array[1024*1024];
void main()
{
  int i;
  double total;
  for (i=0; i<1024*1024; i++)
  {
    total+=array[i];
  }
}
```

The loop is a simple summation of an (uninitialized) array of double-precision floating-point numbers. If this were an integer array, the compiler would optimize the code out, because the value of `total` is unused (also meaningless). However, the compiler in its default mode will honor the floating-point math standard IEEE-754, and will not be allowed to optimize out the floating-point operations.

Example 8.46 shows the process of compiling this code and examining the resulting executable to determine what optimizations the compiler has performed.

Example 8.46 Compiler Commentary Output by `er_src`

```
$ cc -g -O ex8.45.c
$ er_src -src main a.out
Source file: ./loop.c
Object file: ./a.out
Load Object: ./a.out

    1. double array[1024*1024];
    2. void main()
    3. {
        <Function: main>
    4.    int i;
    5.    double total;

   Source loop below has tag L1
   L1 scheduled with steady-state cycle count = 4
   L1 unrolled 4 times
   L1 has 1 loads, 0 stores, 1 prefetches, 1 FPadds, 0 FPmuls, and 0 FPdivs per itera-
tion
   L1 has 0 int-loads, 0 int-stores, 3 alu-ops, 0 muls, 0 int-divs and 0 shifts per
iteration
    6.    for (i=0; i<1024*1024; i++)
    7.    {
    8.       total+=array[i];
    9.    }
   10. }
```

The commentary reports that the loop has been unrolled four times, and that each iteration initially has one load operation, one floating-point addition, and one prefetch. The code generated actually contains fewer prefetch operations than the commentary suggest—only one every four loads because the compiler, in a later optimization stage, eliminates some of the duplicate prefetch statements.

9

Correctness and Debug

9.1 Introduction

The objective of this chapter is to give an overview of the support for code checking at both compile time and runtime.

The correctness of code is sometimes one of the reasons the compiler cannot be instructed to generate highly optimized code. As an example, consider that at -xO2 the compiler assumes that all variables are volatile; that is, their value may change due to other events within the system. At -xO3, the compiler no longer assumes this, and relies on the programmer explicitly inserting the `volatile` keyword. If a program is coded to rely on this assumption of volatility, it will fail to work correctly at -xO3.

In general, the higher the level of optimization, the more aggressive the compiler is in achieving this optimization. As a result, weaknesses in the code can be exposed, causing incorrect results. With that in mind, the next section discusses how the compiler and other tools can assist in identifying problems.

9.2 Compile-Time Checking

9.2.1 Introduction

It is possible for the compiler to check the correctness of the source code during compilation, and for it to produce information on the compilation process (e.g., listing the header files that were included). The compile-time checking features of the compiler are tied to the particular language of the source code. Consequently, we will cover these features on a language-by-language basis.

9.2.2 Compile-Time Checking for C Source Code

The correctness checking of C source code is largely left to lint, which I cover in Section 9.2.3. There are, however, two options for the C compiler to give more detailed feedback on the source code. Table 9.1 summarizes these two options.

Table 9.1 Compiler Options for C Code Checking

Flag	Comment
-v	Run stricter semantic checks on code. Will provide more detailed feedback on possible errors in the code, but not as detailed as lint.
-xtransition	Issue warnings for differences between K&R C and ISO C encountered in the program

9.2.3 Checking of C Source Code Using lint

The lint command is the preferred way to check C source code for errors. Example 9.1 shows the command line for it.

Example 9.1 Invoking lint

```
$ lint <options> <files>
```

The default behavior for lint will provide a reasonable level of analysis, but the tool has options to extend the analysis that it performs, as summarized in Table 9.2.

Table 9.2 Options for `lint`

Flag	Comment
`-Nlevel=<n>`	Specifies the level of analysis done. The default is 2. 1: Do single procedure analysis. 2: Do whole program analysis. 3: Do constant propagation (takes two to four times longer). 4: Maximum level of analysis (takes 20 to 100 times longer).
`-errchk=<text>`	▪ The default is `%none`. ▪ `%all` means do all the checks. ▪ `longptr64` means check for portability to an environment where longs are 64-bits and ints are 32-bits. ▪ `structarg` means check structural arguments passed by value. ▪ `parenthesis` means check for situations where increased parentheses would improve the readability of the code. ▪ `signext` means check for sign extension problems; valid only with longptr64. ▪ `sizematch` means check for assignment of a large integer to a small integer variable.
`-Ncheck=<text>`	▪ The default is `%none`. ▪ `%all` means do all the tests. ▪ `macros` means check for consistency of macro definitions across files. ▪ `extern` means check for a one-to-one mapping of declarations between source files and their headers.

Example 9.2 shows some C code containing errors.

Example 9.2 C Code Containing Errors

```
void main()
{
  int a,b;
  a=0;
  if (a=b) {printf("Equal\n");}
}
```

Example 9.3 shows the output from `lint` when it is run on the C code shown in Example 9.2.

Example 9.3 Output from `lint`

```
$ lint ex9.2.c
(5) warning: assignment operator "=" found where "==" was expected
(5) warning: variable may be used before set: b
(5) warning: implicit function declaration: printf

set but not used in function
    (3) a in main

function returns value which is always ignored
    printf
```

9.2.4 Source Processing Options Common to the C and C++ Compilers

The C and C++ compilers can also generate other useful output, as shown in Table 9.3.

Table 9.3 Other Useful Options for the C Compiler

Flag	Comment
-H	Print the header files that are included during the compilation process
-P	Produce a `.i` file containing the preprocessed source code
-E	Output preprocessed source code to `stdout`, including line number information
-xM	Output Makefile dependency information

The -H, -P, -E, and -xM options are supported by both the C and C++ compilers. The -H option produces a list of all the header files that are included at compile time. This kind of information can be useful in resolving conflicts within the header files. Example 9.4 shows an example of the header file information for a program that includes only `stdio.h`.

Example 9.4 Example of Header File Inclusion Information

```
$ more ex9.4.c
#include <stdio.h>
void main()
{
}
$ cc -H ex9.4.c
/usr/include/stdio.h
        /usr/include/iso/stdio_iso.h
                /usr/include/sys/feature_tests.h
                        /usr/include/sys/isa_defs.h
                /usr/include/sys/va_list.h
                /usr/include/stdio_tag.h
                /usr/include/stdio_impl.h
```

The -P flag preprocesses the source files and outputs the preprocessed source. This can be useful in situations where it is necessary to track down exactly what the compiler is seeing. The resulting file can be very long, as shown in Example 9.5. The original source code had four lines, but the preprocessed source has 311.

Example 9.5 Preprocessing Source Code

```
% wc ex9.4.c
       4        6       35 ex9.4.c
% cc -P ex9.4.c
% wc ex9.4.i
     311      549     4056 ex9.4.i
```

The -xM option is very similar to the -H option in that it reports included files. In this case, the information that is output is meant to be used in generating appropriate dependency information for Makefiles. Example 9.6 shows an example of the -xM option.

Example 9.6 Example of -xM Outputting Information for Makefiles

```
$ cc -xM ex9.4.c
ex9.4.o: ex9.4.c
ex9.4.o: /usr/include/stdio.h
ex9.4.o: /usr/include/iso/stdio_iso.h
ex9.4.o: /usr/include/sys/feature_tests.h
ex9.4.o: /usr/include/sys/isa_defs.h
ex9.4.o: /usr/include/sys/va_list.h
ex9.4.o: /usr/include/stdio_tag.h
ex9.4.o: /usr/include/stdio_impl.h
ex9.4.o: /usr/include/sys/isa_defs.h
```

9.2.5 C++

Table 9.4 shows the C++ compiler options that control the output of warning information.

Table 9.4 C++ Flags for Correctness

Flag	Comment
-xport64=<text>	• no means do not report on errors when porting to 64-bit. • implicit means give warning messages for implicit casts. • full means give all warning messages about code which may not be safe in the 64-bit environment.
-xe	Do not compile the program, check only for syntax and semantic errors

continues

Table 9.4 C++ Flags for Correctness (*continued*)

Flag	Comment
+w	Reports warnings on code which may have problems, such as: • Not being portable • Being inefficient • Likely to have an error
+w2	In addition to +w reports on violations that are probably harmless
-w	Do not print warning messages (some serious warning messages are still printed)

Example 9.7 shows the output of running the C++ compiler on the code from Example 9.2. The C++ compiler picks up the fact that the b variable has not been assigned, but does not warn about the potentially incorrect condition used by the if statement.

Example 9.7 Output from C++ Compiler with More Detailed Warnings Enabled

```
% CC +w2 ex9.2.c
"ex9.2.c", line 2: Warning (Anachronism): main() must have a return type of int.
"ex9.2.c", line 5: Warning: The variable b has not yet been assigned a value.
"ex9.2.c", line 5: Error: The function "printf" must have a prototype.
1 Error(s) and 2 Warning(s) detected.
```

As well as the outputs from the C++ compiler described in Section 9.2.4, there is also -xdumpmacros, as described in Table 9.5.

Table 9.5 -xdumpmacros C++ Compiler Option

Flag	Comment
-xdumpmacros	Prints out information about the definition, use, and undefinition of macros

Example 9.8 shows an example of the -xdumpmacros compiler flag.

Example 9.8 Example of Output from the -xdumpmacros C++ Compiler Flag

```
$ CC -xdumpmacros ex9.4.c
#define __SunOS_5_9 1
#define __SUNPRO_CC 0x580
#define unix 1
#define sun 1
#define sparc 1
#define __sparc 1
#define __sparcv8plus 1
#define __unix 1
#define __sun 1
#define __BUILTIN_VA_ARG_INCR 1
...
```

9.2.6 Fortran

Table 9.6 shows the flags that control the amount of warning information output by the Fortran compiler.

Table 9.6 Flags Controlling Warning Information from the Fortran Compiler

Flag	Comment
-u	Will report an error if a variable is used before it is defined
-w0	Just show error messages (equivalent to -w)
-w1	Show error messages and warnings (default)
-w2	Show error messages, warnings, and cautions
-w3	Show error messages, warnings, cautions, and notes
-w4	Show error messages, warnings, cautions, notes, and comments

Example 9.9 shows an example program that uses a variable without declaring it.

Example 9.9 Fortran Code with Undeclared Variable

```
$ more ex9.9.f
      PROGRAM test
       PRINT *, array(1)
      END
```

This program will compile because the compiler will assume that space has been reserved for the variable in another file. However, it will fail at link time because no space has been declared for the variable; this problem is shown in Example 9.10.

Example 9.10 Link-Time Error Due to Undeclared Variable

```
$ f90 ex9.9.f
Undefined                           first referenced
 symbol                              in file
array_                              ex9.9.o
ld: fatal: Symbol referencing errors. No output written to a.out
```

However, this issue can be identified using the -u flag, as shown in Example 9.11.

Example 9.11 Using -u Flag to Warn of Undefined Variables

```
$ f90 -u ex9.9.f

        PRINT *, array(1)
                 ^
"ex9.9.f", Line = 2, Column = 18: ERROR: An explicit type must be specified for object
"ARRAY", because -u, the IMPLICIT NONE commandline option is specified.

f90comp: 3 SOURCE LINES
f90comp: 1 ERRORS, 0 WARNINGS, 0 OTHER MESSAGES, 0 ANSI
```

The Fortran compiler also supports a more advanced level of source code analysis under the -Xlist flag. This flag will check the source for errors globally across all files. Table 9.7 shows a selection of the available settings for -Xlist. By default, the output from the -Xlist flag is put into a file which is given the same name as the first input file on the command line, but with the file extension replaced by .lst. For example, using -Xlist on a source file called test.f will leave the results in a file called test.lst.

Table 9.7 -Xlist Options That Can Be Used with the Fortran Compiler

Flag	Comment
-Xlist	Output errors, listing, and cross-reference
-XlistE	Output errors only
-XlistL	Output errors and listing
-XlistX	Output errors and cross-reference
-Xlistc	Output errors and call graph
-XlistMP	Check for inconsistencies in OpenMP statements
-Xlistv1	Only check for syntax errors
-Xlistv2	Check for syntax errors, argument consistency, and variable usage. This is the default level.
-Xlistv3	Check common blocks
-Xlistv4	Check equivalence blocks

Example 9.12 shows an example of the output from -Xlist. In this code, the array is declared and then printed, but no value has been assigned to it. A warning is printed in the t2.lst file that the compiler generates.

Example 9.12 Example of Output from -Xlist

```
$ more ex9.12.f
      PROGRAM test
      REAL*8 array(7)
      PRINT *, array(1)
      END
$ f90 -Xlist ex9.12.f
$ more ex9.12.lst
ex9.12.f                    Wed May 10 22:43:35 2006                  page 1

FILE   "ex9.12.f"
     1          PROGRAM test
     2          REAL*8 array(7)
     3          PRINT *, array(1)
                         ^
**** WAR  #424:  array "array" is set to zero value by default
     4          END
....
```

9.3 Runtime Checking

9.3.1 Bounds Checking

The debugger provides the facility to check an application's memory acccess pattern (e.g., to check for situations where it reads uninitialized memory or situations where it accesses memory that has previously been freed), memory usage, and memory leaks. The simplest way to access this is through the `bcheck` utility. Example 9.13 shows the syntax for this command.

Example 9.13 Syntax of the `bcheck` Command

```
$ bcheck <flags> <app> <parameters>
```

You can pass a number of options to `bcheck`, as shown in Table 9.8. The utility will check for memory leaks by default. The `-access` option generates a report on whether the memory was accessed in valid ways. The `-memuse` option produces a report on memory usage; for example, the line at which memory was allocated or freed.

Table 9.8 Available Options for `bcheck`

Flag	Comment
`-leaks`	Check for memory leaks (default)
`-access`	Also perform access checking on the program
`-memuse`	Also perform memory use checking on program

The program shown in Example 9.14 has several issues. The first is that it writes beyond the end of an allocated chunk of memory, and the second is that it writes to a previously freed memory location.

You can run this code under `bcheck` to look for memory access issues, as shown in Example 9.15.

`bcheck` detects and reports the write past the end of the array and the write to previously freed memory.

Example 9.14 Code Demonstrating Bad Memory Access

```c
#include <stdlib.h>
void main()
{
  double *array;
  int count;
  array=malloc(5*sizeof(double));
  for (count=1; count < 6; count++) array[count]=0.0;
  free(array);
  array[1]=1.0;
}
```

Example 9.15 Output from Memory Access Checking under bcheck

```
% cc -g -o bounds ex9.14.c
% bcheck -access bounds
Reading bounds
...
RTC output redirected to logfile 'bounds.errs'
execution completed, exit code is 1
% more bounds.errs
<rtc> Write to unallocated (wua):
Attempting to write 4 bytes at address 0x252c8
    which is just past heap block of size 40 bytes at 0x252a0
This block was allocated from:
        [1] main() at line 6 in "ex9.14.c"
Location of error:
=>[1] main(), line 7 in "ex9.14.c"

<rtc> Write to unallocated (wua):
Attempting to write 4 bytes at address 0x20c78
    which is 896 bytes into the heap; no blocks allocated
=>[1] main(), line 9 in "ex9.14.c"
```

9.3.2 watchmalloc

Solaris provides an alternative memory library, called watchmalloc.so, which helps in detecting usage of previously freed memory. It also ensures that previously freed memory is not returned to the application for reuse. Using the library is enabled through the environment setting LD_PRELOAD, as shown in Example 9.16.

Example 9.16 Preloading watchmalloc

```
$ setenv LD_PRELOAD watchmalloc.so.1
```

The `MALLOC_DEBUG` environment variable determines whether `watchmalloc` checks for writes outside allocated memory, or reads outside allocated memory. Table 9.9 shows the settings for the `MALLOC_DEBUG` environment variable, along with estimates of the slowdown factor for running applications with those settings.

Table 9.9 Settings for the `MALLOC_DEBUG` Environment Variable

Flag	Comment
WATCH	Checks memory for writes to past end of allocated memory, or writes of previously deallocated memory. This will cause a program execution slowdown on the order of ten to 100 times.
RW	Checks for reads past end of allocated memory, or reads of previously deallocated memory. This will cause a program execution slowdown on the order of 1000 times.

You can run the example program from Example 9.14 under `watchmalloc.so`, as shown in Example 9.17. `watchmalloc.so` is able to detect the write to memory after it has been freed.

Example 9.17 Running Code with Bad Memory Accesses under `watchmalloc`

```
% setenv LD_PRELOAD watchmalloc.so.1
% setenv MALLOC_DEBUG WATCH
% bounds
Trace/Breakpoint Trap (core dumped)
% dbx - core
Corefile specified executable: "bounds"
...
program terminated by signal TRAP (write access watchpoint trap)
Current function is main
    9       array[1]=1.0;
```

9.3.3 Debugging Options under Other `mallocs`

A number of alternative libraries are available for memory managment. One such library is `libumem`. `libumem` has some debug capability, which you can enable using environment variables. The `UMEM_DEBUG` environment variable controls the kind of debug action that is taken. The default is to enable guard regions around allocated memory to protect against overwriting, as well as to trace the time, the size, and the contents of allocated and freed memory. It is possible to set the `UMEM_LOGGING` environment variable to record this information to in-memory linked lists. I will discuss using `libumem` to detect memory leaks further in Section 9.6.

The `mtmalloc` library has options that you can access through the programmatic `mallocctl` interface that control whether allocated and freed memory is overwritten with a pattern so that accesses to uninitialized data, or to data after it has been freed, are more apparent.

9.3.4 Runtime Array Bounds Checking in Fortran

The Fortran compiler is able to add runtime array boundss checking to applications using the `-C` flag. Example 9.18 shows an example of using this flag to check for accesses outside the bounds of an array.

Example 9.18 Using the `-C` Fortran Compiler Flag for Runtime Array Bounds Checking

```
% more ex9.18.f
      program
      real*8  b(200)
      index=300
      b(index)=1.0
      end
% f95 -C ex9.18.f
% a.out
 ******   FORTRAN RUN-TIME SYSTEM   ******
Subscript out of range. Location:   line 4 column 10 of 'ex9.18.f'
Subscript number 1 has value 300 in array 'B'
Abort (core dumped)
```

The `-C` flag also gives improved compile-time bounds checking, as shown in Example 9.19. Without the flag, the compiler handles the file without reporting an error; with the flag, an error is reported on the line where the out-of-bounds access is performed.

Example 9.19 Compile-Time Checking with `-C`

```
% more ex9.19.f
      program
      real*8  b(200)
      b(201)=1.0
      end
% f95 ex9.19.f
% f95 -C ex9.19.f
      b(201)=1.0
          ^
"ex9.19.f", Line = 3, Column = 10: WARNING: Subscript out of range. Subscript number 1
has value 201 in array 'B'

f90comp: 5 SOURCE LINES
f90comp: 0 ERRORS, 1 WARNINGS, 0 OTHER MESSAGES, 0 ANSI
```

9.3.5 Runtime Stack Overflow Checking

The stack is the part of memory where local variables are allocated when a routine is called. The amount of memory reserved for the stack is determined in a number of different ways, depending on how the process is set up.

- If the process is either single-threaded or the master thread of a multi-threaded application, the size of the stack can be set using the `ulimit` command. For a 32-bit application, the command `ulimit -s unlimited` will set the stack to be 2GB, which leaves 2GB for the heap, so it is often more appropriate to set the stack to an appropriate size rather than just `unlimited`. The default stack size for the main thread is 8MB.

- If the application is parallelized using either OpenMP or `-xautopar`, the stack size of the worker threads can be controlled using the environment variable `STACKSIZE`, which sets the size of the stack for the worker threads in megabytes. The default is 4MB for 32-bit applications and 8MB for 64-bit applications.

- If an application is parallelized using Pthreads, the stack size of the threads is determined by the attributes passed to the call to `pthread_create`; the stacksize can be set before the thread is created using the `pthread_attr_setstacksize` call. The default is to reserve 1MB of space for 32-bit applications, and 2MB for 64-bit applications.

Given that stack space has to be reserved in advance, it is possible to run out. This may happen if there are many nested calls to routines, or if the local variables are large in size. On SPARC, the compilers support stack overflow checking to protect against the situation where the application runs out of stack space. Table 9.10 shows the compiler options that control whether code to guard against stack overflow is generated.

Table 9.10 Compiler Options for Runtime Stack Overflow Checking

Flag	Comment
-xcheck=stkovf	Inserts code to check for stack overflow in both single-threaded and multithreaded applications. Generate a SIGSEGV if the stack overflows at runtime.

Example 9.20 shows an example of using this flag. In the example, the code is compiled with no optimization to avoid the code being optimized out. Unless the

stack size is set to be greater than 40MB, the code will die at runtime with a SEGV. Running the code under dbx will indicate that the code dies during the initialization loop of the a array. The error indicates a failure due to writing to memory beyond the end of the a array. When the code is run with stack checking enabled, the SEGV occurs in the _stack_grow routine, which indicates that the problem is due to running out of stack space.

Example 9.20 Example of Using -xcheck=stkovf

```
% more ex9.20.c
void main()
{
  int a[10000000];
  int b;
  for (b=0; b<1000000; b++) {a[b]=0;}
}
% cc -g ex9.20.c
% dbx a.out
...
(dbx) run
Running: a.out
(process id 7651)
signal SEGV (no mapping at the fault address) in main at line 5 in file "ex9.20.c"
    5        for (b=0; b<1000000; b++) {a[b]=0;}
dbx: read of 4 bytes at address fd5da0d8 failed -- Error 0
...
% cc -g -xcheck=stkovf ex9.20.c
% dbx a.out
...
(dbx) run
Running: a.out
(process id 7658)
signal SEGV (no mapping at the fault address) in _stack_grow at 0xff2b2b24
0xff2b2b24: _stack_grow+0x0060: ldub        [%o1 - 1], %g0
dbx: read of 4 bytes at address ff400018 failed -- Error 0
Current function is main
    5        for (b=0; b<1000000; b++) {a[b]=0;}
```

9.3.6 Memory Access Error Detection Using `discover`

The SPARC-only tool discover is available as an add-on for Sun Studio 12 from http://cooltools.sunsource.net/discover/. The tool uses the same technology as BIT (discussed in Section 8.13 of Chapter 8) to instrument the application to record memory access patterns such as writes past the end of arrays, writes to previously free memory, or use of uninitialized memory. At the end of running the instrumented version of the code, a report on memory access violations is produced. The binary needs to be built with optimization and the compiler flag -xbinopt=prepare. Example 9.21 shows an example of the code from Example 9.14, which writes to freed memory, being run under discover.

Example 9.21 Example of Code Being Run under `discover`

```
$ cc -g -O -xbinopt=prepare -o bounds ex9.14.c
$ discover bounds
$ bounds
ERROR (FMW): writing to freed memory at address 0x50010 (8 bytes) at:
        main() + 0x19c [bounds:0x3019c]
            <ex9.14.c:9>:
                    6:        array=malloc(5*sizeof(double));
                    7:        for (count=1; count < 5; count++) array[count]=0.0;
                    8:        free(array);
                    9:=>     array[1]=1.0;
                   10:    }
...
DISCOVER SUMMARY:
        unique errors   : 1 (1 total)
        unique warnings : 0 (0 total)
```

9.4 Debugging Using `dbx`

9.4.1 Debug Compiler Flags

Several compiler flags influence the generation of debug information. Table 9.11 summarizes the flags.

Table 9.11 Compiler Flags Associated with Debug Information

Flag	Comment
-g	-g is the flag that tells the compiler to generate debug information. This flag will disable some inlining optimizations in C++.
-g0	This flag is only for C++, and it tells the compiler to both generate debug information and perform inlining optimizations
-xdebugformat=dwarf -xdebugformat=stabs	Prior to Sun Studio 11, the default debug format that the compiler used to store debug information was the stabs format. This flag tells the compiler to use the newer dwarf format, which is the default for Sun Studio 12. I provide more details in Section 9.4.3.
-xs	This flag tells the compiler to include debug information in the executable. Consequently, the size of the executable will increase significantly. If the debug information is recorded in stabs format, it is stored in the object files. When the dwarf format is used the debug information is stored in the executable (and this flag is unnecessary).

9.4.2 Debug and Optimization

As a rule, the generation of debug information should result in little difference in performance. The exceptions to this rule are as follows:

- For C++, the -g flag will disable some of the inlining that the compiler performs. Unfortunately, this can have quite a large impact on performance. Use of the -g0 flag will enable both debug information and inlining; but the resulting code might be slightly trickier to understand.

- For -xO3 and -xO2 optimizations, a single optimization (the tail-call optimization) is disabled on SPARC. At levels of optimization higher than -xO3, the optimization is enabled. It is unlikely that disabling the tail-call optimization will cause a large difference in performance. However, when it is enabled the resulting code (and call stack) might be harder to understand. I provide an example of the difference in call stacks from the tail-call optimization in Section 8.16 of Chapter 8.

- In the absence of any optimization flags the use of -g will result a reduction in performance.

Because in most cases the impact of enabling debug information is negligible, it is a good policy to always generate the information. Debug information is used by both the debugger and the Performance Analyzer, so having it immediately available can be very useful.

9.4.3 Debug Information Format

The Sun Studio compilers have recently begun to support two debug formats. Prior to Sun Studio 11, the C, C++, and Fortran compilers used the stabs format to hold debug information. With Sun Studio 11, the C compiler transitioned to using dwarf format. With Sun Studio 12, all three of the languages default to using the dwarf format. You can use the compiler flag -xdebugformat=[dwarf|stabs] to toggle between the two formats.

The tools handle much of the difference between the two formats transparently. The differences that might be apparent to the developer are as follows.

- When the stabs format is used the debug information is stored in the object (.o) files by default. It is possible to embed the debug information in the executable using the -xs flag. If an application built using the stabs format is being profiled or debugged, it is often helpful to have the object files available, because they will contain the data necessary to map the disassembly code to source.

- The tools used to extract information from the application change. The dump-stabs tool extracts stabs information from an application, and the dwarf-dump tool will read dwarf information from an application. I cover both of these tools in Section 4.5.7 of Chapter 4.

9.4.4 Debug and OpenMP

It is necessary to have an optimization of at least -xO3 to compile programs that are parallelized with OpenMP. Enabling OpenMP support in the compiler using the -xopenmp flag will increase the optimization level to -xO3.

The -g (or -g0) flag will generate debug information for an OpenMP program in the same way it does for a normal program. However, there is a slight problem here. Full debug is only available with no optimization, but OpenMP is only available with some optimization.

To solve this problem, the -xopenmp flag has a setting to enable OpenMP without optimization; this setting is -xopenmp=noopt. Using this flag, the compiler will honor the OpenMP directives in situations when no optimization levels have been specified. This allows full debugging of OpenMP applications.

9.4.5 Frame Pointer Optimization on x86

The -xregs=frameptr compiler flag allows the compiler to use the frame pointer as additional general purpose register on x86, potentially leading to some performance gains. This is the default for 64-bit code, but it is an option for 32-bit code (it is included in -fast for C in Sun Studio 11).

I discuss the frame pointer and the base pointer in Section 3.6 of Chapter 3. They are used as part of the function-calling convention. For 32-bit code the frame pointer is used in reconstructing stack traces for both debugging and performance analysis. Compiling with -xregs=frameptr may stop some tools from being able to reconstruct the stack. On 64-bit code, the ABI uses .eh_frame records to hold stack information, so the frame pointer register can be used as an additional integer register.

9.4.6 Running the Debugger on a Core File

If an application does have the misfortune to dump core, it is relatively straight forward to run dbx on the core file and determine where the program died. Example 9.22 shows a typical command line.

Example 9.22 Running dbx on a Core File

```
$ dbx - core
```

In some cases, the debugger is unable to determine exactly which executable produced the core file. In these cases, you should replace the hyphen with the name (and path) to the executable.

9.4.7 Example of Debugging an Application

Example 9.23 shows an example of a program that will generate an integer division by zero exception. This program will be used to investigate various debug scenarios.

Example 9.23 Example of a Program That Will Cause a Runtime Exception

```
$ more ex9.23.c
int test1(int a,int b)
{
  if (a>b)
  { return a/b;}
  else
  { return a-b;}
}

void test2(int c)
{
  int x,y;
  for (x=1; x<c; x++)
   for (y=c; y>=0; y--)
    test1(x,y);
}

void main()
{
  test2(10);
}
```

When the program is compiled with debug information and no optimization, the compiler is able to produce a very good mapping between the assembly code and the source code, as well as a good mapping between the variables in the source and the variables used in the assembly code, as shown in Example 9.24.

Given the information the debugger displays, it is relatively obvious what the problem might be. However, it is useful to use this to explore the state of the program when it dumped core. It is useful to print out the call stack to see how the program got to this point. The command to show the current location and call

Example 9.24 Compiling and Running dbx on Resulting Core File

```
$ cc -g ex9.23.c
$ a.out
Arithmetic Exception (core dumped)
$ dbx - core
Corefile specified executable: "./a.out"
Reading a.out
core file header read successfully
Reading ld.so.1
Reading libc.so.1
Reading libdl.so.1
Reading libc_psr.so.1
program terminated by signal FPE (integer divide by zero)
Current function is test1
    5        return a/b;
```

stack is the where command, and Example 9.25 shows the output from this command. There is also a whereami command that shows just the current location and not the call stack. In the absence of optimization, the debugger is able to print information about the parameters passed into each routine.

Example 9.25 Printing the Call Stack Using the dbx where Command

```
(dbx) where
=>[1] test1(a = 1, b = 0), line 5 in "ex9.23.c"
  [2] test2(c = 10), line 18 in "ex9.23.c"
  [3] main(), line 23 in "ex9.23.c"
```

The print command will display the current value of variables, as shown in Example 9.26. This shows that, not surprisingly, the value of b was zero, which caused the divide-by-zero exception.

Example 9.26 Printing Out Variables in dbx

```
(dbx) print a,b
a = 1
b = 0
```

When the application is compiled with optimization, it is harder for the compiler to record the same level of debug information. The debugger will usually be able to display the line of source that corresponds to the assembly instruction which caused the error. It can also display the call stack at that point. However, it will not be able to print the values of variables within the routine, and it also cannot show the values of the parameters that were passed into the routine.

For optimized code, it may be necessary to look at the values in the registers (using the `regs` command) to determine what has happened. Example 9.27 shows the same application compiled with optimization.

Example 9.27 Debugging Optimized Code

```
$ cc -O -g ex9.23.c
$ a.out
Arithmetic Exception (core dumped)
$ dbx - core
...
program terminated by signal FPE (integer divide by zero)
Current function is test1 (optimized)
    5        return a/b;
(dbx) where
=>[1] test1(a = ???, b = ???) (optimized), at 0x10c84 (line ~5) in "ex9.23.c"
  [2] test2(c = ???) (optimized), at 0x10ce0 (line ~18) in "ex9.23.c"
  [3] main() (optimized), at 0x10d10 (line ~23) in "ex9.23.c"
```

In Example 9.27, the debugger is able to show the line of source that caused the problem. However, the debugger is unable to display the values of the parameters passed into the routine.

The `regs` command shows the current instruction and the next instruction, together with the status of all the integer registers. Example 9.28 shows output from this command.

Example 9.28 Examining the Registers

```
(dbx) regs
current frame:  [1]
g0-g1     0x00000000 0x00000000 0x00000000 0x0000f000
g2-g3     0x00000000 0x00000000 0x00000000 0x00000000
g4-g5     0x00000000 0x00000000 0x00000000 0x00000000
g6-g7     0x00000000 0x00000000 0x00000000 0x00000000
o0-o1     0x00000000 0x00000001 0x00000000 0x00000000
o2-o3     0x00000000 0x00022f30 0x00000000 0x0009f29c
o4-o5     0x00000000 0xfffffff7 0x00000000 0x00000000
o6-o7     0x00000000 0xffbff988 0x00000000 0x00010ce0
l0-l1     0x00000000 0xff33e688 0x00000000 0xff341f98
l2-l3     0x00000000 0xff341fa8 0x00000000 0xffffffff
l4-l5     0x00000000 0xffffffff 0x00000000 0x00000b00
l6-l7     0x00000000 0x00014bd1 0x00000000 0x00000000
i0-i1     0x00000000 0x00000001 0x00000000 0x00000009
i2-i3     0x00000000 0x00000001 0x00000000 0x00000001
i4-i5     0x00000000 0x00000000 0x00000000 0x0000000a
i6-i7     0x00000000 0xffbff9e8 0x00000000 0x00010d10
y         0x00000000 0x00000000
ccr       0x00000000 0xfe000007
pc        0x00000000 0x00010c84:test1+0x10     sdivcc  %o0, %o1, %o0
npc       0x00000000 0x00010c88:test1+0x14     bvc,pn %icc,test1+0x2c
```

The regs command, as shown in Example 9.28, prints the values of all the integer registers. It also prints the instruction that was being executed, labeled with pc, and the instruction that would have been executed next, labeled with npc. Looking at the instruction being executed, it is no surprise that it is a divide instruction, and it can be translated as "divide register %o0 by register %o1, and place the result in register %o0." Examining the values contained in the registers, and you can see there is a single line of text that contains the values for registers %o0 and %o1. Register %o0 contains the value 1, and register %o1 contains the value 0, which identifies the reason the application failed.

9.4.8 Running an Application under dbx

The alternative way to debug is to run the application under the debugger. Example 9.29 shows the command line for this.

Example 9.29 Running an Application under the Debugger

```
$ dbx a.out
```

If the application requires some arguments to be passed into it, you can set them using the runargs command, as shown in Example 9.30. This example application does not require command-line arguments.

Example 9.30 Setting the Command-Line Arguments

```
(dbx) runargs <params>
```

Using binary compiled with no optimization will demonstrate the richest set of features. It is known that the program dumps core in the test1 routine. Consequently, it makes sense to set a breakpoint at the start of that routine, using the stop in command, as shown in Example 9.31. This command will stop in the named routine; for unoptimized code, the command will cause the program to stop after the prolog function; for optimized code the program will stop at the first instruction of the function. In both cases, the parameters passed into the function will be visible. For optimized code, these parameters may no longer be visible once the program is stepped forward. Other variants of the stop command allow the user to specify the source line or the exact address at which the debugger will stop.

Example 9.31 Setting the Breakpoint Using dbx

```
(dbx) stop in test1
(1) stop in test1
(dbx) run
Running: a.out
(process id 2405)
stopped in test1 at line 3 in file "ex9.23.c"
   3     if (a>b)
```

Once the debugger has stopped in the routine, it is possible to check the incoming variables and see whether the problem occurs. However, in this example, the problem occurs when the b variable has the value zero. It is helpful to insert a conditional breakpoint, as shown in Example 9.32, that will stop execution of the program when the b variable has the value zero.

Example 9.32 Conditional Breakpoint

```
(dbx) stop in test1 -if (b==0)
(1) stop in test1 -if b == 0
(dbx) run
Running: a.out
(process id 2425)
stopped in test1 at line 3 in file "ex9.23.c"
   3     if (a>b)
(dbx) print b
b = 0
```

A few other housekeeping-type functions are useful to know. To list the status of the various breakpoints, there is the status command; there is also the delete command to remove a breakpoint. These are shown in Example 9.33.

Example 9.33 Managing Breakpoints

```
(dbx) status
 (1) stop in test1 -if b == 0
(dbx) delete 1
```

It is possible to use dbx to rapidly determine which routine regularly fails after a certain number of iterations, as the current example does. The example program dumps core with a floating-point exception. dbx needs to be told to catch this exception, using the catch FPE statement, so that program state at the point of failure can be retrieved. This is shown in Example 9.34.

Example 9.34 Catching a Floating-Point Exception Using dbx

```
% dbx bad
Reading bad
Reading ld.so.1
Reading libc.so.1
Reading libdl.so.1
Reading libc_psr.so.1
(dbx) catch FPE
(dbx) run
Running: bad
(process id 11962)
signal FPE (integer divide by zero) in test1 (optimized) at line 5 in file "ex9.23.c"
    5        return a/b;
```

In this case, the failure happens after a fixed number of calls to the test1 routine. It is possible to use the -count infinity breakpoint modifier to obtain a count of the number of times the routine was entered before failure. Once this count is obtained, you can set the breakpoint so that it will stop on the failing entry to the routine. Example 9.35 shows these steps. The debugger is set to stop in the test1 routine with a count setting of infinity. After the program has run and the floating-point exception has been encountered, the status command shows the failure occurred on the eleventh entry to the test1 routine. Running a second time with the breakpoint set to trigger on a count of 11 causes the debugger to stop the program on the eleventh entry to the routine so that the variables can be printed before the floating-point trap ocurrs.

Example 9.35 Setting a Breakpoint for the Failing Entry to a Function

```
(dbx) stop in test1 -count infinity
(2) stop in test1 -count 0/infinity
(dbx) run
Running: bad
(process id 11986)
signal FPE (integer divide by zero) in test1 (optimized) at line 5 in file "ex9.23.c"
    5        return a/b;
(dbx) status
 (2) stop in test1 -count 11/infinity
(dbx) stop in test1 -count 11
(3) stop in test1 -count 0/11
(dbx) run
Running: bad
(process id 11987)
stopped in test1 (optimized) at line 2 in file "ex9.23.c"
    2    {
(dbx) print a,b
a = 1
b = 0
```

The `funcs` command will list the available routines in an executable. This command has a range of options. One way to use it is to request a list of the routines that have the word "test" in their names, as shown in Example 9.36. A related function is `whereis`, which reports the location of a particular function, including the name of the appropriate source file if that is available.

Example 9.36 Returning Routines Containing the Word "Test"

```
(dbx) funcs test
`a.out`ex9.23.c`test1
`a.out`ex9.23.c`test2
`libc.so.1`sigfpe.c`_test_sigfpe_master
`libc.so.1`nss_common.c`retry_test
`libc.so.1`regex.c`test_string
`libc.so.1`regex.c`test_char_against_ascii_class
`libc.so.1`regex.c`test_char_against_multibyte_class
`libc.so.1`regex.c`test_char_against_old_ascii_class
`libc.so.1`regex.c`test_repeated_ascii_char
`libc.so.1`regex.c`test_repeated_multibyte_char
`libc.so.1`regex.c`test_repeated_group
`libc.so.1`_pthread_testcancel
`libc.so.1`pthread_testcancel
(dbx) whereis test1
function:        `a.out`ex9.23.c`test1
```

9.5 Locating Optimization Bugs Using ATS

The Automatic Tuning and Troubleshooting System (ATS) is available for download from `http://cooltools.sunsource.net/ats/`. As its full name suggests, it is a way to automatically locate optimization bugs in a program, and it can automatically tune to find the best compiler options. The novel thing about the tool is that it is able to do this without access to the original source files.

Sun Studio 11 and later compiler versions support the tool. The Sun Studio 11 release was only for SPARC processors; the Sun Studio 12 release is available for x86 processors. It requires the application to be compiled and linked with the `-pec` compiler driver flag. The syntax for passing this option to the compiler depends on the language, as shown in Example 9.37.

Example 9.37 Passing the `-pec` Option to the Compiler

```
cc -Wd,-pec
CC -Qoption CC -pec
f90 -Qoption f90 -pec
```

To understand how `ats` works, it is necessary to have a high-level understanding of how a compiler works. A compiler has four stages.

1. Parsing source code. The frontend of the compiler reads the source files and converts the text into a format that the compiler can understand. This format is called Intermediate Representation, or IR for short.

2. Optimization. The optimization stage attempts to find ways to transform the IR to improve performance.

3. Code generation. The code generation stage converts the IR into assembly code for the processor to execute. This stage will perform further optimizations designed to extract maximum performance from the processor that the compiler is targeting.

4. Linking. Finally, the objected files produced by the compiler are combined into an executable by the linker (as described in Chapter 7).

When the compiler is passed the -pec flag it stores the IR from the source files in the final executable. This can add significant size to the executable, but it has no impact on its runtime performance. The `ats` tool is able to retrieve the stored IR and rebuild the application with different compiler flags. The -pec flag needs to be used in both the compilation of the file and the linking of the executable. If multiple files are compiled separately, `ats` will only be able to recompile the files compiled with the -pec compiler option.

Example 9.38 shows an example of building and recompiling using `ats`. The `ats` command took several parameters. The -i flag either specifies compiler flags to use, or can specify a script to execute. The -r flag tells `ats` how the application should be executed. If this flag is not used, `ats` will invoke the application with no parameters (so, in this case, the flag is unnecessary). The final part of the command to `ats` is the application (or library) that should be recompiled.

The output shows that the application was rebuilt with the -fast compiler flag, and then run. However, the default for `ats` is to remove the binary after `ats` exits, but you can override this by passing the -keepbin flag to `ats`.

In this way, `ats` can, for example, be a convenient way to use profile feedback on an application without having to do two compilation passes of the original source.

If `ats` is not given any compiler flags or script to recompile with, its default behavior is to auto-tune the application. It will try different sets of compiler flags and keep trying the more promising flags until it locates a set that gives the shortest runtime. You can override the metric of shortest runtime by one supplied by a user-supplied metric using the -metric flag (which takes a script to be executed after every run as a parameter). Example 9.39 shows an example of using this feature.

Example 9.38 Recompiling Using ATS

```
% more ex9.38.c
#include <stdio.h>
int main() {
  printf("Hello world\n");
  return 0;
}
% cc -Wd,-pec -O -o test ex9.38.c
Number of recompilable files = 1
% ats -i '-fast' -r 'test' test
Results continuously updated at file:///tmp/ATS/run1/ats_res.html

=== Starting Automatic Tuning System ===
Will try the following set of options:
        -fast
--- Number 1 ---
Recompiling with: /opt/SUNWspro/bin -fast
Hello world
Passed

Results are at file:///tmp/ATS/run1/ats_res.html
```

Example 9.39 Auto-Tuning Using ATS

```
% ats -r 'test' test
Results continuously updated at file:///tmp/ATS/run2/ats_res.html
=== Starting Automatic Tuning System ===
Will try the following set of options:
        script:autotuning
--- Number 1 ---
Recompiling with: /opt/SUNWspro/bin -fast
Hello world
Passed
--- Number 2 ---
Recompiling with: /opt/SUNWspro/bin -xO4
Hello world
Passed
--- Number 3 ---
Recompiling with: /opt/SUNWspro/bin -xO3
Hello world
Passed
...
```

The ATS tool can be very helpful in debugging bugs that appear when a program is compiled with particular compiler flags. The tool has a script called `findbug` that initially locates the compiler flag that causes an application to fail. Then, having found one set of flags for which the application works and another set of flags for which the application fails, `ats` is able to perform a binary search over all the modules in the program and locate the particular object file(s) that cause the failure. Example 9.40 shows the command line to do this. The `findbug` script takes the failing optimization flags as parameters. The rest of the command line should be familiar. If the failure manifests by the application running slowly, never terminating, or terminating early, it is possible to use a timeout to stop the application after a period of time, and use further options to specify whether timing out meant the program was successful or failing.

Example 9.40 Using ATS to Locate an Optimization Problem

```
% ats -i 'script:findbug -fast' -r 'test' test
```

9.6 Debugging Using mdb

The modular debugger (mdb) ships as part of Solaris and is able to debug both the live Solaris kernel and user programs. One use of the tool is to inspect (or even change) kernel variables. Example 9.41 shows an example of using mdb to inspect the page coloring setting. To inspect the kernel, it is necessary to pass the -k flag to mdb. By default, mdb will not write to the kernel, so you also need to add the -w flag. You can display the value of a variable by passing the name of the variable together with the /X format specifier (which instructs mdb to show the word at that address). The ::quit command is used to exit mdb.

Example 9.41 Using mdb to Evaluate the Setting for the Page Coloring Algorithm

```
$ mdb -k
Loading modules: [ unix krtld genunix ip usba nfs random ptm logindmux ipc cpc lofs ]
> consistent_coloring /X
consistent_coloring:
consistent_coloring:            0
> ::quit
```

It is also possible to inspect a user program, as shown in Example 9.42. This shows the process of loading an application under mdb, setting a breakpoint using the <address>::bp command, running the application until the breakpoint, and then printing the current contents of registers.

It is also possible to examine an application for bad memory accesses using libumem and mdb. It is necessary to preload libumem, and set the appropriate environment variables to enable memory activity debug information to be gathered (as described in Section 9.3.3). The application being examined must either still be running or have generated a core file (a core file can be generated from a running process using the gcore <pid> command).

The ::umem_verify command will report whether any of the allocated memory has been corrupted, and the ::umalog command will report where the corrupted memory was allocated and freed. Example 9.43 shows an example of

Example 9.42 Debugging a Program Using mdb

```
% mdb test
Loading modules: [ libc.so.1 ]
> main::bp
> ::run
mdb: stop at main
mdb: target stopped at:
main:           save      %sp, -0x60, %sp
> ::regs
%g0 = 0x00000000                   %l0 = 0x00000001
%g1 = 0x0000f000                   %l1 = 0xffbffbec
%g2 = 0x00000000                   %l2 = 0xffbffbf4
...
> ::step
mdb: target stopped at:
main+4:         sethi     %hi(0x10800), %i5
> ::quit
```

using mdb to locate where corrupted memory was allocated and freed in the
bounds example program from Example 9.14. (The program has been modified
so that it pauses before terminating. The pause allows time to generate a core file
or attach mdb.)

Example 9.43 Using mdb to Locate Memory Corruption

```
% export LD_PRELOAD=libumem.so
% export UMEM_DEBUG=default
% export UMEM_LOGGING=transaction
% umem_bounds &
[1] 12034
% gcore 12034
gcore: core.12034 dumped
% mdb core.12034
Loading modules: [ libumem.so.1 libc.so.1 ld.so.1 ]
> ::umem_verify
Cache Name                   Addr      Cache Integrity
umem_magazine_1               3c008 clean
...
umem_alloc_40                 3dc08 clean
umem_alloc_48                 3ddc8 1 corrupt buffer
...
> ::umalog

T-0.000000000  addr=4bfc0  umem_alloc_48
       libumem.so.1`umem_cache_free+0x4c
       libumem.so.1`process_free+0x6c
       main+0x2c
       _start+0x108

T-0.000023400  addr=4bfc0  umem_alloc_48
       libumem.so.1`umem_cache_alloc+0x13c
       libumem.so.1`umem_alloc+0x44
       libumem.so.1`malloc+0x2c
       main+4
       _start+0x108
```

The `::umalog` command shows that the memory was allocated at the address `main+4` and freed at the address `main+0x2c`. This is not sufficient to determine the address of the store that is corrupting the memory, but it should be sufficient to determine where in the program the corrupted memory was allocated and released.

You can use the `::find_leaks` command to locate the address where memory that has not yet been freed was allocated. If the process is still running, it is likely that this will report memory that the application will free later.

Table 9.12 shows a summary of `mdb` commands and their `dbx` equivalents.

Table 9.12 Mapping of `mdb` Commands to `dbx`

mdb	dbx	Comment
mdb <program> mdb [<program>]<corefile>	dbx <program> dbx <program> <corefile> dbx - <corefile>	Start debugger
::run <arguments>	runargs <arguments> run	Run program under debugger
<address>::bp	stop at <address>	Set breakpoint at address
::regs	regs	Examine registers
::fpregs	regs -f	Examing floating-point registers
::stack	where	Examine call stack
<address>::dis <routine>::dis	dis <address> dis <routine>	Disassemble routine
::step	nexti	Execute next instruction
::quit	quit	Leave debugger

PART III

Optimization

10

Performance Counter Metrics

10.1 Chapter Objectives

Most processors have performance counters that record a variety of hardware events that occur during application execution. These counters are typically able to provide some insight into performance-relevant information such as the number of cache misses, branch mispredictions, and so on. In some cases, it is possible to derive some synthetic metrics, such as bandwidth, which will provide more information about what the system or process is doing, and whether there is a bottleneck.

By the end of the chapter, the reader will have been introduced to the performance counters on a number of platforms, and understand how the events recorded can be synthesized into metrics that are relevant to the execution of an application.

10.2 Reading the Performance Counters

A number of tools can read the performance counters.

- The `cputrack` tool follows a process or a PID and reports the events that occur to just that process. I cover `cputrack` in more detail in Section 4.4.4 of Chapter 4.

- The `cpustat` tool reports events for all available processors. It requires superuser privileges because it will report events that happen to processes that are owned by all users. I cover `cpustat` in more detail in Section 4.4.3 of Chapter 4.

- The `collect` tool is part of the Performance Analyzer, and it can gather a time-based profile of an application and a performance counter event-based profile of an application. The advantage of an event-based profile is that it shows where the events are occurring in the application. I cover `collect` in more detail in Section 8.3 of Chapter 8.

- The programmatic interface to the hardware performance counters is `libcpc`. This interface allows the developer to create tools such as `cpustat`, or to make a program aware of performance counter events during its own runtime.

The easiest way to access the performance counters is to use `cputrack` to follow the events an application encounters. Example 10.1 shows an example command line for `cputrack`.

Example 10.1 Command Line for `cputrack`

```
$ cputrack -c pic0=Instr_cnt,pic1=Cycle_cnt <app> <params>
```

Rather than repeating code, the examples in the next section will use a Perl script to read the performance counters and present the results, as shown in Example 10.2. This script takes as parameters the name of an application and its corresponding parameters. It then runs `cputrack` on this application collecting information on whichever counters are specified in the call to the `track` subroutine. When the program terminates, the return value from `cputrack` is the `exit` line containing the total number of events recorded. The Perl language is ideally suited to processing this kind of textual information. However, it would also be possible to do this without the Perl script.

Example 10.2 Outline of Perl Script, `count`, to Read the Performance Counters

```
$ more count.pl
#!/bin/perl -w

$commandline = "";
while (defined($arg = shift @ARGV))
{
  $commandline = $commandline ." ".$arg;
}

sub track
{
  (my $counters)=@_;
  $text=`cputrack -c $counters $commandline | grep exit`;
  $text=~/\W+(\d+\.\d+)\W*\d+\W*exit\W*(\d+)\W*(\d+)/;
  $counter1=$2;
  $counter2=$3;
}
```

In the next sections, lines will be added to the count script to collect more performance counter data.

10.3 UltraSPARC III and UltraSPARC IV Performance Counters

There are two programmable performance counters on the UltraSPARC III family of processors, labeled pic0 and pic1. Each counter can count a variety of events. Some events (such as instruction counts) can be counted by either counter, and other events (such as second-level cache misses) can be counted on only one of the two counters.

The events available on a given processor, and their distribution between the two counters, depend on the particular type of processor. The following examples assume an UltraSPARC IIICu processor; a section at the end discusses the differences between this processor and the UltraSPARC IV and UltraSPARC IV+ processors.

The performance counters have brief names that assist in determining the type of events counted. This section focuses on the counters that give the most helpful information in determining the events the processor is encountering.

10.3.1 Instructions and Cycles

You can use the performance counters to assess the floating-point content in an application. This is useful in determining the number of floating-point operations as a proportion of the total instruction count. Example 10.3 shows the floating-point code, fp.c.

Example 10.3 Floating-Point Test Program, fp.c

```
% cat fp.c

#include <stdio.h>
void main()
{
  int i,j,k;
  static double x[1024*1024];
  static double y[1024*1024];
  for (i=0; i<1024*1024; i++) x[i]=y[i]=1.0;

  for (k=0;k<100; k++)
    for (i=0; i<1024*1024-k; i++)
      x[i]+=y[k]*x[i];
  if (x[0]<0) printf("Negative");
}
```

The performance counters that are appropriate to measure are as follows.

- `Instr_cnt`, the number of instructions completed.

- `Cycle_cnt`, the number of cycles taken.

- `FA_pipe_completion`, which counts the number of floating-point instructions that were dispatched down the "add" floating-point pipe. This is basically a count of the number of floating-point additions, subtractions, and comparisons.

- `FM_pipe_completion`, which counts the number of floating-point instructions that were dispatched down the "multiply" floating-point pipe. This is basically a count of the number of floating-point multiplies, divides, and square roots.

Example 10.4 shows the Perl code that collects these counters.

Example 10.4 Perl Code to Collect Instruction Mix Counts

```
print("Summary data\n");
track('pic0=Instr_cnt,pic1=Cycle_cnt');
print("Instruction count      = $counter1\n");
print("Cycle count            = $counter2\n");
track('pic0=FA_pipe_completion,pic1=FM_pipe_completion');
print("Floating-point Add insts= $counter1\n");
print("Floating-point Mul insts= $counter2\n");
```

Example 10.5 shows the results of running this on the `fp` test program.

Example 10.5 Instruction Mix Counts from `fp` Program

```
Summary data
Instruction count      = 1687350175
Cycle count            = 2708197832
Floating point Add insts= 104852651
Floating point Mul insts= 104852650
```

The program took 2.7 billion cycles to execute, and during that time 1.6 billion instructions were executed. This translates into 1.6 cycles per instruction (often referred to as CPI), or alternatively, that 0.6 instructions are executed every cycle (called IPC). The counters report 104 million floating-point add and 104 million floating-point multiply instructions; looking back at the source confirms that this is almost exactly correct.

You must be careful when intepreting the floating-point counters, because they also count Visual Instruction Set (VIS) instructions. These instructions are used in the `libc_psr` library to improve the performance of the `memmove` and `memcpy` code. Applications that use these routines may appear to falsely have a high float-ing-point content. You can use the Performance Analyzer to profile the application and show where these floating-point instructions were used, and this information can confirm that the counts are floating-point rather than VIS instructions. Example 10.6 shows the profile of the test program. Although the events do not line up exactly with the floating-point instructions, they do get reported in the same block of code, which is sufficient to be confident that the performance counters are reporting floating-point computation.

Example 10.6 Profiling Application to Locate Floating-Point Instructions

```
$ collect -h FA_pipe_completion,,FM_pipe_completion fp
$ er_print test1.er
(er_print) metrics e.FA_pipe_completion:e.FM_pipe_completion
Current metrics: e.FA_pipe_completion:e.FM_pipe_completion:name
Current Sort Metric: Exclusive FA_pipe_completion Events ( e.FA_pipe_completion )
(er_print) dis main
Excl.                Excl.
FA_pipe_completion   FM_pipe_completion
Events               Events


  ...
                                      <Function: main>
  ...
             0                0     106ec:  sll     %i4, 3, %10
             0                0     106f0:  add     %10, %12, %11
             0                0     106f4:  st      %11, [%fp - 16]
       1000003          1000003     106f8:  ldd     [%11], %f6
##    46000138         46000138     106fc:  sll     %i5, 3, %10
             0                0     10700:  ldd     [%10 + %17], %f4
             0                0     10704:  fmuld   %f4, %f6, %f4
             0                0     10708:  faddd   %f6, %f4, %f4
##    56000224         56000224     1070c:  std     %f4, [%11]
             0                0     10710:  inc     %i4
             0                0     10714:  neg     %i5, %10
             0                0     10718:  add     %10, %16, %10
       1000003          1000003     1071c:  cmp     %i4, %10
             0                0     10720:  bl      0x106ec
             0                0     10724:  nop
```

10.3.2 Data Cache Events

A number of events can be collected for the data cache:

- DC_rd, the number of data cache read events
- DC_rd_miss, the number of data cache read miss events
- DC_wr, the number of data cache write events
- DC_wr_miss, the number of data cache write miss events

The Perl code in Example 10.7 enables the collection of events relating to the data cache.

Example 10.7 Perl Code to Collect Data Cache Events

```
print("\nL1 data cache events\n");
track('pic0=DC_rd,pic1=DC_rd_miss');
print("Data cache reads         = $counter1\n");
print("Data cache read misses   = $counter2\n");
track('pic0=DC_wr,pic1=DC_wr_miss');
print("Data cache writes        = $counter1\n");
print("Data cache write misses  = $counter2\n");
```

Example 10.8 shows the results from running this on the unoptimized `fp` code. This data shows that there are about 200 million load and 200 million store operations, with one memory operation for each floating-point operation.

Example 10.8 Data Cache Events for `fp` Program

```
L1 data cache events
Data cache reads         = 223955118
Data cache read misses   = 26234197
Data cache writes        = 211827185
Data cache write misses  = 118047571
```

Example 10.9 shows the disassembly of the source code from Example 10.3. There are two floating-point loads and two stores in the loop. There is also a floating-point multiply and a floating-point addition. The code has been compiled without optimization, which explains why the compiler has left the unnecessary store of the `i` index variable at `0x106f4`. The floating-point load of `y[k]` at `0x10700` could also be eliminated by optimization.

Example 10.9 Disassembly of Hot Loop of Unoptimized `fp` Program

```
  106ec:  a1 2f 20 03   sll     %i4, 3, %l0   ◄──
  106f0:  a2 04 00 12   add     %l0, %l2, %l1
  106f4:  e2 27 bf f0   st      %l1, [%fp - 16]
  106f8:  cd 1c 60 00   ldd     [%l1], %f6
  106fc:  a1 2f 60 03   sll     %i5, 3, %l0
  10700:  c9 1c 00 17   ldd     [%l0 + %l7], %f4
  10704:  89 a1 09 46   fmuld   %f4, %f6, %f4
  10708:  89 a1 88 44   faddd   %f6, %f4, %f4
  1070c:  c9 3c 60 00   std     %f4, [%l1]
  10710:  b8 07 20 01   inc     %i4
  10714:  a0 20 00 1d   neg     %i5, %l0
  10718:  a0 04 00 16   add     %l0, %l6, %l0
  1071c:  80 a7 00 10   cmp     %i4, %l0
  10720:  06 bf ff f3   bl      main+0x8c        ! 0x106ec
  10724:  01 00 00 00   nop
```

Examining the count of the number of data cache read misses, Example 10.9 shows that one in every 8.5 loads is a data cache miss. One of the loads is always of the same variable, so that load will always be a cache hit. The other load is streaming through memory, so this load should incur one cache miss per data cache line, which translates to one in four of these loads should miss (the cache lines in the data cache are 32 bytes in length). Consider four iterations of the loop. In those four iterations, the load of y[k] will never miss (because k is not changing) and the load of x[i] would miss once, so one load in eight should encounter a cache miss, which agrees with the results from the performance counters.

For the write misses, it appears that half of the stores miss the data cache. The redundant store to the i loop index variable will always hit in the write cache, but because the variable is not loaded in the loop it will not be present in the data cache. Hence, all the stores of the i variable will be data cache misses. The other stores are to the x array, which has previously been loaded from, so stores to this array will always hit in the data cache. Consequently, half the stores will miss the data cache.

10.3.3 Instruction Cache Events

The following performance counters record events associated with the instruction cache.

- IC_ref counts the number of instruction cache references.
- IC_miss counts the number of instruction cache misses.
- IC_miss_cancelled counts the number of instruction cache misses which were canceled because the instructions were not actually needed. An example of this might be when unnecessary instructions are fetched because of a mispredicted branch.
- Dispatch0_IC_miss counts the number of cycles where no instructions were dispatched because the processor was waiting for instruction cache misses.
- EC_ic_miss is a count of the number of instruction cache misses that also missed the second-level cache.

You can extend the script to read these counters by adding the code shown in Example 10.10.

Example 10.11 shows the results of collecting data on the fp program. There are about 800 million instruction cache references. Compared with the instruction count information shown in Example 10.5, this shows that each reference to the

Example 10.10 Reading Instruction Cache Events

```
print("\nL1 instruction cache events\n");
track('pic0=IC_ref,pic1=IC_miss');
print("Inst. cache references  = $counter1\n");
print("Inst. cache misses      = $counter2\n");
track('pic0=Instr_cnt,pic1=IC_miss_cancelled');
print("Inst. cache miss cancel = $counter2\n");
track('pic0=Dispatch0_IC_miss,pic1=EC_ic_miss');
print("Cycles lost to IC misses= $counter1\n");
print("Instruction misses in L2= $counter2\n");
```

instruction cache furnished the processor with an average of two instructions. The processor also speculatively accesses the instruction cache, so the number of references does not correlate strongly with the number of instructions.

Of the instruction cache references, only about 9,000 were misses. Nearly one-third of the misses were canceled, meaning that the processor did not actually need to wait for the instructions to be returned. About a thousand instruction cache misses were also misses in the second-level cache; this is probably due to the initial fetch of the application's instructions. The final counter is the number of cycles lost due to instruction cache misses, and this estimates about 240,000 cycles. This is not a significant portion of the 2.7 billion cycles of runtime for the application.

Example 10.11 Instruction Cache Events for the `fp` Program

```
L1 instruction cache events
Inst. cache references  = 838567620
Inst. cache misses      = 9197
Inst. cache miss cancel = 2539
Cycles lost to IC misses= 241601
Instruction misses in L2= 1046
```

10.3.4 Second-Level Cache Events

Example 10.12 shows the extensions to the counter reading script that are necessary to read a selection of the second-level cache events. I will discuss the counters further in the next two sections. The important second-level cache event counters are:

- `EC_rd_miss` is a count of the number of second-level cache read misses.
- `EC_misses` is a count of all the second-level cache misses (both reads and writes).
- `EC_ref` is a count of the number of speculative references to the second-level cache.
- `Re_EC_miss` is a count of the number of cycles spent waiting for data that was not present in the second-level cache.

Example 10.12 Second-Level Cache Event Counting

```
print("\nL2 cache events\n");
track('pic0=EC_rd_miss,pic1=EC_misses');
print("L2 cache read miss    = $counter1\n");
print("L2 cache misses       = $counter2\n");
track('pic0=EC_ref,pic1=Re_EC_miss');
print("L2 cache references   = $counter1\n");
print("Cycles of L2 miss     = $counter2\n");
```

10.3.5 Cycles Lost to Cache Miss Events

A number of counters of the number of cycles are spent waiting for data that was not present on the processor. These are as follows.

- The Re_DC_miss counter counts the number of cycles spent waiting for data that is not in the data cache. This counter starts counting from the moment the processor determines the data is not in the first-level cache, and completes counting when the data has been returned from either memory or the second-level cache.

- The Re_EC_miss counter counts the number of cycles spent waiting for data that is not in the second-level cache. This counter starts counting from the point at which the processor determines that the data is not in the second-level cache, and stops counting when the data is returned from memory.

- The Re_DC_missovhd counter counts the number of cycles of data cache miss overhead. This counter counts the time between when the processor determines the data is not in the data cache to the point at which the processor determines whether the data is in the second-level cache. It sums over both second-level cache misses and second-level cache hits. The purpose of this counter is to enable a better estimation of the cycles spent waiting on data from memory. Section 10.3.7 discusses the use of this counter in more detail.

The script shown in Example 10.13 will count the cycles lost in data cache miss events.

Example 10.13 Counters for Cycles Lost Due to Data Cache Misses

```
track('pic0=Instr_cnt,pic1=Re_DC_miss');
print("Cycles lost to L1 misses= $counter2\n");
track('pic0=Instr_cnt,pic1=Re_DC_missovhd');
print("Cycles lost to L1 ovrhd = $counter2\n");
```

10.3.6 Example of Cache Access Metrics

Example 10.14 shows code to measure memory latency. This code works by setting up a linked list and then looping through the elements of the linked list. If each element is on a different cache line, and the whole list is too large to fit into the on-chip cache but small enough to fit into the second-level cache, the resulting timing will be proportional to the latency of the second-level cache. If the linked list is too big to fit into the second-level cache, the timing will be proportional to the latency of memory (or the third level of cache if there is one).

Example 10.14 Code to Measure Latency

```
#include <stdio.h>
#include "timing.h"

#define ITERATIONS 1024*1024*2*2
static int** array[SIZE];

void main()
{
  int i;
  int **j;
  for (i=0; i<SIZE-1; i++)
   array[i]=(int**)&array[i+16];
  for (i=0; i<16; i++)
    array[SIZE-i]=(int**)&array[i];

  starttime();
  j=array[0];
  for (i=0; i<4*ITERATIONS; i++)
   j=(int **)*j;
  endtime(4*ITERATIONS);
}
```

The code in Example 10.14 has to be compiled with a value defined for the constant SIZE. Example 10.15 shows the compile lines for three different variants of the code. The three variants define settings for SIZE such that the linked list fits into the on-chip cache, the second-level cache, and memory.

Example 10.15 Three Different Compile Lines for the Latency Code

```
$ cc -DSIZE='1024*4'      -o 16KB  ex10.14.c
$ cc -DSIZE='1024*1024'   -o 4MB   ex10.14.c
$ cc -DSIZE='1024*1024*4' -o 16MB  ex10.14.c
```

Performance data for the code was collected from an UltraSPARC III-based system. The system has an 8MB second-level cache (and no third-level cache), so the largest data set size is resident in memory, the second data set size is resident in the second-level cache, and the smallest data set size is resident in the on-chip data cache.

Table 10.1 tabulates the performance counter values for running these three different tests. This data includes events for both the on-chip cache and the second-level cache.

Table 10.1 Performance Counters for the Latency Set of Benchmarks

Event Counter	On-Chip Data	Data in Second-Level Cache	Data in Memory
Data cache reads	16,846,053	16,846,151	16,846,298
Data cache read misses	3,475	16,780,649	16,780,859
Data cache writes	18,634	1,065,163	4,217,081
Data cache write misses	9,325	1,055,876	4,207,812
Second-level cache references	16,857,134	17,057,175	17,658,899
Second-level cache misses	1,879	79,290	14,773,004
Second-level cache read misses	489	12,213	14,509,060
Cycles lost due to data cache misses	127,209	280,496,955	2,575,746,745
Cycles of data cache miss overhead	25,112	100,676,051	86,406,749
Cycles lost due to second-level cache misses	76,235	2,404,304	2,476,307,980
Runtime in cycles	67,952,940	319,720,440	2,676,577,095

In a number of rows in Table 10.1 the values are similar for all sizes of the data set. The values are not identical, as there will be run-to-run variances on the system due to other tasks running, and how the task being measured is scheduled. The following observations can be made from the data in the table.

- The number of reads of the on-chip data cache is nearly constant. All three codes perform the same number of iterations, so they will do the same number of reads of the on-chip data cache.

- The number of second-level cache references is constant for all three codes. This is because the second-level cache is checked in parallel with the data cache. This results in better performance in the case where the data is not in the data cache.

The next thing to cover is the on-chip cache events for each of the three test programs.

- The number of data cache read miss events is low for the situation where the data is resident in the data cache. When the data is no longer able to fit on the chip, all the data cache reads become data cache read misses.
- The number of writes is correlated with the number of writes of pointers necessary to set up the linked list in the first place.

For the second-level cache, the number of misses is very low when the data fits into either the data cache or the second-level cache, but as soon as the data is larger than the second-level cache, all the references are misses.

10.3.7 Synthetic Metrics for Latency

Using the performance counters, it is possible to estimate the latency and bandwidth for the caches and system. This is an estimate because it is not possible to simultaneously collect data for all the counters, so some margin of error is introduced by having to rotate through the counters or gather the data over separate runs of the application.

The data cache miss overhead counter (Re_DC_missovhd) counts the number of cycles that elapse between the data cache miss and the processor determining whether the data is in the second-level cache. If the data is not in the second-level cache, the Re_EC_miss counter will count the number of cycles from the point at which the processor determines that the data is not present in the second-level cache until the data is returned from memory.

Example 10.1 shows how the counters behave in the presence and absence of second-level cache hits. Memory latency is the sum of the data cache miss overhead counter plus the second-level cache miss time. However, the data cache miss overhead counter records the cycles for both the second-level cache hits and misses, so it is necessary to correct by only taking the proportion of the count that can be attributed to second-level cache misses. Second-level cache latency can be calculated using a similar calculation on the data cache miss time that remains after the cycles lost to second-level cache misses have been taken into account.

A more formal definition of the latencies can be produced as follows. Memory latency is the sum of the Re_EC_miss counter and the proportion of the Re_DC_missovhd counter that is from second-level cache misses. The proportion of second-level cache misses can be calculated from the ratio of the EC_rd_miss and DC_rd_miss counters. The memory latency is the total time spent waiting for second-level

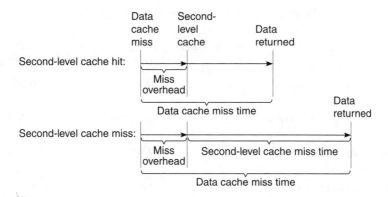

Figure 10.1 Performance Counters Measuring Cache Miss Latency

cache misses divided by the number of second-level cache read misses. Here is the formula for measuring memory latency:

$$\text{Memory latency} = \left(\frac{\text{EC\_rd\_miss}}{\text{DC\_rd\_miss}} \times \text{Re\_DC\_rd\_missovhd} + \text{Re\_EC\_miss}\right)\Big/\text{EC\_rd\_miss}$$

It is also possible to calculate the latency of the second-level cache. This is the time spent waiting on data cache misses minus the time spent waiting for data from memory. Again, the latency per miss is calculated by dividing the total latency by the number of data cache read misses that were second-level cache hits. Here is the formula for determining second-level cache latency:

$$\text{L2 cache latency} = \frac{\left(\text{Re\_DC\_miss} - \left(\frac{\text{EC\_rd\_miss}}{\text{DC\_rd\_miss}} \times \text{Re\_DC\_missovhd} + \text{Re\_EC\_miss}\right)\right)}{(\text{DC\_rd\_miss} - \text{EC\_rd\_miss})}$$

You can use the data gathered in Table 10.1 to derive estimates of second-level cache and memory latency, as shown in Table 10.2.

Table 10.2 Synthetic Latency Metrics

Metric	Data in Data Cache	Data in Second-Level Cache	Data in Memory
DC read misses	3,475	16,780,649	16,780,859
EC read misses	489	12,213	14,509,060
Data cache miss overhead	25,112	100,676,051	86,406,749

continues

Table 10.2 Synthetic Latency Metrics (*continued*)

Metric	Data in Data Cache	Data in Second-Level Cache	Data in Memory
Second-level cache read misses/ data cache read misses	0.14	0	0.86
Cycles spent waiting for data not in data cache	127,209	280,496,955	2,575,746,745
Cycles spent waiting for data not in second-level cache	76,235	2,404,304	2,476,307,980
Estimated second-level cache latency (cycles)	16	17	11
Estimated memory latency (cycles)	163	203	176

The values of between 11 and 17 cycles for the second-level cache latency, and 163 and 203 cycles for memory latency, are reasonable estimates. The most accurate estimates are likely to be when the values are calculated from the majority of events. For the second-level cache latency, the estimate of 17 cycles when the data is principally resident in the second-level cache is likely to be most accurate. Similarly, the estimate of 176 cycles for memory latency when most of the accesses are to memory is also likely to be most the most accurate estimate.

10.3.8 Synthetic Metrics for Memory Bandwidth Consumption

Using the performance counters, it is possible to estimate memory bandwidth consumption for a given application. Each access to memory will bring in a 64-byte cache line from memory, each access to the second-level cache will bring a 32-byte cache line from the second-level cache, and each access to the data cache will bring in the appropriate number of bytes to fill the register. However, for the data cache, each access will be selecting a subset of 32 bytes, so it seems appropriate to consider the size of the data to be 32 bytes. The bandwidth is calculated as the number of bytes transferred per second. If time is measured in cycles, it is necessary to convert to seconds by multiplying by the processor speed. You can determine the bandwidth for a given cache by using the formula shown in the following equation:

$$\text{Bandwidth} = \text{Size in bytes} \times \text{Total number of hits in cache} \times \frac{\text{Processor speed (MHz)}}{\text{Runtime in cycles}}$$

Table 10.3 shows estimates of memory bandwidth consumption for the various levels to cache for the data from a 1200MHz system shown in Table 10.1. There are two ways to present bandwidth data. The bandwidth presented in this table is the contribution from each level of cache, calculated by taking the total reads and writes to that cache and subtracting the misses.

Table 10.3 Estimates of Memory Bandwidth Consumption

Metric	Data in Data Cache	Data in Second-Level Cache	Data in Memory
Cycles taken	67,952,940	319,720,440	2,676,577,095
Data cache reads	16,846,053	16,846,151	16,846,298
Data cache writes	18,634	1,065,163	4,217,081
Data cache read misses	3,475	16,780,649	16,780,859
Data cache write misses	9,325	1,055,876	4,207,812
Estimated total data cache bandwidth	9.5 GB/s	9 MB/s	1 MB/s
Second-level cache misses	1,879	72,290	14,773,004
Estimated second-level cache bandwidth	6 MB/s	2 GB/s	89 MB/s
Estimated memory bandwidth	2 MB/s	19 MB/s	424 MB/s
Total bandwidth from all sources	9.5 GB/s	2 GB/s	514 MB/s

10.3.9 Prefetch Cache Events

The prefetch cache is used by floating-point load instructions. Several counters report how much (and how efficiently) the cache is being used. The addition to the script shown in Example 10.16 reports these additional counters.

There are two read ports on the prefetch cache, labeled 0 and 1. It is possible for the UltraSPARC III family of processors to do two reads from the caches in a single cycle. If this happens, the second read port (port 1) of the prefetch cache will be used. The counters `PC_port0_rd` and `PC_port1_rd` count the number of times each port is used.

Note that if the processor is stalled waiting for data from memory, it will check the prefetch cache roughly every seven cycles to determine whether the data is there. This periodic checking will be counted on the `PC_port0_rd` counter, which

Example 10.16 Prefetch Cache Events

```
print("\nPrefetch cache events\n");
track('pic0=PC_port0_rd,pic1=PC_port1_rd');
print("Prefetch cache port 0 rd= $counter1\n");
print("Prefetch cache port 1 rd= $counter2\n");
track('pic0=Instr_cnt,pic1=Re_PC_miss');
print("Cycles lost to prefetch cache misses = $counter2\n");
track('pic0=Instr_cnt,pic1=PC_soft_hit');
print("Software prefetch hits  = $counter2\n");
track('pic0=Instr_cnt,pic1=PC_hard_hit');
print("Hardware prefetch hits  = $counter2\n");
track('pic0=Instr_cnt,pic1=PC_MS_misses');
print("Prefetch cache ld misses= $counter2\n");
track('pic0=Instr_cnt,pic1=PC_snoop_inv');
print("PC snoop invalidate     = $counter2\n");
```

makes the counter useless as an accurate count of the total number of reads. In addition to these polling events, the counter will also count the number of prefetches emitted.

If the processor predicts that the data is going to be in the prefetch cache, and it turns out that the data is not available there, the processor will stall. The number of cycles lost to prefetch cache stall is counted by the Re_PC_miss counter.

The PC_MS_misses counter counts the number of times data was not found in the prefetch cache.

The performance counters can also track whether the prefetch cache hits are due to hardware prefetch or software prefetch, using the two counters PC_hard_hit and PC_soft_hit.

The PC_snoop_inv counter counts the number of snoop invalidates of the prefetch cache. This covers the situation where the data in the prefetch cache is invalidated by a write (including writes from other processors). Because a write to a cache line will place new data into the cache line, the processor maintains coherence by removing the old value from the prefetch cache.

Example 10.17 shows a program that will test bandwidth. The code reads in two arrays, each 16MB in size. On a 1200MHz UltraSPARC IIICu, this program, when compiled with prefetch, runs for 2.7 seconds. Each array is read 104 times, so the total data accessed in those 2.7 seconds is 32MB*104, which is about 3.2GB of data. The bandwidth consumed works out to be 1.2MB per second.

The inner loop of the bandwidth code will have a load for each variable x[i] and y[i], and a store for the variable x[j] (the compiler has to store x[j] in case j==i). This makes a total of about 400M loads and 200M stores. The compiler also puts out one prefetch for each four elements, or about 100M prefetches. The arrays are padded with 64 bytes so that they do not conflict in the data cache.

Table 10.4 shows the performance counters for the prefetch cache for the bandwidth program. The prefetch cache has about 500M reads from it, which corresponds

Example 10.17 Bandwidth Test Example

```
void main()
{
  int i,j;
  static double x[2*1024*1024+8];
  static double y[2*1024*1024+8];

  for (i=0; i<2*1024*1024; i++) x[i]=y[i]=1.0;

  for (j=0;j<104;j++)
    for (i=0; i<2*1024*1024; i++)
    x[j]+=x[i]*y[i];
    if (x[1024]<0) printf("Negative");
}
```

to the 400M loads and the 100M prefetches. Most of the time the data is being successfully brought in by software prefetches. However, hardware prefetch is fetching some data, and some data is being missed.

Table 10.4 Prefetch Cache Activity During Bandwidth Program

Performance Counter	Value
Prefetch cache read port 0	503,247,280
Prefetch cache read port 1	0
Recycle prefetch cache miss	0
Software prefetch hits	446,587,539
Hardware prefetch hits	5,481,395
Prefetch cache misses	23,780,845
Prefetch cache snoop invalidates	627,095

You can estimate the effectiveness of software prefetch by dividing the number of software prefetch hits by the sum of the software and hardware prefetch hits, and the prefetch cache misses. In the results shown in Table 10.4, the effectiveness of software prefetch can be calculated as being about 94%.

10.3.10 Comparison of Performance Counters with and without Prefetch

Table 10.5 shows the bandwidth code from Example 10.17 compiled with and without prefetch. There is a slight difference in the generated code when compiling with prefetch, as the compiler will unroll loops more aggressively to facilitate prefetch insertion; but in the absence of prefetch insertion, the compiler will not unroll the loops as much.

Table 10.5 Comparison between the Bandwidth Code Compiled with and without Prefetch

Performance Counter	Code with Prefetch	Code without Prefetch
Instruction count	1,480,870,974	1,370,772,062
Cycle count	3,245,081,446	**13,106,565,453**
Data cache miss cycles	1,117,105,661	**10,886,641,871**
Data cache miss overhead	841,727,714	859,868,049
Second-level miss cycles	217,151,127	**9,997,065,676**
Floating-point stall cycles	1,159,122,346	1,418,048,741
Data cache reads	604,270,133	437,262,299
Data cache read misses	20,311,231	**108,316,523**
Data cache writes	233,221,259	276,971,801
Data cache write misses	75,338,101	**275,819,562**
Instruction cache references	525,868,599	1,147,890,473
Prefetch cache port 0 reads	513,008,974	817,243,188
Software prefetch hits	472,392,646	0
Hardware prefetch hits	2,926,857	167,025,448
Prefetch cache misses	32,270,822	325,919,045
Second-level cache read misses	838,315	**53,862,917**
Second-level cache misses	54,487,563	54,387,127
Second-level cache references	620,509,017	492,968,116
Integer stall cycles	41,276	41,290
Store queue stall cycles	32,905,563	**121,493,876**

It is visible from the table that the performance gains come from eliminating the cycles spent waiting on data cache misses; this is apparent from comparing the total cycle count to the number of cycles spent on data cache misses.

The data cache miss overhead counter remains constant between the two scenarios; this count basically measures the time it takes to determine whether a load is a data cache hit, and is proportional to the number of loads (not whether the loads hit or miss).

In the floating-point stall cycles row of Table 10.5, it is apparent that a large number of cycles are spent waiting for floating-point data to be ready. This is an artifact of the code, and the fact that the compiler cannot schedule the code optimally due to potential aliasing between the loads of x[i] and the stores to x[j]. In fact, in the optimal code, this issue now consumes about one-third of the runtime (1 billion cycles out of 3 billion). I discuss this topic in more detail in Section 10.3.12.

In the code without software prefetch, there are correspondingly zero software prefetch hits. There is a higher number of hardware prefetch hits. However, hardware prefetch can only fetch data from the second-level cache, so this does not cause a large gain in performance for this particular code.

The absence of software prefetch has a significant impact on the store queue. The data cache write misses increase significantly, and a large number of cycles are lost to store queue stalls. However, the store queue stall cycles are much lower than the number of cycles lost to second-level cache misses.

Examining the instruction count difference between the two codes, there are about 100M software prefetch-related instructions. Without prefetch, there is also an increase in the number of instruction cache references. This is due to the increased number of processor stalls.

10.3.11 Write Cache Events

Four performance counters are associated with the write cache:

- The WC_miss counter, which counts the number of times a write misses the write cache
- The WC_snoop_cb counter, which counts the number of times a snoop[1] from another processor forces the write cache to copy its data back to memory
- The WC_scrubbed counter, which counts the number of times a store hits a subblock in a clean cache line
- The WC_wb_wo_read counter, which counts the number of sub-blocks that are written to memory without having to be fetched from memory first[2]

---

1. Snooping is the process of watching the address bus and seeing whether one processor is requesting ownership of data that is held in the caches of another processor. If this is happening, the data must be invalidated from the caches so that all the copies of the data are kept in sync.
2. A store is actually more complex than just writing data from memory. In most cases, the data has to be read from memory, and the writing processor needs to obtain "ownership" of the data (so that other processors do not write to the same data at the same time). Once the data has been read from memory, the new data can be written, and the merged result written back to memory.

The code in Example 10.18 shows how these counters can be read.

Example 10.18 Write Cache Performance Counters

```
print("\nWrite cache events\n");
track('pic0=Instr_cnt,pic1=WC_miss');
print("Write cache misses      = $counter2\n");
track('pic0=Instr_cnt,pic1=WC_snoop_cb');
print("Write cache snoop copy back= $counter2\n");
track('pic0=Instr_cnt,pic1=WC_scrubbed');
print("Write cache scrubbed    = $counter2\n");
track('pic0=Instr_cnt,pic1=WC_wb_wo_read');
print("Write cache write back without read= $counter2\n");
```

The code shown in Example 10.19 streams data through the write cache. The code performs 400M reads and 200M writes. Most of the writes are to contiguous memory.

Example 10.19 Code That Performs a Stream of Stores

```
#include <stdio.h>
void main()
{
  int i,j;
  static double x[2*1024*1024+8];
  static double y[2*1024*1024+8];

  for (i=0; i<2*1024*1024; i++) x[i]=y[i]=1.0;

  for (j=0;j<104;j++)
   for (i=j; i<2*1024*1024; i++)
    x[i-j]+=x[i]*y[i];
  if (x[1024]<0) printf("Negative");
}
```

The code in Example 10.19 produces the write cache performance data shown in Example 10.20. There are about 30M write cache misses, and each miss will bring in 64 bytes. This corresponds to about 1.9GB of data, or 240M 8-byte store instructions. There are a small number of copy backs due to snoops. The count of accesses to scrubbed cache lines and the count of the lines written back without reads is twice the number of misses. This is because the lines have 32-byte subblocks, and these counters work on the subblock level.

Example 10.20 Write Cache Performance Counter for Stream Example

```
Write cache events
Write cache misses             =   30,110,789
Write cache snoop copy back    =    4,056,399
Write cache scrubbed           =   55,378,731
Write cache write back without read=   55,368,956
```

10.3.12 Cycles Lost to Processor Stall Events

Several performance counters count the number of cycles during which the processor is stalled on some condition. The important ones are as follows.

- The `Rstall_storeQ` counter counts the number of cycles that the processor spends stalled because the store queue is full. The store queue is an eight-deep structure, so if one store misses to memory, the processor can issue a further seven stores before stalling.

- The `Rstall_IU_use` counter counts the number of cycles that the processor spends stalled because it is waiting for the results of an integer operation. An example of this might be a load which hits data cache (so it is not a load miss), but has a consumer of the data from that load as the next instruction; at this point, there is a stall while the data is fetched from the cache to be used.

- The `Rstall_FP_use` counter counts the number of cycles the processor is stalled waiting for the results of a floating-point operation. Examples of this might be where one floating-point operation is waiting for the result of a previous one. Similar to the integer case, this counter will count the number of cycles of stall between a load that hits in the cache, and the consumption of that data by a floating-point operation. It will also measure the number of cycles between when the processor stalls waiting for the result of a prior floating-point operation.

- The `Re_RAW_miss` counter counts the number of cycles lost due to loads being reissued because of read-after-write hazards. A read-after-write hazard occurs when the data has just been written and the program wants to read the data back again. There is a short time during which the processor has to wait for the write operation to complete.

The code in Example 10.21 shows how these events can be counted.

Example 10.21 Script to Read the Stall Event Performance Counters

```
print("\nStall events\n");
track('pic0=Rstall_IU_use,pic1=Rstall_FP_use');
print("Cycles spent waiting for integer data = $counter1\n");
print("Cycles spent waiting for FP data      = $counter2\n");
track('pic0=Rstall_storeQ,pic1=Re_RAW_miss');
print("Cycles lost to store queue stalls    = $counter1\n");
print("Cycles lost due to Read-After_write   = $counter2\n");
```

10.3.13 Branch Misprediction

A number of counters deal with branches and branch misprediction.

- The `IU_Stat_Br_count_taken` counter counts the number of taken branches.
- The `IU_Stat_Br_count_untaken` counter counts the number of untaken branches. It is worth recalling that most branches will sometimes be taken and sometimes be untaken. For example, the branch at the end of a loop will often be a branch back to the top of the loop, but once all the iterations of the loop have been completed, that branch will not be taken.
- The `IU_Stat_Br_miss_taken` counter counts the number of times the processor predicted that a branch would be untaken, but in fact, the branch was taken.
- The `IU_Stat_Br_miss_untaken` counter counts the number of times the processor predicted that a branch would be taken, but in fact, the branch was untaken.

Some counters count cycles lost due to branches.

- The `Dispatch0_br_target` counter counts the number of cycles where the instruction fetch queue is empty because of a branch target calculation (e.g., when the destination address is the value of a register loaded from memory).
- The `Dispatch0_mispred` counter counts the number of cycles where the instruction fetch queue is empty because of a branch misprediction.
- The `Dispatch0_2nd_br` counter counts the number of cycles where the instruction fetch queue is empty because two branches are sharing a four-instruction group, and it is necessary to refetch the second branch in the group.

The code in Example 10.22 shows how these counters can be read.

Example 10.22 Counters Covering Branches and Branch Misprediction

```
print("\nBranch statistics\n");
track('pic0=Dispatch0_br_target,pic1=Dispatch0_mispred');
print("Cycles lost to branch target mispredict = $counter1\n");
print("Cycles lost to mispredicted branches    = $counter2\n");
track("pic0=Dispatch0_2nd_br,pic1=Instr_cnt");
print("Cycles lost to branches sharing cacheln = $counter1\n");
track("pic0=IU_Stat_Br_miss_taken,pic1=IU_Stat_Br_miss_untaken");
print("Branches mispredicted but taken = $counter1\n");
print("Branches mispredicted but untaken = $counter2\n");
track('pic0=IU_Stat_Br_count_taken,pic1=IU_Stat_Br_count_untaken');
print("Branches taken                   = $counter1\n");
print("Branches untaken                 = $counter2\n");
```

You can calculate the branch misprediction rate by dividing the total number of mispredicted branches by the total number of taken and untaken branches, as shown in the following formula:

$$\text{Branch misprediction rate} = \frac{\text{Branches mispredicted taken} + \text{Branches mispredicted untaken}}{\text{Branches taken} + \text{Branches untaken}}$$

10.3.14 Memory Controller Events

The UltraSPARC IIICu processor has a number of performance counters dedicated to the memory activity. There are four memory controllers and each memory controller is associated with some particular physical memory. If all the memory slots are not filled on a particular board, the associated memory controller will be idle. Performance counters record, for each memory controller, the number of reads, the number of writes, and the number of cycles that a memory request was stalled because the memory controller was busy.

An application running on a system can access the memory held on any processor, not only the processor on which it is running. Hence, it is no longer appropriate to use `cputrack` to report on the memory controller events. These events need to be reported on a system-wide basis, so `cpustat` is the appropriate tool. Examining the results on a system-wide basis will mean that all the processes that are active on the machine will contribute to the measured bandwidth.

The `cpustat` command does not have the facility to track the run of a single process, so the command must be run in parallel with the workload being examined. Example 10.23 shows a script to read the memory controller.

Example 10.23 Script to Read the Memory Controller Performance Counters

```
# cpustat -c pic0=MC_reads_0,pic1=MC_writes_0,sys \
         -c pic0=MC_reads_1,pic1=MC_writes_1,sys \
         -c pic0=MC_reads_2,pic1=MC_writes_2,sys \
         -c pic0=MC_reads_3,pic1=MC_writes_3,sys
```

Example 10.24 shows the results of running the bandwidth test program on a two-processor UltraSPARC IIICu-based machine. The system has only one active memory controller attached to CPU zero.

To calculate the system-wide bandwidth it is necessary to sum all the memory controller events for each second. For the first second, there were 4.8 million read events and 8,000 writes. Each read or write corresponds to 64 bytes of data. For that particular second, the read bandwidth is about 300MB per second and the write bandwidth about 0.5MB per second.

Example 10.24 Output from Memory Controller Performance Counters Running the
                  Bandwidth Test Program

```
# cpustat -c pic0=MC_reads_0,pic1=MC_writes_0,sys \
          -c pic0=MC_reads_1,pic1=MC_writes_1,sys \
          -c pic0=MC_reads_2,pic1=MC_writes_2,sys \
          -c pic0=MC_reads_3,pic1=MC_writes_3,sys 1
  time cpu event      pic0       pic1
 1.007  0  tick    4852308       8668  # pic0=MC_reads_0,pic1=MC_writes_0,sys
 1.007  1  tick          0          0  # pic0=MC_reads_0,pic1=MC_writes_0,sys
 2.007  0  tick    4779037       4687  # pic0=MC_reads_1,pic1=MC_writes_1,sys
 2.007  1  tick          0          0  # pic0=MC_reads_1,pic1=MC_writes_1,sys
 3.007  0  tick    4243420     289528  # pic0=MC_reads_2,pic1=MC_writes_2,sys
 3.007  1  tick          0          0  # pic0=MC_reads_2,pic1=MC_writes_2,sys
 4.007  1  tick          0          0  # pic0=MC_reads_3,pic1=MC_writes_3,sys
 4.007  0  tick    4717364       4927  # pic0=MC_reads_3,pic1=MC_writes_3,sys
...
```

10.4 Performance Counters on the UltraSPARC IV and UltraSPARC IV+

10.4.1 Introduction

The performance counters on the UltraSPARC IV and UltraSPARC IV+ are
broadly the same as the counters on the UltraSPARC IIICu processor. However,
these two processors are dual core, so some of the counters have changed in meaning. The UltraSPARC IV+ introduces a third-level cache which has caused a
change of name for some counters.

10.4.2 UltraSPARC IV+ L3 Cache

The presence of a third-level cache on the UltraSPARC IV+ means that additional
counters are necessary to track the utilization of this cache, and that the names of
the existing counters need to be changed for clarity. The counters that count the
number of cycles lost to second- and third-level cache misses are Re_L2_miss
(changed from Re_EC_miss) and Re_L3_miss. There are counters of references
and misses for both caches (L2_ref, L3_ref, L2_miss, L3_miss).

Example 10.25 shows the script to read the UltraSPARC IV+ third-level cache
performance counters.

Example 10.25 Script to Read UltraSPARC IV+ Third-Level Cache
Performance Counters

```
print("\nL3 cache events\n");
track('pic0=L3_rd_miss,pic1=L3_miss');
print("L3 cache read miss     = $counter1\n");
print("L3 cache misses        = $counter2\n");
track('pic0=Instr_cnt,pic1=L3_write_miss_RTO');
print("L2 cache write misses  = $counter2\n");
track('pic0=Instr_cnt,pic1=Re_L3_miss');
print("Cycles of L3 miss      = $counter2\n");
```

10.4.3 Memory Controller Events

The memory controller is shared between both of the cores on the UltraSPARC IV
and UltraSPARC IV+. This is indicated by appending the suffix _sh to the counter
name. For example, reads of bank 0 are counted using the shared counter MC_
reads_0_sh.

When reading a shared counter, both cores will obtain the same value. This
changes the way bandwidth is calculated for the system. Because both cores will
return the same value, the calculation of bandwidth should either take the value of
just one core, or take the value from both cores and divide by two.

Example 10.26 shows an example of reading the memory controller performance counters on a two-processor (four-core) UltraSPARC IV+-based system. The
two cores share memory contollers, so the total number of events needs to be
divided by two to reflect this.

Example 10.26 Reading Memory Controller Counters on UltraSPARC IV/IV+

```
# cpustat -c pic0=MC_reads_0_sh,pic1=MC_writes_0_sh,sys \
          -c pic0=MC_reads_1_sh,pic1=MC_writes_1_sh,sys \
          -c pic0=MC_reads_2_sh,pic1=MC_writes_2_sh,sys \
          -c pic0=MC_reads_3_sh,pic1=MC_writes_3_sh,sys
  time cpu event   pic0    pic1
 5.011  18  tick  584485  418248 # pic0=MC_reads_0_sh,pic1=MC_writes_0_sh,sys
 5.011  16  tick  601932  421997 # pic0=MC_reads_0_sh,pic1=MC_writes_0_sh,sys
 5.011   0  tick  602500  422088 # pic0=MC_reads_0_sh,pic1=MC_writes_0_sh,sys
 5.011   2  tick  584451  418248 # pic0=MC_reads_0_sh,pic1=MC_writes_0_sh,sys
 ...
```

10.5 Performance Counters on the UltraSPARC T1

10.5.1 Hardware Performance Counters

The UltraSPARC T1 processor can have up to 32 simultaneous threads running, with each thread having two hardware performance counters tracking the events that occur to that particular thread. One of the two counters can count only instructions; the second counter is able to count one of eight different event types at a time. The event types are as follows.

- SB_full. The store buffer full counter is the only counter on the UltraSPARC T1 that counts cycles; all the others count events. This counter counts the number of cycles that the store buffer is full, and no further stores can be issued.

- FP_instr_cnt. This counter counts the number of floating-point instructions executed.

- IC_miss. This counter counts the number of instruction cache misses. Each instruction cache miss will cause the thread to stall waiting for an instruction to be fetched from either memory or the second-level cache.

- DC_miss. This counter counts the number of data cache misses. Each data cache miss will cause the thread to stall until the data is fetched from either the second-level cache or from memory.

- ITLB_miss. This counter counts the number of instruction Translation Lookaside Buffer (TLB) misses. Each instruction TLB miss will cause the thread to stall until the TLB entry can be fetched.

- DTLB_miss. This counter counts the number of data TLB misses.

- L2_imiss. This counter counts the number of second-level cache misses that were caused by instruction cache misses.

- L2_dmiss_ld. This counter counts the number of second-level cache misses that were caused by data cache load misses.

Example 10.27 shows an example of collecting all the events for a single-threaded process using `cputrack`.

It is useful to interpret the performance counters in the context of the architecture of the UltraSPARC T1. The 32 threads execute on eight cores (four threads share each core), so a maximum of eight threads can actually execute instructions in a single cycle (one thread from each core). Taking the four threads that share a single core, every cycle the four threads are polled and one of the threads gets to execute a single instruction. The threads are scheduled using a round robin algorithm among the threads that are able to run on a given cycle. If all four threads

Example 10.27 Collecting Events for a Process Using `cputrack`

```
% cputrack -c SB_full,sys,Instr_cnt,sys \
 -c FP_instr_cnt,sys,Instr_cnt,sys \
 -c IC_miss,sys,Instr_cnt,sys \
 -c DC_miss,sys,Instr_cnt,sys \
 -c ITLB_miss,sys,Instr_cnt,sys \
 -c DTLB_miss,sys,Instr_cnt,sys \
 -c L2_imiss,sys,Instr_cnt,sys \
 -c L2_dmiss_ld,Instr_cnt,sys \
 testapplication
time lwp     event    pic0      pic1
   1.815  1      tick  16719092 242028962  # SB_full,sys,Instr_cnt,sys
   2.173  1      tick         0  68094165  # FP_instr_cnt,sys,Instr_cnt,sys
   3.173  1      tick   7473612 195989449  # IC_miss,sys,Instr_cnt,sys
   4.173  1      tick   2845200 197053479  # DC_miss,sys,Instr_cnt,sys
   5.173  1      tick         0 197594723  # ITLB_miss,sys,Instr_cnt,sys
   7.704  1      tick    353680 385920551  # DTLB_miss,sys,Instr_cnt,sys
   8.103  1      tick       293 104947976  # L2_imiss,sys,Instr_cnt,sys
   9.113  1      tick       321 267404065  # L2_dmiss_ld,Instr_cnt,sys
 ...
```

are ready to execute, this means each thread can execute only one instruction every four cycles. Of course, the threads are not always ready to execute instructions. Most applications have plenty of places where they fetch data from memory, and while one thread is fetching data from memory, the other threads are running on the core.

In fact, the design of the processor relies on the threads having cycles when they are stalled waiting for the completion of some event. These stall cycles give the other threads time to run. Hence, the expectation is that any single thread should get one-quarter of the cycles. This leads to the idea of a cycle budget.

10.5.2 UltraSPARC T1 Cycle Budget

Because four threads are sharing a core, each thread will (in ideal conditions) get one-quarter of the cycles on which to execute an instruction. Each thread will spend three-quarters of the cycles waiting while other threads get to execute their instructions.

If the total count of instructions executed for a given thread is greater than one-quarter of the available cycles, that thread has done better than expected. If it is less, it has done worse than expected.

The performance counters report various events, and each event has a typical cost. For example, a data cache load that misses in the first-level cache will cost about 20 cycles. However, if the load also misses in the second-level cache, it will cost about 100 cycles. Table 10.6 shows values for the costs of the various events; the values selected are round numbers, rather than exact values, because there is no gain from adding extra significant figures.

Table 10.6 Performance Counter Multipliers for Conversion to Cycles

Performance Counter	Multiplier
SB_full	1
FP_instr_cnt	30
IC_miss	20
DC_miss	20
ITLB_miss	100
DTLB_miss	100
L2_imiss	100
L2_dmiss_ld	100

Under an even workload, each thread is expected to execute one instruction every four cycles, leaving three of the four cycles where the thread is unable to execute an instruction. During these three cycles, the thread can be stalled waiting on memory or the completion of some other event. Consequently, the thread can absorb up to three cycles of stall for every instruction executed before the stall cycles start to impact the rate at which instructions are executed by the thread. Another way to express this is that the thread has a budget of stall cycles that it can fill before the stall cycles actually start to consume cycles which could have been used for useful work.

Table 10.7 shows an example of the raw counts from an application run on a 1GHz system. This particular application ran for 60 seconds. The table shows that the application had about 30 seconds of stall time during that minute. Looking at instruction count, the application executed 17 billion instructions, or 17 seconds' worth of instructions. You can convert the performance counter events into estimates of consumed time in seconds by multiplying by the appropriate factor.

Table 10.7 Performance Counter Events Converted into Seconds

Performance Counter	Multiplier	Raw Event Count	Seconds @ 1GHz
SB_full	1	7,772,624,752	7.8
FP_instr_cnt	30	595,352	0
IC_miss	20	33,937,416	0.7
DC_miss	20	562,411,736	11.2
ITLB_miss	100	2,496	0

Table 10.7 Performance Counter Events Converted into Seconds (*continued*)

Performance Counter	Multiplier	Raw Event Count	Seconds @ 1GHz
DTLB_miss	100	2,206,792	0.2
L2_imiss	100	759,904	0.1
L2_dmiss_ld	100	70,120,336	7
Total stall time			27
Instruction count	1	17,316,110,266	17.3

Table 10.8 shows how the performance-counter-derived metrics compare to the fair share that the thread should have obtained if it were competing against three other similar threads. In this case, the thread managed to execute more instructions than might be expected: 17 billion rather than the expected 15 billion. The application also did not record as many stall events as the thread could have handled. The thread could have had 45 seconds of stall time before the stall events started to reduce the actual number of instructions executed. However, it recorded only 27 seconds' worth of stall events.

Table 10.8 Comparison of Theoretical and Actual Performance Metrics

Event	Time	Performance Metrics
Total runtime	60 seconds	
Stall budget	45 seconds	27 seconds
Instruction budget	15 seconds	17.3 seconds

10.5.3 Performance Counters at the Core Level

The performance counters can also be aggregated over the entire core using cpustat. In this case, the most useful metric is the total number of instructions that the core executes. In theory, the core should be able to execute one instruction every cycle. If the core executes fewer instructions than this, it indicates that for some cycles none of the threads had any instructions ready to be executed. Once an UltraSPARC T1 processor is hitting its maximum theoretical instruction issue rate, the only way that its performance can be improved is by reducing the instruction count; hence, measuring the total number of instructions issued is a useful metric of processor utilization.

10.5.4 Calculating System Bandwidth Consumption

The UltraSPARC T1 has performance counters for memory reads and writes that you can access using the `busstat` command (as described in Section 4.4.5 of Chapter 4). Example 10.28 shows an example of reading these counters. In the first second, about 3 million read operations occurred and about 24,000 writes. Each access was of a 64-byte cache line, so the total read bandwidth was about 180MB per second and the total write bandwidth about 1.5MB per second.

Example 10.28 Measuring Bandwidth on an UltraSPARC T1

```
# busstat -w dram0,pic0=mem_reads,pic1=mem_writes \
          -w dram1,pic0=mem_reads,pic1=mem_writes \
          -w dram2,pic0=mem_reads,pic1=mem_writes \
          -w dram3,pic0=mem_reads,pic1=mem_writes
time dev    event0            pic0      event1       pic1
1    dram0  mem_reads         755608    mem_writes   7208
1    dram1  mem_reads         751498    mem_writes   5550
1    dram2  mem_reads         748432    mem_writes   6334
1    dram3  mem_reads         749538    mem_writes   5541
2    dram0  mem_reads         761371    mem_writes   5096
2    dram1  mem_reads         757113    mem_writes   3450
2    dram2  mem_reads         754249    mem_writes   3956
2    dram3  mem_reads         755412    mem_writes   3465
...
```

10.6 UltraSPARC T2 Performance Counters

The UltraSPARC T2 processor has two performance counters per virtual processor. Each counter can select from a set of performance events that is both similar to and more fully featured than the performance counters on the UltraSPARC T1. The events feature information about the on-chip encryption engine as well as details of the more usual concerns, such as cache misses. Table 10.9 summarizes a selection of the countable events.

Table 10.9 UltraSPARC T2 Performance Counters

Counter Name	Description
`Br_completed`	Count of the number of branches
`Br_taken`	Count of the number of taken branches
`Instr_FGU_arithmetic`	Number of instructions dispatched to the floating-point unit (includes VIS instructions)
`Instr_ld`	Load instructions

Table 10.9 UltraSPARC T2 Performance Counters (*continued*)

Counter Name	Description
Instr_st	Store instructions
Instr_cnt	Instruction count
IC_miss	Instruction cache misses
DC_miss	Data cache misses
ITLB_miss	Instruction TLB misses
DTLB_miss	Data TLB misses
L2_imiss	Instruction cache misses that also missed the second-level cache
L2_dmiss_ld	Data cache load misses that also missed the second-level cache

The implementation of the performance counters is more flexible than it appears from the available events. The default sets of events represent those that are anticipated to be commonly occuring. At the implementation level, the events are counted depending on the presence of a control bit. An `emask` value can be applied to a particular event type to include additional events in that count. Example 10.29 shows two methods of counting the total number of load and store instructions. The examples show counting of one type of event with an `emask` value that includes the count of the other event type.

Example 10.29 Counting Both Load and Store Instructions

```
$ cputrack -c Instr_ld,emask=16 sleep 1
   time lwp        event      pic0
  1.014   1         exit     77693
$ cputrack -c Instr_st,emask=8 sleep 1
   time lwp        event      pic0
  1.010   1         exit     77693
```

The UltraSPARC T2 provides the same memory controller interface as the UltraSPARC T1, so it is still possible to calculate system memory bandwidth utilization using `busstat`, as discussed in Section 10.5.4.

10.7 SPARC64 VI Performance Counters

The SPARC64 VI can count up to eight different events simultaneously. Not all event types are available on every counter. Table 10.10 shows the performance counter events relating to cycle and instruction counts.

Table 10.10 SPARC64 VI Cycle and Instruction Count Events

Performance Counter	Description
active_cycle_count	Number of cycles where the strand could issue instructions. A core is shared by two strands, so each strand will get only a portion of the total cycles.
cycle_counts	Total number of cycles
instruction_counts	Number of instructions completed
load_store_instructions	Number of completed load and store instructions
floating_instructions	Number of floating-point instructions (excluding floating-point multiply accumulate instructions)
impdep2_instructions	Number of floating-point multiply accumulate instructions

The processor is also able to provide statistics on cache activity, as shown in Table 10.11.

Table 10.11 SPARC64 VI Cache Events

Performance Counter	Description
trap_IMMU_miss	Instruction TLB miss count
trap_DMMU_miss	Data TLB miss count
if_r_iu_req_mi_go	Instruction cache misses
op_r_iu_req_mi_go	Data cache misses
sx_miss_count_dm	Number of loads or stores that miss in the second-level cache
sx_read_count_dm	Number of load references to second-level caches
sx_miss_count_dm_if	Number of instruction fetches that miss the second-level cache

10.8 Opteron Performance Counters

10.8.1 Introduction

The Opteron processor can simultaneously count up to four different counters recorded with 48 bits of precision. Most events are available on all the counters.

Some counters count events, and some count the number of cycles that a condition is true. The counters also have a rich set of modifiers, as follows.

- The umask flag allows a finer degree of control over the type of event that is recorded. For example, the count of dispatched floating-point operations can be refined to include or exclude the operations dispatched to the Add pipe.

- The invert flag causes the counter to count the opposite event. For example, the counter might count "Cycles with no floating-point operations retired." The invert bit enables the count of cycles where one or more floating-point operations were retired.

- The count mask takes a value from zero to 3, which causes the counter to count the number of cycles where more than the value held in the count mask register events occured. For example, it may be appropriate to count the number of cycles where more than one floating-point instruction was retired.

The use of these modifiers can complicate the syntax of the parameters that need to be passed to cputrack (for example). For example, to read the number of data cache misses that were satisfied with data from memory, it is necessary to specify a umask of 31, as shown in Example 10.30. If it is necessary to specify a umask for one counter, a umask must be specified for all counters.

Example 10.30 Specifying an umask Value

```
% cputrack -c DC_refill_from_system,umask=31 a.out
   time lwp        event        pic0
  1.013    1        tick        7789
...
```

10.8.2 Instructions

There is no cycle counter on the Opteron processor. The best you can do is to use the virtualized tick counter to estimate the number of cycles the processor has been running the code. There are counters for both instructions retired and micro-ops (on the x86, one instruction can get decoded into many micro-ops).

Example 10.31 shows some example code. This code performs some floating-point computation on an array that occupies about 80MB of memory (i.e., the array is sufficiently large not to be resident in cache).

You can calculate the instruction count and CPI for this code using the cputrack command shown in Example 10.32. The code took about 15 seconds to run, and in that time it had about 31 billion execution cycles. Also in that time, the code executed

Example 10.31 Code Demonstrating Floating-Point Computation and Data Streaming

```
#include <stdlib.h>
void main()
{
  int i,j;
  double * array;
  array=(double*)calloc(sizeof(double),1024*1024*10+1024);
  for (i=0;i<1024*1024*10; i++)
    for (j=0;j<1024;j++) {array[i+j]*=array[j];}
}
```

about 97 billion instructions, or about three instructions per cycle (or a CPI of about 0.3 cycles per instruction).

Example 10.32 Instructions Executed and Cycles Used for Example Code

```
% cputrack -t -c FR_retired_x86_instr_w_excp_intr a.out
   time lwp    event       tsc        pic0
  1.062  1     tick 2330773504 6144648944
  2.012  1     tick 2087807799 6217969696
  3.082  1     tick 2357834540 7022124232
  4.062  1     tick 2159143630 6430669324
  5.012  1     tick 2092832142 6232977377
  6.112  1     tick 2424034021 7220773839
  7.012  1     tick 1982731169 5905046364
  8.022  1     tick 2225519971 6627051051
  9.142  1     tick 2467798772 7349139827
 10.042  1     tick 1982781404 5904087586
 11.022  1     tick 2159467178 6430330524
 12.142  1     tick 2467995628 7352116739
 13.042  1     tick 1983093368 5905803554
 14.022  1     tick 2159199769 6429267572
 14.868  1     exit 30881012895 96719537894
```

10.8.3 Instruction Cache Events

Table 10.12 shows the performance counters that record instruction cache events.

Table 10.12 Instruction Cache Events

Counter	Comment
IC_fetch	Number of references to instruction cache. Each reference is typically 16 bytes.
IC_miss	Number of instruction cache misses. Each miss will fetch 64 bytes of data into the instruction cache.
IC_refill_from_L2	Number of instruction cache misses where the instructions were fetched from the second-level cache
IC_refill_from_system	Number of instruction cache misses where the instructions were fetched from memory

Example 10.33 shows the instruction cache events for the example program. As expected, there are very few instruction cache miss events, and most of the misses that occur are satisfied from the second-level cache. Over the run of the program, there are about 22 billion instruction cache fetches. Comparing this with the number of instructions executed from Example 10.32, it is apparent that each fetch pulls in more than one instruction.

Example 10.33 Instruction Cache Events from Example Program

```
% cputrack -c IC_fetch,IC_miss,IC_refill_from_L2,\
IC_refill_from_system a.out
   time lwp     event     pic0    pic1    pic2   pic3
  1.025   1     tick 1266669483   42756   41900    856
  2.095   1     tick 1567169246      17      12      5
  3.095   1     tick 1467051425      14      13      1
  4.025   1     tick 1364361538      18      14      4
  5.095   1     tick 1569819889      10       6      4
  6.095   1     tick 1467046643      18      16      2
  7.015   1     tick 1350016237      10       7      3
  8.095   1     tick 1584361418      15       9      6
  9.035   1     tick 1378986055      17      12      5
 10.035   1     tick 1466815005      21      20      1
 11.095   1     tick 1555371634       9       6      3
 12.095   1     tick 1467000757      17      15      2
 13.025   1     tick 1364455072      11       9      2
 14.025   1     tick 1467513432      11      10      1
 14.904   1     exit 21625197419   43244   42105   1139
```

10.8.4 Data Cache Events

Table 10.13 shows the performance counters that record data cache events.

Table 10.13 Data Cache Events

Counter	Comment
DC_access,umask=0	Number of accesses to the data cache. Each access is for up to eight bytes.
DC_miss,umask=0	Number of data cache misses. Each miss will fetch 64 bytes.
DC_refill_from_L2,umask=30	Number of data cache misses where the instructions were fetched from the second-level cache. The umask specifies that the count is only of the data returned by the second-level cache.
DC_refill_from_system,umask=31	Number of data cache misses where the instructions were fetched from memory. The umask setting specifies that the count should include lines fetched regardless of their status (shared, etc.) in memory.

As mentioned previously, if one event type needs to be specified using a `umask` value, all the events need to have a `umask` value specified. Example 10.34 shows the output. The results show that there are few misses of the data cache, and that for most of these misses, the data is returned by the second-level cache.

Example 10.34 Data Cache Miss Behavior

```
%  cputrack -c DC_access,umask0=0,DC_miss,umask1=0,\
DC_refill_from_L2,umask2=30,\
DC_refill_from_system,umask3=31 a.out
   time lwp      event      pic0       pic1       pic2       pic3
  1.038  1       tick 2013160055    6697863      81992       8888
  2.018  1       tick 2141777473      91700      84629       7880
  3.108  1       tick 2387248456     102058      94262       8075
  4.108  1       tick 2190410280      95050      87802       7898
  5.138  1       tick 2255645393      96741      89253       8665
  6.038  1       tick 1970982313      84715      78189       7461
  7.018  1       tick 2147518809      88654      81701       7301
  8.158  1       tick 2496684673     106585      98393       8725
  9.028  1       tick 1904474513      87048      80581       7580
 10.018  1       tick 2168389992      90452      83364       7665
 11.018  1       tick 2189554810      94334      87151       7591
 12.018  1       tick 2189179065     100109      92803       7615
 13.108  1       tick 2386460592     105704      97767       8661
 14.108  1       tick 2189517756      99117      91814       7628
 14.862  1       exit 32280794785   8014500    1298478     117358
```

10.8.5 TLB Events

The Opteron processor has two levels of TLB. The penalties associated with a TLB miss are higher for a second-level TLB miss than for a first-level miss. The first-level TLBs are quite small (8–32 entries), so first-level misses are likely. The second-level data TLBs are larger—512 entries—and able to map a total of 2MB with 4KB pages. On some processors, there are only eight entries for large page (2MB) sizes, mapping a total of 16MB. You need to be careful when attempting to use these large page sizes because applications that have more than eight streams of data may encounter more TLB misses when using the large page sizes. Table 10.14 shows the performance counters that count TLB events.

Table 10.14 Counters of TLB Miss Activity

Counter	Comment
DC_dtlb_L1_miss_L2_hit	Data TLB misses that hit in the second-level data TLB
DC_dtlb_L1_miss_L2_miss	Data TLB misses that miss in the second-level data TLB
IC_itlb_L1_miss_L2_hit	Instruction TLB misses that hit in the second-level instruction TLB
IC_itlb_L1_miss_L2_miss	Instruction TLB misses that miss in the second-level instruction TLB

Example 10.35 shows the TLB miss events for the example code from Example 10.31. As might be expected, there are very few ITLB miss events because the code has a small footprint. There are a number of data TLB miss events, and again this is not surprising given that the code accesses 80MB of data. For both instructions and data, most of the TLB miss events also miss the second-level TLB.

Example 10.35 TLB Miss Events for Example Code

```
% cputrack -c DC_dtlb_L1_miss_L2_hit,DC_dtlb_L1_miss_L2_miss,\
IC_itlb_L1_miss_L2_hit,IC_itlb_L1_miss_L2_miss a.out
   time lwp     event      pic0      pic1      pic2      pic3
  1.021   1      tick       846     42416        24       127
  2.021   1      tick       539      1438         0         7
  3.021   1      tick       525      1446         0         7
  4.021   1      tick       462      1483         0        14
  5.021   1      tick       498      1452         0        10
  6.021   1      tick       466      1472         0        13
  7.021   1      tick       458      1469         0        12
  8.021   1      tick       471      1465         0        12
  9.021   1      tick       434      1481         0        14
 10.021   1      tick       528      1477         0        13
 11.021   1      tick       554      1443         0         7
 12.021   1      tick       404      1526         0        20
 13.021   1      tick       519      1473         0        13
 14.021   1      tick       497      1465         0        11
 14.878   1      exit      7641     62779        24       312
```

10.8.6 Branch Events

A number of counters deal with branches and whether the branches are successfully predicted. Table 10.15 summarizes these counters.

Table 10.15 Performance Counters for Branch Instructions

Counter	Comment
FR_retired_branches_w_excp_intr	Count of the number of branch instructions
FR_retired_taken_branches	Count of the number of taken branches
FR_retired_branches_mispred	Count of the number of mispredicted branches
FR_retired_taken_branches_mispred	Count of the number of taken branches that were mispredicted (as untaken)

Example 10.36 shows the branch behavior for the code in Example 10.31. This shows that about 11 billion branch instructions were executed, and almost all the branches were taken (as might be expected given that the example code is basically a loop). A small number of branches were mispredicted.

Example 10.36 Branch Behavior

```
% cputrack -c \
FR_retired_branches_w_excp_intr,FR_retired_taken_branches,\
FR_retired_branches_mispred,FR_retired_taken_branches_mispred a.out
   time lwp      event       pic0         pic1         pic2       pic3
   1.046   1      tick 674328909   673660467       682027      24454
   2.016   1      tick 705745215   705056684       688639        108
   3.015   1      tick 729519932   728808205       711822         95
   4.035   1      tick 744173761   743447738       726090         67
   5.016   1      tick 714629491   713932291       697314        114
   6.016   1      tick 729264976   728553498       711588        110
   7.045   1      tick 750978557   750245896       732795        134
   8.016   1      tick 707517145   706826884       690350         89
   9.015   1      tick 729256449   728544979       711556         86
  10.035   1      tick 743999905   743274052       725937         84
  11.016   1      tick 714664639   713967405       697335        101
  12.016   1      tick 729288385   728576884       711606        105
  13.045   1      tick 751130083   750397274       732914        105
  14.016   1      tick 707452148   706761951       690312        115
  14.862   1      exit 10749271174 10738773002   10513206      26364
```

10.8.7 Stall Cycles

A number of counters count the cycles where the processor is stalled waiting for some resource to become available. The FR_dispatch_stalls counter counts the cycles that the processor is stalled for any reason. Other counters count the cycles for particular reasons. The processor can be stalled waiting for several resources, so the sum of the counts of particular events may be greater than the total number of stall cycles. Table 10.16 shows the counters of the more common processor stall events.

Table 10.16 Counters of Cycles Lost to Common Processor Stall Events

Performance Counter	Comment
FR_dispatch_stalls	Cycles where the processor is stalled for any reason
IC_instr_fetch_stall	Cycles where the instruction fetcher is stalled waiting for an instruction to be returned
FR_nothing_to_dispatch	Cycles where the instruction decoder is stalled waiting for the next instruction to be fetched
FR_dispatch_stall_branch_abort_to_retire	Cycles where the processor is stalled waiting for the pipeline to empty after a mispredicted branch

Table 10.16 Counters of Cycles Lost to Common Processor Stall Events (*continued*)

Performance Counter	Comment
`FR_dispatch_stall_reorder_buffer_full`	Cycles where the processor is stalled waiting for space to place new instructions into the reorder buffer
`FR_dispatch_stall_fpu_full`	Cycles where the processor is stalled waiting for floating-point resources to become available
`FR_dispatch_stall_ls_full`	Cycles where the processor is stalled because it has issued the maximum number of outstanding loads and stores

Example 10.37 shows the results of collecting stall counters from running the code from Example 10.31. The program runs for nearly 33 billion cycles, and during this time it records about 100 million cycles where it is stalled. The largest contributors to these stall cycles are cycles where the load-store buffer is full, and cycles where the processor is waiting for the pipeline to drain after a mispredicted branch.

Example 10.37 Stall Counters

```
% cputrack -t -c \
FR_dispatch_stalls,FR_dispatch_stall_branch_abort_to_retire,\
FR_dispatch_stall_reorder_buffer_full,FR_dispatch_stall_ls_full a.out
   time lwp     event       tsc        pic0      pic1      pic2      pic3
  1.028  1      tick 2257800536  51512069   3150726    275872  45447395
  2.038  1      tick 2220385161   3821357   3366804    387113     40268
  3.038  1      tick 2203667201   3697187   3322315    318420     32508
  4.038  1      tick 2203055193   3717391   3327498    331802     33993
  5.018  1      tick 2159219395   3647666   3253087    337027     33507
  6.018  1      tick 2203399406   3621695   3312054    260876     24048
  7.028  1      tick 2225631783   3670077   3347347    271383     26683
  8.038  1      tick 2225205871   3740950   3390102    295452     34314
  9.028  1      tick 2181306304   3692344   3297329    338405     32002
 10.028  1      tick 2203192240   3859867   3390965    404749     46720
 11.018  1      tick 2181210235   3709892   3343766    311055     35354
 12.028  1      tick 2225275668   3847361   3463826    324485     44459
 13.028  1      tick 2203488398   3690767   3361926    274976     31906
 14.018  1      tick 2180422293   3845446   3396229    384203     43124
 14.861  1      exit 32730289452 103315019  49571951   4843149  45947444
```

11

Source Code Optimizations

11.1 Overview

The objective of this chapter is to introduce some common coding situations and to demonstrate how performance can be improved either by using the appropriate compiler flags or by modifying the source code.

As an adjunct to this, the code samples also demonstrate how to read the performance counters, and to identify what the bottleneck is in various situations.

11.2 Traditional Optimizations

11.2.1 Introduction

Many texts will list a number of optimizations that you can apply to source code. You should be careful if the code looks like it is susceptible to one of these optimizations. In many cases, the compiler may already be performing the optimization. If such an opportunity is identified, the first step is to determine whether the compiler is already doing the optimization, usually by checking the disassembly of the routine or examining the profile of where the time is spent in the routine. If the compiler is not doing the optimization, the next step is to determine whether the problem can be solved with more aggressive compiler options, or with source code changes.

This section describes a number of traditional optimizations that, in most situations, the compiler will perform. The section discusses how to identify and improve situations where the compiler is unable to perform the optimization. The issues that typically stop the compiler from performing the optimizations are pointer aliasing and complex program flow.

11.2.2 Loop Unrolling and Pipelining

Loop unrolling is when multiple iterations of a loop are combined into a single iteration of a loop. Further optimization of pipelining the loop occurs when the compiler mixes operations from different iterations of the loop so that multiple computations can be overlapped. I discuss loop unrolling and pipelining in Section 5.12.6 and Section 5.12.8 of Chapter 5. Figure 11.1 shows the loop optimizations of unrolling and pipelining. The original loop has a trip count of 10. When the loop is unrolled by two, the trip count is halved to 5. Pipelining the loop keeps the same trip count, but mixes instructions from the two unrolled iterations. The advantage of unrolling the loop is that it reduces the number of branch statements encountered at runtime. A consequence of this is that some other instructions can also be eliminated. It is also possible that by unrolling the loop, the compiler can schedule better prefetch instructions. When the loop is also pipelined, the latency of the instructions from one iteration of the loop can often be hidden by instructions from other iterations.

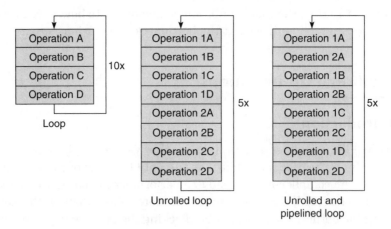

Figure 11.1 Unrolling and Pipelining Loops

A related optimization occurs when the compiler fully unrolls the loops, eliminating the need for branches. It can do this if it is able to determine the exact trip count of the loop, and if the optimization is likely to be beneficial.

There are downsides to this optimization. Unrolled loops take up more space in the instruction cache and can use more registers to hold temporary values, and the trip count of the loop has to be greater than the unroll for the unrolled code to actually be used.

Example 11.1 shows an example in which complex program flow inhibits loop unrolling. The `if` condition can inhibit the compiler from performing loop unrolling and pipelining. For this situation, you can replace the `if` condition with equivalent code that uses conditional move instructions on hardware that supports them, as I discuss further in Section 11.8.2.

Example 11.1 Complex Program Flow Inhibiting Loop Unrolling

```
int calc(int* array, int count)
{
  int total =0;
  for (int i=0; i<count; i++)
  {
    total +=array[i];
    if (total<0) {total=0;}
  }
  return total;
}
```

11.2.3 Loop Peeling, Fusion, and Splitting

When several adjacent loops perform calculations over the same range of values, and the later loops do not depend on a value calculated by the earlier loops, it can often make sense to combine the loops into a single loop; this is called *loop fusion*.

In some cases, it may not be possible to combine the initial or final iterations of the two loops. In these cases, those iterations are peeled off into separate code. Loop peeling is also useful in situations where the behavior of a loop changes depending on the index variable—perhaps the first iteration of the loop has code that initializes values; this first iteration can be peeled off, reducing the complexity of the rest of the code.

The example in Example 11.2 shows a pair of loops that can be fused after suitable peeling. If the first iteration of the first loop is peeled, the first loop becomes much simpler and can be coded efficiently. After loop peeling, the bounds of the two loops end up being the same, and the two loops can be fused, reducing the total instruction count and the amount of data that needs to be fetched from memory (the `array[i]` value is used in both loops, and fusing the loops means the value can be reused).

Example 11.2 Loops Suitable for Peeling and Fusing

```
int calc(int * array, int count)
{
  int total =0;
  for (int i=0; i<count; i++)
  {
    if (i==0) {total = 1<<array[i];}
        else  {total += array[i];}
  }
  for (int i=1; i<count; i++)
  {
    total+=array[i-1]*array[i];
  }
  return total;
}
```

Example 11.3 shows the equivalent transformed code.

Example 11.3 Transformed Code after Loop Peeling and Fusing

```
int calc(int * array, int count)
{
  int total =1<<array[0];
  for (int i=1; i<count; i++)
  {
    total += array[i];
    total += array[i-1]*array[i];
  }
  return total;
}
```

The opposite of loop fusion is *loop splitting*; this is when a loop has a complex body which can be split into two independent parts. An advantage of doing this could be to reduce the number of registers used by each iteration of the loop and avoid the compiler having to store partial results to memory and then having to load them back (this is called *spilling and filling registers*).

11.2.4 Loop Interchange and Tiling

Many codes have nested loops which iterate over matrices of values. The performance of the loops depends on whether the loops are arranged optimally. The factors you need to consider when determining the layout of the loops are the amount of reuse of values from previous iterations, whether the data is contiguous in memory, and how much data needs to be fetched from memory for each iteration. Selecting the appropriate loop nesting leads to better performance due to accessing memory locations contiguously, as well as reusing previously loaded values.

Typically, the compiler is good at determining the appropriate nesting for the loops, but a number of issues can stop it from being able to pick appropriately. One obvious issue is pointer aliasing between the stored values and loaded values. A more subtle issue is where the compiler determines that a dependency exists between one iteration and a previous iteration. In this case, it may not be possible for the compiler to perform the loop interchange. The code in Example 11.4 shows an example where loop interchange would improve memory access patterns. The innermost loop accesses the matrices a and b by stride rather than contiguously. Interchanging the inner and outer loops will access the arrays in a contiguous way, leading to a performance gain.

Example 11.4 Code with Potential Loop Interchange Opportunity

```
void mmmul(float ** a, float ** b, int n, int m)
{
  for (int i=0; i<n; i++)
    for (int j=0; j<m; j++)
    {
        b[j][i]+=a[j][i];
    }
}
```

Another optimization that applies to loop nests is that of *loop tiling*. As the name suggests, this takes nested loops and splits the loop nests into smaller tiles, where all the data can be fit into on-chip cache. These optimizations can lead to significantly better performance for optimizations such as matrix-matrix multiplication. They are also optimizations that the compiler may have difficulty performing. Example 11.5 shows an example of matrix-matrix multiplication code that could be tiled. Tiling is effective for this code because in the original loop, accesses to b[k][j] are read as striding through memory, so there is poor use of the caches.

Example 11.5 Matrix-Matrix Multiplication Code

```
void mmmul(float ** a, float ** b, float **c, int n, int m)
{
  for (int i=0; i<n; i++)
    for (int j=0; j<m; j++)
    {
      c[i][j]=0.0;
      for (int k=0; k<m; k++)
      {
        c[i][j]+=a[i][k]*b[k][j];
      }
    }
}
```

Example 11.6 shows a simple version of loop tiling. In this variant of the code, two iterations for the loop variable j are combined. This allows reuse of the matrix element a[i][k]. This code is missing the cleanup loop necessary to handle matrices where m is odd. A more complex form of tiling could be used to further increase the reuse of matrix elements.

Example 11.6 Simple Loop Tiling Example

```
void mmmul(float ** a, float ** b, float **c, int n, int m)
{
  for (int i=0; i<n; i++)
    for (int j=0; j<m; j+=2)
    {
      c[i][j  ]=0.0;
      c[i][j+1]=0.0;
      for (int k=0; k<m; k++)
      {
        c[i][j  ]+=a[i][k]*b[k][j  ];
        c[i][j+1]+=a[i][k]*b[k][j+1];
      }
    }
}
```

11.2.5 Loop Invariant Hoisting

Loop invariant hoisting refers to the process of removing calculations that do not change with the loop iterations out of the loop. Pointer aliasing is probably the main reason the compiler would leave loop invariant calculations inside a loop body. Example 11.7 shows an example of this. In this code, the calculation of squaring the scale variable could be hoisted out of the loop if the compiler could be sure that the stores to the result array would not change its value.

Example 11.7 Loop Invariant Code

```
int calc(int * array, int * scale, int * result, int n)
{
  for (int i=0; i<n ; i++)
  {
    result[i] =(*scale)*(*scale)*array[i];
  }
}
```

Example 11.8 shows a transformed version of the source that has the loop invariant code hoisted.

Example 11.8 Loop Invariant Code

```
int calc(int * array, int * scale, int * result, int n)
{
  int tmp=(*scale)*(*scale);
  for (int i=0; i<n ; i++)
  {
    result[i] =tmp*array[i];
  }
}
```

11.2.6 Common Subexpression Elimination

A lot of code has some amount of repetition in it. It can be clearer to recalculate a value rather than hold it in a temporary register. The compiler is very efficient at recognizing common calculations and holding the partial results for later use. This is referred to as *common subexpression elimination* (CSE). Adherence to the IEEE-754 standard may inhibit some CSE optimizations.

Example 11.9 shows an example this. In this example, the base * width expression can be calculated first and then used as part of the following calculations.

Example 11.9 Common Subexpressions

```
volume = base * width * height;
area = base * width;
```

11.2.7 Strength Reduction

Strength reduction is the substitution of a cheap calculation for a more expensive one. A simple example is where multiplication of an integer by two can be achieved by shifting the integer value left by one bit. Multiplication by three can be achieved using a shift and an add.

In general, the compiler is able to perform many of these optimizations, but in some circumstances the developer has either more insight into the common values encountered by the code, or can find an algorithm that requires fewer cycles to execute than the original code.

11.2.8 Function Cloning

The compiler is often able to detect functions that can be cloned and replaced by a specialized version. The cloned function is identical to the original function, but it is tailored to a particular call of the original function where the calling parameters are known. Example 11.10 shows an example of a function that could be cloned. In this case, the f function is called with the j parameter set to the value 2. A specialized version of the function could be produced where the j parameter is replaced throughout the function by the value 2. For this example, inlining would be a more appropriate optimization because the body of the cloned function is small, but cloning can be a very useful optimization when the function is called in the same way from multiple locations or when the function body is too large for inlining to be effective.

Example 11.10 Code with Function Cloning Opportunities

```
int f(int i, int j)
{
  return (i*j);
}

main()
{
  ...
  j = f(i,2);
  ...
}
```

11.3 Data Locality, Bandwidth, and Latency

11.3.1 Bandwidth

Applications can often access memory as a long array of data. Typically this happens when doing mathematical calculations; for example, calculating the average of a series of numbers. Each number is read and added, and then the next number is fetched. In this situation, the memory access is predictable, and the performance is basically driven by *memory bandwidth*—the rate at which data can be transferred from memory into the processor. Example 11.11 shows an example program.

The -xprefetch compiler flag determines whether prefetch instructions are inserted into the code. Since the Sun Studio 9 compiler, the generation of prefetch instructions has been enabled by default. Adding prefetch instructions can make a signficant difference to performance. For example, in Example 11.12

Example 11.11 Program to Sum a Series of Numbers

```
#include "timing.h"

#define SIZE 2*1024*1024
#define RPT 100

double array[SIZE];

int main()
{
  int index,count;
  double totalf;

  for (index=0; index<SIZE; index++) array[index]=0;

  totalf=0;
  starttime();
  for (count=0; count<RPT; count++)
  {
    for (index=0;index<SIZE;index++)
      totalf+=array[index];
    totalf=totalf*5.7;
  }
  endtime(SIZE*RPT);

  return (int)totalf;
}
```

the application takes about 24ns per iteration without prefetch, and 5ns per iteration with prefetch.

Example 11.12 Code Run with and without Prefetch

```
% cc -xO3 -xtarget=ultra3 -xprefetch=no ex11.11.c
% time a.out
Time per iteration 23.86 ns
% cc -xO3 -xtarget=ultra3 -xprefetch stream_13.c
% time a.out
Time per iteration  5.14 ns
```

11.3.2 Integer Data

Prefetch also makes a significant difference for integer data. However, for the UltraSPARC III family of processors, integer data can be fetched only into the second-level cache (not the on-chip cache). Example 11.13 shows example code that streams integer data.

Example 11.13 Streaming Integer Data

```
#include "timing.h"

#define SIZE 4*1024*1024
#define RPT 100

int array[SIZE];

int main()
{
  int index,count;
  int totalf;

  for (index=0; index<SIZE; index++) array[index]=0;

  totalf=0;
  starttime();
  for (count=0; count<RPT; count++)
  {
    for (index=0;index<SIZE;index++)
      totalf+=array[index];
    totalf=totalf*5.7;
  }
  endtime(SIZE*RPT);

  return totalf;
}
```

Example 11.14 shows the results of compiling this code with and without prefetch. The code takes 13ns per iteration without prefetch compared to 4ns with prefetch. Rather surprisingly, the integer code runs faster than the floating-point code because the latency of the floating-point add and load instructions is four cycles. In comparison, an integer load takes two cycles, and an integer add only one cycle. It is the latency of these floating-point instructions that significantly determines the performance of the loop.

Example 11.14 Streaming Integer Data with and without Prefetch

```
% cc -xO3 -xtarget=ultra3 -xprefetch=no time ex11.13.c
% a.out
Time per iteration 12.90 ns
% cc -xO3 -xtarget=ultra3 -xprefetch ex11.13.c
% a.out
Time per iteration  3.81 ns
```

11.3.3 Storing Streams

Performance can also be improved with prefetch when storing streams of data, as shown in Example 11.15.

Example 11.15 Streams of Stored Data

```
#include "timing.h"

#define SIZE 2*1024*1024
#define RPT 100

double array[SIZE];

int main()
{
  int index,count;
  double totalf;

  for (index=0; index<SIZE; index++) array[index]=0;

  totalf=0;
  starttime();
  for (count=0; count<RPT; count++)
  {
    for (index=0;index<SIZE;index++)
    {
      array[index]=totalf;
      totalf+=index;
    }
    totalf=totalf*5.7;
  }
  endtime(SIZE*RPT);

  return (int)totalf;
}
```

Example 11.16 shows the results of compiling the test code for storing streams of data. With prefetch the code takes 10ns per iterations; without prefetch it takes 30ns per iteration.

Example 11.16 Results of Storing a Stream of Data with and without Prefetch

```
% cc -x03 -xtarget=ultra3 -xprefetch=no ex11.15.c
% a.out
Time per iteration 29.30 ns
% cc -x03 -xtarget=ultra3 -xprefetch ex11.15.c
% a.out
Time per iteration  9.76 ns
```

11.3.4 Manual Prefetch

Sometimes the compiler is unable to insert prefetches into the code. This may happen where a loop contains `if` statements or other control flow. It may also happen where the access pattern is apparent to the developer because of some characteristic of the application, but that characteristic is not apparent to the compiler; perhaps a linked list has a generally predictable access pattern.

In Fortran, this is done using pragmas inserted into the source code. For C/C++, it is necessary to include the `sun_prefetch.h` header file. In Sun Studio 12, the manual prefetch for the x86 was included in the header. The platform-agnostic versions of the functions start with `sun` rather than `sparc`. Table 11.1 summarizes the actions of the various prefetch types.

Table 11.1 Manual Prefetch

Construct	Description

`sparc_prefetch_read_once(<address>)`
`sun_prefetch_read_once(<address>)`
`$PRAGMA SPARC_PREFETCH_READ_ONCE (address)`
	Fetch data to be read once. Try to avoid polluting the caches with the data.

`sparc_prefetch_read_many(<address>)`
`sun_prefetch_read_many(<address>)`
`$PRAGMA SPARC_PREFETCH_READ_MANY (address)`
	Fetch data to be read multiple times. Install data in caches.

`sparc_prefetch_write_once(<address>)`
`sun_prefetch_write_once(<address>)`
`$PRAGMA SPARC_PREFETCH_WRITE_ONCE (address)`
	Fetch cache line for it to be written to once

`sparc_prefetch_write_many(<address>)`
`sun_prefetch_write_many(<address>)`
`$PRAGMA SPARC_PREFETCH_WRITE_MANY (address)`
	Fetch cache line for it to be written to multiple times

You need to be careful to ensure that manually inserted prefetch instructions are actually prefetching the correct address. Consequently, it is often worth checking the disassembly for the section of code containing the manual prefetch call.

For the code shown in Example 11.17, Sun Studio 12 does not insert prefetch instructions at `-O` unless the flag `-xprefetch_level=2` is also specified.

Example 11.17 Code Where the Compiler Does Not Insert Prefetches

```
#include "timing.h"

#define SIZE 2*1024*1024
#define RPT 100

double array[SIZE];

int main()
{
  int index,count;
  double totalf;

  for (index=0; index<SIZE; index++) array[index]=0;

  totalf=0;
  starttime();
  for (count=0; count<RPT; count++)
  {
    for (index=0;index<SIZE;index++)
    {
      if (array[index]>0) totalf+=array[index];
    }
    totalf=totalf*5.7;
  }
  endtime(SIZE*RPT);

  return (int)totalf;
}
```

Example 11.18 shows analyzer output for the hot part of the code. The time is being attributed to the floating-point branch instruction, although it is caused by the load instruction at `0x10ee4`.

Example 11.18 Analyzer Output for the Hot Part of the Code

```
    0.              10ec8:  fcmped      %fcc0, %f2, %f6
## 6.124            10ecc:  fbule,pn    %fcc0, 0x10ed8
    0.040           10ed0:  inc         8, %l7
    0.              10ed4:  faddd       %f8, %f2, %f8
    0.040           10ed8:  inc         %l6
    0.060           10edc:  cmp         %l6, %l0
    0.              10ee0:  ble,a,pt    %icc,0x10ec8
    0.030           10ee4:  ldd         [%l7], %f2
```

Having identified which load instruction is missing cache, and the source line that generates this load instruction, it is relatively easy to add a manual prefetch to get the data ready for the load. The source code in Example 11.19 has been modified to contain the appropriate manual prefetch code.

Example 11.19 Modified Source Showing Manual Prefetch Insertion

```
#include "timing.h"
#include <sun_prefetch.h>
#define SIZE 2*1024*1024
#define RPT 100

double array[SIZE];

int main()
{
  int index,count;
  double totalf;

  for (index=0; index<SIZE; index++) array[index]=0;

  totalf=0;
  starttime();
  for (count=0; count<RPT; count++)
  {
    for (index=0;index<SIZE;index++)
    {
      sparc_prefetch_read_many(&array[index+16]);
      if (array[index]>0) totalf+=array[index];
    }
    totalf=totalf*5.7;
  }
  endtime(SIZE*RPT);

  return (int)totalf;
}
```

Example 11.20 shows the analyzer output for the modified source code with the manually inserted prefetch.

Example 11.20 Analyzer Output for the Modifed Code

```
    0.060        10ed4:  ldd        [%16], %f2      ◄
    0.           10ed8:  fcmped     %fcc0, %f2, %f6
##  2.542        10edc:  fbule,pn   %fcc0, 0x10ee8
    0.020        10ee0:  inc        8, %16
    0.           10ee4:  faddd      %f8, %f2, %f8
    0.060        10ee8:  inc        %15
    0.           10eec:  inc        8, %17
    0.100        10ef0:  cmp        %15, %10
    0.           10ef4:  ble,pt     %icc,0x10ed4
    0.           10ef8:  prefetch   [%17], #n_reads
```

As mentioned previously, the compiler is able to insert prefetches for this loop when it is compiled with the options -O and -xprefetch_level=2. Example 11.21 shows the performance from the two variants of the code under different levels of prefetch insertion. The original code with no prefetch takes 30ns per iteration; when manual prefetch is added this time is reduced to 13ns per iteration. However, when the compiler adds prefetch instructions for this loop, it is able to achieve 10.5ns per iteration. So, given the right options, the compiler is able to do better than a manually inserted prefetch instruction.

Example 11.21 Comparison of Compiler and Manual Prefetch Insertion

```
% cc -xO3 -xtarget=ultra3 -xprefetch ex11.17.c
% a.out
Time per iteration 29.84 ns
% cc -xO3 -xtarget=ultra3 -xprefetch ex11.19.c
% a.out
Time per iteration 13.11 ns
% cc -xO3 -xtarget=ultra3 -xprefetch -xprefetch_level=2 ex11.17.c
% a.out
Time per iteration 10.50 ns
```

11.3.5 Latency

Latency is a measure of how long it takes to fetch a single item of data from memory. Code to measure latency can be hard to write because it has to ensure the following.

- The data has to be entirely resident in a particular level of cache. The simplest way to achieve this is to make the data set slightly smaller than the level of cache being measured and to iterate through every element in the data set before repeating the access to any element.

- Each access must bring in a different cache line to always be fetching new data from memory; otherwise, the latency calculated will be some average of cache miss and cache hit costs.

- You must write the access pattern such that the compiler cannot detect a regular stride pattern and add prefetch instructions to reduce the latency. The easiest way to achieve this goal is to make the loop a pointer chasing loop. In this way, the compiler cannot have insight into the next address except from loading the current address.

- In the presence of hardware stride predictors, the memory access pattern needs to be sufficiently complex to avoid the hardware prefetch being able to predict the next location. One way to achieve this is to randomize the addresses used. The degree of complexity needed in the software will depend on the complexity of the hardware prefetch unit.

The code shown in Example 11.22 sets up a simple test of memory latency. A linked list is traversed, each location is a new fetch from memory, and the latency is measured as the time per iteration of the inner loop. Because the UltraSPARC IIICu processor that this test has been run on does not have a hardware prefetch unit that fetches data from memory, there is no need to complicate the linked list. Notice that at the end of the code there is a redundant operation on the pointer to ensure that the compiler is unable to optimize out of the loop.

Example 11.22 Test of Memory Latency

```
#include <stdio.h>
#include "timing.h"

#define SIZE 1024*1024*2*2
#define ITERATIONS 1024*1024*2*2
static int** array[SIZE];

void main()
{
  int i;
  int **j;
  for (i=0; i<SIZE-16; i++)
    array[i]=(int**)&array[i+16];
  for (i=0; i<16; i++)
    array[SIZE-1-i]=(int**)&array[i];

  starttime();
  j=array[0];
  for (i=0; i<4*ITERATIONS; i++)
  {
    j=(int **)*j;
  }
  endtime(4*ITERATIONS);
  if (j==0) {printf("Null element\n");}
}
```

Example 11.23 shows the results of running the program in Example 11.22 on a two-processor 1056MHz UltraSPARC IIICu system. This indicates that the memory latency is about 150ns.

Example 11.23 Latency Results

```
% cc -xO3 -xprefetch -xtarget=ultra3 -xmemalign=8s ex11.22.c
% a.out
Time per iteration 155.15 ns
```

Looking at the program, it is possible to determine that the stride pattern is completely predictable, and having determined this, it is possible to add prefetches for the appropriate distance ahead. In the first instance, the next iteration is going to be at an offset of 16 elements (i.e., 16*4 = 64 bytes) from the current iteration.

You can modify the code as shown in Example 11.24 to take advantage of this information.

Example 11.24 Adding Prefetch to the Latency Test

```
#include <stdio.h>
#include "timing.h"
#include <sun_prefetch.h>

#define SIZE 1024*1024*2*2
#define ITERATIONS 1024*1024*2*2
static int** array[SIZE];

void main()
{
  int i;
  int **j;
  for (i=0; i<SIZE-16; i++)
   array[i]=(int**)&array[i+16];
  for (i=0; i<16; i++)
    array[SIZE-1-i]=(int**)&array[i];

  starttime();
  j=array[0];
  for (i=0; i<4*ITERATIONS; i++)
  {
   j=(int **)*j;
   sparc_prefetch_read_many(j+16);
  }
  endtime(4*ITERATIONS);
  if (j==0) {printf("Null element\n");}
}
```

Now when the code is compiled, the latency is noticieably reduced, as shown in Example 11.25.

Example 11.25 Running the Latency Code with Prefetch Inserted

```
% cc -xO3 -xprefetch -xtarget=ultra3 -xmemalign=8s ex11.24.c
% a.out
Time per iteration 98.08 ns
```

Inserting prefetch for the next cache line does improve performance, but it does not achive the best possible performance because at any one time two cache line accesses at most will be fetched from memory. Fetching a cache line that is farther ahead should improve performance, as more prefetches will be active at the same time, and each prefetch will have more time to retrieve the data before it is needed. The data presented in Table 11.2 shows the changes in performance as the prefetch-ahead distance is modified.

Table 11.2 Memory Latency As a Function of Number of Cache Lines
Prefetched Ahead

Prefetch Ahead-Cache Lines	Measured Memory Latency
None	155ns
1	98ns
2	69ns
3	55ns
4	47ns
5	43ns
6	39ns
7	38ns
8	44ns
9	52ns

As you might expect, the big gains in performance come from emitting prefetches for one or two cache lines ahead, and that further prefetches give diminishing gains. One way to look at these results is that the degree of memory-level parallelism (the amount of data that is being fetched from memory simultaneously) is being increased as more cache lines are prefetched in parallel. In effect, the latency bound code is being converted to one that is bound by bandwidth.

You can confirm this by calculating the bandwidth both initially and when prefetches are emitted for two cache lines ahead. Initially, the code attains one cache line every 155ns, so a bandwidth of 64 bytes * 1,000,000,000ns/155ns = 394MB per second. When the code is prefetching for two cache lines ahead the bandwidth is 64 bytes * 1,000,000,000ns / 69ns = 885MB per second—a doubling of the utilized bandwidth.

The other situation to consider is when it is possible to determine that some degree of pointer chasing is going on, and it is not possible to determine the pattern at compile time but it is predictable at runtime. The code shown in Example 11.26 demonstrates one way to issue speculative prefetches at runtime. In this simplified case, the code is the latency test program, and consequently, the memory access pattern is very predictable. However, rather than doing a static speculation of where the next memory access might be, the code uses a simple stride predictor which assumes that the accesses are regularly spaced. The stride predictor attempts to predict for two accesses in advance.

Example 11.26 Speculative Stride Prediction

```
#include <stdio.h>
#include "timing.h"
#include <sun_prefetch.h>

#define SIZE 1024*1024*2*2
#define ITERATIONS 1024*1024*2*2
static int** array[SIZE];

void main()
{
  int i;
  int **j;
  int ** old;
  for (i=0; i<SIZE-16; i++)
   array[i]=(int**)&array[i+16];
  for (i=0; i<16; i++)
    array[SIZE-1-i]=(int**)&array[i];

  starttime();
  j=array[0];
  old = j;
  for (i=0; i<4*ITERATIONS; i++)
  {
   j=(int **)*j;
   sparc_prefetch_read_many(j + 2*(j-old));
   old = j;
  }
  endtime(4*ITERATIONS);
  if (j==0) {printf("Null element\n");}
}
```

It is worth observing that one successful prefetch will save significant memory access time, and if the code that emits the prefetch adds only a few cycles, even a moderately successful prediction scheme can improve performance.

Consider a system where a successful prefetch will save 150 cycles, and where the code to emit the prefetch takes ten cycles. After N prefetches, the prefetch scheme has cost $10*N$, but it has successfully prefetched R cache lines, which results in a savings of $150*R$ cycles. When $150*R > 10*N$ the prefetch scheme has improved performance. The success rate (R/N) of the prefetch scheme has to be greater than 1/15 (or 7%).

Of course, there are downsides to speculatively emitting prefetch.

- Emitting prefetches takes up instruction slots which could be usefully used by the rest of the code. As pointed out earlier, this can be factored into the decision of whether to emit the prefetches.

- The speculative prefetches may knock useful data out of the caches.

- The speculative prefetches may use system bandwidth that could be better used by another thread running on the processor.

11.3.6 Copying and Moving Memory

As pointed out in Section 7.3.1 of Chapter 7 the library routines for memcpy and
memset are contained both in the generic libc and in the libc_psr, the version
of the library optimized for the target platform. For short calls to these routines,
the cost of calling them is greater than the work performed by the routines.

In these cases, the compiler, if given the -xbuiltin flag (see Section 5.10.1 of
Chapter 5), will inline the calls to memset or memcpy. If the length of the memory
copy or memory clear is unknown at runtime, the compiler will generate code to
test whether it is worth doing the call. The code shown in Example 11.27 demonstrates these optimizations.

Example 11.27 Program to Demonstrate Inlining of memcpy and memset

```
#include <string.h>

void newcopy(int* a, int *b)
{
  memcpy(a,b,10);
}

void newzero(int* a)
{
  memset(a,0,10);
}

void copylen(int* a, int* b, int n)
{
  memcpy(a,b,n);
}

void zerolen(int* a, int n)
{
  memset(a,0,n);
}
```

When the code in Example 11.27 is compiled with -fast and the disassembly is
examined, it is possible to determine that the calls to memcpy and memset in the
first two routines are entirely removed, whereas the calls in the second two routines are performed only for lengths longer than 32 bytes. Example 11.28 shows a
snippet of the code for the newcopy routine.

The code in Example 11.28 is interesting because it is a fully unrolled, byte-by-byte
copy of ten bytes. The first part of the code is a test to see whether the source and destination addresses are aligned on a 4-byte boundary. If this is the case, 4-byte loads
and stores can be used instead.

Example 11.28 Part Disassembly for the Inlined `memcpy` Routine

```
% cc -fast -S ex11.27.c
% more ex11.27.s
...
                        newcopy:
/* 000000      4 */       and      %o0,3,%g2
/* 0x0004       */        and      %o1,3,%g3
/* 0x0008       */        orcc     %g2,%g3,%g0
/* 0x000c       */        be,a     .L900000125
/* 0x0010       */        ld       [%o1],%f0
                        .L900000107:
/* 0x0014      4 */       add      %o0,10,%o0
/* 0x0018       */        ldub     [%o1],%g4
/* 0x001c       */        add      %o1,10,%o1
/* 0x0020       */        stb      %g4,[%o0-10]
/* 0x0024       */        ldub     [%o1-9],%g3
/* 0x0028       */        stb      %g3,[%o0-9]
/* 0x002c       */        ldub     [%o1-8],%g2
/* 0x0030       */        stb      %g2,[%o0-8]
/* 0x0034       */        ldub     [%o1-7],%g1
/* 0x0038       */        stb      %g1,[%o0-7]
/* 0x003c       */        ldub     [%o1-6],%o5
/* 0x0040       */        stb      %o5,[%o0-6]
/* 0x0044       */        ldub     [%o1-5],%o4
/* 0x0048       */        stb      %o4,[%o0-5]
/* 0x004c       */        ldub     [%o1-4],%o3
/* 0x0050       */        stb      %o3,[%o0-4]
/* 0x0054       */        ldub     [%o1-3],%g5
/* 0x0058       */        stb      %g5,[%o0-3]
/* 0x005c       */        ldub     [%o1-2],%o2
/* 0x0060       */        stb      %o2,[%o0-2]
/* 0x0064       */        ldub     [%o1-1],%g4
/* 0x0068       */        retl     ! Result =
/* 0x006c       */        stb      %g4,[%o0-1]
...
```

11.4 Data Structures

11.4.1 Structure Reorganizing

When coding with data structures, it is important to realize that the processor will load parts of the structure at cache line granularity. So, when a single member from a structure is loaded, the processor will fetch the entire cache line containing that structure member, and will consequently bring in some of the surrounding structure members. Obviously, you can use this to your advantage when the application uses several members of the structure at the same time.

The code in Example 11.29 defines a structure that (when compiled as SPARC v8 code) takes up 64 bytes. The data cache has 32-byte cache lines, and i1 is the first item on one 32-byte cache line and `i3` is the first item on the next 32-byte cache line.

Example 11.29 Code That Shows Cross-Cache Line Accesses to Structure Members

```
#include <stdio.h>
#include "timing.h"

#define SIZE 8*16*1024
#define RPT 1000

struct s1
{
  int i1,i2;   double d1,d2,d3;
  int i3,i4;   double d4,d5,d6;
};
static struct s1 s[SIZE];
#pragma align 64 (s1)

int main()
{
  int index,count,total=0;
  float totalf=0.0;

  for (index=0; index<SIZE; index++) {
    s[index].i1=s[index].i2=s[index].i3=s[index].i4=0;
    s[index].d1=s[index].d2=s[index].d3=s[index].d4
             =s[index].d5=s[index].d6=0.0; }

  starttime();
  for (count=0; count<RPT; count++) {
    for (index=0;index<SIZE;index++) total+=s[index].i1 + s[index].i3;
      total = total *2; }
  endtime(SIZE*RPT);

  starttime();
  for (count=0; count<RPT; count++) {
    for (index=0;index<SIZE;index++) total+=s[index].i1 + s[index].i2;
      total = total *2; }
  endtime(SIZE*RPT);

  return( total );
}
```

Compiling and running this code produces the results shown in Example 11.30. In the first loop, the structure members `i1` and `i3` are accessed. These two structure members are 32 bytes apart, and consequently, they do not share the same 32-byte cache line. The load of `i1` will ensure that the entire 64-byte structure is brought into the second-level cache (because this larger cache has a 64-byte line size), but it will bring only 32 of the 64 bytes into the on-chip cache. So, the load of `i3` will still have to fetch more data from the second-level cache. Timing shows the near doubling of performance in the second loop where these two items share the same 32-byte cache line.

Example 11.30 Compiling and Running 64-byte Structure Code

```
% cc -fast ex11.29.c
% a.out
Time per iteration 38.07 ns
Time per iteration 21.27 ns
```

Integer data was used in the code in Example 11.30, which means that for an UltraSPARC III processor, it gets read through the 32-byte lines of the data cache. If floating-point data is used, it will be fetched through the prefetch cache with its 64-byte lines. Example 11.31 shows the same loops from Example 11.29 recoded to use the floating-point members of the data structure.

Example 11.31 Accessing Floating-Point Structure Members

```
...
  starttime();
  for (count=0; count<RPT; count++) {
    for (index=0;index<SIZE;index++) totalf+=s[index].d1 + s[index].d4;
      totalf = totalf *2; }
  endtime(SIZE*RPT);

  starttime();
  for (count=0; count<RPT; count++) {
    for (index=0;index<SIZE;index++) totalf+=s[index].d1 + s[index].d2;
      totalf = totalf *2; }
  endtime(SIZE*RPT);

  return( totalf );
}
```

In this case, the data is fetched through the prefetch cache with a 64-byte line size, so there is no difference between loading any pair of the elements in the 64-byte structure. You can see the results in Example 11.32.

Example 11.32 Loading Floating-Point Structure Elements

```
% cc -fast ex11.31.c
% a.out
Time per iteration 11.72 ns
Time per iteration 11.61 ns
```

In general, data structures do not necessarily align to cache line boundaries. Because of this, it is more important to consider how the elements in the structure are used, and how likely they are to be fetched in the same memory access. Consider one final variant of this code, shown in Example 11.33.

Example 11.33 Compressed Structure

```
#include <stdio.h>
#include "timing.h"

#define SIZE 8*16*1024
#define RPT 1000

struct s1 {
  int i1,i2;
  int i3,i4; };
static struct s1 s[SIZE];
#pragma align 64 (s1)

int main()
{
  int index,count,total=0;

  for (index=0; index<SIZE; index++) {
    s[index].i1=s[index].i2=s[index].i3=s[index].i4=0; }

  starttime();
  for (count=0; count<RPT; count++) {
    for (index=0;index<SIZE;index++)
      total+=s[index].i1 + s[index].i3;
      total = total *2; }
  endtime(SIZE*RPT);
  return total;
}
```

In the code shown in Example 11.33, the redundant floating-point members of the structure have been removed. Hence, each structure takes 16 bytes, so two structures can fit onto a single 32-byte data cache line. Example 11.34 shows the results of compiling and running the code.

Example 11.34 Results of Running Compressed Structure Code

```
% cc -fast ex11.33.c
% a.out
Time per iteration 11.37 ns
```

The results shown in Example 11.34 are about twice as fast as the best numbers from Example 11.30 because the data is contained within a single cache line, and because one cache line contains the data for two iterations of the loop. In fact, it would be possible to further improve performance by removing the remaining two redundant members.

In these examples, structure elements have been removed. In real code, it is likely that most of the structure elements will be used. However, some will be used frequently, and some will be used infrequently. In this situation, the structure can be split to gather all the frequently used elements together, and place all the infrequently used elements into a separate location.

The mapping between the frequently used elements and their infrequently used counterparts can be achieved either through a pointer or by indexing into an array.

Where there are a sizeable number of members in the structure, it may be appropriate to consider the order in which the elements are placed in the structure. The elements could be grouped in order of frequency of access, or perhaps so that elements that are usually accessed together can be placed together in the structure.

11.4.2 Structure Prefetching

The compiler will pick up situations in which prefetches can be inserted for a structure. However, in some cases—possibly when the pattern of accessing the structures is not predictable—the compiler will be unable to insert prefetches for the structures. At that point, it is possible to insert manual prefetch for the structures. Consider the structure shown in Example 11.35.

Example 11.35 Large Structure

```
struct s1
{
  int i1,i2;
  double d1,d2,d3,array[16];
  int i3,i4;
  double d4,d5,d6;
};
```

The structure in Example 11.35 spans several cache lines; consequently, a fetch of the structure member i1 will not also fetch structure member d5. In the case where this structure is accessed "randomly"—for example, through a pointer—it may well improve performance to prefetch the structure member d5 while i1 is being loaded. Example 11.36 shows an example of how this might be achieved.

Example 11.36 Prefetching Structure Members

```
int threshold(struct s1* s)
{
  sparc_prefetch_read_many(&s->d5);
  if (s->i1>0) && (s->d5>1.0) {return 1;} else {return 0;}
}
```

Given the size of the structure defined in Example 11.35, it is not possible for the two critical structure members to share a cache line. Consequently, prefetching the appropriate structure members can lead to a significant performance gain. Example 11.37 shows the full code for this test of prefetching large structures.

Example 11.37 Full Code for Test of Prefetching Large Structures

```
#include <stdio.h>
#include <sun_prefetch.h>
#include "timing.h"

#define SIZE 8*16*1024
#define RPT 1000

struct s1 {
  int i1,i2; double d1,d2,d3,array[16];
  int i3,i4; double d4,d5,d6; };
static struct s1 s[SIZE];
#pragma align 64 (s1)

int threshold(struct s1* s) {
  sparc_prefetch_read_many(&s->d5);
  if ( (s->i1>0) && (s->d5>1.0))  {return 1;} else {return 0;} }

int main()
{
  int index,count,total=0;

  for (index=0; index<SIZE; index++)   {
    s[index].i1=s[index].i2=s[index].i3=s[index].i4=0;
    s[index].d1=s[index].d2=s[index].d3=s[index].d4
             =s[index].d5=s[index].d6=0.0; }

  starttime();
  for (count=0; count<RPT; count++) {
    for (index=0;index<SIZE;index++) total+=threshold(&s[index]);
    total = total *2; }
  endtime(SIZE*RPT);

  return total;
}
```

Example 11.38 shows the results of compiling the code in Example 11.37 both with and without prefetch.

Example 11.38 The Benefits of Compiling with Prefetch

```
% cc -xO3 -xtarget=ultra3 -xprefetch ex11.37.c
% a.out
Time per iteration 117.42 ns
% cc -xO3 -xtarget=ultra3 -xprefetch=no ex11.37.c
% a.out
Time per iteration 182.78 ns
```

Example 11.39 shows another example of how a structure might be prefetched. This code demonstrates the difference in performance between randomly accessing the elements in an array, accessing them serially, and emitting prefetch for a future random access to an element.

Example 11.39 Random Structure Access

```
#include "timing.h"
#include <sun_prefetch.h>
#define SIZE 2*1024*1024
#define RPT 10

struct data {
        int i1,i2,i3,i4,i5,i6,i7,i8;
        double d1,d2,d3,d4; };

struct data d[SIZE];

int main()
{
  long index,count;
  float totalf=0,value;

  for (index=0; index<SIZE; index++) d[index].d1=0;

  starttime();
  for (count=0; count<RPT; count++) {
    for (index=0;index<SIZE;index++) totalf+=d[index ^345678].d1;
    totalf*=5.7; }
  endtime(SIZE*RPT);

  starttime();
  for (count=0; count<RPT; count++) {
    for (index=0;index<SIZE;index++) totalf+=d[index].d1;
    totalf*=5.7; }
  endtime(SIZE*RPT);

  starttime();
  for (count=0; count<RPT; count++) {
    for (index=0;index<SIZE;index++) {
      sparc_prefetch_read_many(&d[(index+2)^345678].d1);
      totalf+=d[index ^345678].d1; }
    totalf*=5.7; }
  endtime(SIZE*RPT);

  return (int)totalf;
}
```

Example 11.40 shows the results of compiling and running the code shown in Example 11.39.

Example 11.40 Results of Random Access Code

```
% cc -xO3 -xtarget=ultra3 -xprefetch ex11.39.c
% a.out
Time per iteration 186.56 ns
Time per iteration 51.87 ns
Time per iteration 80.60 ns
```

The results in Example 11.40 show that the random access pattern exposes the application to the entire memory latency of nearly 200ns. If the data is accessed as a predictable stream, the cost of each access is significantly less because the compiler is able to prefetch it. However, because only one element is used from each cache line, the cost of fetching that single element is still signficant.

The compiler is unable to predict the "random" access pattern, but in the third case it is possible to insert manual prefetch using knowledge of how the access pattern is derived—and this approach is very successful, though not reaching the same performance as the streaming case.

11.4.3 Considerations for Optimal Performance from Structures

You can consider a number of optimizations when dealing with structures in a program.

- Order the members in the structure so that frequently accessed members are close together. This optimization will ensure that when a hot structure member is fetched from memory, it will bring other useful data with it. The corollary to this is to place rarely used structure members together, because it is unlikely that any of them will be needed.

- A similar consideration is the idea that if a structure has members which are always accessed together, these should be grouped together in the structure.

- If the application streams through an array of structures, it may be best to consider splitting the array of structures into two arrays of structures: one array of structures which comprise only the frequently accessed members of the original structure, and one array of structures which comprise only the rarely accessed members of the original structure. If you do this, fetching one structure from memory will probably fetch part of the next structure from memory.

- Some structures may contain distinct sets of members, in which case, even though all the sets of members are hot, it may improve performance to split the structure into several structures, each being used in a different part of the application.

- If structures are accessed at random (i.e., an access to a particular structure does not make it likely that structures adjacent to it in memory will be accessed next), it is important that the hot structure members are placed together (to maximize the chance that they will all be fetched in the same memory access).

11.4.4 Matrices and Accesses

Matrices are one of the common data structures used in a great many applications. However, they can potentially be one of the areas where performance suffers.

Because of the cache line structure, memory has a kind of grain, much like wood. Memory that is accessed sequentially (with the grain) gets performance equivalent to the available memory bandwidth. Memory that is accessed either randomly or by stride (across the grain) gets performance equivalent to memory latency.

With matrices it is very easy to forget about this and to think in terms of the higher-level abstraction. In an ideal world, this would be perfectly acceptable, but currently it is possible to lose a lot of performance this way.

For example, the code in Example 11.41 allocates a matrix, and then accesses the matrix both in rows and in columns.

Example 11.41 Accessing a Matrix by Rows and Columns

```c
#include <stdlib.h>
#include "timing.h"
#define SIZE 2024
#define RPT 10

double **d;
int main()
{
  long x,y,count;
  float totalf,value;

  d=(double**)malloc(SIZE*sizeof(double*));
  for (y=0; y<SIZE; y++)
    d[y]=(double*)malloc(SIZE*sizeof(double));

  for (y=0; y<SIZE; y++)
    for (x=0; x<SIZE; x++) d[y][x]=x+y;

  totalf=1;
  value=1.556;
  starttime();
  for (count=0; count<RPT; count++) {
    for (y=0; y<SIZE; y++) {
      for (x=0; x<SIZE; x++) totalf+=d[x][y];
      totalf*=5.7;
    }
  }
  endtime(SIZE*SIZE*RPT);

  starttime();
  for (count=0; count<RPT; count++) {
    for (y=0; y<SIZE; y++) {
      for (x=0; x<SIZE; x++) totalf+=d[y][x];
      totalf*=5.7;
    }
  }
  endtime(SIZE*SIZE*RPT);

  return (int)totalf;
}
```

Example 11.42 shows the results of compiling and running the code in
Example 11.41. It takes about 100ns for each loop iteration when the data is
accessed by striding through memory (taking a cache miss on every access). In comparison, it takes about 12ns per iteration when memory is accessed contiguously.

Example 11.42 Compiling and Running Matrix Code

```
% cc -fast ex11.41.c
% a.out
Time per iteration 97.08 ns
Time per iteration 11.59 ns
```

However, it is often not as simple as just modifying the code to transpose the
matrix; in some cases, the matrix will be accessed by rows, and then later accessed
by columns. For situations like this, it may be necessary to examine how the structure is most often used, and to optimize for that case. Alternatively, if the structure is used heavily in one way and then heavily in another way, it may be best to
transpose the matrix between the two uses.

One of the quirks that makes this issue slightly more confusing is that the default
access patterns for C and Fortran are different. Fortran is *column major*, so columns
are laid out to be contiguous in memory, whereas C is *row major*, so rows are laid out
to be contiguous in memory. Generally, this should not be a problem, but when codes
are ported between C and Fortran, it is very easy to trip up on these kinds of things.

11.4.5 Multiple Streams

In some cases, the application might be using multiple streams of data. Although
each stream of data may be contiguous, the overall effect may be that the performance is not as good as it could be. An application that handles multiple streams
of data might have suboptimal performance for several reasons.

- When there are multiple streams of data, the likelihood that two or more of
  the streams suffer from some kind of conflict in memory is increased. For
  example, the streams might all map to the same set of lines in the caches, or
  to the same Translation Lookaside Buffer (TLB) entries. This will be apparent as high numbers of cache misses or TLB misses. This is particularly a
  problem in programs where the dimensions of the arrays are a power of two.

- It may not be possible for the compiler to insert sufficient prefetches to get all
  the streams onto the processor. Recall that for the UltraSPARC III/IV, there
  can be, at most, eight outstanding prefetches at any one time, and if there are
  more streams than this, some of the streams may not get the full benefit of

prefetch. On the other hand, if the streams are staggered in memory, it may well be that by the time the prefetch for one stream is issued, the prefetch for another stream has completed. So, although eight streams may seem quite a small number, it can be sufficient for many cases.

- A final possibility is that the complexity of the calculations in the application requires more registers than are available on the processor. In this case, the compiler will spill some registers to memory and reload them later. This additional memory traffic can reduce performance. It is possible to detect register spills and fills as they will appear as loads and stores to the same location on the stack.

There are two principal ways to improve the performance of code with multiple streams of data. Fundamentally, the approaches are ways of reducing the number of streams of data it is necessary to fetch from memory at any one time.

One approach is to split the calculation such that fewer streams are necessary at any one time—for example, by splitting a single large loop into multiple smaller loops. The compiler has the capability to split and merge loops, so doing this manually is necessary only when the calculation performed in the loop is complex or a programmer has insight into a particular way of splitting the loops.

An alternative approach is to use a single array of structures rather than a set of arrays of data. The observation in this case is that all the items of data are used at the same time, so it makes sense to store them in a structure so that the memory accesses fetch the greatest amount of useful data.

11.5 Thrashing

11.5.1 Summary

Thrashing in the caches occurs when one read or write pulls data into the cache, but due to unfortunate circumstances, a later memory access brings data into the same cache line and knocks the first data out before all of it is used, so the next reference to the first cache line has to fetch it again. In general, this should not be a problem. The on-chip caches for the UltraSPARC III family of processors are four-way associative (meaning that five or more streams of data are necessary before thrashing occurs), the second-level cache is two-way associative on the UltraSPARC III/IV, and the UltraSPARC IV+ has four-way associative second- and third-level caches. The UltraSPARC T1 processor has a 12-way second-level cache which helps it to avoid thrashing.

Thrashing can also happen to the TLBs. As previously discussed, the TLBs hold the translations from virtual memory to physical memory. One TLB entry holds the data for a "page" in memory. For UltraSPARC processors, the default size of a page is 8KB.

However, using multiple page size support (MPSS) in Solaris 9 and beyond, it is possible to select other page sizes, up to a maximum of 256MB. For the UltraSPARC III family of processors, the TLBs are either four-way associative if only one page size is in use, or two-way associative if multiple page sizes are being used.

The code shown in Example 11.43 demonstrates thrashing in the data TLB. This code has two loops. The first loop accesses data that is contained on pages that map to different TLB entries. The second loop is set up so that the data is contained on pages that map to the same TLB entries. There are five loads, so the second loop will thrash TLBs that have less than five-way associativity.

Example 11.43 Code to Demonstrate Thrashing in TLBs

```
#include "timing.h"
#define SIZE 1024*1024
#define RPT 100


double array[2*SIZE+1024*4];

int main()
{
  int index,count;
  double totalf=0.0;
  for(index=0; index<SIZE+1024*4; index++) {array[index]=0;}
  /*No thrashing - each access offset by a page*/
  starttime();
  for (count=0; count<RPT; count++)
  {
    for(index=0;index<SIZE/5;index++)
    {
      totalf+=array[index];
      totalf+=array[index+SIZE/4+1024];
      totalf+=array[index+SIZE/2+2048];
      totalf+=array[index+3*SIZE/4+3072];
      totalf+=array[index+SIZE+4095];
    }
  }
  endtime(SIZE*RPT/5);

  /*Using multiple parallel points - and thrashing*/
  starttime();
  for (count=0; count<RPT; count++)
  {
    for(index=0;index<SIZE/5;index++)
    {
      totalf+=array[index];
      totalf+=array[index+SIZE/4];
      totalf+=array[index+SIZE/2];
      totalf+=array[index+3*SIZE/4];
      totalf+=array[index+SIZE];
    }
  }
  endtime(SIZE*RPT/5);
}
```

Running this code with 8KB pages on a 900MHz UltraSPARC IIICu system produces the results shown in Example 11.44. It is apparent that each iteration costs about 130ns more when there is a TLB miss than when there is no such miss. However, there can be multiple TLB misses during a single iteration, so it is not a good estimate of the cost of a single TLB miss.

Example 11.44 Timing Information for TLB Thrashing

```
$ cc -O -xpagesize=8K ex11.43.c
$ a.out
Time per iteration 40.34 ns
Time per iteration 171.18 ns
```

It is possible to use large, 4MB pages under Solaris 9 (or later) to run this same code, as shown in Example 11.45. To do this the code is recompiled with the -xpagesize compiler flag, which sets the preferred page size for the application. Under these conditions, the TLB thrashing disappears.

Example 11.45 Running with Large Pages

```
$ cc -O -xpagesize=4M ex11.43.c
$ a.out
Time per iteration 37.72 ns
Time per iteration 49.66 ns
```

11.5.2 Data TLB Performance Counter

You can diagnose TLB miss problems using the performance counters. Example 11.46 shows the code from Example 11.43 running under cputrack. The output from cputrack is interleaved with the output from the application. The output shows nearly 40,000 TLB misses during the first half second of runtime when the application is mainly performing the first timed loop, but 3 million data TLB misses during each of the subsequent half seconds.

Example 11.47 shows the same code recompiled to use large pages. Note that in this case, the number of data TLB misses drops significantly. The number of data TLB misses actually drops for both loops, but the most significant drop is for the second loop, which previously "thrashed" the TLB.

Example 11.46 Collecting Data TLB Miss Data Using `cputrack`

```
$ cc -O ex11.43.c
$ cputrack -c Cycle_cnt,sys,DTLB_miss,sys -T 0.5 a.out
   time lwp       event       pic0        pic1
  0.586   1        tick   521170187       39611
Time per iteration 40.86 ns
  1.196   1        tick   547745025     2843144
  1.556   1        tick   322703361     3114752
  2.136   1        tick   520862693     5056245
  2.536   1        tick   359048691     3502039
  3.186   1        tick   583925403     5740212
  3.676   1        tick   440179419     4374420
  4.103   1        tick   382964175     3810607
  4.656   1        tick   497185847     4902241
Time per iteration 180.88 ns
  4.692   1        exit  4206350026    33684344
```

Example 11.47 Data TLB Misses on Code Run with Large Pages

```
$ cc -O -xpagesize=4M ex11.43.c
$ cputrack -c Cycle_cnt,sys,DTLB_miss,sys -T 0.5 a.out
   time lwp       event       pic0        pic1
  0.606   1        tick   538310671       13088
Time per iteration 39.03 ns
  1.076   1        tick   420190029         615
  1.626   1        tick   492992859         396
Time per iteration 52.63 ns
  1.977   1        exit  1765294966       14361
```

11.6 Reads after Writes

A general problem in processors is the reading of data just after it has been written. The processor will want to fetch the data for the load as early as possible, while at the same time leaving as much time as possible before committing the data from the store to memory. Hence, it is quite possible for loads to require data that the store is writing, and the processor must detect and compensate for this condition. The UltraSPARC III family of processors detects this condition, and in many cases is able to pass the data from the store directly to the waiting load. This is called a *bypass* (because it bypasses storing the data to memory). Unfortunately, in some cases the processor is not able to achieve this and ends up stalling while the processor waits for the store to complete; these stalls are counted by the `Re_RAW_miss` hardware performance counter.

The code in Example 11.48 demonstrates the fact that bypassing cannot occur when there are multiple stores to the same location in the store queue.

Example 11.48 Code Demonstrating RAW Recycles

```
#include "timing.h"

struct block
{
  float * i1;
  float *i2;
  float i3,i4;
};
#define RPT 100
#define SIZE 400000
struct block array[SIZE];

int main()
{
  int i,r;
  float tmp;
  for (i=0; i<SIZE; i++) array[i].i1=array[i].i2=&array[i].i3;

  starttime();
  for (r=0; r<RPT; r++)
  for (i=0; i<SIZE; i++)
  {
    *array[i].i1=tmp;
    *array[i].i2=tmp;
    tmp=array[i].i3;
  }
  endtime(SIZE*RPT);

  for (i=0; i<SIZE; i++) array[i].i1=&array[0].i3;

  starttime();
  for (r=0; r<RPT; r++)
  for (i=0; i<SIZE; i++)
  {
    *array[i].i1=tmp;
    *array[i].i2=tmp;
    tmp=array[i].i3;
  }
  endtime(SIZE*RPT);

  return array[50].i3;
}
```

The first loop of the code in Example 11.48 does two stores to the same location in cache; the second loop does only one store to this location, but does a second store to a loop invariant location, so the amount of work done in the loop is the same, and the difference is just whether the same location has one or two stores. Example 11.49 shows the result of running this code.

Example 11.49 Timing Difference Due to RAW Recycles

```
% cc -O -o storeqraw ex11.48.c; storeqraw
Time per iteration 45.50 ns
Time per iteration 35.78 ns
```

Of course, when looking at this code, it is hard to determine whether the problem is due to RAWs, or to something else. Example 11.50 shows the same code run under `cputrack`. The elapsed time for the code was about three seconds. In these three seconds, the application ran for around 3 billion cycles, and of these cycles about 700 million cycles were lost in RAW events. Looking at the tick events, it is apparent that all of the RAW events occurred during the first two seconds of the runtime, while the program was running the first loop.

Example 11.50 Using `cputrack` to Diagnose RAW Recycle Stalls

```
$ cputrack -c pic0=Cycle_cnt,pic1=Re_RAW_miss -T 0.1 storeqraw
   time lwp      event      pic0       pic1
   0.135   1       tick  112070175   41474094
   0.215   1       tick   80337891   31415479
   0.405   1       tick  197275657   85670349
   0.535   1       tick  134027271   46209804
   0.635   1       tick  102887411   35337929
   0.795   1       tick  165542688   64723434
   0.905   1       tick  113576452   37968193
   1.065   1       tick  165790082   56343951
   1.235   1       tick  176385576   59758571
   1.315   1       tick   82219157   27279044
   1.415   1       tick  103153311   39265904
   1.515   1       tick  103057459   67316587
   1.645   1       tick  133953232   45847683
   1.715   1       tick   71622390   28445114
   1.814   1       tick  101593208   54344345
Time per iteration 44.11 ns
   1.945   1       tick  135442423        584
   2.015   1       tick   71587341          0
   2.155   1       tick  144634395          0
   2.365   1       tick  218608250          0
   2.505   1       tick  144791619         15
   2.695   1       tick  197614220         15
   2.775   1       tick   82260779         15
   2.865   1       tick   92813310         15
   2.945   1       tick   81870516          0
   3.015   1       tick   71703014          0
Time per iteration 32.98 ns
   3.139   1       tick  128353970       1234
   3.141   1       exit 3213235301  721402359
```

11.7 Store Queue

11.7.1 Stalls

The store queue on the UltraSPARC III family of processors is a list of up to eight stores that are waiting to be written to the write cache. The queue is there to cover the time until the cache line is returned from memory to the write cache. If consecutive stores are to the same 32-byte cache line, the stores will be coalesced in the write cache before the data is returned from memory. Sometimes stores are issued more quickly than the rate at which the store queue can empty. In this situation, the store queue becomes full, which causes the processor to stall.

11.7.2 Detecting Store Queue Stalls

The `Rstall_storeQ` performance counter counts the number of cycles lost to the store queue being full. The store queue is eight entries deep, so the point at which a store queue full condition is signaled is at least eight stores after the store that caused the problem.

The code shown in Example 11.51 demonstrates the problem. In the code, there are two stores to adjacent cache lines.

Example 11.51 Code to Generate Store Queue Stalls

```
#include "timing.h"
#define SIZE 2*1024*1024

struct s
{
  int i;
  long long c1[7];
  int j;
  long long c2[7];
};

struct s array[SIZE];
#pragma align 64 (array)

int main()
{
  long index,count;

  starttime();
  for(int rpt=0; rpt<50; rpt++)
  for (index=0; index<SIZE; index++)
  {
   array[index].i=0;
   array[index].j=0;
  }
  endtime(50*SIZE);

  return (int)array[1000].c1[4];
}
```

The code in Example 11.51 can be run under `cputrack`, as shown in Example 11.52.

Example 11.52 Using `cputrack` to Diagnose Store Queue Stalls

```
$ cc -O -xprefetch=no ex11.51.c
$ cputrack -c pic0=Rstall_storeQ,pic1=Cycle_cnt a.out
   time lwp       event       pic0        pic1
  1.060   1        tick   644804272    649558373
  2.060   1        tick   796943266    801122930
  3.070   1        tick  1000911386   1005635125
 ...
 47.020   1        tick   928484629    933084884
Time per iteration 454.59 ns
 47.678   1        exit 46531663044  46766729365
```

As you can see from the results shown in Example 11.52, almost all the cycles are spent in store queue stalls. One way to reduce the cycles lost to store queue stalls is to insert prefetches into the source to fetch the data from memory in advance of the processor needing to store to the line. Example 11.53 shows this modification.

Example 11.53 Manually Inserting Prefetches to Improve Store Performance

```c
#include "timing.h"
#include "sun_prefetch.h"
#define SIZE 2*1024*1024

struct s
{
  int i;
  long long c1[7];
  int j;
  long long c2[7];
};
struct s array[SIZE];
#pragma align 64 (array)

int main()
{
  long index,count;
  starttime();
  for(int rpt=0; rpt<50; rpt++)
  for (index=0; index<SIZE; index++)
  {
   sparc_prefetch_write_many(&array[index+4].i);
   sparc_prefetch_write_many(&array[index+4].j);
   array[index].i=0;
   array[index].j=0;
  }
  endtime(50*SIZE);

  return (int)array[1000].c1[4];
}
```

Example 11.54 shows the results of running the code with the manual prefetch statements.

Example 11.54 Performance of Code with Manual Prefetch Statements

```
$ cc -O ex11.53.c
$ cputrack -c pic0=Rstall_storeQ,pic1=Cycle_cnt a.out
   time lwp        event          pic0          pic1
   1.127    1         tick    522959825    540753639
...
  21.177    1         tick   1002783584   1028022465
Time per iteration 204.31 ns
  21.434    1         exit  20368619655  20913555870
```

It is apparent that the code runs twice as fast as the original code, but still spends much of its time stalled on store queue full conditions. This is not surprising, because the code is doing only stores, and each store is using only part of a cache line; also observe that although the code is doing only stores, the processor still has to fetch the data, update it, and then return the data to memory, so the bandwidth consumption is actually twice that of just the store stream.

Because the stores are coalesced in the write cache, there is some benefit to organizing the stores such that stores to the same 32-byte cache line are consecutive.

11.8 If Statements

11.8.1 Introduction

Most code has a number of conditional statements. These can be critical decision statements for the code, or possibly just an assertion statement that checks that nothing is going wrong. For each if statement, the compiler generally has to generate at least one branch. In the absence of information that suggests that one branch of the if statement is more likely, the compiler will generate a balanced version of the code, as shown in Figure 11.2. In this figure, both possibilities for the if statement have two branch statements.

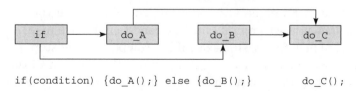

if(condition) {do_A();} else {do_B();}   do_C();

Figure 11.2 Code Generated in the Absence of Information about Branch Taken Probability

At runtime, the processor has a branch predictor that determines whether a given branch is taken. Consequently, misprediction of branches is not a huge problem for most codes. However, there are a couple of problems with branches.

First, the compiler (in the absence of profile feedback information) has little idea whether a branch is going to be taken (even if the programmer knows). Consequently, the compiler usually generates code that assumes that the branch will be taken half the time and not taken the other half of the time.

Second, the compiler has to assume that the codes for the taken case and the untaken case are equally likely, and so both need to be in close proximity. If a branch is rarely taken, the compiler could place the rarely taken code further away, and make the critical portion of the code smaller (and fit into the instruction cache better).

Compiling the application using profile feedback (discussed in Section 5.7.4 of Chapter 5) gives the compiler some idea about how the branches are taken, and often leads to better arrangement of code, and hence, better performance.

11.8.2 Conditional Moves

Some processors have support for replacing some types of branches with conditional moves. A conditional move statement tells the processor to move data between two registers only if a condition is true.

Consider how often an application might contain logic such as "if A is greater than B, let A equal B." Normally this would be encoded as a test comparing A and B, followed by a branch that directs the processor over an assignment statement.

The problem with this code construct is that the branch is going to be unpredictable, so the processor may spend some time dealing with mispredicted branches. Also, a branch statement will inhibit the compiler from doing some loop optimizations.

If the compiler can generate a conditional move, there is no branch statement, just a single instruction that is executed conditionally. This helps performance by avoiding the unpredictable branch, and by allowing the compiler to do loop optimizations. The code shown in Example 11.55 is an example of where the compiler can use a conditional move statement instead of a branch.

When the code in Example 11.55 is compiled, you receive the disassembly for the main loop shown in Example 11.56. The conditional move instruction, `fmovdg`, updates the value held in register `%f16` if the compare of registers `%f12` and `%f16` indicates that the value in register `%f12` is greater than that in `%f16`.

An alternative way to get branchless sequences of code is for the compiler to use logical operations. Example 11.57 shows an example where the compiler is able to do this. The first loop has an `if` test that either increments a value or not. In this case, the compiler will often generate code that contains a branch over the increment operation. In the second loop, the increment operation takes the value of the comparison as a parameter, so the compiler does not need to generate a branch.

Example 11.55 Example of Code Where a Conditional Move Statement Can Be Used

```
#include "timing.h"

double array[1024*1024];

void main()
{
 int i;
 double max;
 for (i=0; i<1024*1024;i++){array[i]=i;}
 max=0;
 starttime();
 for (i=0; i<1024*1024; i++)
 {
   if (array[i]>max) {max=array[i];}
 }
 endtime(1024*1024);
 if (max!=1024*1024) {printf("NE\n");}
}
```

Example 11.56 Disassembly for Code Using Conditional Moves

```
    10ef4:  81 ab 0a d0   fcmped  %fcc0, %f12, %f16
    10ef8:  ae 05 e0 01   inc       %l7
    10efc:  ac 05 a0 08   inc       8, %l6
    10f00:  a1 a9 80 4c   fmovdg    %fcc0, %f12, %f16
    10f04:  80 a5 c0 19   cmp       %l7, %i1
    10f08:  24 4f ff fb   ble,a,pt  %icc, 0x10ef4
    10f0c:  d9 1d a0 00   ldd       [%l6], %f12
```

Example 11.57 Two Alternative Formulations of Counting a Loop

```
#include "timing.h"
int array[1024*1024];

void main()
{
  int i;
  int count;
  count=0;
  for(i=0; i<1024*1024; i++) array[i]=i-1024*512;

  starttime();
  for (i=0; i<1024*1024; i++)
  { if (array[i]>0) {count++;} }
  endtime(1024*1024);
  if (count==0) {printf("Zero\n");}

  count=0;
  starttime();
  for (i=0; i<1024*1024; i++)
  { count+=(array[i]>0); }
  endtime(1024*1024);
  if (count==0) {printf("Zero\n");}

}
```

Example 11.58 shows timing information for the code shown in Example 11.57.

Example 11.58 Timing Comparison of Branching and Branchless Versions

```
$ cc -O ex11.57.c
$ a.out
Time per iteration 10.73 ns
Time per iteration  7.73 ns
```

Example 11.59 shows the disassembly of the branching version of the code.

Example 11.59 Version of Code Using Branches to Increment the Count Variable

```
10dc4:  80 a2 60 00  cmp      %o1, 0
10dc8:  04 40 00 03  ble,pn   %icc, 0x10dd4
10dcc:  86 00 e0 04  inc      4, %g3
10dd0:  aa 05 60 01  inc      %l5
10dd4:  84 00 a0 01  inc      %g2
10dd8:  80 a0 80 04  cmp      %g2, %g4
10ddc:  24 4f ff fa  ble,a,pt %icc, 0x10dc4
10de0:  d2 00 e0 00  ld       [%g3], %o1
```

Example 11.60 shows an equivalent branchless version of the code generated for the second timed loop from the source in Example 11.57. To perform the logical operation, the compiler takes more instructions, but can avoid a branch statement.

Example 11.60 Branchless Version of the Loop to Increment the Count Variable

```
10eb4:  97 3c e0 00  sra      %l3, 0, %o3
10eb8:  a8 05 20 01  inc      %l4
10ebc:  94 20 00 0b  neg      %o3, %o2
10ec0:  ba 07 60 04  inc      4, %i5
10ec4:  a3 32 b0 3f  srlx     %o2, 63, %l1
10ec8:  80 a5 00 17  cmp      %l4, %l7
10ecc:  a4 04 80 11  add      %l2, %l1, %l2
10ed0:  24 4f ff f9  ble,a,pt %icc, 0x10eb4
10ed4:  e6 07 60 00  ld       [%i5], %l3
```

One big advantage of conditional code over branches is that it is possible to perform multiple conditional calculations in parallel. Multiple conditional tests end up coded as separate blocks of code. However, if conditional operations are used, instructions from different conditional blocks of code can be mixed together. Mixing instructions together will give the compiler more opportunities to perform better code scheduling, and have fewer stalls.

11.8.3 Misaligned Memory Accesses on SPARC Processors

As discussed in Section 5.8.5 of Chapter 5, the SPARC processors typically do not handle misaligned memory accesses in hardware. Instead, the application will trap to the operating system, which can either perform the misaligned load in software, or cause the application to dump core. The behavior is determined using the -xmemalign compiler flag. Using this flag, it is possible to specify the alignment to be assumed by the compiler. For example, if the data is always aligned on 4-byte boundaries, the compiler can generate code using that assumption.

Example 11.61 shows an example of some code that can benefit from being told to assume an 8-byte alignment. The example code mallocs two arrays of doubles, each double is 9 bytes in size. In the inner loop is a vector product, so it requires two loads of double-precision values per iteration. When compiled with an assumed alignment of eight bytes, each of these two values can be loaded with a single memory operation. When compiled with a memory alignment of four bytes, the compiler has to use two memory operations to load each value.

Example 11.61 Vector Product Example

```
#include <stdlib.h>
#include "timing.h"

#define SIZE 2*1024*1024
#define RPT 10

int main()
{
  int index,count;
  double *value,*value2,totalf;
  void* memory;

  memory=malloc(8*SIZE+64);
  value=(double*)(memory);
  memory=malloc(8*SIZE+64);
  value2=(double*)(memory);

  for (index=0; index<SIZE; index++) value[index]=value2[index]=0;

  totalf=1;
  starttime();
  for (count=0; count<RPT; count++)
  {
    for (index=0;index<SIZE;index++)
      totalf+=value[index]*value2[index];
    totalf=totalf*5.7;
  }
  endtime(SIZE*RPT);


  return (int)totalf;
}
```

Example 11.62 shows the timing of the code under various settings of the -xmemalign flag. Notice that the best performance comes from using -xmemalign=8s. Notice also that using -xmemalign=1s adds significant overhead to the code.

Example 11.62 Vector Product Code under Various -xmemalign Settings

```
$ cc -xO5 -xmemalign=4s ex11.61.c
$ a.out
Time per iteration 54.27 ns
$ cc -xO5 -xmemalign=8s ex11.61.c
$ a.out
Time per iteration 49.49 ns
$ cc -xO5 -xmemalign=1s ex11.61.c
$ a.out
Time per iteration 74.11 ns
```

Example 11.63 shows code that just sums up a vector. Notice that when a value is assigned, it is set to be 1-byte misaligned. If this code was run with -xmemalign= 8s or 4s, the code would dump core with a SIGBUS error. However, it can be compiled and safely run with -xmemalign= 8i or 4i or 1s.

Example 11.63 Example of a Misaligned Vector

```c
#include <stdlib.h>
#include "timing.h"

#define SIZE 2*1024*1024
#define RPT 10

int main()
{
  int index,count;
  float *value,totalf;
  char* memory;

  memory=(char*)malloc(4*SIZE+64);
  value=(float*)(memory+1);
  for (index=0; index<SIZE; index++) value[index]=0;

  totalf=1;
  starttime();
  for (count=0; count<RPT; count++)
  {
    for (index=0;index<SIZE;index++)
      totalf+=value[index];
    totalf=totalf*5.7;
  }
  endtime(SIZE*RPT);


  return (int)totalf;
}
```

Example 11.64 shows the handling of misalignment through various settings of the -xmemalign flag.

Example 11.64 Handling Misaligned Data

```
$ cc -xO5 -xmemalign=8i ex11.63.c
$ a.out
Time per iteration 1466.51 ns
$ cc -xO5 -xmemalign=1s  ex11.63.c
$ a.out
Time per iteration 18.30 ns
```

When it is compiled with -xmemalign=8i the compiler assumes that the data is 8-byte aligned, but it installs a trap handler to catch the case when the data is misaligned. So, instead of dumping core, the program runs. But on every misaligned memory access the processor traps, the trap handler corrects the misalignment, and the program continues. Trapping is a slow process, so the program runs, but slowly. The other alternative is to use -xmemalign=1s. This doesn't trap, but tells the compiler to assume that every memory access could potentially be misaligned by a single byte. So instead of emiting an 8-byte load, the compiler produces eight single-byte loads. This is a very slow way of working, but it is significantly faster than the trap handler.

The trap mechanism used to correct alignment differs between V8 and V9 code. In V9 code, the trap handler is present in the user code. When the application is profiled, time spent handling traps will be reported on the user-land trap handler. In V8 code, the kernel handles the alignment trap, so time spent in misalignment traps will be reported as system time. Example 11.65 shows an example of the profile of a V8 instruction that traps with misalignment. The misaligned memory access causes a trap into the kernel for the alignment to be corrected. Hence, the instruction after the misaligned access (the instruction waiting to be executed) accumulates system time.

Example 11.65 V8 Code with Misaligned Store Instruction Corrected by Trap to Kernel

```
Excl.      Excl.
User CPU   Sys. CPU
  sec.       sec.
   0.         0.              [ 9]   10ccc:  std     %f32, [%o2]
## 0.370     1.081           [ 8]   10cd0:  add     %15, 696, %16
   0.         0.              [ 9]   10cd4:  add     %g2, 64, %g3
```

Example 11.66 shows an equivalent code snippet compiled for V9 architecture. In this case, the misaligned memory access accumulates a small amount of system time where the trap enters the kernel. For V9 code, the kernel will call user code to correct the alignment.

Example 11.66 V9 Code with Misaligned Store Instruction Corrected by User-Land Trap

```
Excl.      Excl.
User CPU   Sys. CPU
  sec.       sec.
   0.         0.           [ 8] 100002738:  or      %l6, 258, %l7
## 0.         0.560        [ 9] 1000273c:  std     %f32, [%o7]
   0.         0.           [ 8] 100002740:  or      %g2, 258, %g3
```

The V9 code also shows significant time in the user-land trap handler, as demonstrated in Example 11.67.

Example 11.67 User-Land Trap Handler in V9 Code

```
Excl.      Excl.       Name
User CPU   Sys. CPU
  sec.       sec.
0.570      0.
0.460      0.          __misalign_trap_handler
0.050      0.          __do_misaligned_ldst_instr
...
```

For a program with misaligned data, a rough guideline for choosing between -xmemalign=1s and -xmemalign=8i is that if there are only a few misaligned accesses, -xmemalign=8i (and the trap handler) should be used. On the other hand, if most memory assesses are misaligned, it is more appropriate to pick -xmemalign=1s. The program will run correctly with either setting, so the decision can be made entirely based on which setting provides the best performance.

11.9 File-Handling in 32-bit Applications

11.9.1 File Descriptor Limits

The fopen call has a limit of 256 open file descriptors when used in 32-bit applications; 64-bit applications do not have this limitation. If it is necessary to open more than 256 simultaneous files, it is better to use the open call, which does not have this limitation. However, the total number of file descriptors is limited by the file descriptors' environment setting (you can change this using the ulimit or limit command). The code shown in Example 11.68 demonstrates the issue.

Example 11.68 Code Demonstrating File Descriptor Limits

```
#include <stdio.h>

/*Necessary for open*/
#include <sys/types.h>
#include <sys/stat.h>
#include <fcntl.h>
/*Necessary for close*/
#include <unistd.h>

#define MAX 1000

void main()
{
  FILE* filep[MAX];   /*for fopen*/
  int filei[MAX];     /*for open*/
  int total;
  char name[256];

  total=0;
  for (total=0; total<MAX; total++)
  {
    sprintf(name,"/tmp/file_%i",total);
    if ( (filep[total]=fopen(name,"w"))==NULL) {break;}
  }

  printf("fopen opened %i files\n",total);

  for(int i=0;i<total; i++) {fclose(filep[i]);}

  total=0;
  for (total=0; total<MAX; total++)
  {
    sprintf(name,"/tmp/file_%i",total);
    if ( (filei[total]=open(name, O_CREAT | O_RDWR, 0644 ))==-1) {break;}
  }

  printf("open opened %i files\n",total);

  for(int i=0;i<total; i++) {close(filei[i]);}
}
```

Example 11.69 shows the results of running this test code for both 32-bit and 64-bit binaries. The output shows that originally only 256 file descriptors were available for an application to use. Three of these file descriptors are already assigned to stdin, stdout, and stderr. The rest are available for the application to use. When the number of file descriptors is increased these new descriptors become available for the open function call, but not for fopen. When the application is compiled to be 64-bit, all the file descriptors are available for both open and fopen.

Example 11.69 File Descriptors for 32-bit and 64-bit Applications

```
$ ulimit -n
256
$ cc ex11.68.c
$ a.out
fopen opened 253 files
open opened 253 files
$ ulimit -n 300
$ a.out
fopen opened 253 files
open opened 297 files
$ cc -xtarget=generic64 ex11.68.c
$ a.out
fopen opened 297 files
open opened 297 files
```

11.9.2 Handling Large Files in 32-bit Applications

There is a default file size limit of 2GB for files handled by 32-bit applications. This limitation is due to the file pointer being held as a signed 32-bit integer. For 64-bit applications, the file pointer is a signed 64-bit integer, so there is no practical limitation on file size.

If a 32-bit application needs to handle files larger than 2GB, it needs to be recompiled with the flags `-D_FILE_OFFSET_BITS=64` and `-D_LARGEFILE_SOURCE`. Example 11.70 shows source code for an application that creates a file of greater than 2GB.

Example 11.70 Application That Creates a File of Greater Than 2GB

```
#include <stdio.h>
#include <stdlib.h>
#include <sys/types.h>
#include <sys/stat.h>
#include <fcntl.h>
#include <unistd.h>

void main()
{
  int filei;
  long long index;
  if ( (filei=open("/tmp/largefile_test", O_CREAT | O_RDWR, 0644 ))==-1)
    {exit(1);}
  for (index=0; index<(long long)3*1024*1023*1024; index+=8*1024)
  {
    if (lseek(filei,index,SEEK_SET)==-1) {printf("Seek failed\n"); break;}
    if (write(filei,".",1)==-1) {printf("Write failed\n"); break;}
    printf("File size=%lli\n",index);
  }
  close(filei);
}
```

Example 11.71 shows the results of compiling this test code with and without large file support. With the appropriate flags, the application is able to write a file greater than 2GB in size.

Example 11.71 Application Compiled with Large File Support

```
% cc -O -o smallfile ex11.70.c
% cc -O -D_FILE_OFFSET_BITS=64 -D_LARGEFILE_SOURCE -o largefile ex11.70.c
% smallfile | tail
File size=2147409920
File size=2147418112
File size=2147426304
File size=2147434496
File size=2147442688
File size=2147450880
File size=2147459072
File size=2147467264
File size=2147475456
Seek failed
% largefile | tail
File size=3217997824
File size=3218006016
File size=3218014208
File size=3218022400
File size=3218030592
File size=3218038784
File size=3218046976
File size=3218055168
File size=3218063360
File size=3218071552
```

Threading and Throughput

12

Multicore, Multiprocess, Multithread

12.1 Introduction

Systems that can execute only a single task at a time are becoming increasingly rare. Most processors can simultaneously execute multiple threads, and systems typically have multiple processors.

The objective of this chapter is to cover various techniques for using multiple processors. By the end of the chapter, the reader will have a good understanding of the various alternatives, and a high-level view of their strengths and weaknesses.

12.2 Processes, Threads, Processors, Cores, and CMT

It is necessary to start this section with an outline of some useful terminology.

A processor, or CPU, is the physical chip that is plugged into the system. A processor can have multiple cores (a *core* is the part of the chip that is capable of executing instructions). A core can appear to the operating system as multiple virtual processors if it is capable of simultaneously executing multiple threads (a *thread* is a single sequence of instructions).

A *process* is another name for an application. Generally, processes are independent of each other. If one process dies, it does not cause another process to also die. It is possible for processes to communicate, or share resources such as memory or I/O.

The most common example of a process is the act of starting new executables. For example, imagine using gzip to compress a file, as shown in Example 12.1. In this instance, the gzip process is started. It is possible to start multiple instances of gzip at the same time, and if one of them hits a problem (i.e., the file to be compressed does not exist), that process will stop, but the other processes will continue.

Example 12.1 Using gzip to Compress a File

```
$ gzip text.txt
```

Each process has a separate address space and stack. A process can contain multiple threads, each able to execute instructions simultaneously. All the threads in a process share the same address space, but each thread will have its own stack. If one thread encounters a problem, that problem may cause the entire process to die. The threads can be tightly integrated or loosely integrated. For a tightly integrated example, consider multiple threads rendering an image, each thread working on part of the image until the entire image is drawn. A Web server is an example of loosely integrated threads; each request for a Web page is handled by a separate thread.

A Web server is an example of functionality that could be implemented using either processes or threads. Every time a request for a page comes in, the server could either use a thread to handle the request, or spawn a new process to handle the request. Some trade-offs are involved in deciding which is more appropriate. For example, the cost of starting a new process is typically greater than the cost of starting a new thread; threads within a single process can share the same Translation Lookaside Buffer (TLB) mappings; different processes require new sets of TLB mappings, which increases the number of active TLB mappings required.

It is the operating system's role to schedule each thread onto a virtual processor for it to run. If multiple virtual processors are available, multiple threads can be active at the same time. If there are more threads than there are virtual processors, each thread will get scheduled onto a virtual processor for a short interval before another thread gets scheduled onto that virtual processor.

As described in the introduction to this chapter, it is now common to find a single system that is capable of running multiple threads at the same time. This can be achieved in the hardware in a number of ways.

The traditional approach is often called symmetric multiprocessing (SMP), whereby a large system is built by combining many boards, each board containing multiple physical processors. This approach has an advantage in that it typically scales the available memory together with the number of processors. However, it has the disadvantage that as the number of processors increases, the complexity of parts of the system, such as the interconnect between processors, increases exponentially.

The complexity can be addressed by each physical processor having multiple cores that share resources (i.e., one physical processor is plugged into the system, and that physical processor has many cores). This increases the number of cores in the system, without requiring an increase in the external wiring between those cores. In this way, system complexity is controlled, at the expense of an increase in CPU complexity.

One way to make it appear as though there are two cores in a single physical processor is to fit two cores into the packaging for an existing single processor. Each core is placed on its own die, or piece of silicon, and the two pieces of silicon are wired together into the single package. A similar approach is to place two cores onto the same piece of silicon. Although there may be performance trade-offs between the two approaches, from a software perspective it is hard to discern any difference. In both cases, twice as many cores are available on the system as there are physical processors plugged into the system. This is often called chip multiprocessing (CMP).

Another way to make multiple cores available using one single physical processor is to make each core on the processor capable of simultaneously running multiple threads. You can achieve this at multiple granularities. For example, the switch between threads could be every instruction, or perhaps one thread runs for a number of instructions before switching, or even instructions from multiple threads can be dispatched at the same time. This is often described as *vertical threading*. Vertical threading is related to the idea of virtual processors. Each core can handle multiple threads, and from the perspective of the operating system it appears that there are multiple processors. These operating-system-visible processors are often called *virtual processors*, because if the die of the processor was inspected it would be possible to identify the core of the processor, but not the threads or the virtual cores.

It should be apparent that there are many ways to develop a processor that can run multiple simultaneous threads, whether it's multiple cores each running one thread, or multiple cores running multiple threads. Regardless of the approach, the process generally goes by one name: chip multithreading (CMT).

Sun has delivered a number of CMT processors. Examples include the UltraSPARC IV+, which has two threads per processor, the UltraSPARC T1, which has 32 threads, and the UltraSPARC T2, with 64 threads.

From a software developer's point of view, it is most convenient to focus mainly on the number of threads available. I will do that in this section, as well as describe some features that give further advantage to CMT systems over SMP systems.

12.3 Virtualization

One of the simplest uses of a system that is capable of running multiple threads is to consolidate multiple workloads from a number of existing systems and run them on the new box. This is one way to increase the utilization of the new system, and to reduce running costs. Obviously, you can achieve this just by installing and running the existing applications. However, in some cases, the applications will have constraints that prevent them from being installed on one system at the same time. For example, the tasks might require different versions of the software, or perhaps one common software component needs to be configured differently for the two workloads.

Another common scenario is that the workload may have to be run on separate systems to ensure that one application dumping core will not impact the other running applications; or perhaps one application cannot interfere with data being held in another.

The use of virtualization technologies enables multiple applications to share a single system without the applications being able to either see or interfere with each other.

Solaris Containers, or Zones, provide one level of virtualization. A system can be configured with multiple Zones. All Zones share the same Solaris kernel, but each Zone appears (for the applications running in the Zone) to be an entirely separate system with its own file system. There is a root Zone which has the ability to see into all the Zones running on the system.

Zones are configured on top of resource pools, so a particular Zone can be configured with a fixed amount of processor resources, or memory. Or multiple Zones can dynamically share resources, with limits so that none of them need be resource-starved. Figure 12.1 shows two resource pools set up on a system. One pool hosts a single Zone, and the second resource pool hosts two Zones, which will share the pool's resources. Each Zone runs the same version of Solaris, but has no insight into the activity in other Zones.

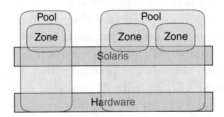

Figure 12.1 Virtualization Achieved through Zones

Zones work very well in situations where the underlying operating system is the same over all applications, and in situations where it is an acceptable risk that the entire system will go down in the event that the kernel panics in any of the Zones. In some situations, these are not acceptable constraints. For these situations there is a further form of virtualization where the many different operating systems can be mounted on the same hardware; this is provided by Sun xVM.

Figure 12.2 shows a schematic of a complete virtualization. This diagram shows multiple instances of Solaris running on one system. Each Solaris instance is entirely independent of the other instances. The technology is not limited to running multiple copies of Solaris; other operating systems can be hosted on the same machine. For example, one system could host both a Solaris and a Linux operating system. The only way that the two operating systems would be visible to each other is through communication utilities such as ssh and telnet.

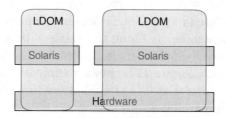

Figure 12.2 Virtualization Achieved through Sun xVM

12.4 Horizontal and Vertical Scaling

You can scale to multiple processors in two ways.

- Vertical scaling uses multiple processors within the same system. The processors will share the same system resources, so an application may become limited by a system-wide resource constraint. However, the cost (in terms of time) of communication between multiple processes is very low because sharing between the processes can occur through the system memory (or through OS features such as pipes or doors). Because the costs of sharing data between processes or threads is very low, vertical scaling is most effective for situations where the many threads (or processes) have to share significant amounts of data, or where a low response time is necessary.

- Horizonal scaling uses multiple systems. One advantage of this approach is that each system has its own resources, so the resources (e.g., bandwidth) scale with the number of systems added. However, the cost of sharing data between systems is high, because it typically requires some kind of system-to-system connectivity, such as Ethernet or Infiniband. Horizontal scaling is most effective in situations where there are small amounts of data to be shared between processes.

12.5 Parallelization

Generally speaking, applications have portions of code that have to be computed in sequence, and portions of code where tasks, or computation, can be spread over multiple CPUs. As an example of parallelizing a task, consider making a cup of tea. To make the drink the following steps are necessary. The kettle needs to be filled with water, the water needs to be boiled, a MUG needs to be fetched from the cupboard, a tea bag needs to be placed in the cup, the boiled water needs to be poured into the cup, and milk (and perhaps sugar) needs to be added. Some of these steps can be completed in parallel; for example, one person can fetch the cup from the cupboard while another is filling the kettle with water. Some of the steps need to be completed serially; for example, the water needs to be boiled before it can be poured into the cup. Figure 12.3 shows a comparison of serial and parallel approaches. The figure shows that it is possible to reduce the time it takes by performing multiple steps in parallel.

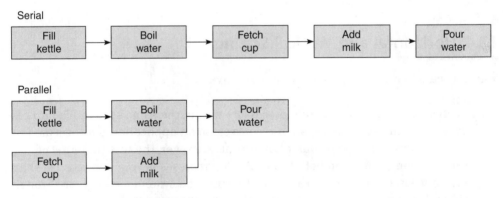

Figure 12.3 Serial and Parallel Tasks

The limit to how fast a task can be completed is the time it takes to complete the serial portion of the task. Assuming that the parallel portions of the task can be spread over infinite numbers of CPUs, those portions of the application will complete in zero time, but the serial portion will take the same amount of time regardless of the number of CPUs. This is known as *Amdahl's Law*.

In theory, performing steps in parallel should mean that the work is completed more quickly than if all the steps were completed serially. However, there are costs associated with parallelization. These are the costs of coordinating the work of the threads (it may take a small amount of time to coordinate the work between the threads). In the case of making a hot drink, this might be when explaining where to find the cup or the milk takes longer than actually going and fetching it yourself. There may also be locality costs where the act of splitting the work between processors means the data becomes spread to memory that is remote from some of the CPUs.

The communication costs typically increase as the number of threads increases. This adds a limit to the amount of parallelism that can be extracted from a given problem. The limit is when the communication costs of adding an additional thread outweigh the performance gains from the computation resource that the thread provides.

One way to minimize the communication costs is to make the chunks of work performed by each thread as large as possible. In this way, the threads need to communicate only when all of them complete their chunks of work, which hopefully is an infrequent event. The other way to reduce communication costs is to minimize the cost of sharing data that needs to be communicated. In some situations, this could be realized by exchanging the smallest possible message; in other situations, this could be achieved by sharing the data between threads using the closest possible memory (perhaps through a shared level of cache rather than through memory).

This brings up an interesting benefit of CMT processors. A single thread on a CMT processor may not be as fast as a single thread on an SMP system. However, the CMT processor has plenty of threads ready to work on a task, and the cores of the processor will usually share caches at some close level of the memory hierarchy. So, the cost of sharing data between cores can be significantly lower than the cost of utilizing the same number of cores on an SMP system. This is a very good situation, because the communication and synchronization costs are low (the communication can often take place at the level of the shared caches), and the work can be spread over more cores before the communication costs outweigh the performance benefits. Similarly, the lower communication costs potentially mean that parts of the code that were not previously profitable to parallelize become parallelizable. All of this contributes to a situation where the performance of a single thread might be lower, but the ability for the performance to scale with multiple threads is greater, leading to better total system performance, measured as throughput.

12.6 Scaling Using Multiple Processes

12.6.1 Multiple Processes

This simplest way to utilize more processor cores is often to run multiple copies of the application. This is an effective approach when each task is completely independent. An example of this is processing multiple independent files, which you can simulate using the script shown in Example 12.2, which runs a number of copies of gzip in parallel. The script can be timed to determine how long it takes to compress and then decompress, in parallel, the given number of copies of the input data set.

Example 12.2 Script to Invoke a Number of Parallel Copies of `gzip`

```
#!/bin/bash

count=0
for ((i=1; i<=$1; i++))
do
  gzip -c --best graphic.raw | gzip -dc - >/dev/null&
done
wait
```

The UltraSPARC T1 processor has eight cores. Each core can execute four threads; hence, up to 32 threads can be active at the same time. Example 12.4 shows the results of running this script on an UltraSPARC T1-based system, compressing between one and 32 copies.

Because the gzip workload is largely CPU-bound, there is some increase in elapsed time as the number of copies increases; it takes less than 2.5 times as long to run 32 copies as it did to run a single copy. The throughput of the system, which is the number of copies completed per unit time, increases to nearly 15 times the throughput of the system running just a single workload.

This is idea of throughput computing—having multiple threads share a processor may cause each individual thread to run slightly slower, but the work performed by the whole processor is much higher than can be achieved by a processor that is capable of running only a single thread.

12.6.2 Multiple Cooperating Processes

Running multiple copies of the same task works in a number of situations, often you need to use multiple cooperating processes to complete one single task. There are two steps to using multiple processes. The first is to spawn the processes, and the second is to establish some way of communicating between the processes.

The UNIX `fork()` call allows a process to spawn a child process. The child process is a copy of the parent process with a different process ID (PID). The

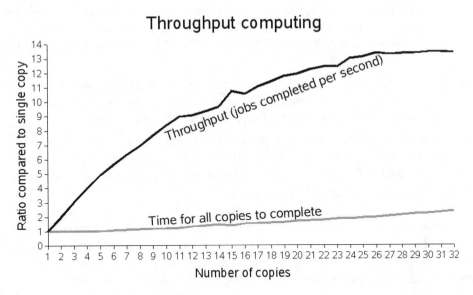

Figure 12.4 Achieved Throughput and Elapsed Time as Number of Threads Increases

`fork()` call is often paired with the `exec()` call, which can be used to start an entirely different executable. However, in this case the child processes will be used to cooperate to complete a single task. Example 12.3 shows how `fork()` can be used to spawn a child process. The return value from the `fork()` call is either zero for the child process or the PID of the child process for the parent process. In this example, the child process will print a message and then immediately exit, and the parent process will print a message and then wait for the child process to exit.

Example 12.3 Using `fork()` to Spawn a Child Process

```
#include <sys/types.h>
#include <sys/wait.h>
#include <unistd.h>
...
   int returned_pid = 1;
   returned_pid=fork();
   if (returned_pid==-1) { perror(); exit(1); }      /* Fork failed   */
   if (returned_pid==0) {printf("Child\n"); exit(0);}  /* child process */
   else { printf("Parent\n"); wait(0);}                /* parent process */
...
```

Having been able to start a child process, it is necessary for that child process to communicate back to the parent process. You can use various strategies to communicate between processes.

- Intimate Shared Memory (ISM). In this situation, all the processes share the same area of virtual memory. Communication costs between the processes are reduced to memory latency levels with no overhead from calls to the operating system.

- Messages queues, named pipes, or signals. All three of these approaches allow one process to send a message to another process. However, sending messages between processes using this interface takes some time.

- Solaris doors. Doors allow one process to ask another process to complete a calculation for it. They are useful where a message goes from one process to another and then back, because the latency of using doors in this situation is less than the latency of two messages.

Example 12.4 and Example 12.5 show the code for an example program that forks multiple threads to calculate a summation. The code uses message queues to pass the results calculated by each child process to the parent process. Example 12.4 shows how the variables are initialized and how the message queue is set up.

Example 12.4 Example of Multiprocess Code: Setting Up Message Queue

```
#include <stdio.h>
#include <stdlib.h>
#include <unistd.h>
#include <sys/types.h>
#include <sys/wait.h>
#include <sys/time.h>
#include <sys/ipc.h>
#include <sys/msg.h>
#include "timing.h"

typedef struct {
  long mtype;
  long long value;
} message;

int * volatile array;
#define SIZE (long long) 128*1024*1024

void main(int argc,const char** argv)
{
  long long sum, i,j, rtn,id,array_length;
  long threads=1;
  int queue_id;
  key_t key=1100;

  if ( (queue_id=msgget(key,IPC_CREAT | 0666)) == -1) {
    fprintf(stderr,"Could not create message queue.\n");
    exit(1);
  }
  array=(int*)malloc(sizeof(int)*SIZE);
  if (argc==2) { threads=atoi(argv[1]); }

  array_length=SIZE/threads;
```

The code in Example 12.5 shows the remaining part of the program—how the processes are forked, and how each process uses the message queue to send its results to the parent process. The parent process gathers all the results together before removing the message queue and exiting. There are two inner loops—one that iterates over the entire array using the i variable, and an outer loop around this which uses the j variable. These two loops ensure that there is sufficient work to actually use the 32 threads. The data array has been declared to be volatile to stop the compiler from optimizing the outer loop away.

Example 12.5 Example of Multiprocess Code: Dividing Task

```
rtn=1;
starttime();
for (id=0;id<threads;id++)
{
    if (rtn !=0){ rtn=fork(); if (rtn==-1) {perror("");} } /*main thread*/
    else {break;}              /*Don't fork child*/
}

if (rtn==0)
{
  /* Child thread*/
  sum=0;
  for (j=0; j<10 ; j++)
    for (i=(id-1)*array_length; i<id*array_length; i++)
    {
      sum+=array[i];
    }

  message message_out;
  message_out.mtype=1;
  message_out.value=sum;
  if (msgsnd(queue_id,&message_out,sizeof(message_out),0)==-1){
     fprintf(stderr,"Unable to send message\n");
     exit(1);
  }
  exit(0);
}
else
{
  sum=0;
  for (id=0; id<threads; id++) {
    message message_in;
    if (wait(0)!=-1) {
      if (msgrcv(queue_id,&message_in,sizeof(message_in),1,0) == -1) {
        fprintf(stderr,"Unable to receive message\n");
        exit(1);
      }
    }
    sum+=message_in.value;
  }
  endtime(SIZE);
  printf("Sum = %i\n",sum);
}
if (msgctl(queue_id,IPC_RMID,NULL) != 0) {
  fprintf(stderr,"Could not remove queue.\n");
  exit(1);
}
}
```

Example 12.5 shows the resulting scaling. The application demonstrates 24x scaling when run on 32 virtual processors.

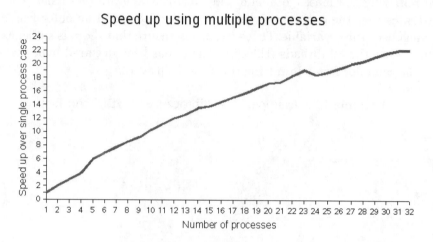

Figure 12.5 Scaling Achieved Using Multiple Processes

12.6.3 Parallelism Using MPI

The Message Passing Interface (MPI) is an approach to process-level parallelism. MPI programs run as a set of cooperating and communicating processes that can span multiple systems (referred to as *nodes* in a *cluster*). Using multiple systems means the resources the application can use (e.g., bandwidth, memory) can scale linearly with the number of processors used. The tricky part of using MPI is that the processes must communicate using messages, and the gains in performance of using multiple nodes must overcome the costs of communication between the nodes. Because the communication is between nodes, it is much more costly (often by an order of magnitude) than communication within a single node. However, a further advantage of MPI is that the problems that can be solved are not constrained to fit into the memory of a single node, which means that much larger problems can be tackled.

In practice, this means it is necessary to partition the algorithm such that minimal communication is required between the nodes. This often means that at least part of the data set is replicated over the nodes, and each node works on a portion of it. A master node is often used to dispatch messages to the other nodes instructing them what to do, and the master node is also responsible for gathering the results of the calculations.

The simple example of summing a series of numbers is not really appropriate for MPI, because the costs of communication will outweigh the performance gains from multiple processors in all but the largest arrays of numbers. Although the example is not interesting from a performance perspective, it does illustrate the basic features of using MPI.

Example 12.6 shows the outline of an MPI program. The first step the program needs to take is to initialize the MPI library using the `MPI_Init` call. Similarly, the last thing the program needs to do is to call the `MPI_Finalize` function of the MPI library before exiting. Because every process will be running exactly the same code, the process must first find out its position, or rank, in the list of processes using the `MPI_Comm_rank` call. It is usually necessary for the process to discover the total number of processes using the `MPI_Comm_size` call. Once the process has this information, it can perform the calculation. Once the process has completed its part of the calculation, it calls `MPI_Barrier` to wait for all the other processes to complete before calling `MPI_Finalize` and exiting.

Example 12.6 Outline of MPI Program

```
#include <mpi.h>

int main(int argc, char **argv)
{
    int    rank;    /*Rank of this node*/
    int    nodes;   /*Number of nodes*/

    MPI_Init(&argc, &argv);
    MPI_Comm_rank(MPI_COMM_WORLD, &rank);
    MPI_Comm_size(MPI_COMM_WORLD, &nodes);

    ...

    MPI_Barrier(MPI_COMM_WORLD);
    MPI_Finalize();
    return 0;
}
```

The processes use `MPI_Send` and `MPI_Recv` for basic communications. These routines pass around arrays of elements.

Example 12.7 shows the program to sum a series of integers using multiple processes. Each process sets up the same array, but performs the calculation over only the part of the array that is assigned to it. An optimization used in most real applications is that they may hold only the part of the data that the particular process will work on, and not the entire data set.

The process of rank zero waits for all the other processes to return their partial sums, and then calculates and prints the final result. In fact, this example could be greatly simplified using the `MPI_REDUCE` function to perform the reduction calculation. All processes would contribute their partial sum as one of the parameters to the MPI_REDUCE call, and the return from the call would be the sum of these values over all the processes.

Example 12.7 MPI Program to Sum Array of Integers

```
#include <mpi.h>
#include <stdlib.h>
#include <stdio.h>

int * array;
#define SIZE 256*1024*1024

int main(int argc, char **argv)
{
  int      rank;     /*Rank of this node*/
  int      nodes;    /*Number of nodes*/
  int      i,length,tmpsum,sum=0;
  MPI_Status status;

  MPI_Init(&argc, &argv);
  MPI_Comm_rank(MPI_COMM_WORLD, &rank);
  MPI_Comm_size(MPI_COMM_WORLD, &nodes);

  array=(int*)malloc(sizeof(int)*SIZE);
  for (i=0; i<SIZE;i++) { array[i]=1; }

  length=SIZE/nodes;
  for (i=rank*length; i<(rank+1)*length; i++) { sum+=array[i]; }
  if (rank!=0)
  {
    MPI_Send(&sum, 1, MPI_INT, 0, rank, MPI_COMM_WORLD);
  }
  else
  {
    for (int j=1; j<nodes; j++)
    {
      MPI_Recv(&tmpsum, 1, MPI_INT, j, j, MPI_COMM_WORLD,&status);
      sum+=tmpsum;
    }
    printf("Total is %i\n",sum);
  }

  MPI_Barrier(MPI_COMM_WORLD);
  MPI_Finalize();
  return 0;
}
```

It is possible to directly use the Sun Studio compilers to build an MPI application. However, you will need to add various additional options to the command line (such as specifying the location of include files and the required libraries). To simplify this, Sun HPC ClusterTools (which provides the MPI library) provides scripts that invoke the compilers with the appropriate options. Example 12.8 shows the ClusterTools 7 command line for compilation of the example program.

Example 12.8 Compiling a C Language MPI Program

```
% mpicc -O -o mpi_sum ex12.7.c
```

Example 12.9 shows the command to run the program using five processes. Before you can run the program, you need to install the ClusterTools software on all the nodes in the cluster.

Example 12.9 Running MPI Program Using Five Nodes

```
% mpirun -np 5 mpi_sum
```

It is possible to mix MPI with thread-level parallelism. An example of doing this would be to split the work over multiple nodes and use thread-level parallelism (such as OpenMP) to extract more performance from each node.

The MPI specification provides a much richer environment than this example code illustrates. Exploring the entire API is beyond the scope of this text.

12.7 Multithreaded Applications

12.7.1 Parallelization Using Pthreads

POSIX threads (or Pthreads) allow a program to use multiple threads, all sharing common memory. Each thread has its own stack (and local variables), and may also have "global" variables local to that thread (i.e., all the routines in the thread can see the same "global" variable, but the value of that variable is local to the thread). All threads share the same heap and global variables, so it is acceptable to pass pointers to objects between threads. Hence, the cost of sharing data between threads is very low, which makes Pthreads an attractive proposition when the algorithm cannot easily be divided into entirely independent calculations.

With the Pthreads approach, the main application will create various worker threads, which will complete a task and then update the results held by the master thread (which has been waiting for the worker threads to complete) before exiting. Of course, the process of creating threads may not be cheap, so the threads can be programmed so that they complete one task and then wait to be told their next task.

When a thread is created it is given the address of a function. The thread will enter this function, and once the function is completed, the thread will wait to rejoin the master thread. In Example 12.10, the threads are created by the master thread calling `pthread_create`. The worker threads will complete the summation, and update their results in the `results` array. The master thread waits by calling `pthread_join` for each created thread. Once the worker thread has joined the master thread, the worker thread ceases to exist.

Example 12.10 Example of Summation Using Pthreads

```
#include <pthread.h>
#include <stdio.h>
#include <stdlib.h>
#include "timing.h"

int *array;
int nthreads=1;
#define SIZE 256*1024*1024

void *dowork(void *params)
{
  int id=*(int*)params;
  int i,sum=0;
  for (i=(id*SIZE)/nthreads;i<(id*SIZE+SIZE)/nthreads;i++) {sum+=array[i];}
  *(int*)params=sum;
}

int main(int argc, char **argv)
{
  int i;
  pthread_t threads[100];
  int thread_data[100];
  int sum=0;
  array=(int*)malloc(sizeof(int)*SIZE);
  for (i=0; i<SIZE;i++) { array[i]=1; }

  if (argc==2) {nthreads=atoi(argv[1]);}
  starttime();
  for (i=0; i<nthreads; i++)
  {
    thread_data[i]=i;
    pthread_create(&threads[i],NULL,dowork,&thread_data[i]);
  }

  for (i=0; i<nthreads; i++)
  {
    pthread_join(threads[i],NULL);
    sum+=thread_data[i];
  }
  endtime(SIZE);
}
```

The program uses an array to pass data into and out of the thread. The data is passed in using the array because that enables each thread to get a separate area in memory. It is tempting to consider passing the address of the i variable, but the variable may well have changed value before the thread starts to execute. Passing data back to the main thread uses the same mechanism, for the same reason that it allows each thread to have a unique location in memory to hold its result. Example 12.11 shows the results of compiling and running the code with various numbers of threads on an UltraSPARC T1-based system.

Example 12.11 Compiling and Running Code That Uses Pthreads

```
% cc -O ex12.10.c -mt -lpthread
% a.out 1
Time per iteration 13.01 ns
% a.out 2
Time per iteration  6.63 ns
% a.out 4
Time per iteration  3.45 ns
```

12.7.2 Thread Local Storage

It is useful for each thread to have data that is visible only to that thread. One way to achieve this is to assign each thread a unique numeric identifier, and use this identifier to index into an array where the thread can store its own data. This is the approach used in Example 12.10. The advantage of this approach is that data can be shared relatively easily between the threads using the thread identifier.

The Pthread API also provides a way to hold data for each thread. The master thread creates a key, and each worker thread can use this key to reach thread-specific data. The code in Example 12.12 uses this API. A key is created by the call to the `pthread_key_create` function. This takes an optional parameter of a destructor routine which is called when the thread exits. Each thread can use this key to store data using the `pthread_setspecific` call, which stores a value into the key for that specific thread. The value can subsequently be retrieved using the `pthread_getspecific` call. A key is deleted at the end of the run by the `pthread_key_delete` call.

Example 12.12 Using the Pthread API for Thread Local Data

```
#include <pthread.h>
#include <stdio.h>
#include <stdlib.h>

long long  nthreads=1;

pthread_key_t globalkey=0;

void KeyDestructor(void *value)
{
  free(value);
  pthread_setspecific(globalkey,NULL);
}

void domorework()
{
  int* data=pthread_getspecific(globalkey);
  printf("Address of data = %x\n",data);
}
```

continues

Example 12.12 Using the Pthread API for Thread Local Data (*continued*)

```
void *dowork(void *params)
{
  int* data;
  data=(int*)malloc(1024*sizeof(int));
  pthread_setspecific(globalkey,data);
  domorework();
}

int main(int argc, char **argv)
{
  int i;
  pthread_t threads[100];
  if (argc==2) {nthreads=atoi(argv[1]);}

  pthread_key_create(&globalkey,KeyDestructor);

  for (i=0; i<nthreads; i++)
  {
    pthread_create(&threads[i],NULL,dowork,NULL);
  }

  for (i=0; i<nthreads; i++)
  {
    pthread_join(threads[i],NULL);
  }
  pthread_key_delete(globalkey);
}
```

Although the use of the Pthread API does standardize the handling of thread local data, it is rather cumbersome to use. Fortunately, there is a much easier way to achieve the same result.

Thread Local Storage is implemented by the compiler to allow variables to be declared as being local to a thread, using the __thread specifier. Example 12.13 shows an example that is analogous to the previous one, using Thread Local Storage. In this instance, all that is necessary is to declare the thread_data global variable as being thread local, and the compiler is able to generate the appropriate code so that each thread gets its own copy.

Example 12.13 Example of Using Thread Local Storage

```
#include <pthread.h>
#include <stdio.h>
#include <stdlib.h>

long long  nthreads=1;

__thread int* thread_data;

void domorework()
{
  printf("Address of data = %x\n",thread_data);
}
```

Example 12.13 Example of Using Thread Local Storage (*continued*)

```
void *dowork(void *params)
{
  int* data;
  thread_data=(int*)malloc(1024*sizeof(int));
  domorework();
  free(thread_data);
}

int main(int argc, char **argv)
{
  int i;
  pthread_t threads[100];
  if (argc==2) {nthreads=atoi(argv[1]);}

  for (i=0; i<nthreads; i++)
  {
    pthread_create(&threads[i],NULL,dowork,NULL);
  }

  for (i=0; i<nthreads; i++)
  {
    pthread_join(threads[i],NULL);
  }
}
```

12.7.3 Mutexes

In many situations, it is necessary to share access to a single copy of a particular item. Examples of this range from sharing a particular part of the hardware (e.g., the serial port) to sharing a single variable. In these situations, it is normal to require a lock to ensure that only one thread can be changing the object at any one time. The most common approach to providing a lock is to use a mutex lock (abbreviated from mutually exclusive lock). A mutex can be acquired by only a single thread at a time; any other threads have to wait for that thread to release the lock before they can acquire it. Hence, it is a useful mechanism for ensuring that only one thread can access a particular variable at any one time, or ensuring that only one thread executes a particular region of code at any one time.

If shared data is not protected by a mutex, it will become corrupted. A *data race* is the situation where a thread updates a shared item of data without that item of data being protected by a mutex. Example 12.14 shows a data race condition. This code has a problem where the shared_sum variable can be simultaneously updated by multiple threads.

Example 12.15 shows the results of this data race. The program takes the number of threads to use as an argument. The output shows the value returned if one, two, or four threads are used to perform the calculation. The compiler has produced code that holds the shared_sum variable in a register, which means that it is only written back to memory at the end of the calculation. So, rather than

Example 12.14 Code with Data Race

```c
#include <pthread.h>
#include <stdio.h>
#include <stdlib.h>

int *array;
long long  nthreads=1;
#define SIZE 256*1024*1024
long long  shared_sum=0;

void *dowork(void *params)
{
  long long id=*(int*)params;
  long long i;
  for (i=(id*SIZE)/nthreads;i<(id*SIZE+SIZE)/nthreads;i++)
  {
    shared_sum+=array[i];
  }
}

int main(int argc, char **argv)
{
  int i;
  pthread_t threads[100];
  int thread_data[100];

  array=(int*)malloc(sizeof(int)*SIZE);
  for (i=0; i<SIZE;i++) { array[i]=1; }

  if (argc==2) {nthreads=atoi(argv[1]);}
  for (i=0; i<nthreads; i++)
  {
    thread_data[i]=i;
    pthread_create(&threads[i],NULL,dowork,&thread_data[i]);
  }

  for (i=0; i<nthreads; i++)
  {
    pthread_join(threads[i],NULL);
  }
  printf("Sum = %lli\n",shared_sum);
}
```

getting the sum of the results from all threads, the program is just returning the value calculated by the last thread to complete.

Example 12.15 Error Due to Data Race Condition

```
% cc -O ex12.14.c -mt -lpthread
% a.out 1
Sum = 268435456
% a.out 2
Sum = 134217728
% a.out 4
Sum = 67128444
```

The compiler is not able to determine that the shared_sum variable is shared between multiple threads, which is why the compiler considers it safe to hold in a register. Example 12.16 shows the disassembly for the critical loop. The shared_sum variable is stored every iteration, but it is never loaded, so the changes to shared_sum from other threads are never used in the calculation. The value reported at the end of the run is the value for shared_sum reported by the thread that last performed the store operation.

Example 12.16 Disassembly for the Loop

```
10d50:   97 2b 20 02    sll    %o4, 2, %o3
10d54:   9a 03 60 01    inc    %o5                    ! i++
10d58:   d4 02 c0 04    ld     [%o3 + %g4], %o2       ! load from array[i]
10d5c:   80 a3 40 08    cmp    %o5, %o0
10d60:   93 3a a0 00    sra    %o2, 0, %o1            ! extend int to long long
10d64:   8a 01 40 09    add    %g5, %o1, %g5          ! shared_sum += array[i]
10d68:   ca 70 e0 00    stx    %g5, [%g3]             ! store to shared_sum
10d6c:   04 6f ff f9    ble,pt %xcc, 0x10d50
10d70:   99 3b 60 00    sra    %o5, 0, %o4
```

If the variable were declared to be volatile, the compiler would load and store the variable on every iteration. Example 12.17 shows the modified loop. The "improvement" in the code is that each thread will use the most recently stored value for shared_sum in the summation.

Example 12.17 Loop with shared_sum Declared as Volatile

```
10d4c:   97 2b 20 02    sll    %o4, 2, %o3
10d50:   c6 59 20 00    ldx    [%g4], %g3             ! load shared_sum
10d54:   9a 03 60 01    inc    %o5                    ! i++
10d58:   d4 02 c0 08    ld     [%o3 + %o0], %o2       ! load from array[i]
10d5c:   80 a3 40 05    cmp    %o5, %g5
10d60:   93 3a a0 00    sra    %o2, 0, %o1            ! extend int to long long
10d64:   84 00 c0 09    add    %g3, %o1, %g2          ! shared_sum += array[i]
10d68:   c4 71 20 00    stx    %g2, [%g4]             ! store to shared_sum
10d6c:   04 6f ff f8    ble,pt %xcc, 0x10d4c
10d70:   99 3b 60 00    sra    %o5, 0, %o4
```

This does not solve the data race condition. In fact, it looks like it makes the problem worse because there is much greater variance in the calculated value. The reason for this increased variance is that each thread is reading the value calculated by other threads, so the final result depends on the order in which the threads loaded and stored the value. Example 12.18 shows the variance from this code change. In this example, two runs of the same program both utilizing two threads produce different results.

Example 12.18 Results of Data Race on Volatile Variable

```
% cc -O ex12.17.c -mt -lpthread
% a.out 1
Sum = 268435456
% a.out 2
Sum = 66810147
% a.out 2
Sum = 66214387
```

It is straightforward to add a mutex to the code so that only one thread can update the variable sum at a time. Example 12.19 shows the code. In this code, the shared_sum variable needs to be declared as volatile because it is shared between threads, and as such it needs to be loaded and stored every time it is changed. The mutex ensures that only one thread can make a change at a time. The mutex is created by the pthread_create_mutex call, and it must be destroyed at the end of the run with the pthread_mutex_destroy call. Before updating the shared_sum variable, a thread must acquire the mutex by calling pthread_mutex_lock. After updating the variable, the thread must release the mutex through the pthread_mutex_unlock call.

Example 12.19 Protecting the Variable Sum with a Mutex

```
#include <pthread.h>
#include <stdio.h>
#include <stdlib.h>

int *array;
long long  nthreads=1;
#define SIZE 256*1024*1024
volatile long long  shared_sum=0;

pthread_mutex_t mutex;

void *dowork(void *params)
{
  long long id=*(int*)params;
  long long i;
  for (i=(id*SIZE)/nthreads;i<(id*SIZE+SIZE)/nthreads;i++)
  {
    pthread_mutex_lock(&mutex);
    shared_sum+=array[i];
    pthread_mutex_unlock(&mutex);
  }
}
```

Example 12.19 Protecting the Variable Sum with a Mutex (*continued*)

```
int main(int argc, char **argv)
{
  int i;
  pthread_t threads[100];
  int thread_data[100];

  pthread_mutex_init(&mutex,NULL);

  array=(int*)malloc(sizeof(int)*SIZE);
  for (i=0; i<SIZE;i++) { array[i]=1; }

  if (argc==2) {nthreads=atoi(argv[1]);}
  for (i=0; i<nthreads; i++)
  {
    thread_data[i]=i;
    pthread_create(&threads[i],NULL,dowork,&thread_data[i]);
  }

  for (i=0; i<nthreads; i++)
  {
    pthread_join(threads[i],NULL);
  }
  printf("Sum = %lli\n",shared_sum);
  pthread_mutex_destroy(&mutex);
}
```

The changes in the code mean that it produces the correct answer, but unfortunately, there is considerable overhead in using mutex locks. Example 12.20 shows the difference in performance when two threads, on an SMP system, are attempting to cooperate to perform the calculation. The calculation takes about twice as long, and uses about four times the CPU time, when two threads are used.

Example 12.20 Overhead of Using Mutex Locks

```
% cc -O ex12.19.c -o mutex -mt -lpthread; timex mutex 1
Sum = 268435456

real    1:23.14
user    1:19.69
sys        2.49

% timex mutex 2
Sum = 268435456

real    3:12.09
user    6:00.15
sys        8.76
```

It takes longer with multiple threads because on a traditional SMP system (such as the one used to produce the results in Example 12.20) the cache lines containing the mutex and the `shared_sum` variable need to be written back to memory before the CPU running the second thread can access them. Hence, performance is limited by memory latency. On a CMT system, such as the UltraSPARC T1, the sharing of data between cores can be performed at the on-chip second-level cache, which has much lower latency than memory. Example 12.21 shows the results of running this code on an UltraSPARC T1-based system. Although the CMT system runs slightly slower than the SMP system for the single-threaded case, the system does not slow down when two threads are contending for the same mutex.

Example 12.21 Mutexes on a CMT System

```
% timex mutex 1
Sum = 268435456

real    2:03.62
user    1:52.46
sys       10.06

% timex mutex 2
 Sum = 268435456

real    2:01.22
user    3:29.92
sys       12.00
```

This demonstrates an important point. CMT systems are a better match for threaded programs. Not only can the systems run multiple threads, but also the costs of the traditional impediments to scaling (such as mutexes) are substantially reduced. This means applications that were hitting scaling limits because of mutexes should be able to scale further on a CMT system than they would on a traditional SMP system.

When a thread cannot acquire a mutex, it can either keep trying (spin busy), or sleep for a short period of time before retrying. If the thread keeps trying, it will acquire the mutex as soon as the mutex is released, but it will take up CPU time that another thread could possibly use. Consequently, best performance may be obtained for an application by spinning busy, but best throughput for a system may be obtained if the threads sleep when the mutex is busy. The default for Solaris mutexes is to sleep if the lock cannot be acquired within a small number of tries. However, this protocol does not make a difference for the example code because the lock is held for only very short periods of time.

Consideration needs to be given to the granularity of the mutex used. If large amounts of data are protected by a single mutex, multiple threads may need to update different parts of the data at the same time. This will cause the application to run slowly—the other threads will have to wait while each thread performs its update on independent data. The situation where multiple threads want the same lock is called a *contended lock*.

Of course, the other extreme is having too many mutex locks, and each thread having to acquire multiple locks to complete its work. Because acquiring each lock will take some time, this will also lead to lost performance.

The pragmatic approach is to add the mutex locks that are necessary for the code to function correctly, identify locks that are contended (and therefore are limiting scaling), and replace these locks with a more finely granular mutex-locking scheme or recode to use some form of mutex-free algorithm.

One further area of concern when using mutex locks is that of deadlocks. This is the situation where one thread has one lock and needs to acquire a second, and another thread holds the second lock but needs to acquire the first. In this situation, neither thread can make any progress because each has resources that the other thread needs. To avoid this, always aquire the locks in the same order. That way, if a thread has acquired only the second lock, it knows it will never need the first lock, so a thread that has the first lock but needs the second lock will be guaranteed to eventually get the second lock.

12.7.4 Using Atomic Operations

Atomic operations are ones that appear to be a single operation. As an example, consider a traditional increment of a variable. To do this it is necessary to load the value of the variable, add the increment to this value, and then store the value back to memory. It would be possible for another thread to change the value of the variable while this thread is also changing it. With an atomic operation, it is not possible for another thread to change the value while the operation is completing.

Solaris 10 provides a set of atomic operations[1] that you can use for atomically updating the value of variables. You can use them as a way to avoid the need for mutexes for simple operations on variables, because it is not possible for another thread to update the value of the variable at the same time as the current thread is updating it with an atomic operation. You can rewrite the code in Example 12.19 using atomic operations, as shown in Example 12.22. The use of atomic operations simplifies the code considerably.

Example 12.23 shows the results of compiling and running this code on a CMT system. Compare these numbers with the results shown in Example 12.21. Not only is the overall performance improved by using the simpler construct (the serial program runs in one minute rather than two), but also the scaling is improved—using two threads on a CMT system gives better performance than using just one.

---

1. See `atomic_ops` in the Solaris 10 documentation.

Example 12.22 Using Atomic Operations to Update Variables

```
#include <pthread.h>
#include <stdio.h>
#include <stdlib.h>
#include <atomic.h>

int *array;
long long  nthreads=1;
#define SIZE 256*1024*1024
volatile unsigned long long  sum=0;

void *dowork(void *params)
{
  long long id=*(int*)params;
  long long i;
  for (i=(id*SIZE)/nthreads;i<(id*SIZE+SIZE)/nthreads;i++)
  {
    atomic_add_64(&sum,array[i]);
  }
}

int main(int argc, char **argv)
{
  int i;
  pthread_t threads[100];
  int thread_data[100];


  array=(int*)malloc(sizeof(int)*SIZE);
  for (i=0; i<SIZE;i++) { array[i]=1; }

  if (argc==2) {nthreads=atoi(argv[1]);}
  for (i=0; i<nthreads; i++)
  {
    thread_data[i]=i;
    pthread_create(&threads[i],NULL,dowork,&thread_data[i]);
  }

  for (i=0; i<nthreads; i++)
  {
    pthread_join(threads[i],NULL);
  }
  printf("Sum = %lli\n",sum);
}
```

Example 12.23 Performance of Atomic Operations

```
% cc -O ex12.22.c -mt -lpthread
% timex a.out 1
Sum = 268435456

real      1:12.30
user      1:01.28
sys          9.92

% timex a.out 2
Sum = 268435456

real        45.11
user      1:02.36
sys          9.85
```

12.7.5 False Sharing

Scaling can be worse than expected in another situation, but in this case, the problem is due to the unfortunate layout of the data used by various threads in memory. In this case, data that different threads require resides on the same cache line. As each thread updates its data, it is necessary to fetch the data from the last processor that updated the line before the data can be modified. This situation is referred to as *false sharing*.

False sharing can typically be detected when accesses to particular variables seem unexpectedly expensive. Example 12.24 shows an example of false sharing. In this code, the sum variable is declared to be a pointer to a volatile integer. Because the data is volatile, it needs to be loaded and stored for every operation

Example 12.24 Example of False Sharing

```
#include <pthread.h>
#include <stdio.h>
#include <stdlib.h>
#include "timing.h"

int *array;
int nthreads=1;
#define SIZE 32*1024*1024

void *dowork(void *params)
{
  int id=*(int*)params;
  int i;
  int * volatile restrict sum=(int*)params;
  *sum = 0;
  for (i=(id*SIZE)/nthreads;i<(id*SIZE+SIZE)/nthreads;i++) {*sum+=array[i];}
}

int main(int argc, char **argv)
{
  int i;
  pthread_t threads[100];
  int thread_data[100];
  int sum=0;
  array=(int*)malloc(sizeof(int)*SIZE);
  for (i=0; i<SIZE;i++) { array[i]=1; }

  if (argc==2) {nthreads=atoi(argv[1]);}
  starttime();
  for (i=0; i<nthreads; i++)
  {
    thread_data[i]=i;
    pthread_create(&threads[i],NULL,dowork,&thread_data[i]);
  }

  for (i=0; i<nthreads; i++)
  {
    pthread_join(threads[i],NULL);
    sum+=thread_data[i];
  }
  endtime(SIZE);
}
```

performed on sum; this artificial coding construct is to ensure that the effect of false sharing is readily apparent. The sum pointer is also declared as restricted so that it does not interfere with the calculations of the bounds of the loop. Each thread has its own copy of the sum variable, but all copies are adjacent in memory, and up to 16 threads will share variables on the same cache line.

Example 12.25 shows the performance of this code on a traditional SMP system using one and two threads. You would expect that using two threads would cause the time per iteration to be cut in half, but false sharing in the case where there are two threads causes each iteration to take twice as long.

Example 12.25 Effect of False Sharing on Performance

```
% cc -O -o false_sharing ex12.24.c -mt -lpthread
% false_sharing 1
Time per iteration 19.21 ns
% false_sharing 2
Time per iteration 39.49 ns
```

It is interesting to compare this with the situation on a CMT system, as shown in Example 12.26. The UltraSPARC T1-based system is able to share the data through the second-level cache. Consequently, the performance impact of false sharing is minimal; more impressive is the fact that the gains from using two threads outweigh the additional costs of false sharing.

Example 12.26 False Sharing on a CMT System

```
% false_sharing 1
Time per iteration 29.90 ns
% false_sharing 2
Time per iteration 17.52 ns
```

To fix false sharing, it is necessary to pad data so that each thread's data resides on a different cache line. The size of the padding required is system-dependent, and is the size of data that is necessary to push the two items onto separate cache lines. Example 12.27 shows the modified code to achieve this for the example program. The padding is determined by there being 64 bytes to a cache line, and each item of data being an integer (taking four bytes in a 32-bit application). Hence, there are 16 locations per cache line.

With the padding inserted into the data structures, performance is improved particularly on the SMP system (which reduces from ~39ns per iteration to ~8ns). Similarly, performance improves on the CMT system, but the magnitude of the gain is less because the original performance cost was less. Unfortunately, adding padding may

Example 12.27 Padding Data to Avoid False Sharing

```
starttime();
for (i=0; i<nthreads; i++)
{
  thread_data[i*16]=i;
  pthread_create(&threads[i],NULL,dowork,&thread_data[i*16]);
}

for (i=0; i<nthreads; i++)
{
  pthread_join(threads[i],NULL);
  sum+=thread_data[i*16];
}
endtime(SIZE);
```

reduce the performance of the single-threaded code because elements that could be placed on a single cache line are now spread out onto multiple cache lines.

12.7.6 Memory Layout for a Threaded Application

When a program is parallelized using Pthreads, one of the attributes that you can specify when the thread is created is the amount of stack space. The *stack* is where variables that are local to a function are held. Space on the stack is used as the depth of the call stack increases. Running out of stack space is referred to as a stack overflow. It is possible for the compiler to add code to detect stack overflows, as described in Section 9.3.5 of Chapter 9. By default, the created threads will get 1MB of stack space for 32-bit applications, whereas 64-bit applications will get 2MB.

The Pthread API contains routines to manipulate the attributes of a Pthread. The `pthread_attr_init` function sets up a variable of type `pthread_attr_t` with the default attributes. The `pthread_attr_setstacksize` function changes the stack size setting for the Pthread attribute variable. The variable describing the Pthread attributes can be passed as one of the parameters to the `pthread_create` function, which creates the new thread. Example 12.28 shows an example of changing the stack size for a Pthread. In the example, the thread is requesting stack space for 3MB of data. However, a fixed amount of stack space is required by the thread that also needs to be included in the amount of stack space reserved. This minimum stack size is held in the `PTHREAD_STACK_MIN` constant, which is defined in `limits.h`.

When setting the stack size it is worth considering the total amount of space assigned to each stack, and the number of active threads in the application. For 32-bit applications, it is relatively easy to run out of address space by assigning excessive amounts of stack to each thread.

Example 12.28 Changing Default Stack Size for a Pthread

```
#include <pthread.h>

pthread_attr_t attr;
pthread_t thread;
int ret;

size_t size=PTHREAD_STACK_MIN + 3*1024*1024;
...
  ret=pthread_attr_init(&attr); /*get default values*/
  ret=pthread_attr_setstacksize(&attr,size); /*change stack size attribute*/
  ret=pthread_create((&thread,&attr, starting_routine, parameters);
```

The program shown in Example 12.29 prints out the addresses for various structures in the code's address space. These structures are the stacks for the main thread

Example 12.29 Program to Print the Address of Various Program Structures

```
#include <pthread.h>
#include <stdio.h>
#include <stdlib.h>
#include <unistd.h>

int *array;
int nthreads=1;
#define SIZE 1024*1024

void printstacklocal(int id) {
  int i;
  printf("Address of subroutine stack (for thread %i) = %x\n",id,&i);
}

void *dowork(void *params) {
  int i=*(int*)params;
  printf("Address of stack for thread %i = %x\n",i,&i);
  printstacklocal(i);
  sleep(10);
}

int main(int argc, char **argv) {
  int i;
  pthread_t threads[100];
  int thread_data[100];
  printf("Address of main routine = %x\n",&main);
  printf("Address of dowork routine = %x\n",&dowork);
  printf("Address of printf routine = %x\n",&printf);
  printf("Address of stack for master thread = %x\n",&i);
  printstacklocal(-1);
  for (i=0;i<4; i++) {
    array=(int*)malloc(sizeof(int)*SIZE);
    printf("Address of malloc'd memory %x\n",array);
  }
  if (argc==2) {nthreads=atoi(argv[1]);}
  for (i=0; i<nthreads; i++) {
    thread_data[i]=i;
    pthread_create(&threads[i],NULL,dowork,&thread_data[i]);
  }
  for (i=0; i<nthreads; i++) { pthread_join(threads[i],NULL); }
}
```

and the various created threads, together with the address of allocated memory and the routines that are used. The program's objective is to demonstrate how memory is assigned to the various structures. The `sleep` statement in the program is necessary to avoid the space assigned to each thread being reused by a subsequent thread.

Example 12.30 shows the output from the program, creating two child threads. As you can see, the code is located in the lower part of memory, the stacks are located at the top of memory, and memory is `malloc`'d after the addresses allocated to code. It is also apparent that stacks grow downward, whereas `malloc`'d memory grows upward.

Example 12.30 Output Showing Memory Addresses

```
% cc -O -o layout ex12.29.c -mt -lpthread
% layout 2
Address of main routine = 10d98
Address of dowork routine = 10d64
Address of printf routine = 21070
Address of stack for master thread = ffbffb5c
Address of subroutine stack (for thread -1) = ffbff7d4
Address of malloc'd memory 211d8
Address of malloc'd memory 4211e0
Address of malloc'd memory 8211e8
Address of malloc'd memory c211f0
Address of stack for thread 0 = ff1fbf9c
Address of subroutine stack (for thread 0) = ff1fbf34
Address of stack for thread 1 = ff0fbf9c
Address of subroutine stack (for thread 1) = ff0fbf34
```

An alternative way to view the address space is to use `pmap` (see Section 4.4.7 of Chapter 4), as shown in Example 12.31. This clearly shows the `malloc`'d memory coming from the region that `pmap` labels as *heap*. The stack for the master thread is labeled as *stack* by `pmap`, and the regions for the stack for the worker threads are labeled as *anon* by `pmap`. The `main` and `dowork` routines fall into the region that `pmap` labels with the name of the executable. It is interesting to observe that the address for the `printf` routine is within pages that `pmap` labels with the name of the executable, but `libc` where `printf` actually resides is loaded in higher memory. The address that is printed for `printf` is actually a jump to a lookup table which redirects the code to the real library routine held in higher memory.

Figure 12.6 shows a schematic of how memory is laid out for this application. The application code is located in the lower area of memory, above which the heap grows toward upper memory. The master stack is located at the top of memory, below which the libraries are loaded. The stacks for the threads are placed in memory below the libraries and growing downward. There is unused address space between the top of the heap and the base of the stacks. This memory can be allocated to either increase the heap in use or increase the number of threads.

Example 12.31 Output from `pmap` Showing Memory Layout

```
$ pmap 3261
3261:   layout 2
00010000      8K r-x--  layout
00020000      8K rwx--  layout
00022000  16392K rwx--    [ heap ]
FF0FA000      8K rwx-R    [ anon ]
FF1FA000      8K rwx-R    [ anon ]
FF230000    112K rw---    [ anon ]
FF258000      8K rwxs-    [ anon ]
FF260000     16K rw---    [ anon ]
FF270000      8K rwx--    [ anon ]
FF280000    688K r-x--  /usr/lib/libc.so.1
FF33C000     32K rwx--  /usr/lib/libc.so.1
FF350000     96K r-x--  /usr/lib/libthread.so.1
FF378000      8K rwx--  /usr/lib/libthread.so.1
FF37A000      8K rwx--  /usr/lib/libthread.so.1
FF380000     24K r-x--  /usr/lib/libpthread.so.1
FF396000      8K rwx--  /usr/lib/libpthread.so.1
FF3A0000      8K r-x--  /usr/platform/sun4u-us3/lib/libc_psr.so.1
FF3B0000    184K r-x--  /usr/lib/ld.so.1
FF3EE000      8K rwx--  /usr/lib/ld.so.1
FF3F0000      8K rwx--  /usr/lib/ld.so.1
FF3FA000      8K rwx--  /usr/lib/libdl.so.1
FFBFA000     24K rwx--    [ stack ]
 total   17672K
```

Low memory   High memory

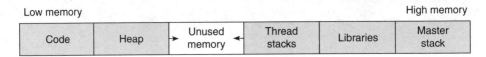

Figure 12.6 Schematic Showing Memory Layout

12.8 Parallelizing Applications Using OpenMP

OpenMP is a specification for a set of compiler directives, library routines, and environment variables that you can use to specify shared memory parallelism in Fortran and C/C++ programs. The approach is to add directives into the application's source code. Under the -xopenmp compiler flag, the Sun Studio compiler will use these directives to produce parallel code. OpenMP has a number of advantages over parallelizing using Pthreads.

- The directives are added to the code. If the compiler flag is not present, the directives are ignored, and the compiler sees the original serial version of the code. Hence, the same source code can easily provide both serial and parallel versions of the application.

- The directives can be added to the source incrementally. Hence, just part of an application can be parallelized and the rest left untouched. This makes it easy to cherry-pick the parts of the application where parallelization is a certain win, while leaving the remaining code untouched.

Because OpenMP uses directives, parallelization of a loop can often be achieved with the addition of a single line of code. This makes it very easy to add parallel regions to an application. However, there will still be situations where calls to the OMP runtime routines are necessary. These calls and any other differences between the serial and multithreaded versions of the code will have to be protected using `#ifdef _OPENMP`.

OpenMP is suited for codes containing either loops, or clearly defined tasks that can be completed in parallel. It may be necessary to use Pthreads for situations where the control flow through the application is less well defined, although this will change with the tasking model in the OpenMP 3.0 specification. In fact, OpenMP is often built on top of Pthreads, so the same libraries are used, and the overall performance characteristics are the same. The major advantage of OpenMP is the convenience of only requiring the addition of high-level directives to the source code.

12.9 Using OpenMP Directives to Parallelize Loops

The most common use of OpenMP directives is to parallelize loops. As an example, consider the summation loop shown in Example 12.32.

Example 12.32 Example of a Summation Loop

```
#include <stdio.h>
#include <stdlib.h>
#include "timing.h"

#define SIZE 128*1024*1024

void main(int argc,const char** argv)
{
  int i;
  int * array;

  array=(int*)malloc(sizeof(int)*SIZE);
  int sum=0;

  for (i=0; i<SIZE; i++) {array[i]=1;}

  starttime();
  for(i=0; i<SIZE; i++) {sum+=array[i];}
  endtime(SIZE);
  printf("Total is %i\n",sum);
}
```

You can use the `omp parallel for` directive to tell the compiler that the following `for` loop should be parallelized. It is also necessary to tell the compiler whether the variables used in the parallel region should be shared between threads, or whether each thread should have a private copy. For simple cases such as this one, it is relatively straightforward to identify that the `array` variable should be shared between threads, and that the `sum` variable is a "reduction" operation. With a *reduction operation*, a number of elements are reduced to a single value through some operations such as addition.

The `-xvpara` compiler flag will output warnings about possible errors in the parallelization. The `-xloopinfo` compiler flag will report whether regions have been parallelized. The compiler will select default settings for the scope of variables. Unfortunately, the defaults will not always be appropriate. To ensure that all the variables are correctly scoped you can switch off the default scoping using the `default(none)` directive. When the resulting program is compiled, the compiler will emit errors for variables that have not been scoped. Example 12.33 shows an example. The error message indicates that the `sum` and `array` variables must be scoped.

Example 12.33 Warning for Variables That Have Not Had Scope Specified

```
$ more ex12.33.c
...
  starttime();
  #pragma omp parallel for default(none)
  for(i=0; i<SIZE; i++) {sum+=array[i];}
  endtime(SIZE);
...
$ cc -O -xvpara -xloopinfo -xopenmp ex12.33.c
"ex12.33.c", line 19: "sum" must be explicitly listed in a data attribute clause of
enclosing omp pragma parallel for
"ex12.33.c", line 19: "array" must be explicitly listed in a data attribute clause of
enclosing omp pragma parallel for
cc: acomp failed for ex12.33.c
```

The `array` variable is shared between all threads, so it should be scoped as `shared(array)`. The `sum` variable, as indicated earlier, is a reduction variable. The reduction scoping clause is used to specify that the variable is used in a reduction operation, and the type of reduction in which the variable occurs. Example 12.34 shows the results of successfully compiling the corrected code.

The Sun Studio compiler contains a Sun-specific extension to the OpenMP specification that requests that the compiler identify the correct scope for variables in the parallel region. The extension is called *autoscoping*, and it is enabled using the `default(__auto)` clause or the `__auto(<list of variables>)` clause. In many cases, this is sufficient to correctly parallelize the code. When

Example 12.34 Compiling Fully Specified Directive

```
$ more ex12.34.c
...
   starttime();
   #pragma omp parallel for default(none) shared(array) reduction(+:sum)
   for(i=0; i<SIZE; i++) {sum+=array[i];}
   endtime(SIZE);
...
$ cc -O -xvpara -xloopinfo -xopenmp ex12.34.c
"ex12.34.c", line 20: PARALLELIZED, user pragma used
```

the `-xvpara` compiler flag is present the compiler will emit a warning if it is unable to autoscope the variables. To identify the scoping that the compiler has applied it is necessary to compile with the `-g` flag to generate debug information, and use the `er_src` tool to extract the compiler commentary for the parallelized code. Example 12.35 shows an example of using autoscoping. The compiler commentary for the file is rather verbose, but the commentary messages show that the compiler was able to correctly identify the `array` variable as being shared and the `sum` variable as being a reduction.

Example 12.35 Example of Autoscoping

```
$ more ex12.35.c
...
   starttime();
   #pragma omp parallel for default(__auto)
   for(i=0; i<SIZE; i++) {sum+=array[i];}
   endtime(SIZE);
...
$ cc -g -O -xvpara -xloopinfo -xopenmp ex12.35.c
"ex12.35.c", line 19: PARALLELIZED, user pragma used
$ er_src a.out
...
   Source OpenMP region below has tag R1
   Variables autoscoped as SHARED in R1: array
   Variables autoscoped as REDUCTION of operator + in R1: sum
   Private variables in R1: i
   Shared variables in R1: array
   Reduction variables of operator + in R1: sum
   18.    #pragma omp parallel for default(__auto)
...
   19.    for(i=0; i<SIZE; i++) {sum+=array[i];}
   20.    endtime(SIZE);
```

To handle reductions, each thread has a private copy of the reduction variable. In this example, each thread would have a private copy of the `sum` variable. All the threads perform the calculation on their private copy of the `sum` variable for the range of data they have been assigned. Once all the threads have completed, the private copies of the reduction variable are combined to produce the final value that will be visible outside the parallel region. Because the work has been spread over multiple threads, the order of the computations is not identical to the serial case. Consequently, for floating-point computations, the use of reductions will result in a different order of computation, which may cause a rounding difference in the computed value; that is, the use of reductions may cause a difference in the results between the serial and parallel code.

Not all computations are reductions, and other OpenMP clauses handle different cases. For example, the `lastprivate` directive produces code that results in the specified variable in the parallel version of the code holding the value that would be calculated from the last iteration of the serial code.

For loop-based parallelism, there are some constraints on the type of loop that can be parallelized. Because the work needs to be divided over the available threads at runtime, the bounds on the loop must be computable before the loop is entered. The same constraint is true for the increments. It is not possible to parallelize loops that have complex exit conditions.

12.10 Using the OpenMP API

The OpenMP specification defines an API that allows the developer to dynamically query and change some of the variables that control parallelization. For example, normally the environment variable OMP_NUM_THREADS is used to specify the number of threads the application will use, but the `omp_set_num_threads()` runtime routine or the `num_threads()` clause can be used to set this value.

To use the API it is necessary to include the `omp.h` header file. If the same code is being used to generate serial and parallel versions of the application, the calls to the API should be protected by `#ifdef _OPENMP`. Example 12.36 shows an example of changing the number of threads depending on the argument passed into the application.

Example 12.36 Using the OpenMP API to Change the Number of Threads

```
void main(int argc, const char** argv)
{
  int threads=1;

  if (argc==2) {threads=atoi(argv[1]);}
#ifdef _OPENMP
  omp_set_num_threads(threads);
#endif
  ...
```

12.11 Parallel Sections

Loop-based parallelism is not the only kind that OpenMP supports. It is also possible to use section-based parallelizm. In this situation, there are two or more independent sections of code to be performed. Using the OpenMP parallel sections directive, it is possible to assign each section to a different thread and have the sections performed in parallel. In Example 12.37, there are two independent parallel sections to be performed. If `OMP_NUM_THREADS` is set to be greater than one, each section will be assigned to a different thread, and overall performance will improve.

Example 12.37 Section-Based Parallelization

```
#include <stdio.h>
#include <stdlib.h>
#include "timing.h"

#define SIZE 128*1024*1024

void main(int argc,const char** argv)
{
  int i;
  int * array;
  int * fib;

  array=(int*)malloc(sizeof(int)*SIZE);
  fib = (int*)malloc(sizeof(int)*SIZE);
  starttime();
  #pragma omp parallel sections default(none) private(i) shared(array,fib)
  {
    #pragma omp section
    for (i=0; i<SIZE; i++) {array[i]=1;}
    #pragma omp section
    {
      fib[0]=0;
      fib[1]=1;
      for (i=2; i<SIZE; i++) {fib[i]=fib[i-1]+fib[i-2];}
    }
  }
  endtime(SIZE);
  int sum =0;
  for(i=0; i<SIZE;i++){sum+=array[i]+fib[i];}
  printf("Sum = %i",sum);
}
```

12.11.1 Setting Stack Sizes for OpenMP

For OpenMP code, the stack size is controlled in two ways. The stack size for the master thread is controlled by the `ulimit` command. The stack size for each worker thread is controlled by the `STACKSIZE` environment variable. This environment variable takes values in kilobytes by default, but you can use specifiers such as B, K, M, or G to conveniently represent other sizes. The defaults for OpenMP threads are 4MB for 32-bit applications and 8MB for 64-bit applications. You can check for stack overflow by building with the -xcheck=stkovf compiler flag, as described in Section 9.3.5 of Chapter 9.

12.12 Automatic Parallelization of Applications

The compiler is able to automatically parallelize loops in an application. The flag to enable this is -xautopar. For some applications, this can be a quick way to utilize multiple cores. However, in many instances it is not possible for the compiler to determine whether parallelization is safe. If the compiler cannot determine that parallelization is safe, it will not perform it. The -xloopinfo flag reports whether the compiler was able to parallelize each loop in a program.

Example 12.38 shows a simple program. This program first initializes an array of doubles, and then sums the values in the array.

Example 12.38 Simple Program to Be Auto-Parallelized

```
#include <stdio.h>
#include <stdlib.h>
#include "timing.h"

double * a;
#define SIZE 10*1024*1024

void main()
{
  int i;
  double t=0.0;
  a=(double*)malloc(sizeof(double)*SIZE);
  for (i=0; i<SIZE;i++)                    // line 13
  {
    a[i]=(double)i;
  }
  starttime();
  for (i=0; i<SIZE;i++)                    // line 18
  {
    t+=a[i];
  }
  endtime(SIZE);
  printf("t=%f\n",t);
}
```

When the program is first compiled, the compiler generates warnings about the safety of both loops, as shown in Example 12.39.

For the first loop at line 13, the compiler is concerned that one of the stores to the a array will overwrite the base address of the array. The best way to avoid this

Example 12.39 Initial Parallelization Warnings

```
% cc -O -xautopar -xloopinfo ex12.38.c
"ex12.38.c", line 13: not parallelized, unsafe dependence (a)
"ex12.38.c", line 18: not parallelized, unsafe dependence (t)
```

issue is to label the a pointer to be restricted. An alternative way to achieve the same result is to specify that pointers to different basic types do not alias, using the -xalias_level=basic compiler flag (you can find more details on this compiler flag in Section 5.9.4 of Chapter 5). The disadvantage of using the flag is that it will apply to the whole file, and in some instances it is not appropriate.

For the second loop at line 18, the t variable is used in a summation reduction. The compiler does not parallelize the loop because this may change the order in which the summation is calculated and could produce a different result. The compiler requires the -xreduction flag to be specified on the compile line for it to generate code that parallelizes reductions. Example 12.40 shows the results of making these two changes (declaring the a variable to be a restrict qualified pointer, and using the -xreduction compiler flag).

Example 12.40 Auto-Parallelization Performed on Both Loops

```
% cc -O -xautopar -xloopinfo -xreduction ex12.40.c
"ex12.40.c", line 13: PARALLELIZED
"ex12.40.c", line 18: PARALLELIZED, reduction
```

As with OpenMP, you can control the number of threads the program uses using the OMP_NUM_THREADS environment variable. Example 12.41 shows the results of running this auto-parallelized code. The program performs the same calculation, but the work is spread over multiple threads, achieving nearly linear speedup.

Example 12.41 Performance of Auto-Parallelized Code

```
% setenv OMP_NUM_THREADS 1 ; a.out
Time per iteration  8.60 ns
t=54975576145920.000000
% setenv OMP_NUM_THREADS 2 ; a.out
Time per iteration  4.53 ns
t=54975576145920.000000
% setenv OMP_NUM_THREADS 4 ; a.out
Time per iteration  2.56 ns
t=54975576145920.000000
```

12.13 Profiling Multithreaded Applications

You can profile multithreaded applications using the Performance Analyzer in the same way as single-threaded codes, as discussed in Section 8.3 of Chapter 8. Example 12.7 shows the profile of the program demonstrating mutex locking from Example 12.19.

The columns show the time spent in user code, as previously, but this being multi-threaded code two threads are contributing user time. The wall time reflects where the master thread spent time, however the master thread was idle waiting for the worker threads to complete their tasks. Hence, the master thread gathers time in the _lwp_wait routine (not shown in Figure 12.7) where it is waiting for the worker threads to complete. The LWP time reflects the total amount of time spent by the threads regardless of whether they were working or sleeping in a wait state.

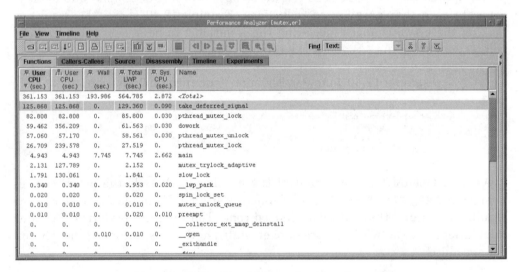

Figure 12.7 Profile of Mutex Locking Example

As you might expect, the majority of the time is spent in code related to the handling of mutex locks. Because the mutexes are locked and unlocked in critical sections, the handling of interrupts is disabled. Hence, the time is accumulated on the take_deferred_signal routine, that is responsible for servicing all the signals that accumulate during a critical region. Calls to malloc and free would also cause time to accumulate on this routine. Figure 12.8 shows the call stack for take_deferred_signal. This call stack shows that almost the entire time attributed to the routine comes from mutex_trylock_adaptive, which is part of the mutex lock code.

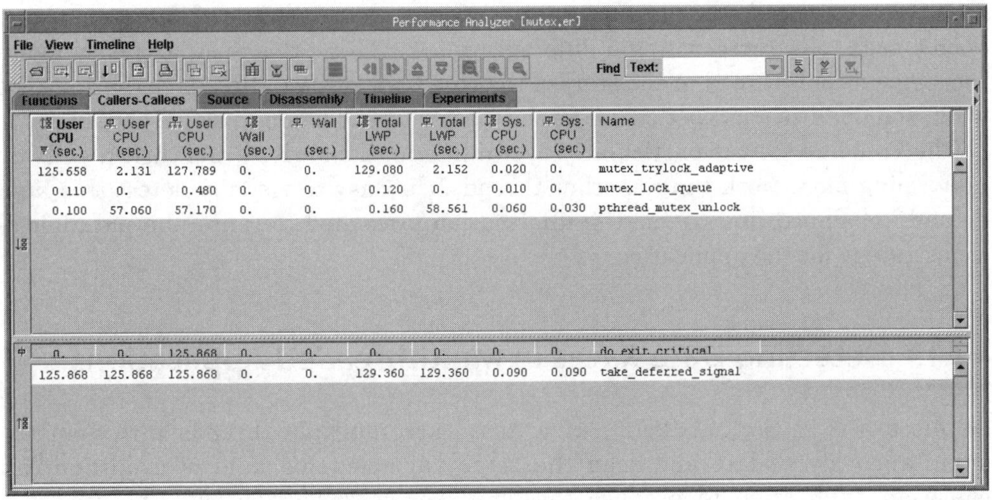

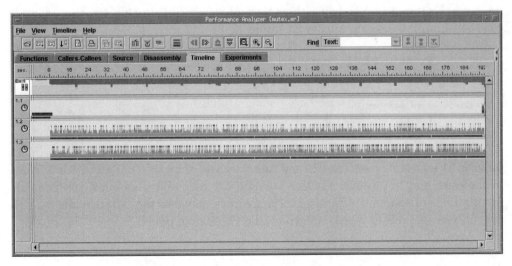

Figure 12.8 Call Stack for `take_deferred_signal`

The Timeline is the other view that can be useful for multithreaded applications. Figure 12.9 shows this view for the mutex application.

Figure 12.9 Timeline for the Mutex Example

In the Timeline view, time runs from left to right. The top line is the user/system/wait state over the course of the run, and each thread is shown as a horizontal line. For each thread, the call stack is shown for every sample as a stack of different colored points (each color representing a different routine). Using this view, it is easy to see the single master thread at the start of the run, then the two threads performing the work, and finally a short period where the master thread becomes active once more.

The Timeline view is particularly useful in situations where one thread ends up performing more work than another thread. It is easy to visually detect this kind of load imbalance, and to use the information presented to refine the parallelization strategy for the application.

12.14 Detecting Data Races in Multithreaded Applications

As discussed in Section 12.7.3, in a data race multiple threads are trying to simultaneously update and read the same variable; this kind of condition can cause an application to produce the wrong answer. The Thread Analyzer was introduced in Sun Studio 12 to detect and report race conditions. The tool will work on any multithreaded applications compiled with the -xinstrument=datarace compiler flag. The programming models supported are Pthreads, Solaris threads, and OpenMP. It is best to compile with debug information and without optimization, as this gives the most accurate mapping of any data races to lines of source. The program should then be run under the collect tool with the -r on flags. Example 12.42 shows the steps necessary to do this for the example code containing a data race from Example 12.14.

Example 12.42 Compiling and Running to Detect Data Races

```
% cc -g -xinstrument=datarace -o nomutex ex12.14.c -mt -lpthread
% collect -r on nomutex 2
```

You can be display the output from the tool by loading the resulting experiment into the Thread Analyzer. The Thread Analyzer will show a list of all the data races in the code, and the user can select a particular race and then show the two conflicting lines of source. In Figure 12.10, the race between the two threads modifying the sum variable is clearly shown on the two source panels.

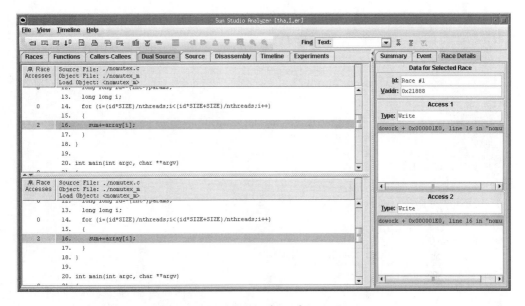

Figure 12.10 Display of Data Races

12.15 Debugging Multithreaded Code

To obtain the best quality of debug information you should compile an application without optimization and the -g compiler flag. However, the flag to enable OpenMP directive recognition (-xopenmp) will force the compiler to use an optimization level of -xO3 (although this behavior will change in a future compiler). To use OpenMP directives with no optimization it is necessary to use the -xopenmp=noopt flag.

Once an application is built, it can be debugged in the same way as serial applications. However, there are some additional commands that specifically deal with threads. Example 12.43 shows code parallelised using OpenMP. This code will be used to demonstrate how the debugger handles multiple threads.

Example 12.43 Code Parallelized Using OpenMP

```c
#include <stdio.h>
#include <stdlib.h>
#include <omp.h>
#include <sys/time.h>
#include "timing.h"

int * array;
int * results;
int array_length;
int round_off;
long threads=1;
#define SIZE 128*1024*1024

void main(int argc,const char** argv)
{
  int i,rtn,id;

  array=(int*)malloc(sizeof(int)*SIZE);
  int sum=0;

  if (argc==2) {threads=atoi(argv[1]);}
#ifdef _OPENMP
omp_set_num_threads(threads);
#endif

  starttime();
#pragma omp parallel sections private(i)
  {
#pragma omp section
  for (i=0; i<SIZE/2;i++) {array[i]=1;}
#pragma omp section
  for (i=SIZE/2; i<SIZE;i++) {array[i]=0;}
  }
  endtime(SIZE);

  starttime();
#pragma omp parallel for reduction (+:sum)
  for (i=0; i<SIZE; i++)
  {
    sum+=array[i];
  }
  endtime(SIZE);
  printf("Total is %i\n",sum);
}
```

Example 12.44 shows how to compile the OpenMP program in Example 12.43 for debugging.

Example 12.44 Compiling an OpenMP Program for Debugging

```
$ cc -g -xopenmp=noopt -o debug ex12.44.c
```

Example 12.45 shows how to set up the program to run under dbx with two threads.

Example 12.45 Setting Up to Run under dbx with Two Threads

```
% dbx debug
Reading debug
Reading ld.so.1
Reading libmtsk.so.1
Reading libthread.so.1
Reading libc.so.1
Reading libdl.so.1
Reading libpthread.so.1
Reading libm.so.1
Reading libc_psr.so.1
(dbx) runargs 2
```

Example 12.46 shows how to add a breakpoint in the second parallel region.

Example 12.46 Setting a Breakpoint in the Second Parallel Region

```
(dbx) list 40,45
   40     #pragma omp parallel for reduction (+:sum)
   41     for (i=0; i<SIZE; i++)
   42     {
   43        sum+=array[i];
   44     }
   45     endtime(SIZE);
(dbx) stop at 43
(2) stop at "ex12.44.c":43
```

The program stops when the first thread hits a breakpoint, as shown in Example 12.47. The `threads` command shows the status of all the threads in the application. In this case, the t@1 thread has reached the breakpoint, and the t@2 thread is in mutex lock code. Once the thread is at the breakpoint, it is possible to print out the variables that are visible at that point.

Example 12.47 One Thread Reaching the Breakpoint

```
(dbx) run
Running: debug 2
...
t@1 (l@1) stopped in _$d1B40.main at line 43 in file "ex12.44.c"
   43        sum+=array[i];
(dbx) threads
*>   t@1  a  l@1   ?()   breakpoint in _$d1B40.main()
     t@2  b  l@2   slave_startup_function() running in __lwp_mutex_lock()
(dbx) print i
i = 0
```

You can use the cont command to specify that just one of the threads should continue to run. In this way, the second thread can also reach the breakpoint, as shown in Example 12.48. The second thread is completing the second half of the calculation, so the value for the i variable starts halfway through its range.

Example 12.48 Allowing the Second Thread to Reach the Breakpoint

```
(dbx) cont t@2
t@2 (1@2) stopped in _$d1B40.main at line 43 in file "ex12.44.c"
   43        sum+=array[i];
(dbx) print i
i = 67108864
```

The sum variable is a reduction variable. Consequently, each thread will see a different value. You can see this in Example 12.49, after the program has completed a few iterations of the loop. The thread command allows the selection of the thread to be examined.

Example 12.49 Printing Thread Local Variable Values

```
(dbx) thread t@1
t@1 (1@1) stopped in _$d1B40.main at line 43 in file "ex12.44.c"
   43        sum+=array[i];
(dbx) print sum
sum = 14
(dbx) thread t@2
t@2 (1@2) stopped in _$d1B40.main at line 43 in file "ex12.44.c"
   43        sum+=array[i];
(dbx) print sum
sum = 0
```

The where command can take the thread ID as a parameter and show the current call stack for that particular thread, as shown in Example 12.50.

Example 12.50 Using the where Command to Show the Call Stack for a
Particular Thread

```
(dbx) where t@2
current thread: t@2
=>[1] _$d1B40.main(), line 43 in "ex12.44.c"
  [2] run_job_invoke_mfunc_once(0x0, 0x0, 0xffbff780, 0x1, 0x1, 0x1), at 0xff36954c
  [3] run_my_job(0xfef13300, 0xffbff884, 0xffbff780, 0x2, 0x1, 0x2), at 0xff36987c
  [4] slave_startup_function(0xfef13350, 0xff397680, 0xff39edd8, 0x3, 0xffffffff, 0x0),
at 0xff375048
```

12.16 Parallelizing a Serial Application

12.16.1 Example Application

This section examines the process of improving the performance of and parallelizing a serial application. The example application calculates whether points are inside or outside the Mandlebrot set. Example 12.51 shows the iterative computation to determine whether a point is inside or outside of the set. The return value of the calculation is either the number of iterations that were required to prove that the point was outside the set, or 1000 if the point was still within the set at that iteration limit.

Example 12.51 Determining Whether a Point Is Inside or Outside the Mandelbrot Set

```
int inset(double ix, double iy)
{
    int iterations=0;
    double x=ix, y=iy, x2=x*x, y2=y*y;
    while ((x2+y2<4) && (iterations<1000))
    {
        y = 2 * x * y + iy;
        x = x2 - y2 + ix;
        x2 = x * x;
        y2 = y * y;
        iterations++;
    }
    return iterations;
}
```

The example code is going to set up a large matrix and then record for each cell the value returned by the inset() function. Example 12.52 shows the code to do this.

Example 12.52 Iterating over the Matrix of Points

```
void calculate()
{
    int x,y;
    double xv,yv;
    for (x=0; x<SIZE; x++)
    {
        for (y=0; y<SIZE; y++)
        {
            xv = ((double)(x-SIZE/2))/(double)(SIZE/4);
            yv = ((double)(y-SIZE/2))/(double)(SIZE/4);
            data[x][y]=inset(xv,yv);
        }
    }
}
```

The code uses a couple of other routines. These routines set up the matrix and validate it, together with the required `main()` function, as shown in Example 12.53.

Example 12.53 Other Necessary Routines

```
#include <stdio.h>
#include <stdlib.h>

#define SIZE 2000
int ** data;

int ** setup()
{
   int i;
   int **data;
   data=(int**)malloc(sizeof(int*)*SIZE);
   for (i=0; i<SIZE; i++)
   {
     data[i]=(int*)malloc(sizeof(int)*SIZE);
   }
   return data;
}
...
void validate()
{
   int x,y;
   for (x=0; x<SIZE; x++)
     for (y=0; y<SIZE; y++)
       {if (data[x][y]<0) {printf("Error");} }
}

void main()
{
   data = setup();
   calculate();
   validate();
}
```

12.16.2 Impact of Optimization on Serial Performance

The first experiment is to examine the impact of optimization on the performance of the code. Table 12.1 shows the results of running this code on a V880, an eight-way UltraSPARC-III-based system.

Table 12.1 Effect of Optimization on Runtime

Optimization Flags	Runtime (Seconds)
None	18.5
-g	33.1
-O / -g -O	12.3
-fast / -g -fast	11.8

When compiled with full debug information and no optimization, the performance of the application drops significantly. When compiled with optimization, adding debug information has no performance impact. Interestingly, there is only a small difference between -O and -fast.

12.16.3 Profiling the Serial Application

The profile is gathered from the application compiled with -fast because this flag produced the fastest runtime. As you may have predicted, most of the time is attributed to the inset routine, whose profile is shown in Example 12.54.

Example 12.54 Profile of the Hot Part of the Application

```
     Excl.
     User CPU
       sec.
                        20. int inset(double ix, double iy)
     0.                 21. {
                              <Function: inset>
     0.                 22.    int iterations=0;
     0.                 23.    double x=ix, y=iy, x2=x*x, y2=y*y;

  ## 7.075              24.    while ((x2+y2<4) && (iterations<1000))
                        25.    {
     1.901              26.       y = 2 * x * y + iy;
     0.400              27.       x = x2 - y2 + ix;
     0.270              28.       x2 = x * x;
     1.231              29.       y2 = y * y;
     0.490              30.       iterations++;
                        31.    }
     0.                 32.    return iterations;
                        33. }
```

The disassembly for this routine is also revealing, as shown in Example 12.55. It shows many dependent floating-point operations. Because of the dependency, the processor will stall waiting for the previous calculation to complete. Some of these dependencies are shown in the code.

Example 12.55 Disassembly for the Hot Loop

```
     0.        [27]   10a48:   fsubd    %f28, %f24, %f0
     0.861     [26]   10a4c:   faddd    %f10, %f6, %f4
     0.360     [27]   10a50:   faddd    %f0, %f8, %f20
     1.351     [26]   10a54:   faddd    %f4, %f6, %f22
     0.440     [28]   10a58:   fmuld    %f20, %f20, %f28
     1.141     [29]   10a5c:   fmuld    %f22, %f22, %f24
     1.691     [24]   10a60:   faddd    %f28, %f24, %f26
     1.731     [24]   10a64:   fcmped   %fcc1, %f26, %f12
  ## 3.302     [24]   10a68:   fbuge,pn %fcc1, 0x10a7c
     0.        [30]   10a6c:   inc      %o1
     0.420     [24]   10a70:   cmp      %o1, 1000
     0.        [24]   10a74:   bl,a,pt  %icc, 0x10a48
     0.        [26]   10a78:   fmuld    %f20, %f22, %f6
```

12.16.4 Unrolling the Critical Loop

Given that there are a number of floating-point use stalls, it makes sense to try to schedule other operations in the gaps where the processor would otherwise be waiting for results. There are a couple of ways to do this. One way is to calculate multiple points at once. Another way is to unroll the loop for the single point. Example 12.56 shows the unrolled code.

Example 12.56 Unrolled Version of `inset()` Routine

```
int inset2(double ix, double iy)
{
   int iterations=0;
   double x=ix, y=iy, x2=x*x, y2=y*y;
   double x3=0,y3=0;
   while ((x3+y3<4) && (x2+y2<4) && (iterations<1000))
   {
      y = 2 * x * y + iy;
      x = x2 - y2 + ix;
      x2 = x * x; x3 = x2;
      y2 = y * y; y3 = y2;
      iterations++;
      y = 2 * x * y + iy;
      x= x2 - y2 + ix;
      x2 = x * x;
      y2 = y * y;
      iterations++;
   }
   if (x3 + y3 >=4) {iterations--;}
   return iterations;
}
```

The manually unrolled code ends up looking rather complex. Two steps are calculated each iteration. The loop will terminate if either of the two steps produced a result that was outside the Mandlebrot set. Also, to return the same number of iterations as the "nonunrolled" loop the iteration count needs to be reduced by one if it was the first computation that exceeded the set. This optimization is not currently performed by the compiler because it introduces an additional loop boundary condition.

With every optimization of this complexity it is a good practice to check that the new routine returns the same values as the old routine. Example 12.57 shows the test harness for this.

Compiling the test harness with `-fast` and running it produces the rather unexpected result that many of the iterations do not match. The `-fast` flag contains the `-fsimple=2` optimization flag, which enables floating-point simplication. Disabling this optimization using `-fsimple=0` causes the results from the two methods to agree.

Example 12.57 Test Harness Comparing the Original and Unroll Versions

```
void calculate()
{
    int x,y;
    double xv,yv;
    for (x=0; x<SIZE; x++)
    {
        for (y=0; y<SIZE; y++)
        {
            xv = ((double)(x-SIZE/2))/(double)(SIZE/4);
            yv = ((double)(y-SIZE/2))/(double)(SIZE/4);
            if (inset(xv,yv)!=inset2(xv,yv))
            {
                printf("(%i %i %i %i) ",x,y,inset(xv,yv),inset2(xv,yv));
            }
        }
    }
}
```

The compiler performs a number of optimizations when the -fsimple=2 flag is specified. For example, the compiler optimizes the calculate routine by hoisting the two divide operations out of the loop and replacing them with an add operation. This is a strength reduction optimization. Example 12.58 shows equivalent code after the optimization has been performed.

Example 12.58 Strength Reduction Optimization Performed on the calculate Routine

```
void calculate()
{
    int x,y;
    double xv,yv;
    double increment;
    increment = 1/(double)(SIZE/4);
    xv = -2.0;
    for (x=0; x<SIZE; x++)
    {
        yv = -2.0;
        for (y=0; y<SIZE; y++)
        {
            if (inset(xv,yv)!=inset2(xv,yv))
            {
                printf("(%i %i %i %i) ",x,y,inset(xv,yv),inset2(xv,yv));
            }
            yv+=increment;
        }
        xv+=increment;
    }
}
```

Within the inset and inset2 routines, the compiler is free to replace the code as written with code sequences that it considers equivalent. One example of this is that the compiler is free to replace $2*x*y$ with $(x+x)*y$ or even $(x*y)+(x*y)$. There is an advantage in removing the constant 2, as the constant has to be loaded from memory, so the compiler is replacing a load operation with one additional floating-point operation.

The change to the code that actually causes the difference in output is that the compiler is free to replace $x2-y2+xi$ with $xi-y2+x2$. Both expressions are equivalent, but there is a difference in rounding depending on whether the addition or the subtraction is performed first. Because the algorithm to determine whether a point is in the Mandlebrot set is an iterative algorithm, a difference in rounding can lead to a difference in the number of iterations required to determine whether a point is in the set. (This is particularly the case for the Mandlebrot algorithm because it is this sensitivity to starting conditions that causes the Mandlebrot set in the first place.)

However, although the two versions of the algorithm do differ in reporting the iteration count for some points in the set, the difference, in this context, is not significant. Using the $-fsimple=0$ compiler flag will stop the compiler from performing the optimizations, and this removes the variance in the output.

In terms of performance, the code with the unrolled loop compiled without floating-point simplication runs in 9.39 seconds compared to the original 11.8 seconds—about a 20% gain in performance. The cost of this 20% gain in performance is that the original code has become slightly more convoluted. One way you might reduce this complexity is by accepting that the exact number of iterations is unimportant. Under that assumption, it is no longer necessary to track the results of the first of the two unrolls, and therefore, the $x3$ and $y3$ variables can be eliminated from the code; however, this does not materially impact performance.

12.16.5 Parallelizing Using Pthreads

Although a 20% performance gain from modifying the source code is a useful performance improvement, it is hard to resist the idea that the application might run many times faster if multiple processors are used.

The source code changes necessary to use Pthreads are quite significant. The validate, inset, and setup routines do not need to be changed; the bulk of the changes occur to the calculate and main routines.

The main routine needs to set up a group of worker threads, set the worker threads to calculate separate parts of the image, and then wait until all the threads complete their work before calling the validate routine. To allocate a section of work to each thread, each thread is given a unique ID, which is then used in the calculate routine to determine which part of the image to compute.

The `calculate` routine requires some small changes to compute the start point and end point of the range of data that the thread will evaluate.

The modified source code is shown in Example 12.59; in the example, the text in bold indicates parts of the code that specifically support threads.

Table 12.2 shows the runtime in seconds for different numbers of threads. The user time is reasonably constant over the variations in the numbers of threads. This is to be expected because the same amount of work is being completed, and that work will take the same number of CPU seconds. The elapsed time is the indicator of how well the work is scaling, and you can see from the table that performance doubles when eight threads are used. This level of performance gain is far from ideal; the ideal performance gain from using eight threads would be for the application to run eight times faster.

Table 12.2 Performance Using Different Numbers of Threads

Threads	User Time (Seconds)	Elapsed Time (Seconds)	Speedup
1	11.68	11.78	1.0
2	11.39	8.4	1.4
3	11.38	9.42	1.25
4	11.4	7.45	1.58
5	11.37	7.39	1.59
6	11.42	6.38	1.85
7	11.42	5.81	2.03
8	11.38	5.23	2.25

Example 12.59 Using Pthreads to Calculate the Mandlebrot Set

```
#include <stdio.h>
#include <stdlib.h>
#include <pthread.h>

#define SIZE 2000
int **  data;

int num_threads=2;
...
```

continues

Example 12.59   Using Pthreads to Calculate the Mandlebrot Set (*continued*)

```
void *calculate(void * arg)
{
    int x,y;
    double xv,yv;
    int id = *(int*)arg;
    int start = (int)(1.0*id/num_threads*SIZE);
    int end =   (int)(1.0*(id+1)/num_threads*SIZE);
    for (x=start; x<end; x++)
    {
        for (y=0; y<SIZE; y++)
        {
            xv = ((double)(x-SIZE/2))/(double)(SIZE/4);
            yv = ((double)(y-SIZE/2))/(double)(SIZE/4);
            data[x][y]=inset(xv,yv);
        }
    }
}

void main(int argc, char** argv)
{
    pthread_t threads[20];
    int id[20];
    if (argc==2) {num_threads=atoi(argv[1]);}
    data = setup();
    for (int i=0; i<num_threads; i++)
    {
        id[i]=i;
        pthread_create(&threads[i],0,calculate,(void*)&id[i]);
    }
    for (int i=0; i<num_threads; i++)
    {
        pthread_join(threads[i],0);
    }
    validate();
}
```

12.16.6 Parallelization Using OpenMP

In contrast to using Pthreads, parallelization using OpenMP is much simpler. All that is necessary is to pick the loop that is to be parallelized and to place the appropriate directive into the source code at that point.

It is best to parallelize such that each thread has the largest possible chunk of work before synchronization is necessary. In this case, the obvious place to put the directive is before the outermost loop in the calculate routine. Example 12.60 shows the resulting code.

The xv, yv, and y variables are used in the parallel region. The default for these variables would be to make them shared between threads, so all the threads use the same copy of the variable. However, this is not desirable for this code. For this code each thread needs its own copy of each of the three variables. You can achieve this by specifying in the OpenMP directive that the variables are private.

Example 12.60 Parallelization Using OpenMP

```
void calculate()
{
   int x,y;
   double xv,yv;
#pragma omp parallel for default(none) shared(data) private (y,xv,yv)
   for (x=0; x<SIZE; x++)
   {
     for (y=0; y<SIZE; y++)
     {
       xv = ((double)(x-SIZE/2))/(double)(SIZE/4);
       yv = ((double)(y-SIZE/2))/(double)(SIZE/4);
       data[x][y]=inset(xv,yv);
     }
   }
}
```

The code should be compiled with the -xopenmp compiler flag to enable the compiler to recognize the OpenMP directives. The -xvpara compiler flag will cause the compiler to emit warnings if there are any issues with the parallelization directives. If the directive had not specified the three variables as private, the compiler would warn of this potential error when the -xvpara flag is specified. The number of threads that the application uses to complete the parallel code is set by the OMP_NUM_THREADS environment variable. Example 12.61 shows the entire sequence for compiling and running the code.

Example 12.61 Compiling and Running the OpenMP Code

```
% cc -fast -xopenmp -xvpara ex12.60.c
% setenv OMP_NUM_THREADS 2
% timex a.out

real        8.40
user       11.41
sys         0.06
```

The performance of the OpenMP code is identical to that of the code parallelized using Pthreads. This is not surprising, because the OpenMP library is built on top of Pthreads.

12.16.7 Auto-Parallelization

Although using OpenMP significantly reduces the number of lines of source code it is necessary to add to achieve parallelization, it would be ideal if the compiler were able to do the parallelization automatically. In fact, this is possible for a range of codes. However, the compiler is able to do this only for situations where it can be sure that the parallelization is safe.

It is possible for the compiler to automatically parallelize this particular code. The flag to enable auto-parallelization is -xautopar. It is best to use this flag together with the -xloopinfo flag, which reports on which loops the compiler has been able to successfully parallelize. Example 12.62 shows the results of using this optimization on the original code.

Example 12.62 Auto-Parallelization of Original Mandlebrot Code

```
% cc -fast -xautopar -xloopinfo ex12.62.c
"m1.c", line 12: not parallelized, call may be unsafe
"m1.c", line 24: not parallelized, loop has multiple exits
"m1.c", line 24: not parallelized, loop has multiple exits (inlined loop)
"m1.c", line 38: not parallelized, unsafe dependence, interchanged
"m1.c", line 40: PARALLELIZED, interchanged
"m1.c", line 52: not parallelized, call may be unsafe
"m1.c", line 53: not parallelized, call may be unsafe
"m1.c", line 12: not parallelized, call may be unsafe (inlined loop)
"m1.c", line 24: not parallelized, loop has multiple exits (inlined loop)
"m1.c", line 38: not parallelized, unsafe dependence, interchanged (inlined loop)
"m1.c", line 40: PARALLELIZED, interchanged (inlined loop)
"m1.c", line 52: not parallelized, call may be unsafe (inlined loop)
"m1.c", line 53: not parallelized, call may be unsafe (inlined loop)
```

The compiler reports that line 40 has been parallelized twice. The first time is when the calculate routine is processed, and the second time is after the calculate routine has been inlined into the main routine. The compiler also reports that the loop has been interchanged. The interchange optimization is where the inner and outer loops are swapped over; the inner loop becoming the new outer loop.

Two flags are included in -fast that enable the compiler to perform the automatic parallelization of this code. The first necessary flag is an optimization level of at least -xO4. At -xO4, the compiler performs inlining of routines within the same file (cross-file inlining is enabled with the -xipo flag). It is necessary for the inset routine to be inlined into the calculate routine for the compiler to determine that the inset routine does not read or write data that would be shared across threads. It is possible to use the no_side_effect pragma (as I discussed in Section 5.12.4 of Chapter 5) to provide the compiler with the same information, and allow it to perform the auto-parallelization even without inlining the inset routine. Example 12.63 shows the use of this pragma.

The other necessary compiler flag that is included in -fast is -xalias_level=basic. As described in Section 5.9.7 of Chapter 5, this flag tells the compiler that pointers to different basic types do not alias; for example, pointers to integers do not point to the same location in memory as pointers to floats. This is critical for the compiler to parallelize the loop in the calculate routine. Without this flag, the compiler would have to assume that stores to data[x][y] may touch

Example 12.63 Use of the `no_side_effect` Pragma

```
int inset(double ix, double iy)
{
    int iterations=0;
    double x=ix, y=iy, x2=x*x, y2=y*y;
    while ((x2+y2<4) && (iterations<1000))
    {
        y = 2 * x * y + iy;
        x = x2 - y2 + ix;
        x2 = x * x;
        y2 = y * y;
        iterations++;
    }
    return iterations;
}
#pragma no_side_effect(inset)
```

memory that is pointed to by `data[x]`, and consequently that the loop is not safe to parallelize.

Table 12.3 shows the elapsed and user time for the auto-parallelized code. There are two surprising results from this. The first result is that the auto-parallelized code gets nearly a doubling of performance from using two threads compared to the case where just a single thread is used. The second surprising result is that the performance of three threads is nearly the same as the performance of a single thread (and all scaling beyond two threads is poor).

Table 12.3 Performance of Auto-Parallelized Code Using Different Numbers of Threads

Threads	User Time (Seconds)	Elapsed Time (Seconds)	Speedup
1	11.67	11.77	1.0
2	11.71	5.99	1.96
3	11.74	10.98	1.07
4	11.69	5.88	2
5	11.70	8.16	1.44
6	11.70	5.60	2.1
7	11.75	6.42	1.83
8	11.71	4.86	2.42

The problem that is causing poor scaling for more than two threads, and poor scaling for the codes parallelized using Pthreads and OpenMP, is load balancing. You can see this when examining the Timeline view of the performance of the code parallelized using Pthreads and run with two threads, as shown in Figure 12.11.

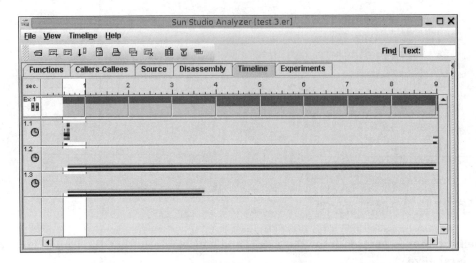

Figure 12.11 Timeline View of Thread Utilization for Pthread Code

The Timeline view shows the activity of the threads as horizontal lines; whenever a thread is active the line is in color, and when the thread is inactive the line is not shown. The figure shows the master thread as being active initially and at the end of the run. In between, the two worker threads are active. It is readily apparent that one of the two worker threads is active for a much shorter time than the other thread. This is an example of load imbalance, where the work is unevenly distributed between the two threads.

The reason for this load imbalance is obvious when you consider the shape of the Mandlebrot set. Figure 12.12 shows the output from this program rendered as an image.

Figure 12.12 Rendered Output from Mandlebrot Program

If two threads divide the work along the horizontal axis, both threads end up with identical computations to perform. However, if the work is divided vertically, the two threads end up with different amounts of computation to perform, and the runtime for the entire application is dependent on the time it takes for the longest-running thread to complete. For three threads, the thread that computes the middle of the set ends up performing the bulk of the calculations.

12.16.8 Load Balancing with OpenMP

For this calculation, it is not possible, in general, to statically schedule the work so that each thread has an equivalent amount of computation. The only way to load-balance between the threads is to allocate work dynamically. With dynamic allocation, the threads that complete their work faster end up performing more of the computations, and the threads that take longer end up performing fewer of the computations. It is not possible for auto-parallelization to choose dynamic scheduling. It is also hard to implement dynamic scheduling using Pthreads. However, OpenMP provides dynamic scheduling as an option when inserting the parallelization directive. Example 12.64 shows the modified OpenMP code for the `calculate` routine.

Example 12.64 Specifying Dynamic Scheduling in an OpenMP Directive

```
void calculate()
{
    int x,y;
    double xv,yv;
#pragma omp parallel for default(none) shared(data) \
                        private(y,xv,yv) schedule(dynamic)
    for (x=0; x<SIZE; x++)
    {
      for (y=0; y<SIZE; y++)
      {
        xv = ((double)(x-SIZE/2))/(double)(SIZE/4);
        yv = ((double)(y-SIZE/2))/(double)(SIZE/4);
        data[x][y]=inset(xv,yv);
      }
    }
}
```

The dynamic scheduling causes the work to be split into a number of small chunks and each thread requests a new chunk as it completes them. In this way, slower threads will complete fewer chunks of work, but the work should be relatively evenly distributed across all the threads. Table 12.4 shows the results of this change in the code. The elapsed time of the code shows roughly linear scaling as the number of threads increases.

Table 12.4 Performance of OpenMP Code with Dynamic Scheduling

Threads	User Time (Seconds)	Elpased Time (Seconds)	Speedup
1	11.70	11.79	1
2	11.42	5.83	2.02
3	11.40	3.96	2.98
4	11.43	3.02	3.9
5	11.41	2.46	4.79
6	11.40	2.08	5.67
7	11.41	1.81	6.51
8	11.40	1.62	7.28

12.16.9 Sharing Data between Threads

The Mandlebrot example used so far is an example of computation that is "embarrassingly parallel." Each thread performs its part of the calculation, and does not use the results of the computation from the other threads. Many times the threads in code need to share a single item of data, or cooperate to produce a single item of data. An artificial example of this would be to produce the sum of all the results from the `inset` routine rather than assigning them to a matrix.

The Pthread code shown in Example 12.59 can be modified to provide an example of multiple threads cooperating to produce a single value. Example 12.65 shows the modified code for the `calculate` routine. It is necessary for the code to use (or in this case, print) the calculated value `sum` for the compiler not to eliminate it. It is also necessary to declare the `sum` variable as being volatile because it is shared among multiple threads.

This code contains a data race for the `sum` variable. The two threads will attempt to update `sum` at the same time, and only one of the threads will be successful. You can detect this using the Thread Analyzer, as shown in Example 12.66.

The tool detects a single race condition at line 50, which is the write to the `sum` variable. There are multiple ways to resolve this condition.

A mutex lock could be added to protect the addition of the return value from the `inset` routine to the `sum` variable. An undesirable way to do this would be to wrap the existing statement with a mutex lock and unlock. This would have the unfortunate side effect of ensuring that only a single thread could enter the `inset` routine, causing the code to become effectively single-threaded. To only protect the addition, you can use a temporary value to hold the result of the call, and place the mutex lock around the addition. Example 12.67 shows the necessary modifications. The mutex is initialized and destroyed in the `main` routine, and the `calculate` routine updates

Example 12.65 Using Multiple Pthreads to Calculate a Single Value

```
volatile int sum=0;

void *calculate(void * arg)
{
   int x,y;
   double xv,yv;
   int id = *(int*)arg;
   int start = (int)(1.0*id/2*SIZE);
   int end =  (int)(1.0*(id+1)/2*SIZE);
   for (x=start; x<end; x++)
   {
     for (y=0; y<SIZE; y++)
     {
       xv = ((double)(x-SIZE/2))/(double)(SIZE/4);
       yv = ((double)(y-SIZE/2))/(double)(SIZE/4);
       sum+=inset(xv,yv);                          // line 50
     }
   }
}

void validate()
{
   int x,y;
   for (x=0; x<SIZE; x++)
     for (y=0; y<SIZE; y++)
       {if (data[x][y]<0) {printf("Error");} }
   printf("sum = %i\n",sum);
}
```

Example 12.66 Detecting Data Races Using the Thread Analyzer

```
$ cc -xinstrument=datarace -g ex12.65.c -mt -lpthread
$ collect -r on a.out
Creating experiment database tha.1.er ...
sum = 383659083
$ er_print -races tha.1.er

Total Races:  1 Experiment: tha.1.er

Race #1, Vaddr: 0x21ab8
     Access 1: Write, calculate + 0x000001DC,
                   line 50 in "ex12.65.c"
     Access 2: Write, calculate + 0x000001DC,
                   line 50 in "ex12.65.c"
  Total Traces: 1
```

the sum variable within a section of code enclosed by a mutex lock/unlock. This code change removes the data race condition.

Of course, the summation of the results of calling the inset routine could be held in the local variable tmp, and this variable could be added onto sum after the loop. The advantage of doing this would be in removing the calls to mutex lock/ unlock from the inner loop and placing them in a less-performance-sensitive region of code. You can achieve a similar effect using thread local variables.

Example 12.67 Avoiding a Data Race Using a Mutex

```
pthread_mutex_t mutex;
...
void *calculate(void * arg)
{
   int tmp;
...
       tmp=inset(xv,yv);
       pthread_mutex_lock(&mutex);
       sum+=tmp;
       pthread_mutex_unlock(&mutex);
...
}
...
void main()
{
...
   pthread_mutex_init(&mutex,NULL);
...
   pthread_mutex_destroy(&mutex);
}
```

A final alternative is to use atomic operations to update the value held by the sum variable. Such operations would have a lower cost than using mutexes, and would not require each thread to hold a copy of a temporary value.

12.16.10 Sharing Variables between Threads Using OpenMP

It is trivial to use OpenMP to reduce the return values from the inset function into the single value held in the sum variable. Example 12.68 shows the code for this. Each thread has a private copy of the sum variable, which it updates. These private values are combined to produce the result that is available after the parallel region.

It is also possible to use approaches in OpenMP equivalent to mutex locks and atomic operations. These depend on a single variable being shared among all the threads. Consequently, the variable needs to be declared as shared, and in some situations it may be necessary to declare the variable as volatile.

A more efficient alternative to declaring the variable as volatile is to use the flush directive, which ensures consistency of the variable between threads. A flush directive should be used before a shared variable is read to ensure that the value read is the value from memory and not a value held in a register. Similarly, a flush directive should be used after a shared variable is updated to ensure that the new value is written back to memory. The use of flush results in a finer grain of control over the locations in the code where the variable must be synchronized across threads. In comparison, the declaration of a variable as volatile will result in all reads of the variable having an implicit flush operation before the

Example 12.68 Using the `reduction` Directive

```
int sum = 0;
...
void calculate()
{
   int x,y;
   double xv,yv;
#pragma omp parallel for default(none) shared(data) private(y,xv,yv) \
      schedule (dynamic) reduction(+:sum)
   for (x=0; x<SIZE; x++)
   {
     for (y=0; y<SIZE; y++)
     {
       xv = ((double)(x-SIZE/2))/(double)(SIZE/4);
       yv = ((double)(y-SIZE/2))/(double)(SIZE/4);
       sum+=inset(xv,yv);
     }
   }
}
```

read, and all writes having an implicit flush after the write. Many OpenMP directives contain an implicit flush operation on all shared variables, so it is necessary to explicitly include the directive in only a small number of situations.

The strategies used for Pthreads are also possible using OpenMP. An OpenMP critical region is equivalent to acquiring and releasing a mutex lock—only a single thread can be in that region at any one time. Example 12.69 shows the source code modification for this. The `critical` directive has an implied flush operation on entry and exit, so there is no need to make the `sum` variable `volatile` or to add flush directives.

Example 12.69 Using a Critical Region to Avoid a Data Race Condition

```
int sum = 0;
...
void calculate()
{
   int x,y;
   double xv,yv;
#pragma omp parallel for private (y,xv,yv) \
      schedule (dynamic) shared(sum)
   for (x=0; x<SIZE; x++)
   {
     for (y=0; y<SIZE; y++)
     {
       xv = ((double)(x-SIZE/2))/(double)(SIZE/4);
       yv = ((double)(y-SIZE/2))/(double)(SIZE/4);
       #pragma omp critical
       {
         sum+=inset(xv,yv);
       }
     }
   }
}
```

The code containing a critical region would serialize performance, because only a single thread could be in the critical region at a time. The same optimization as used in the Pthread code could be used to improve this. A private temporary variable could be used to hold the return value from the `inset` routine, and the addition of this variable to `sum` would be the only code left in the critical region.

It is also possible to make the addition atomic using the `atomic` directive. Example 12.70 shows an example of this code. The `atomic` directive implies a flush directive on the shared variable. It also applies only to the addition operation, so it avoids serializing the code.

Example 12.70 Using an `atomic` Directive to Avoid a Data Race Condition

```
int sum = 0;
...
void calculate()
{
    int x,y;
    double xv,yv;
#pragma omp parallel for private (y,xv,yv) \
        schedule (dynamic) shared(sum)
    for (x=0; x<SIZE; x++)
    { for (y=0; y<SIZE; y++)
        {
            xv = ((double)(x-SIZE/2))/(double)(SIZE/4);
            yv = ((double)(y-SIZE/2))/(double)(SIZE/4);
            #pragma omp atomic
            sum+=inset(xv,yv);
        }
    }
}
```

PART V

Concluding Remarks

13

Performance Analysis

13.1 Introduction

This final chapter will discuss the process of performance analysis. By the end of the chapter, the reader will have insight into such topics as how best to apply optimization, and some guidelines regarding what to expect as the result of performing particular optimizations.

13.2 Algorithms and Complexity

Finalizing the optimal compiler options is something that might be completed late in the development process. However, by that point many of the important decisions that impact the performance of the application have already been made; and once the final code is delivered, it can be hard to improve performance just through minor changes of the code, or by selecting different compiler options. Hence, performance is something that needs to be considered as an early part of the design, or possibly redesign, of an application.

Three major factors can have an impact on a program's performance. One factor is coding rules. For example, this can define how pointers are to be used in the program; as discussed in Section 5.9 of Chapter 5, being able to provide better aliasing information to the compiler can lead to improved performance. The second factor to consider is the algorithmic complexity of the various parts of the application. The final factor is how the various data structures in an application are used.

As an example of how selecting data structures and algorithms can impact performance, consider a discrete event simulation package. In discrete event simulation, the program holds a list of events sorted in time order. The program steps through the list, removing the earliest event and adding new events into the list according to when they will occur.

There are a number of different data structures that can hold such a list. A simple approach is to use an array to hold the sorted list of events; then, every time a new event is added, it will be necessary to first locate the insertion point in the array, and then to add the new event at that point. The easiest way to locate the insertion point is to start at the beginning of the array and find the first event in the array that has a time greater than the time of the event to be inserted. Example 13.1 shows code for this kind of search.

If the times of the events are randomly distributed, it would not be unexpected to find that, on average, new events get inserted into the middle of the array. This would mean that the `for` loop would have to perform an average of $N/2$ comparisons for a list containing N events. As the list of events grows, the number of comparisons will grow linearly with the length of the list; hence, these are referred to as Order(N) comparisons, or just that the algorithm has complexity O(N).

Example 13.1 Inserting an Event into a Sorted Array Using Linear Search

```
typedef struct
{
  float time;
  int   type;
} event_t

#define SIZE 10*1024
event_t events[SIZE];
int total_events=0;

void insert_event(event_t event)
{
  if (total_events>=SIZE) {
    printf("Insufficient space to insert new event\n");
    exit(1);
  }
  int current_event=0;
  for (current_event=0;
       ( (current_event<total_events) &&
         (events[current_event].time<event.time) );
       current_event++);

  memmove(&events[current_event+1],
          &events[current_event],
          sizeof(event_t)*(SIZE-current_event));
  events[current_event].time=event.time;
  events[current_event].type=event.type;
  total_events++;
}
```

Most programmers will immediately recognize that there are faster ways to search a sorted array; a significant improvement is to use a binary search, as shown in Example 13.2.

The binary search algorithm works by partitioning the array into two halves at each comparison. This means that there will be $\log_2(N)$ comparisons for an array containing N events, or a complexity of $O(\log(N))$.

Example 13.2 Inserting an Event into a Sorted List of Events Using Binary Search

```
typedef struct
{
  float time;
  int   type;
} event_t;

#define SIZE 10*1024
event_t events[SIZE];
int total_events=0;

void insert_event(event_t event)
{
  if (total_events>=SIZE) {
    printf("Insufficient space to insert new event\n");
    exit(1);
  }
  int min_event=0;
  int max_event=total_events;
  int current_event=0;
  while (max_event-min_event>1)
  {
    current_event = (max_event-min_event)>>1 + min_event;
    if (event.time>events[current_event].time)
      {min_event=current_event;}
    else
      {max_event=current_event;}
  }
  memmove(&events[current_event+1],
          &events[current_event],
          sizeof(event_t)*(SIZE-current_event));
  events[current_event].time=event.time;
  events[current_event].type=event.type;
  total_events++;
}
```

From the notation, it is hard to gather some idea of the costs of the two strategies. Table 13.1 shows numerical values for the complexities of these two approaches.

By comparing the two approaches, it is apparent that if the array is going to hold more than about ten events, it will be more efficient to use a binary search rather than a linear search to determine the location in the array where the event should be inserted.

Table 13.1 Comparison of O(N) Complexity with O(log(N)) Complexity

Length of Array	Comparisons for O(N)	Comparisons for O(log(N))
10	5	3
100	50	6
1,000	500	10
10,000	5,000	13

However, the code to insert the new event is only half of the routine. The second part of the routine requires that the elements be shifted by one element every time a new event is added. Consider the average insertion point to be the midpoint. Then, for an array containing 1,000 events, each new event will require a memmove operation of 500*8 bytes = 2KB. memmove is an O(N) operation, so it will take a significant amount of time in the routine.

The total time taken in the routine is the sum of the time taken to search the array and the time taken to insert the new element. Assume that initially, with the linear search code, the time taken for the two parts was equal for an array with 1,000 elements. So, half the time was taken by the linear search algorithm. Moving to binary search reduced the number of comparisons fiftyfold; so, the time taken by the search part of the algorithm is now about one-fiftieth of what it was. However, the time taken in the insertion code is unchanged. Consequently, the performance of the function has only doubled.

This is an example of Amdahl's Law, where the total speedup is limited by the amount of time spent in the part of the code that is improved. In this example, only half the time is spent in the code that is being improved, so the maximum performance gain from optimizing this code would be to make the whole function run twice as fast.

By looking at the performance of the routine used in the example, it is apparent that the bottleneck to be improved is the amount of memory that has to be moved around. The most obvious way to change this is to use pointers to events rather than an array. Adding an event would then just be a case of changing a few pointers rather than moving large amounts of memory.

If the code was implemented as a doubly linked list, adding a new event would require changing four pointers, which would have almost zero cost. However, searching for the point at which to insert the event would take a linear search from the start of the linked list, which, as discussed earlier, is an O(N) activity.

Fortunately, many more efficient data structures are available to solve this problem. If the program is written with good encapsulation, replacing the original implementation with a new, more efficient algorithm should be as simple as using a different file in the build. Of course, using this kind of encapsulation might mean that performance gains are available from performing crossfile optimization (see Section 5.7.2 of Chapter 5).

One further consideration in this domain is how the choice of algorithm can be influenced by the characteristics of the system. In the example, the best performance, purely from an algorithmic viewpoint, is likely to be some form of linked list. However, linked lists require pointer chasing, and depending on the cache configuration of the system, the size of the linked list, and the frequency over which it is iterated, the act of iterating over the list may cause data to be fetched from memory, so performance will be determined by memory latency. In comparison, when searching through an array, it is possible to prefetch array elements in advance, so the performance of the code is determined by the available bandwidth of the system.

Consequently, for a particular number of elements, depending on system characteristics it may be more efficient to use arrays than linked lists. As a consequence, you should avoid prematurely optimizing an application to suit a particular platform, and you should ensure that a particular source code optimization is neither a quirk of the workload or the platform, nor due to a poor choice of compiler flags.

As an example of premature optimization, consider the situation where a short array of structure elements is to be zeroed out in memory, as shown in Example 13.3.

Example 13.3 Zeroing Out an Array of Structure Elements

```
for (int i=0; i<5 ; i++)
{
  a[i].var1=0;
  a[i].var2=0;
}
```

The developer times this bit of code and discovers that for his system, the test code runs faster if the loop is entirely unrolled. Hence, the unrolled version of the code appears in the application.

At a later stage, the developer uses a different set of compiler flags that includes enabling prefetch. If the original code had been left, the compiler would have inserted prefetch statements leading to an improvement in performance. However, because the loop has been removed, the compiler does not insert prefetch statements, so the code runs slower than optimal.

Many times a developer will do some code optimization to improve performance, but the optimization makes the code harder to read and unable to exploit future optimizations. Generally speaking, you should avoid manually performing optimizations that the compiler should be able to perform. On the other hand, optimizations that improve the algorithm or reduce memory traffic are often sufficiently general that they work for most platforms, under most compiler optimization levels.

13.3 Tuning Serial Code

The most important action for improving the performance of an application is to profile the code. The profile will quickly indicate where the hot points are in the code, and once the hot points have been identified, it is often relatively easy to improve their performance.

However, the process of tuning an application starts earlier than this. The first steps are to be able to build the application and to locate a workload and choose an appropriate metric that will provide information about the behavior of the application before the tuning started.

Once baseline performance has been established and a profile of the application has been obtained, it is necessary to consider the next steps. The first questions you should ask are as follows.

- Is the application spending time in the appropriate parts of the code? For example, if an application that searches a database for a particular string spends all of its time loading the database from disk before it starts the search, the application is not spending time in the appropriate parts of the code. Problems such as this can indicate that the architecture of the application is incorrect (perhaps multiple queries need to be performed at the same time, or maybe the application needs to be run as a daemon).

- Are there any hot points in the code? A hot point is a routine, or a few lines of code, where considerable time is being spent. Again, the issue here could be structural (perhaps the data could be laid out better in memory), or possibly due to something that is fixable by the compiler (perhaps there is an aliasing issue that stops the compiler from performing an optimization).

- Is the profile of the application flat, without any hot spots? It is often hardest to improve the performance of applications where time is evenly distributed over many routines. If this is the case, it is worth considering whether inlining routines would improve performance (inlining has the advantage that it will produce routines which have more time attributed to them), or perhaps there is something structural in the code that can be changed to reduce the cost of the commonly executed routines at the expense of increasing the complexity of the rarely executed routines. Profile feedback is another optimization technique that might be considered in this situation.

When a hot region of code has been identified it is useful to estimate the value of improving the performance of that routine. This comes down to Amdahl's Law. For example, if it was possible to double the performance of that particular routine, how much extra performance would be gained for the whole application? You need to weigh the extra performance against the cost of changing the source code and the implicit cost of adding complexity to the code base (changing the source code to improve performance can sometimes cause the source code or algorithms to be harder to follow or maintain).

Once you have determined that a particular part of the code is worth performance tuning, you should consider the following questions.

- Can any algorithmic changes be applied here to improve performance? Although algorithmic changes may involve significant changes to the source code, they typically give the largest performance gains. The compiler will usually implement what is written in the source code. It will not often remove an algorithm that the developer has implemented and replace it with a more optimal one.

- Will any minor source code changes enable the compiler to do a better job? Qualifying pointers with the `restrict` keyword will often enable the compiler to perform more optimization. Moving some small and hot routines into header files will enable the compiler to inline them where they are called, avoiding the need to use crossfile optimization to achieve the same result. Perhaps it is possible to manually insert prefetch statements to reduce the time spent on cache misses.

- Will source code changes clarify the algorithm for the compiler? For example, using a local variable to hold a copy of the value of a global variable will allow the compiler to perform some optimizations that may otherwise be inhibited by aliasing issues.

- Can any optimization flags be used? For example, it may be that compiling at `-xO4` causes some routines to be inlined, leading to better performance. Similarly, adding profile feedback might enable the compiler to make better decisions for the scheduling of the code. Adding `-xipo` will allow the compiler to do crossfile inlining.

- Can any assertion flags be used? It may be possible to safely use the `-xrestrict` flag because the assertion it makes is known to be true for the entire application.

- Are all the instructions on the hot code path necessary? In some cases, it may be possible to reduce the instruction count (and increase performance) by replacing code that takes a number of instructions with precomputed, or easy-to-compute values, making the common case for the program take fewer instructions.

Generally, you need to examine hot points in the code carefully to determine whether the compiler is doing exactly what you intended. Sometimes, the compiler is not performing some optimization that you expected, perhaps because the code contains aliasing issues or the compiler is just unable to perform an optimization of the required complexity. It is normally the best course of action to make minor changes to the source or the compiler flags so that the compiler can perform the optimization that you expected.

Once you have decided on and tried a strategy, it is important to rerun the test workload and determine whether the change gave a gain in performance (or not), and to decide whether sufficient time is still being spent at the hot spot to support further work.

13.4 Exploring Parallelism

If one large performance gain can come from changing the algorithms used in serial programs, the other potential gain comes from using multiple processors to share the work. In an ideal case, using two processors would double application performance. However, things are rarely ideal, and once again Amdahl's Law helps to estimate the performance gains that could be attained through parallelizing an application. The performance gain from parallelizing an application depends on how much of the application can be parallelized, and how much remains serial code.

There is an additional complexity in parallelizing an application, because parallelization does incur some overhead every time the threads need to synchronize (or share data). At some point, the overhead of communication across $N+1$ processors outweighs the benefit of sharing the work with the additional processor.

As in the serial case, it is necessary to identify where the time is being spent. However, having identified this, the next question to answer is "What is the largest unit of work that can be performed in parallel?"

- Some applications handle multiple tasks or queries, so it makes sense to parallelize the application at the level of the individual task—each task is assigned to a different thread. This kind of application is often a good fit for using `pthreads`, or perhaps multiple processes to achieve parallelization.

- Other applications do not have obvious tasks, but iterate over the same loop or blocks of code. These applications can often be parallelized using OpenMP (or auto-parallelization) to share the iterations of the loops across multiple threads.

- Another class of parallelization occurs where roles are assigned to different threads or processes. For example, one thread may be responsible for maintaining a queue of calculations to perform, another thread may be responsible for gathering the input required for these calculations before placing them on the queue, and a third thread may be responsible for taking the results of the calculations and rendering them into a comprehensive format.

Searching out the largest chunk of work that can be parallelized will (usually) also indicate the work that can be performed in parallel with a minimum amount of communication between threads. It is often the communication that causes an application to fail to scale well beyond a certain number of processors.

To use multiple threads (or processes), some data will be shared among threads. This data will normally need to be protected so that multiple threads do not attempt to update and read it at the same time. The usual way to do this is through mutexes or similar constructs. It is critical for correctness that all the shared variables are identified and appropriately protected.

Once an application has been parallelized, you should compare its performance to the original serial code. Sometimes, if the parallelization has been only partially implemented, the performance may be lower than that of the serial code. If this is the case, you should carefully decide whether to proceed, bearing in mind that the additional parallel code will have to compensate for the time already lost.

Once parallel code is developed that does improve performance, the next step is to examine the scaling of that code as the number of processors or threads is increased. As the work is shared among more threads, the profile will change, and the places where work has been successfully spread over multiple threads should consume a constant amount of CPU time (but that time will be spread over many threads and will represent diminishing amounts of elapsed time). At some point, the CPU time for the parallel regions will start to increase, as the overhead of parallelizing the code outweighs the benefits obtained from the additional threads. At this point, it is important to determine where the additional time is coming from; whether it is purely that there is insufficient work for each thread, or whether there is some kind of synchronization constraint (e.g., mutexes).

If you can track down the scaling problem to a hot mutex, consider whether the data protected by the mutex could be better shared among threads. Perhaps it is possible to break the mutex, into multiple mutexes each one protecting different data. Alternatively, there may be a way to assign a copy of the data to each thread and to synchronize the data after all the threads have completed a section of work.

For multithreaded programs, the ideal limiting factor for performance is when all the available processors are continuously busy doing useful work. So, one final consideration is to check whether threads are idle for an excessive amount of time (which might indicate load imbalance), or if the threads are spending significant time in the operating system (which may indicate that the application is stalled on disk, or other resource limitations). Assuming that all the threads are doing useful work, further optimization depends on reducing the time each thread spends doing work, which is the same situation as for the serial code.

13.5 Optimizing for CMT Processors

There is a subtle difference between optimizing for chip multithreading (CMT) processors and optimizing for single-threaded processors. For a processor that executes only a single thread, it is only possible to optimize for latency, so it becomes important to obtain performance by prefetching data or changing data layout to improve cache hits. It is also possible to improve performance by reducing the instruction count, but this is not often a key concern because the single-threaded processors are typically super-scalar, and as such, they can dispatch many instructions in a single cycle.

In contrast, a CMT processor is less sensitive to stalls induced by cache misses. The latency of the code will still be impacted by these cache misses, but the cache misses give other threads the opportunity to use the core, so the throughput of the system will remain high even with cache misses.

A CMT processor will still benefit from optimizations that improve cache hit rates or reduce memory stalls, but the improvements from these are more limited. Once the processor is executing its full capacity of instructions every cycle, reductions in memory stall time do not improve performance. Once the CMT processor is approaching full utilization, the only opportunity for performance gains is to reduce the instruction count.

The difference in approach when targetting a CMT processor is that it is much more important to use multiple threads, which will enable more instructions to be issued per cycle, as one of the first steps to take when improving performance. Once the application is using multiple threads, it is necessary to check how much of the peak instruction issue rate is being used. If few instructions are being issued, it may be necessary to work on eliminating the traditional performance inhibitors (such as cache misses). On the other hand, if the utilization of the processor is high—in which many instructions are being issued every cycle—it is necessary to look for optimizations that reduce the instruction count.

Index

Numbers

32-bit applications, file handling in, 364–367
32-bit architecture, specifying in compiler, 103
32-bit code on UltraSPARC processors, 30
64-bit architecture, specifying in compiler, 103
286 processor, 39
386 processor, 39
    SSE instruction sets on, 95–96
    -xtarget=generic compiler option, 99
80286 processor, 39
80386 processor, 39
    SSE instruction sets on, 95–96
    -xtarget=generic compiler option, 99
8086 processor, 39

A

,a adornment (SPARC instruction), 25
.a files (static libraries), 182
access to memory
    error detection for, 261–262, 274
    metrics on (example), 288–290
accessing matrix data, 347–348
active_cycle_count counter, 310

activity reports. *See* system status reporting
addition operations, 9
address, memory, 16, 18
address space for process, reporting on, 78–79
addressing modes, SPARC, 24–25
aggressively optimized code, compiler
    options for, 93–95. *See also* Sun
    Studio compiler, using
algorithmic complexity, 437–442
alias_level pragma, 143–144
alias pragma, 144–145
aliasing control pragmas, 142–147
aliasing of pointers. *See* pointer aliasing in C
    and C++
align pragma, 136–137
-aligncommon=16 compiler option, 101
alignment of variables, specifying, 135, 136–137
AMD64 processors, 40
    compiler performance, 105
Amdahl's Law, 377, 440, 443
analyzer GUI, 207, 210–212
AND operation (logical), 9
application profiles. *See* profiling performance

ALSO AVAILABLE IN THE SOLARIS SERIES

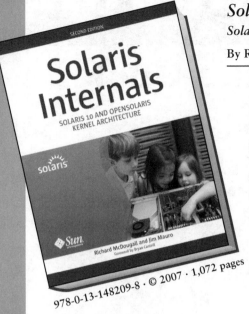

978-0-13-148209-8 · © 2007 · 1,072 pages

Solaris™ Internals, Second Edition
Solaris 10 and OpenSolaris Kernel Architecture

By Richard McDougall and Jim Mauro

Solaris™ Internals, Second Edition, describes the algorithms and data structures of all the major subsystems in the Solaris 10 and OpenSolaris kernels. The text has been extensively revised since the first edition, with more than 600 pages of new material. Integrated Solaris tools and utilities, including DTrace, MDB, kstat, and the process tools, are used throughout to illustrate how the reader can observe the Solaris kernel in action. The companion volume, *Solaris™ Performance and Tools*, extends the examples contained here, and expands the scope to performance and behavior analysis. Coverage includes

- Virtual and physical memory
- Processes, threads, and scheduling
- File system framework and UFS implementation
- Networking: TCP/IP implementation
- Resource management facilities and zones

The *Solaris™ Internals* volumes make a superb reference for anyone using Solaris 10 and OpenSolaris.

978-0-13-156819-8 · © 2007 · 496 pages

Solaris™ Performance and Tools
DTrace and MDB Techniques for Solaris 10 and OpenSolaris

By Richard McDougall, Jim Mauro, and Brendan Gregg

Solaris™ Performance and Tools provides comprehensive coverage of the powerful utilities bundled with Solaris 10 and OpenSolaris, including the Solaris Dynamic Tracing facility, DTrace, and the Modular Debugger, MDB. It provides a systematic approach to understanding performance and behavior, including

- Analyzing CPU utilization by the kernel and applications, including reading and understanding hardware counters
- Process-level resource usage and profiling
- Disk IO behavior and analysis
- Memory usage at the system and application level
- Network performance
- Monitoring and profiling the kernel, and gathering kernel statistics
- Using DTrace providers and aggregations
- MDB commands and a complete MDB tutorial

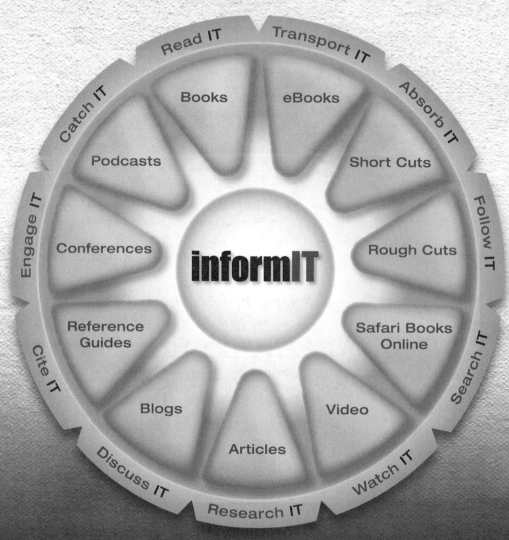

THIS BOOK IS SAFARI ENABLED

INCLUDES FREE 45-DAY ACCESS TO THE ONLINE EDITION

The Safari® Enabled icon on the cover of your favorite technology book means the book is available through Safari Bookshelf. When you buy this book, you get free access to the online edition for 45 days.

Safari Bookshelf is an electronic reference library that lets you easily search thousands of technical books, find code samples, download chapters, and access technical information whenever and wherever you need it.

TO GAIN 45-DAY SAFARI ENABLED ACCESS TO THIS BOOK:

- Go to **http://www.prenhallprofessional.com/safarienabled**

- Complete the brief registration form

- Enter the coupon code found in the front of this book on the "Copyright" page

PRENTICE HALL

If you have difficulty registering on Safari Bookshelf or accessing the online edition, please e-mail customer-service@safaribooksonline.com.